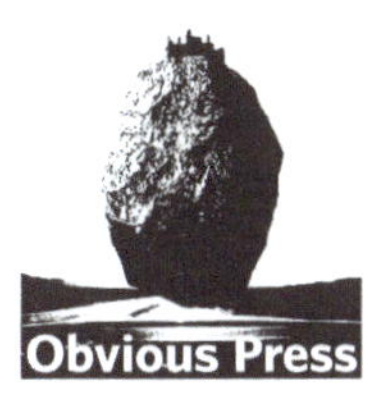

Museyrooms

Intersections of People and Art in Museums

Mikesch W. Muecke

Obvious Press
918 5th Street
Ames, IA, 50010-5906
USA
www.obviouspress.com

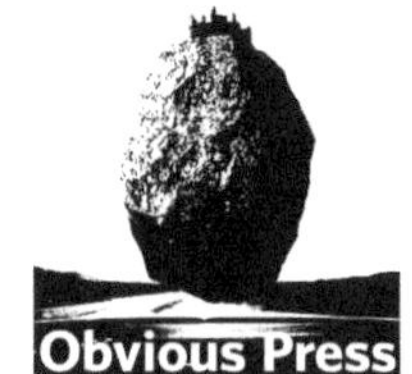

First published in 2010
MUSEYROOMS: INTERSECTIONS OF PEOPLE AND ART IN MUSEUMS.

For information address Obvious Press, 918 5th Street, Ames, IA 50010-5906 or write to editor@obviouspress.com

ISBN-13:978-1-941892-15-2

ISBN-10:1941892159

Graphic design, layout, and typesetting by polytekton.com

Table of Contents

About the Book	6
Chicago Art Institute	8
Musée des Arts et Metiérs in Paris	20
Musée du Louvre in Paris	30
MARTA in Herford	36
Westfälisches Freilichtmuseum in Detmold	38
National Gallery of Art in Washington DC	54
Smithsonian National Air and Space Museum	106
National Building Museum in Washington DC	108
French Icarian Colony Living History Museum in Corning, IA	114
St. Louis Art Museum	118
Nelson-Atkins Museum of Art in Kansas City, MO	174
Kemper Museum of Contemporary Art in Kansas City, MO	194

Dedicated to
J.B., J.J., A. L. P., M.Z., and Z.Z.

Collecting seems to be instinctive for many human beings. It may be based upon the search for physical security (today collections often are considered good investments), social distinction (Thorstein Veblen would call it "conspicuous consumption"), the pursuit of knowledge and connoisseurship (genuine love for objects and desire to find out everything about them), and a wish to achieve a kind of immortality, as witness the great number of named collections in museums.

Edward Alexander. *Museum in Motion,* p. 9

About the Book

In *Babel's Tower* Francis Taylor called museums evidence of the "magpiety of mankind." Over the last years I visited several of these spaces of manic collecting and, where non-flash photography was permitted, I began to take images of the interiors. Soon I noticed that a large number of my photographs were blurred. Before discarding these obviously flawed images I observed—by taking a second look—a certain lightness in these pictures that stood in marked contrast to the rigidity of the physical museum spaces and their contents. The sense of power and control that museal architecture always represents, seemed to have been countered by photographs that captured not only the art but also the museums' inhabitants in motion. At times I felt compelled to include some non-blurry pictures of the artwork as well but for the most time I was amazed and detained by that subtle intersection of architecture, space, and inhabitants in motion.

This book contains photographs I took in the following museums: the Art Institute in Chicago, IL, the Musée des Arts et Métiers in Paris, the Louvre, the MARTa in Herford, Germany, the Freilichtmu- seum in Detmold, Germany, the National Gallery in Washington, DC, the Building Museum in Washing- ton, DC, the French Icarian Colony Living History Museum in Corning, IA, the St. Louis Art Museum in St. Louis, MO, and finally both the Nelson-Atkins and the Kemper Museum in Kansas City, MO.

About the Title

This book and its title is a not-so-oblique nod to my erstwhile teacher and mentor Dr. Jennifer Bloomer who published an article, in February 1988, about the John Soane Museum in London, entitled "In the Museyroom", in *Assemblage* No. 5 (The MIT Press). In that essay she refers to James Joyce who, as far as I know, coined the word 'museyroom' and mentions it at least three times in *Finnegans Wake* in a reference to what might as well be the Wellington Museum (page 8, lines 9 and 10): "This way to the museyroom. Mind your hats goan in! Now yiz are in the Willingdone Museyroom." And, on page 11, line 22: "This way the museyroom. Mind your boots goan out."

As Bloomer writes in her essay, Joyce's words are 'switching mechanisms'—especially for those of us who know more than one language—and in a different but related sense the images on the following pages work as visual switches between what we expect to see in a museum, and what people actually do in these collective and collecting spaces.

In those first pages of *Finnegans Wake* Joyce makes ample use of starting his sentences with the declarative "This is...". Bloomer borrows his writing technique for her essay, amplifying the two words to "THIS IS...", and breaks the text into paragraphs that mimic the language of museum guides, ergo:

THIS IS the least I could do in naming the book...

MM, Ames, November 2010

Whenever a poet or preacher, chief or wizard spouts gibberish, the human race spends centuries deciphering the message.
Umberto Eco, *Foucault's Pendulum*: 104

What better hiding place for the true Templar than in the crowd of his caricatures?
Umberto Eco, *Foucault's Pendulum*: 355

Chicago Art Institute: 2 + 0 + 1 = 3 (trinity)

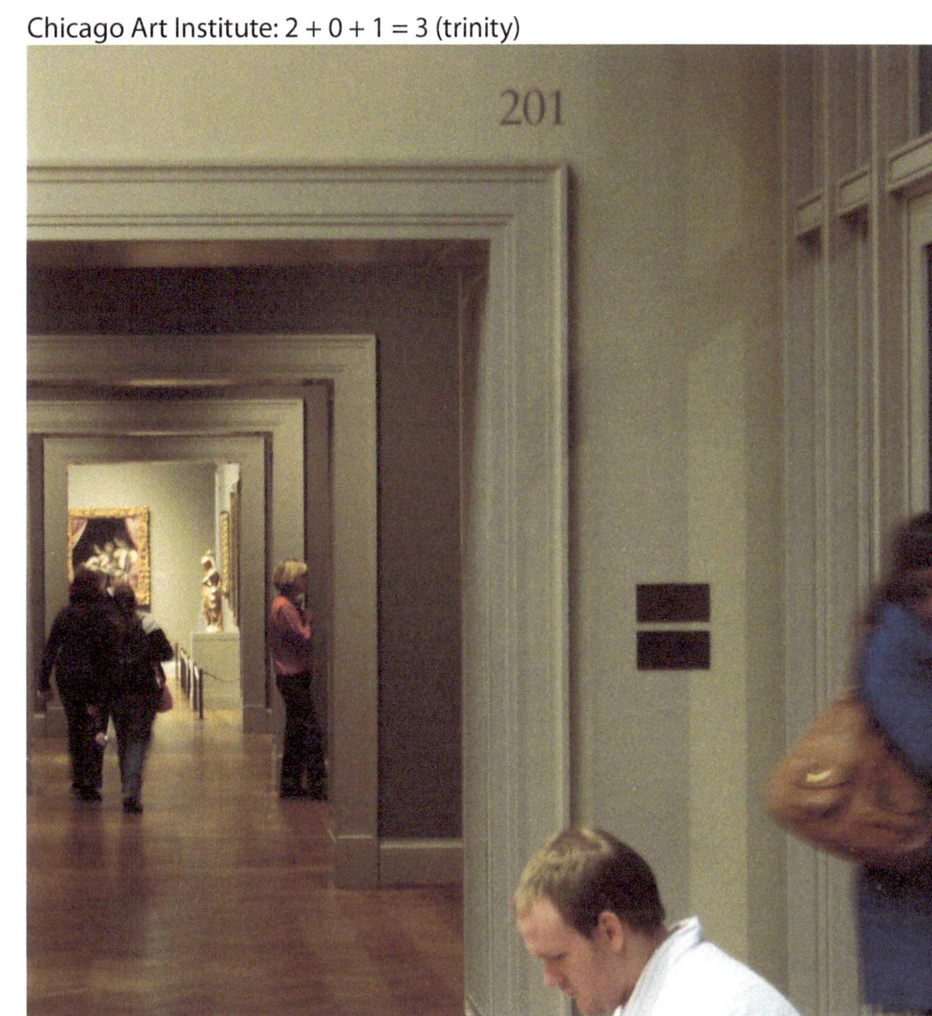

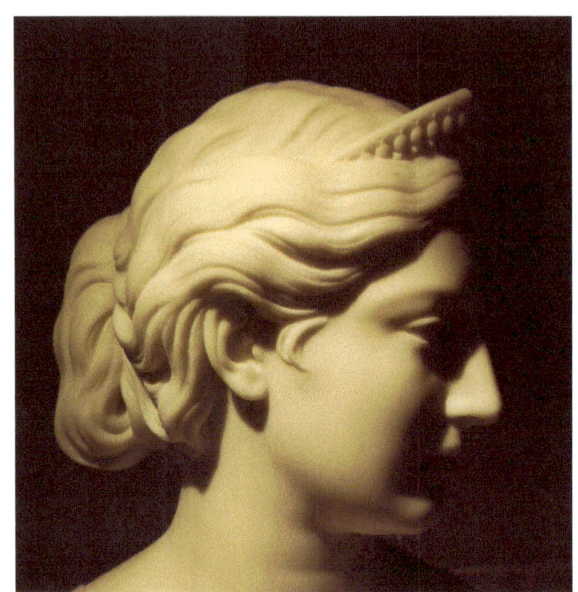

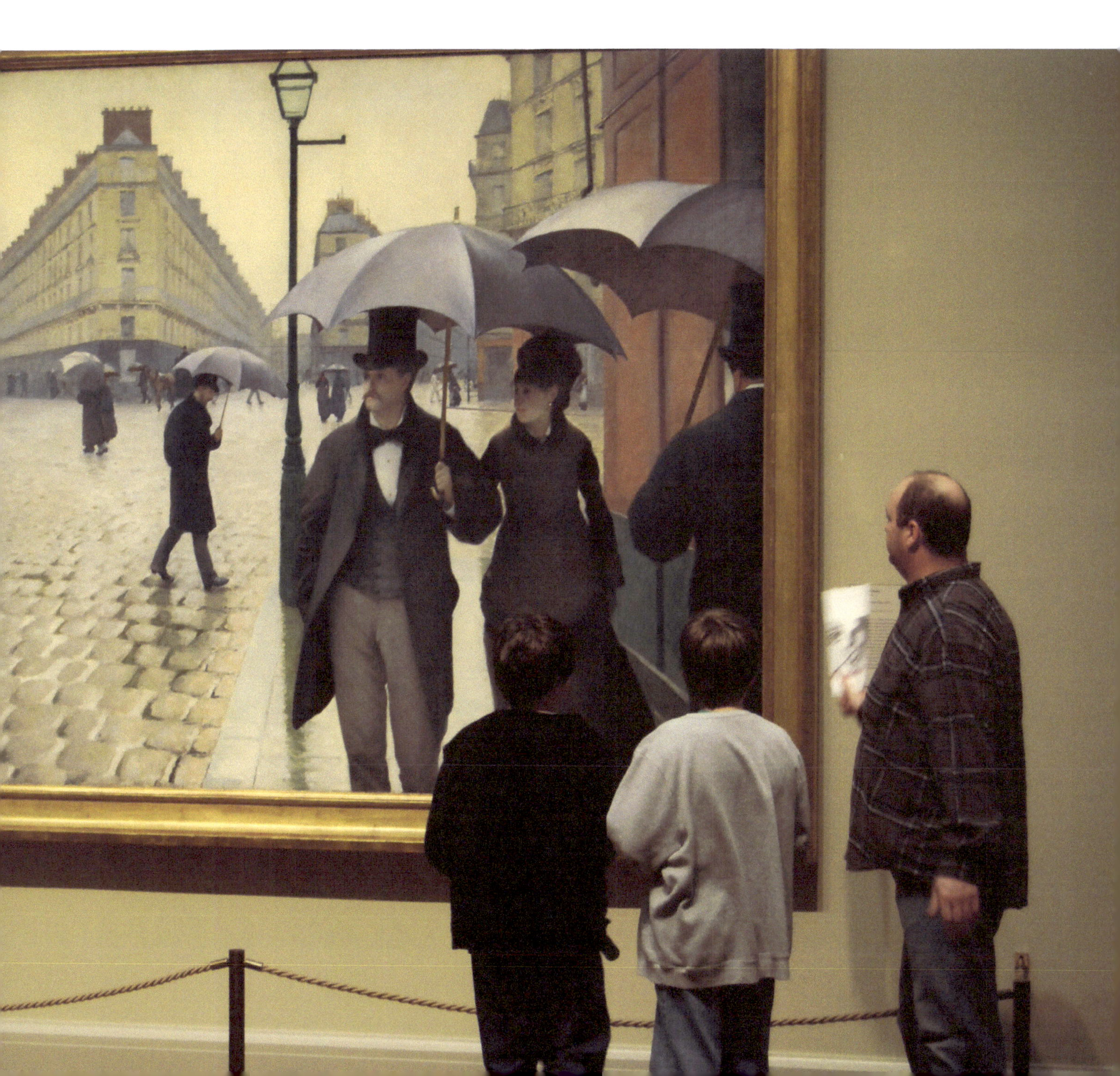

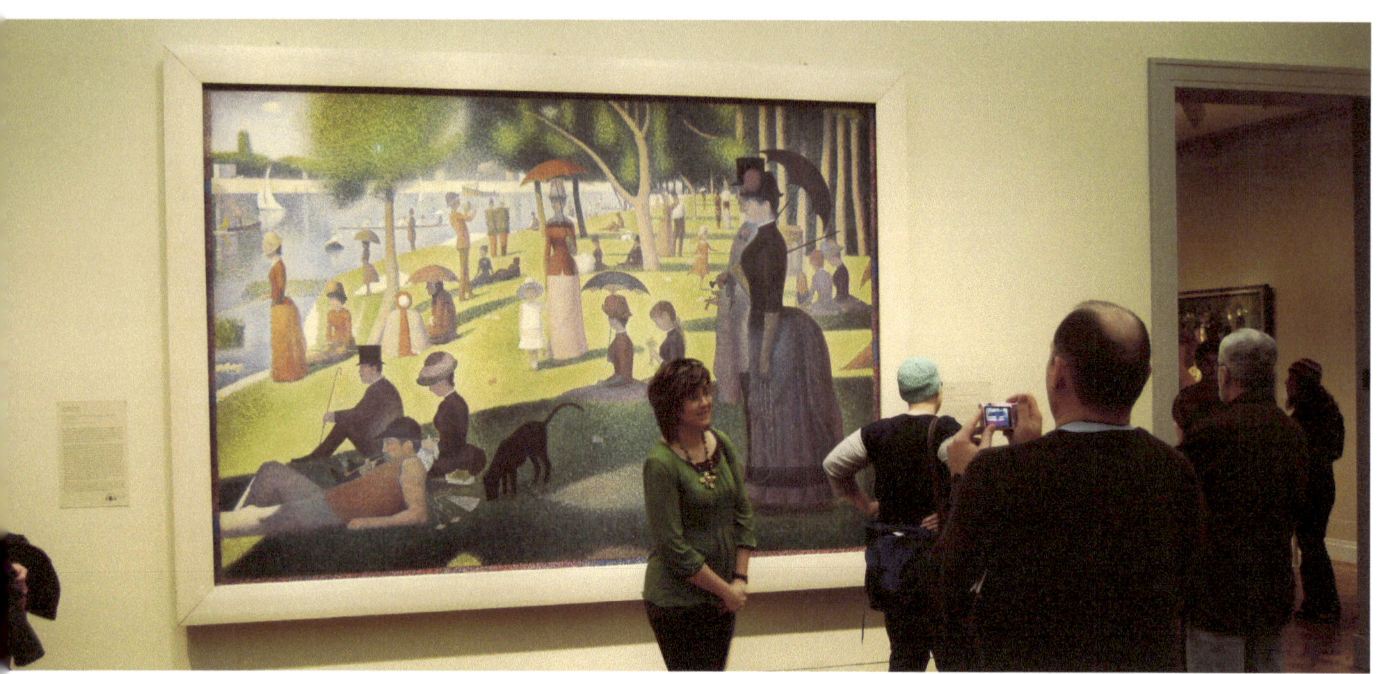

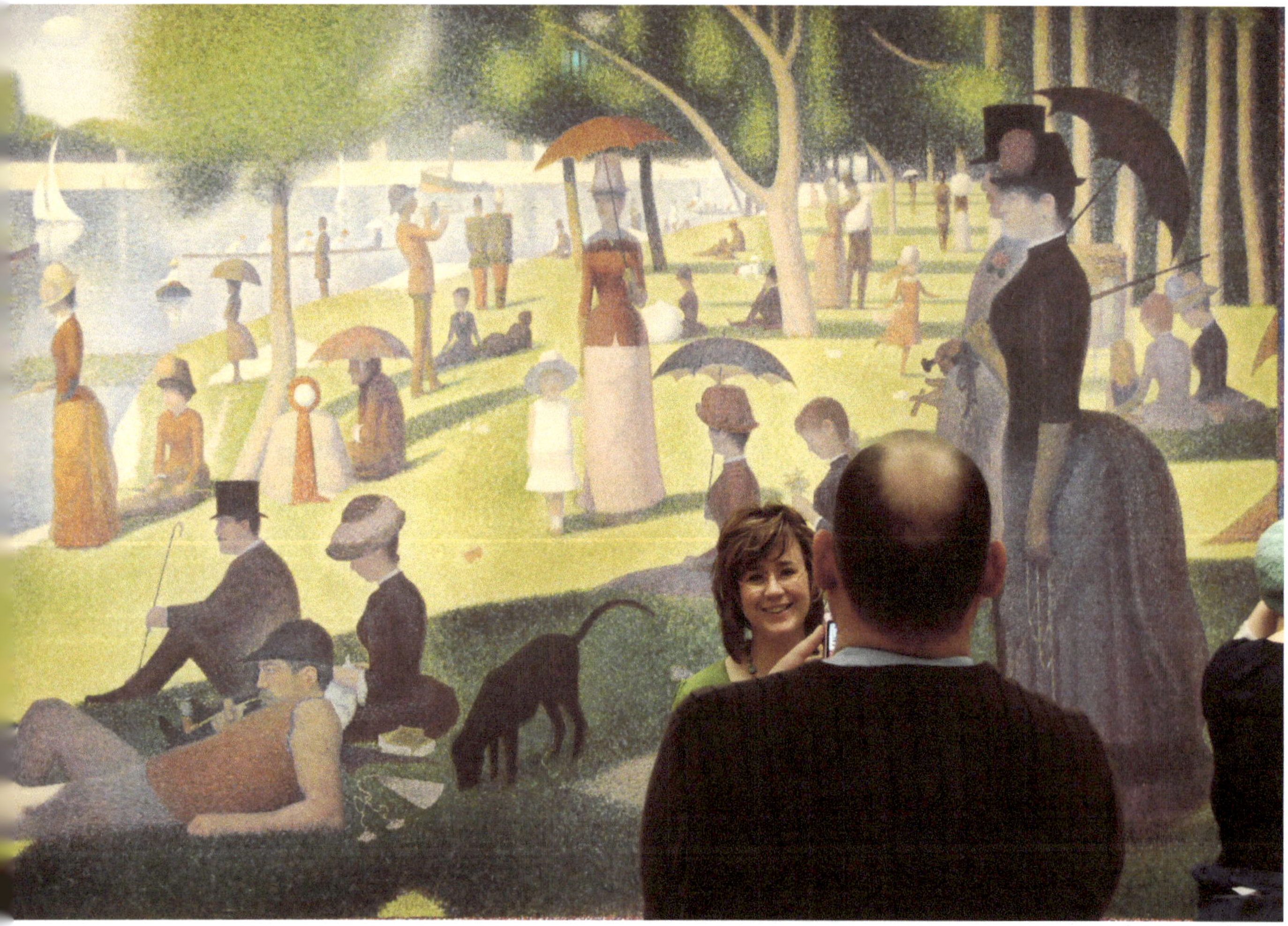

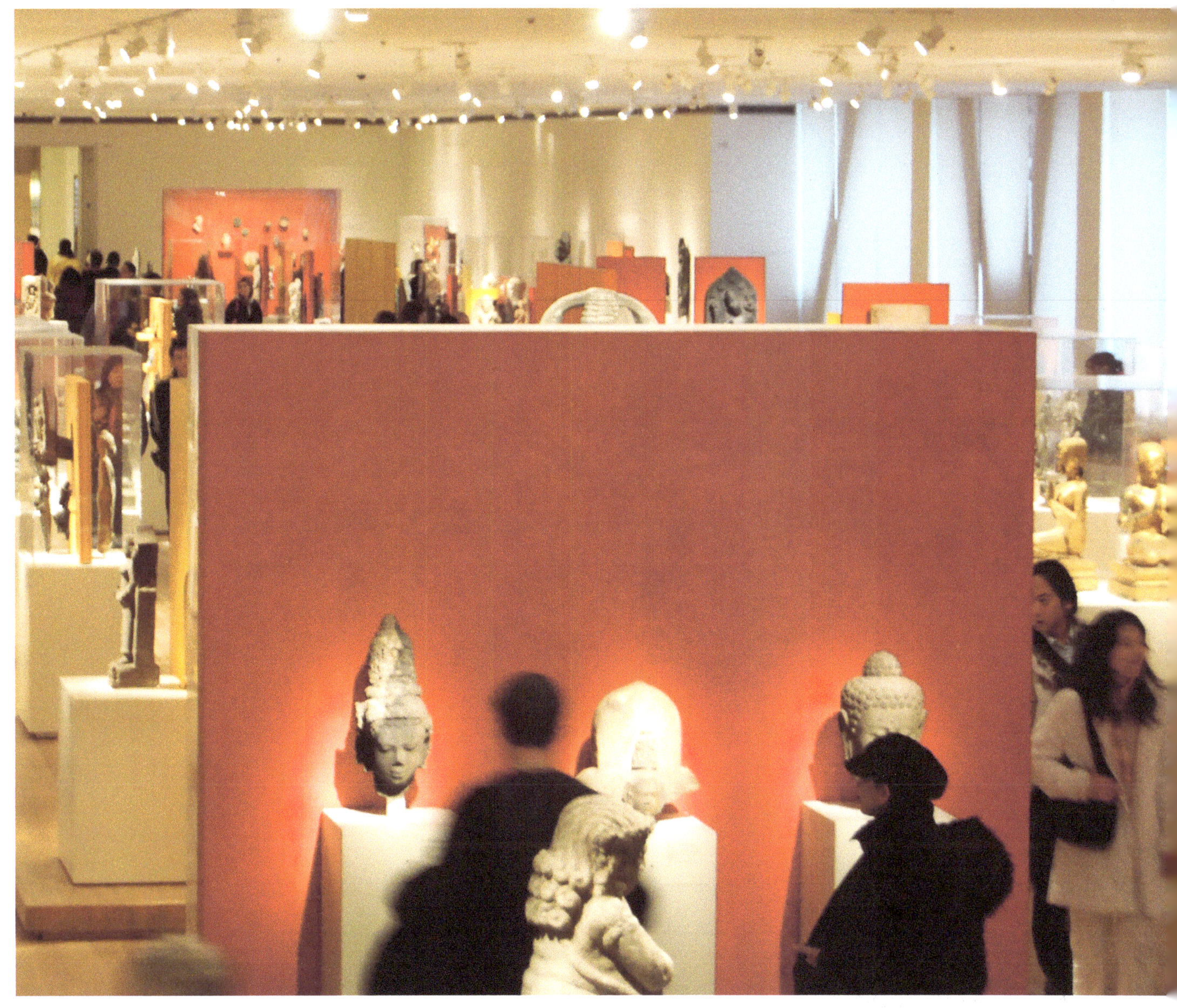

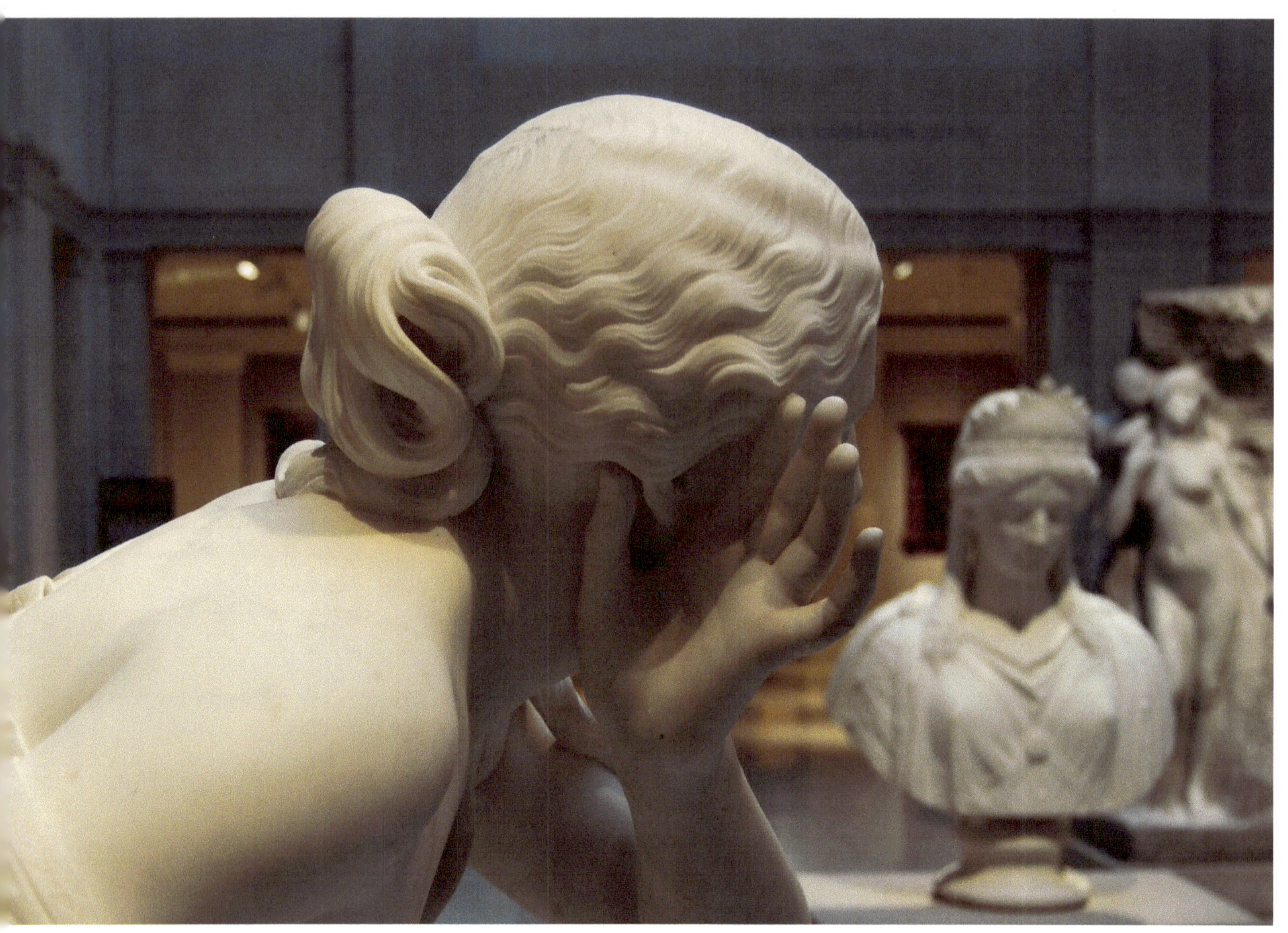

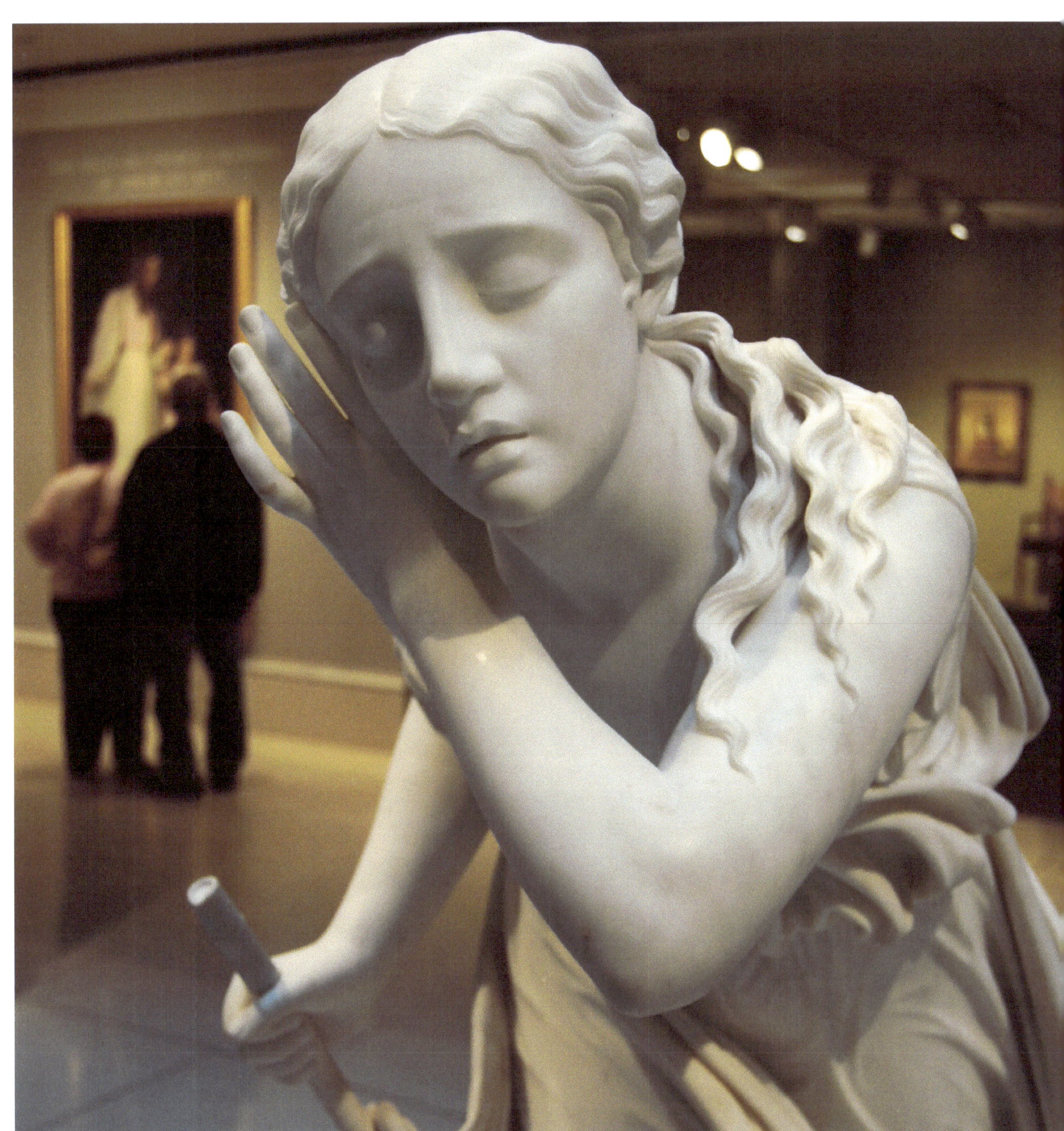

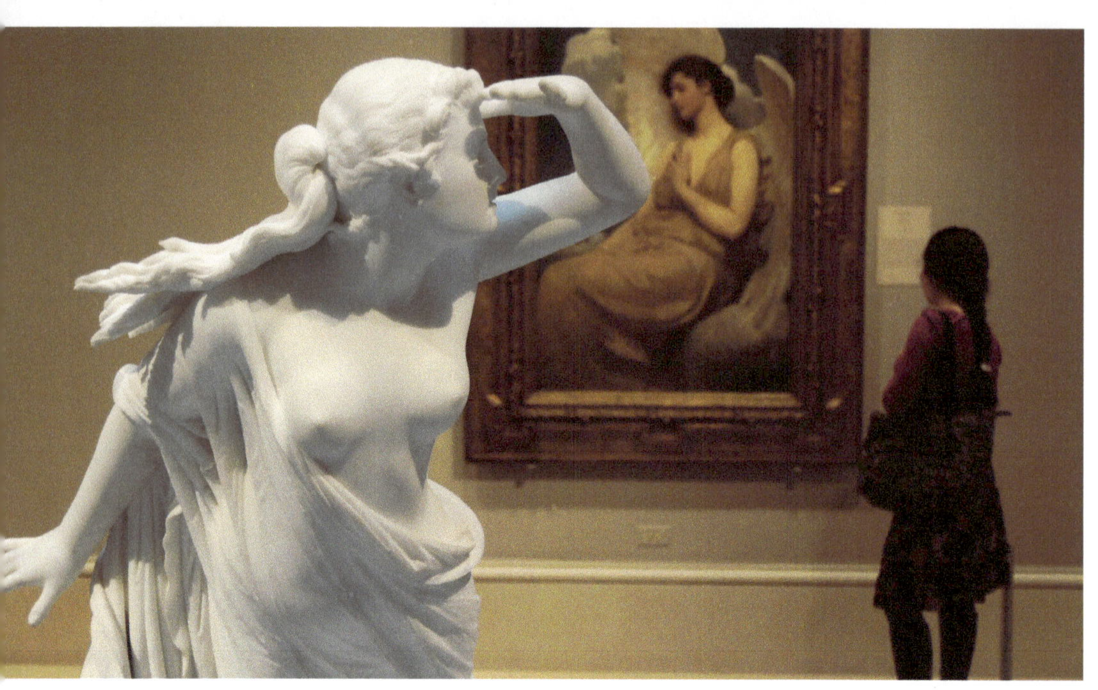

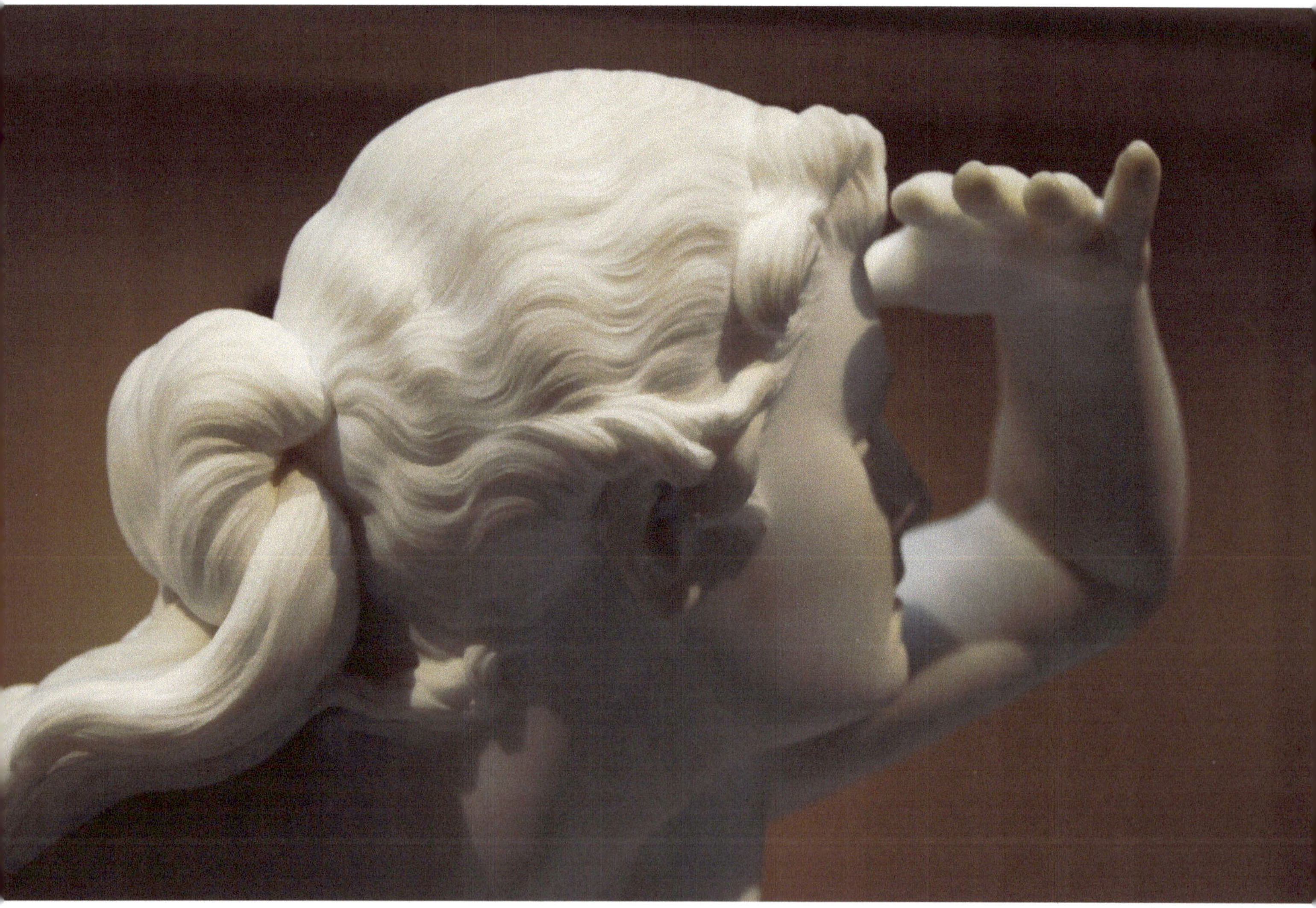

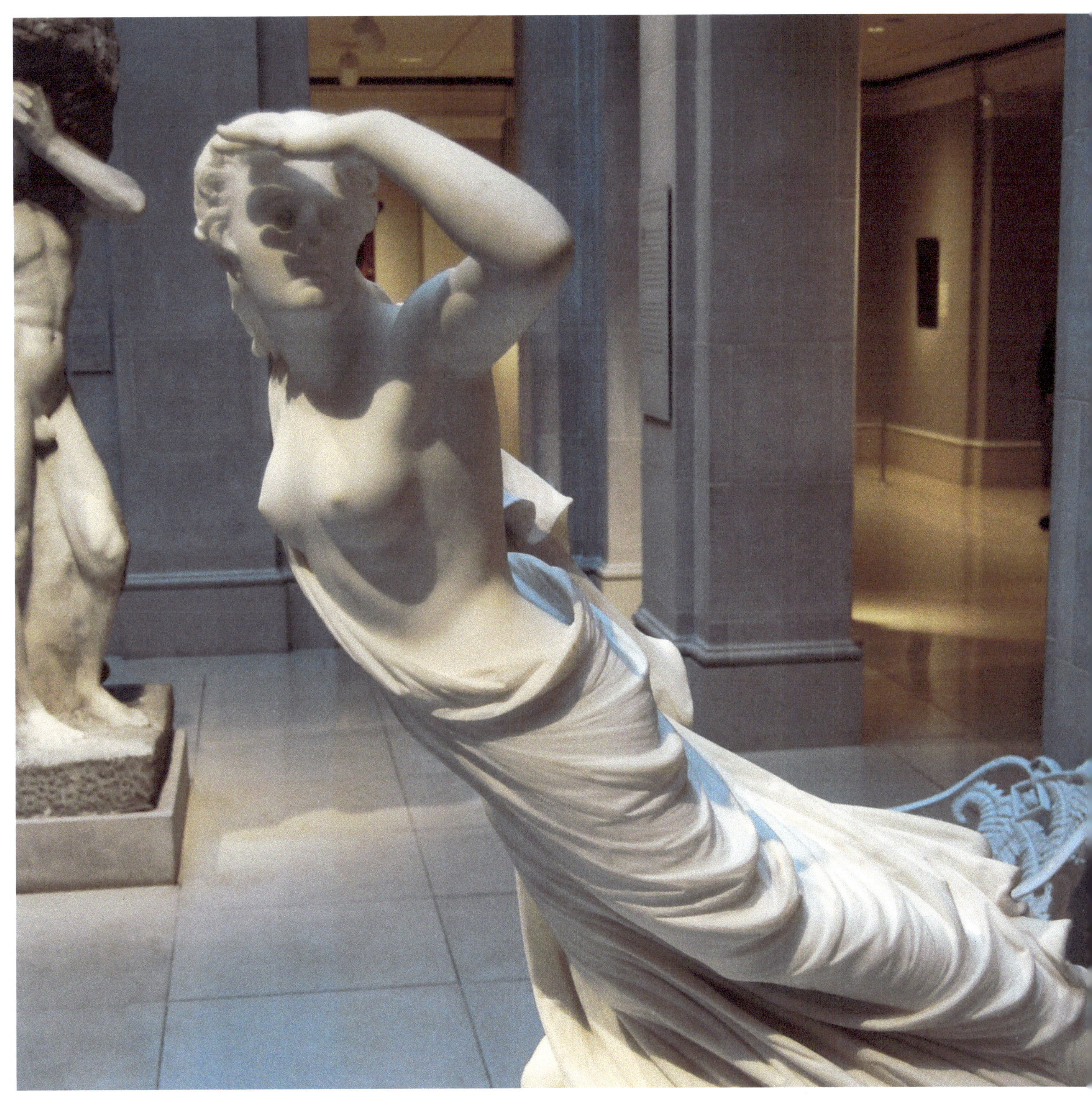

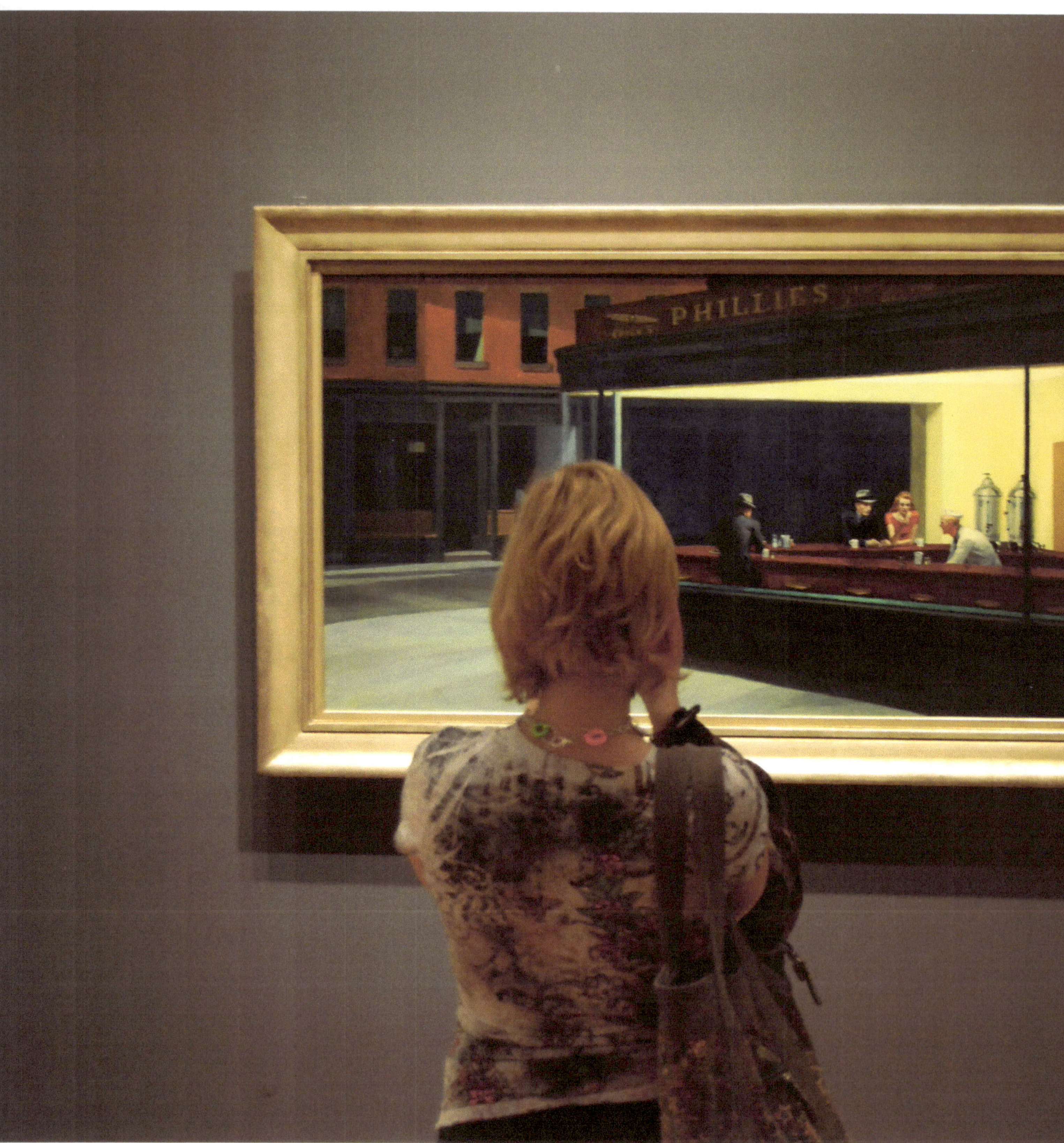
PHILLIES

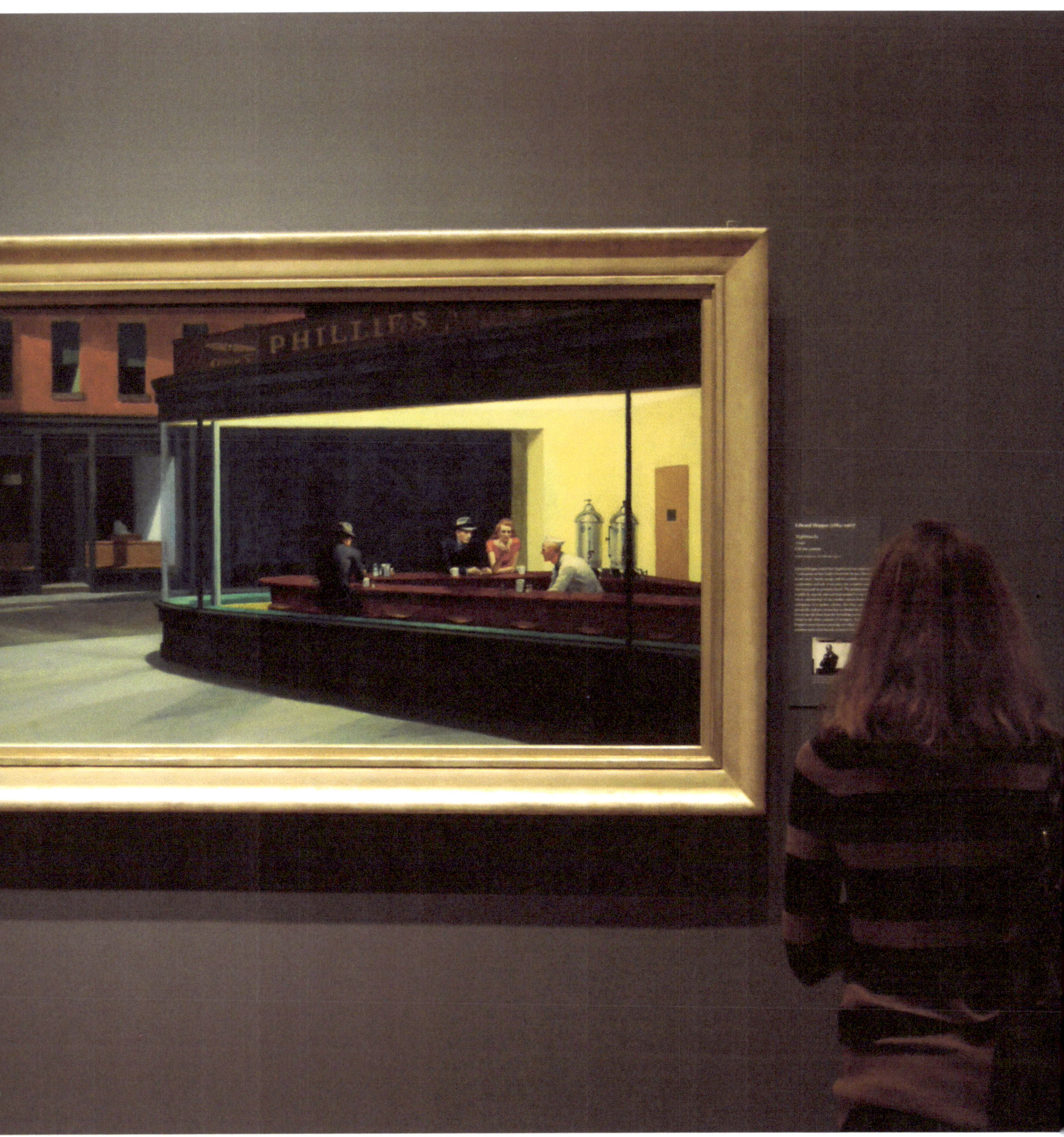
PHILLIES

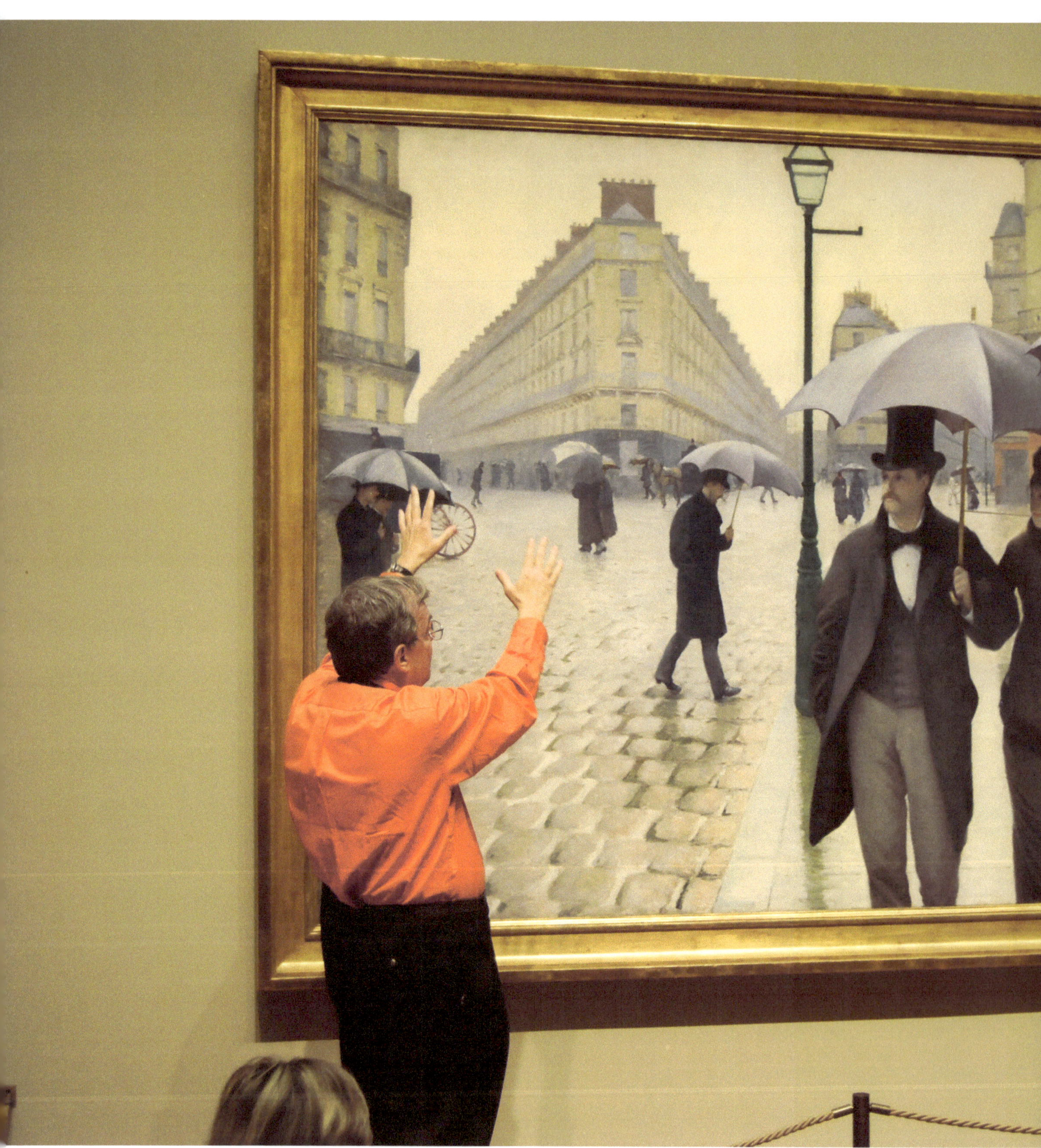

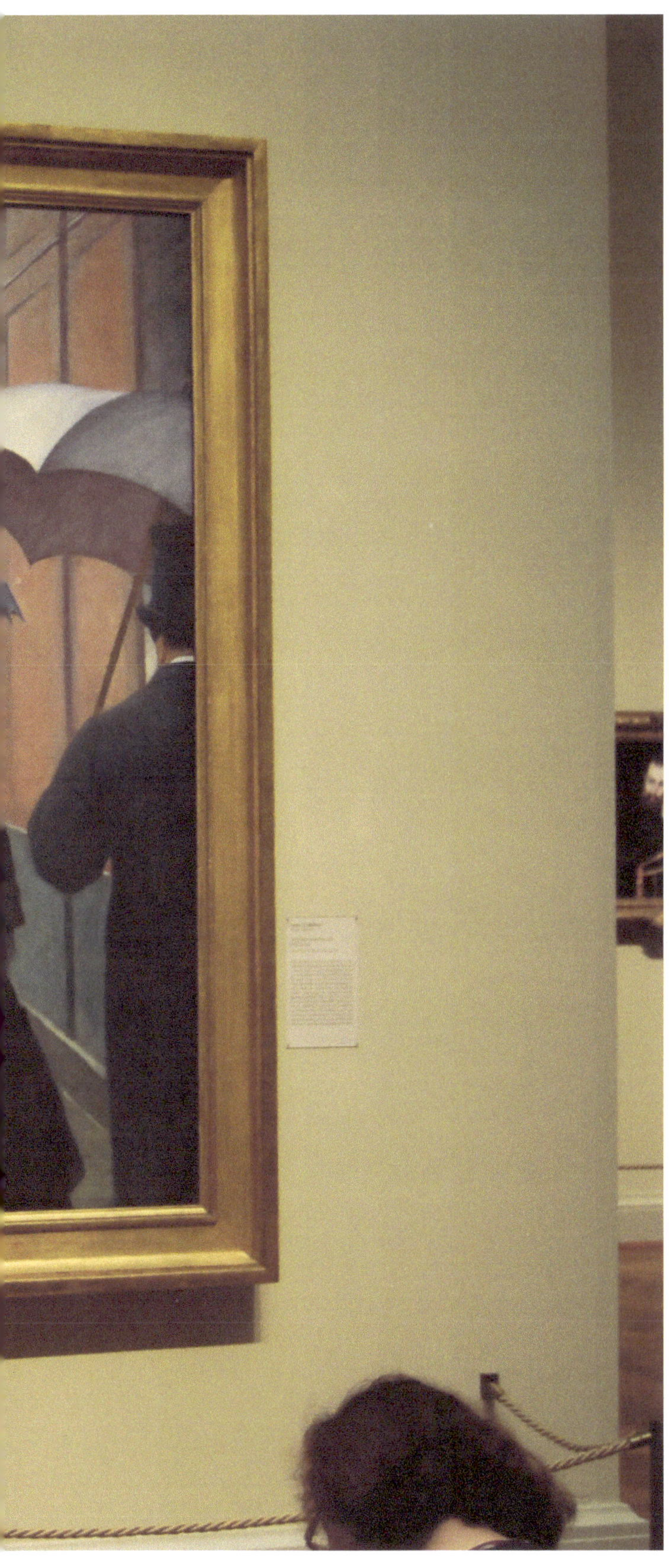

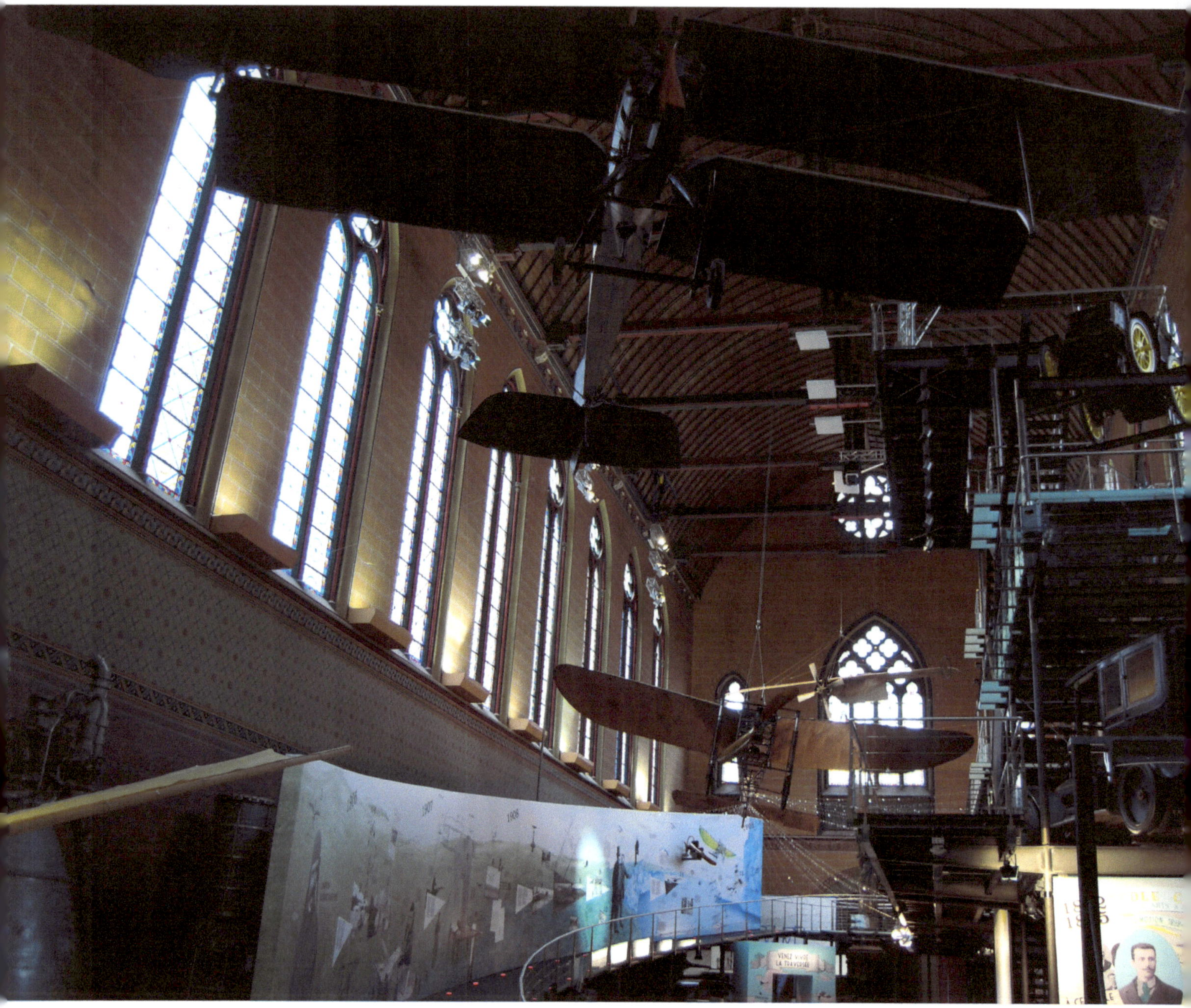

On the floor stretches a line of vehicles: Bicycles, horseless carriages, automobiles; from the ceiling hang planes. Some of the objects are intact, though peeling and corroded by time, and in the ambiguous mix of natural and electric light they seem covered by a patina, an old violin's varnish. Others are only skeletons or chassis, rods and cranks that threaten indescribable tortures. You picture yourself chained to a rack, something digging into your flesh until you confess.
Umberto Eco, *Foucault's Pendulum*: 7

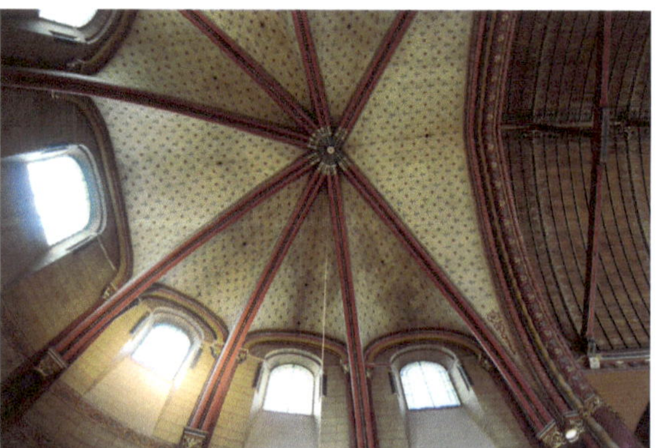

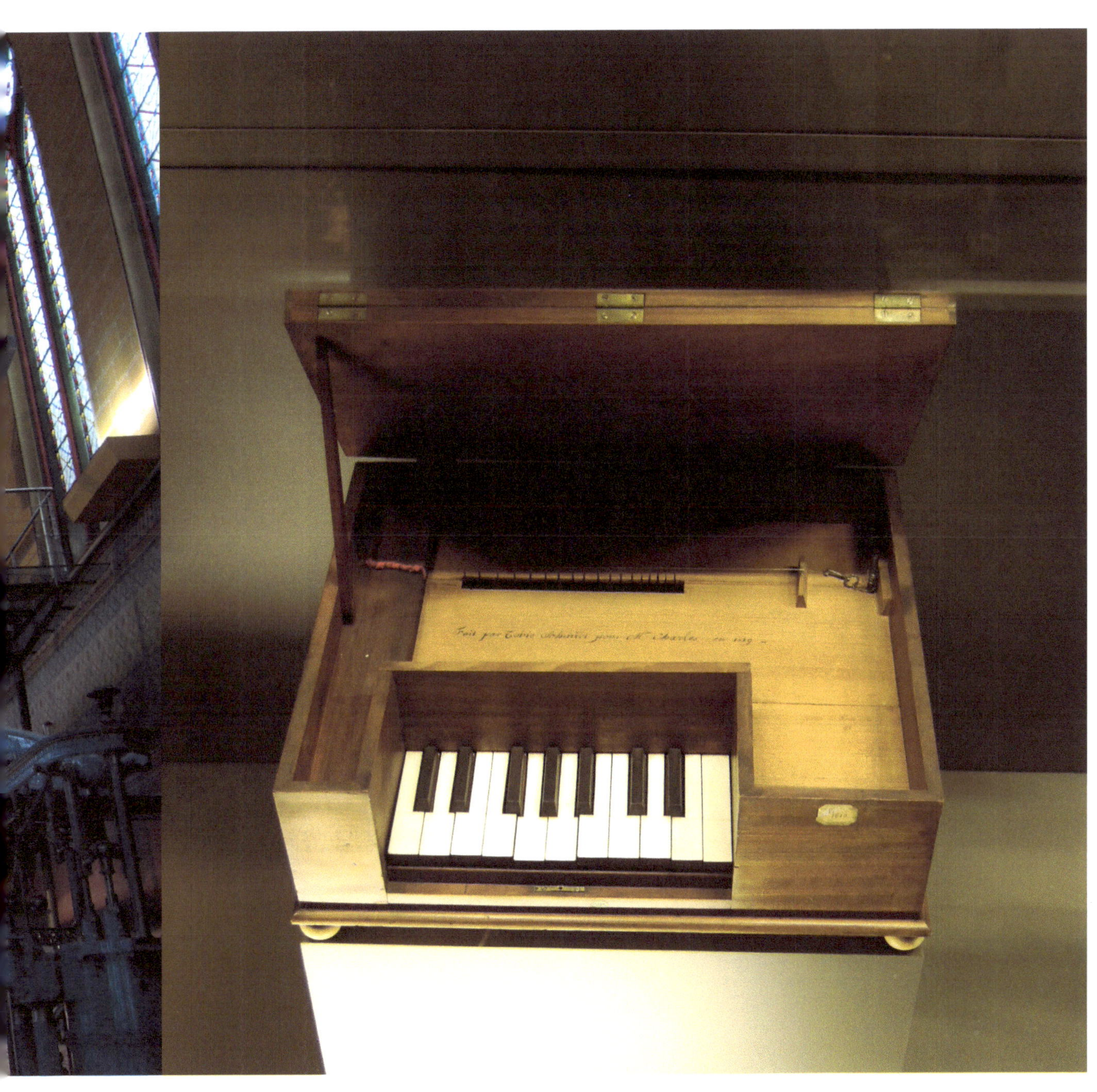

We're here to see connections.
Umberto Eco, *Foucault's Pendulum*: 478

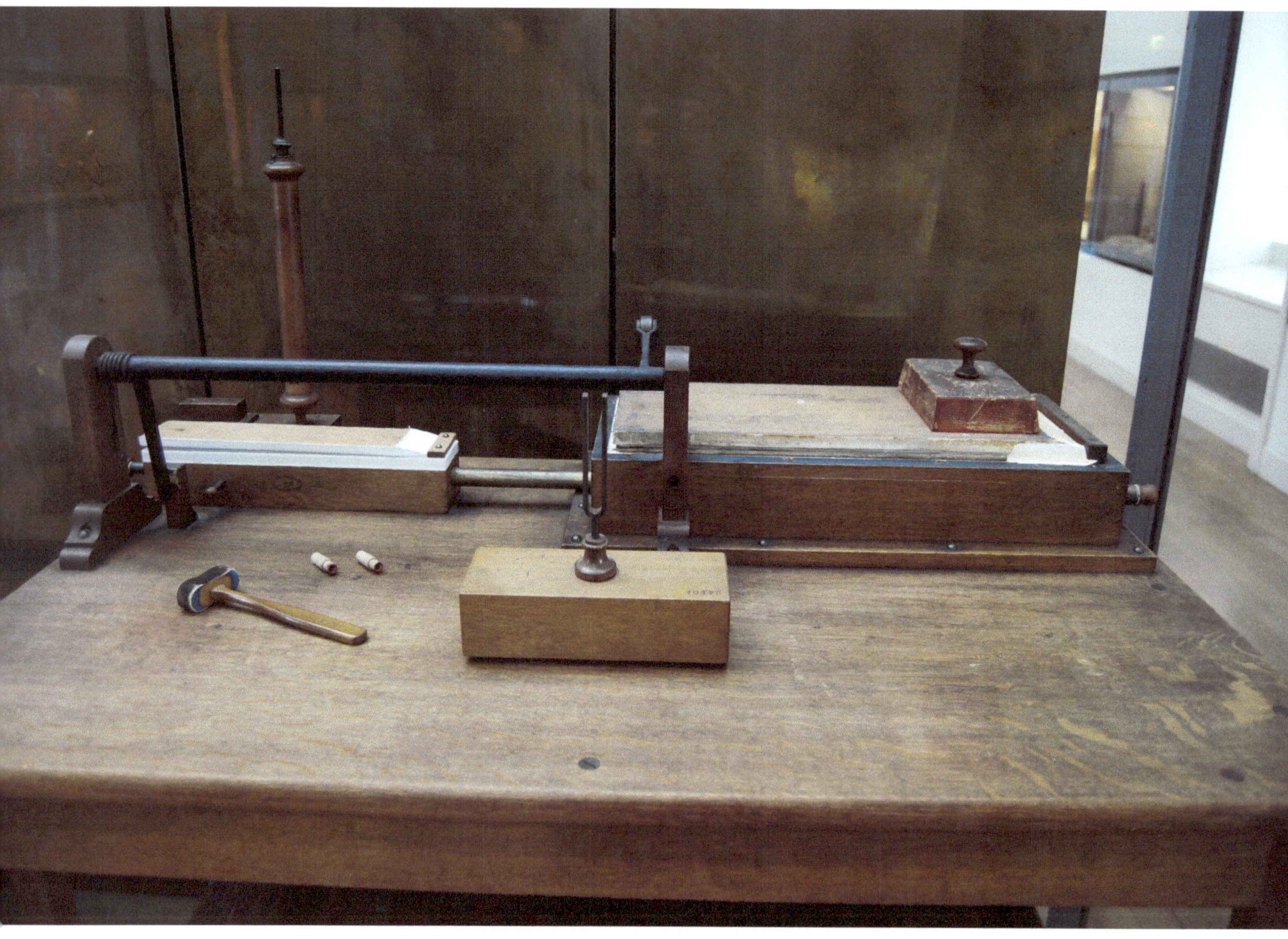

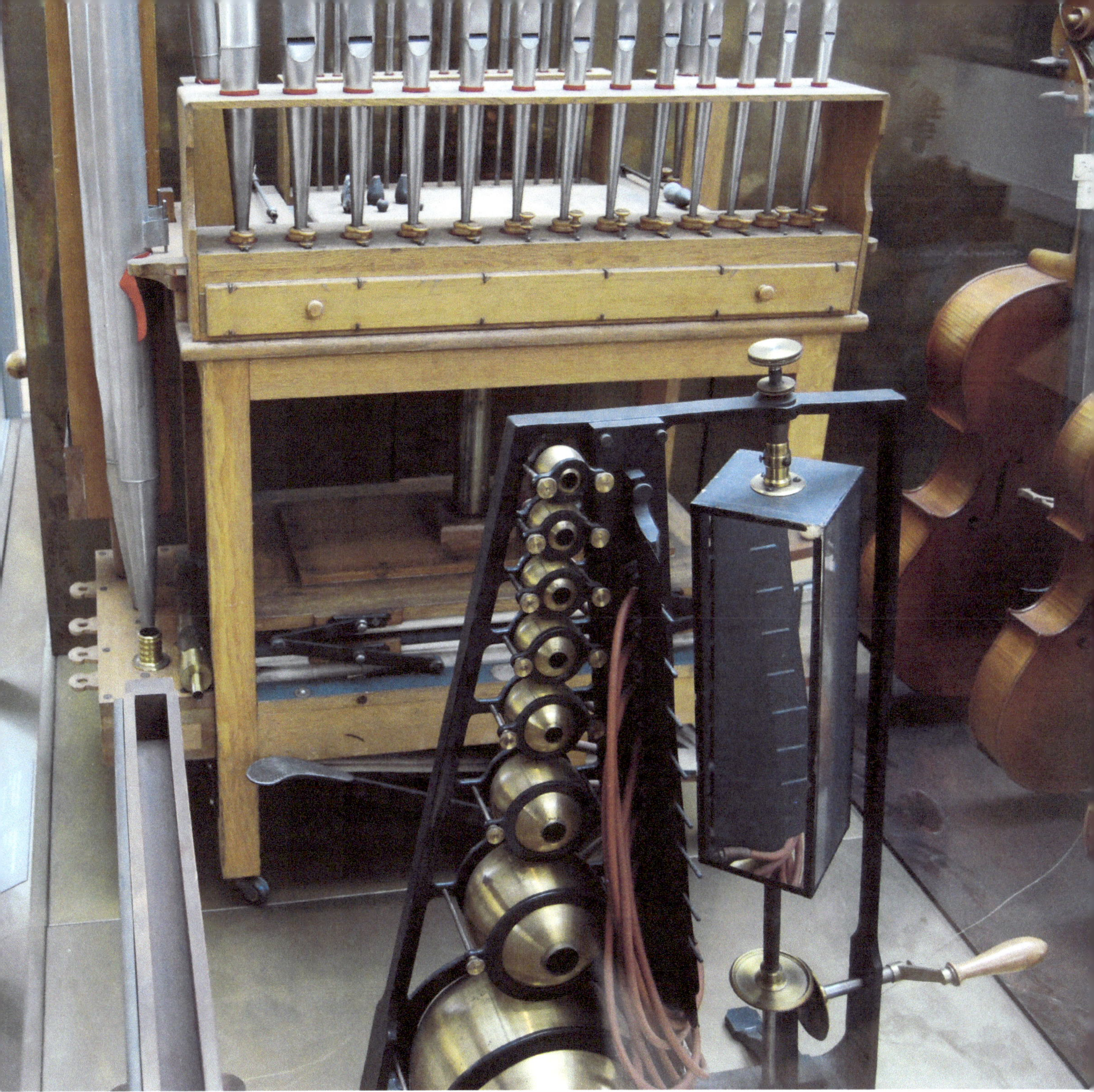

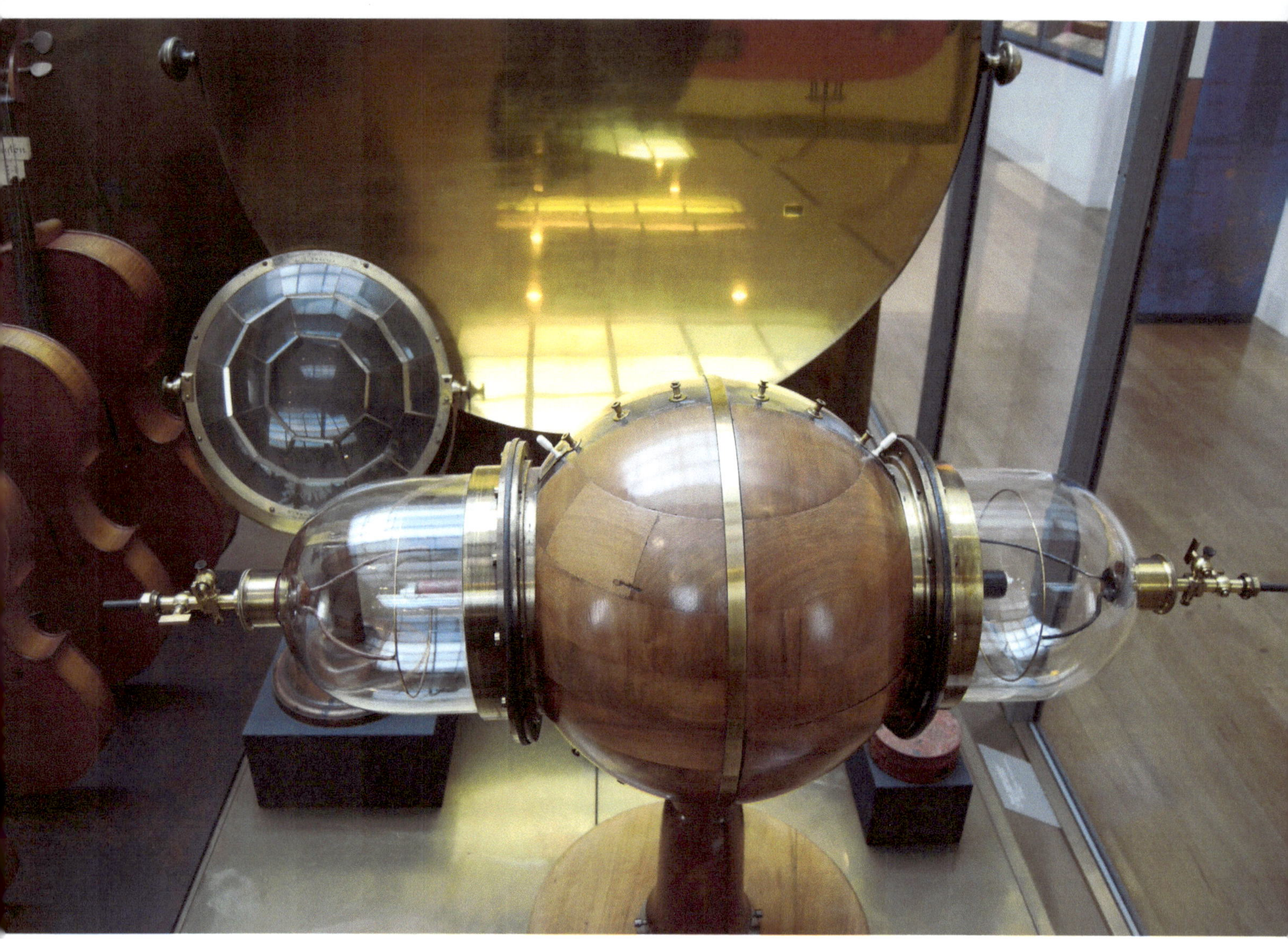

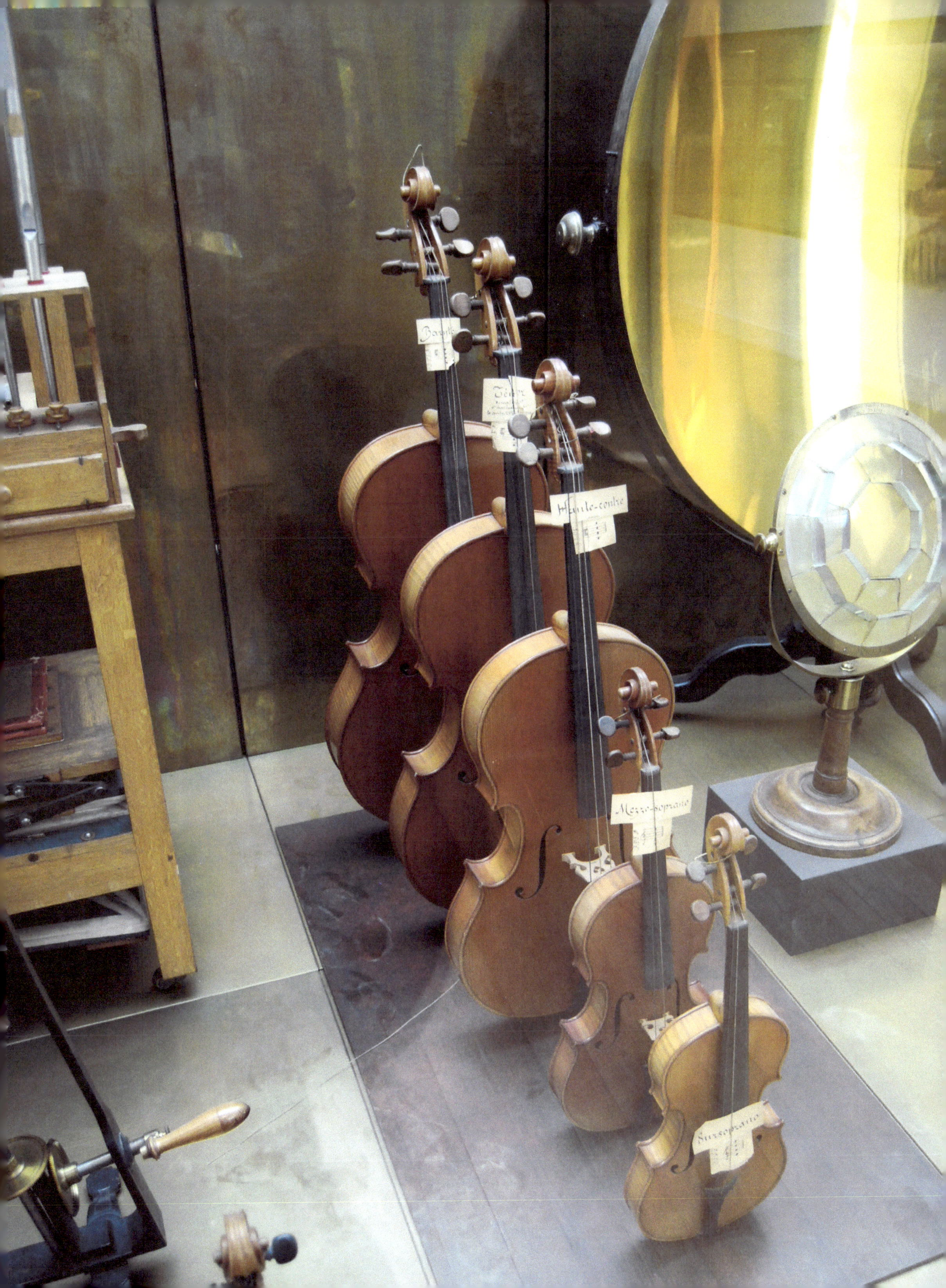
Mezzo-soprano
Sursoprano

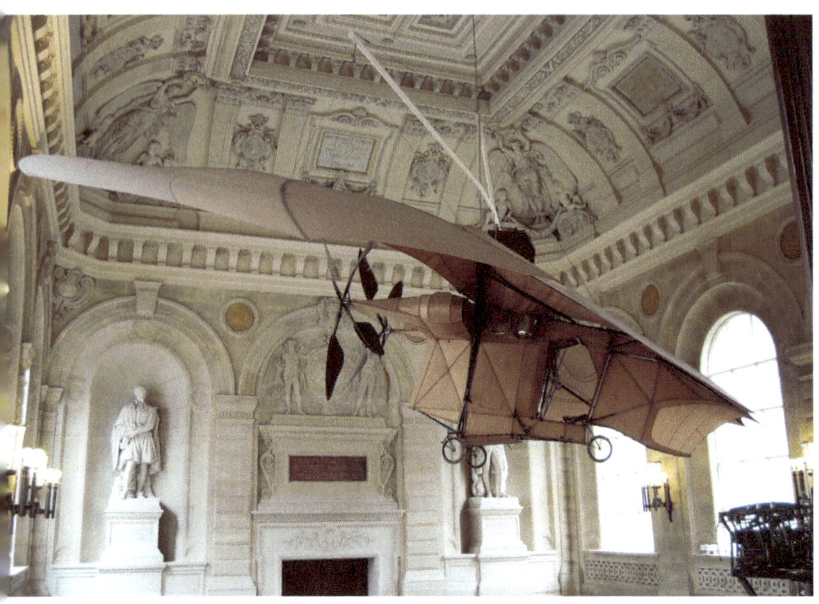

Aéroplane de Clément Ader, *Avion 3*, 1893-1897

You live on the surface. You sometimes seem profound, but it's only because you piece a lot of surfaces together to create the impression of depth, solidity. That solidity would collapse if you tried to stand it up.
Umberto Eco, *Foucault's Pendulum*: 56

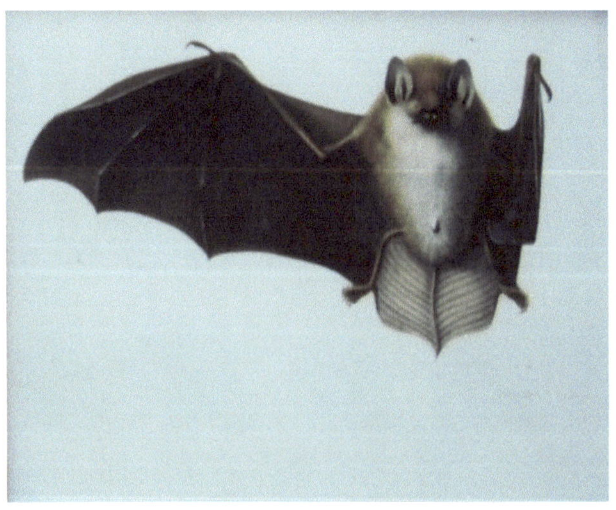

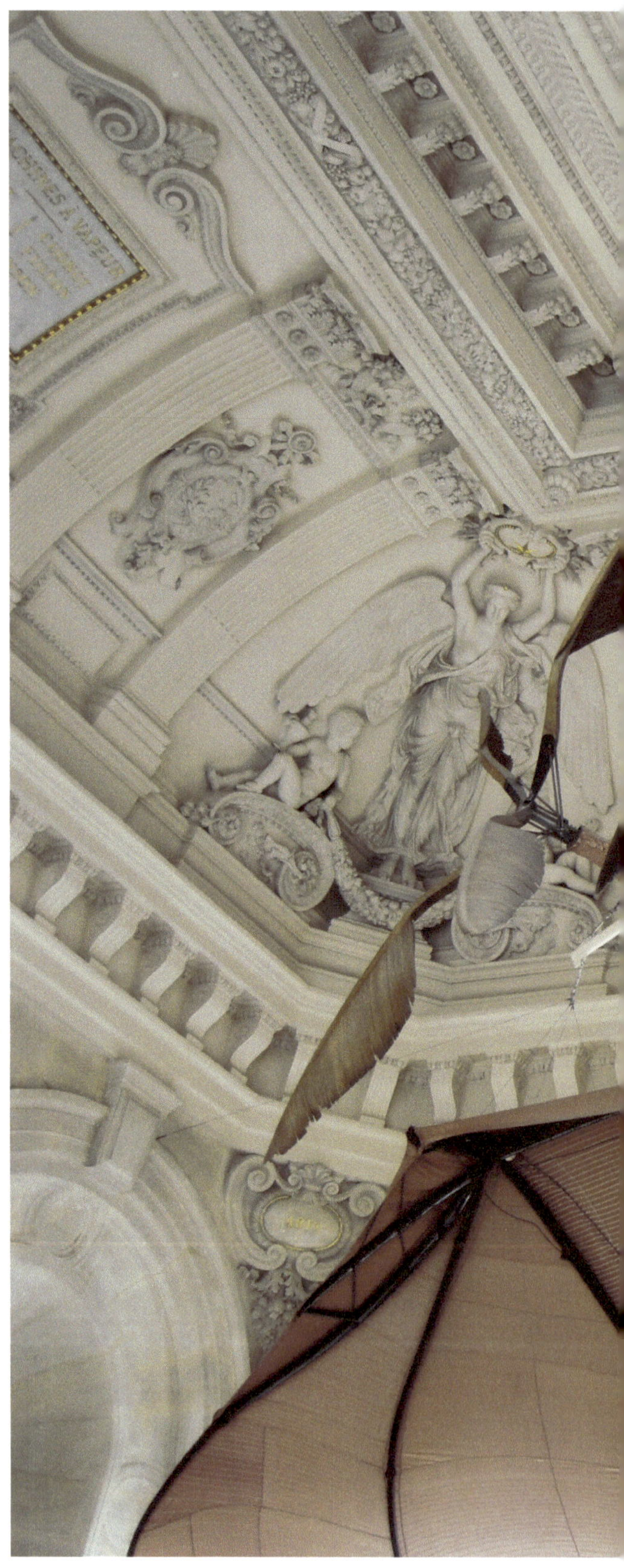

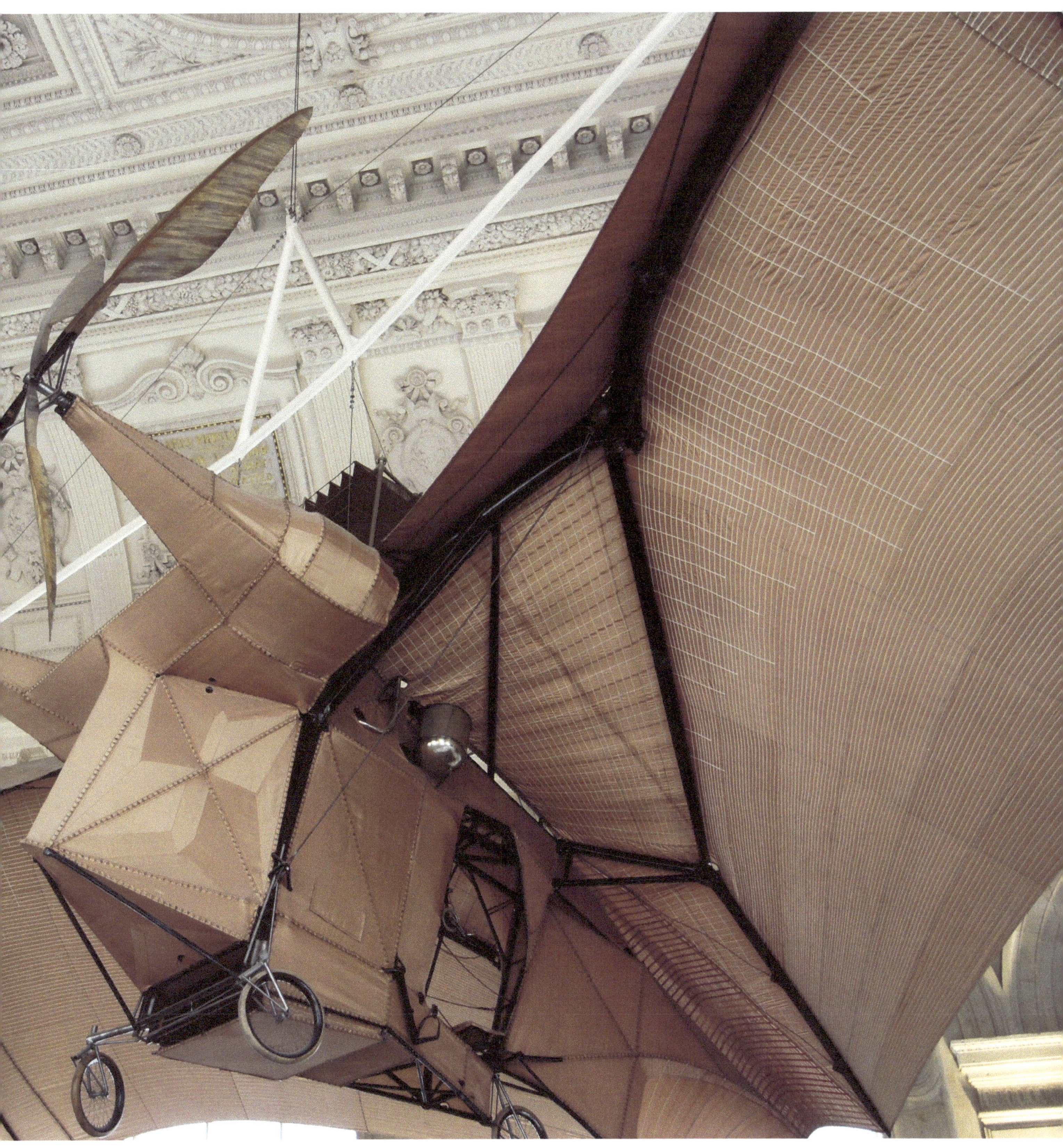

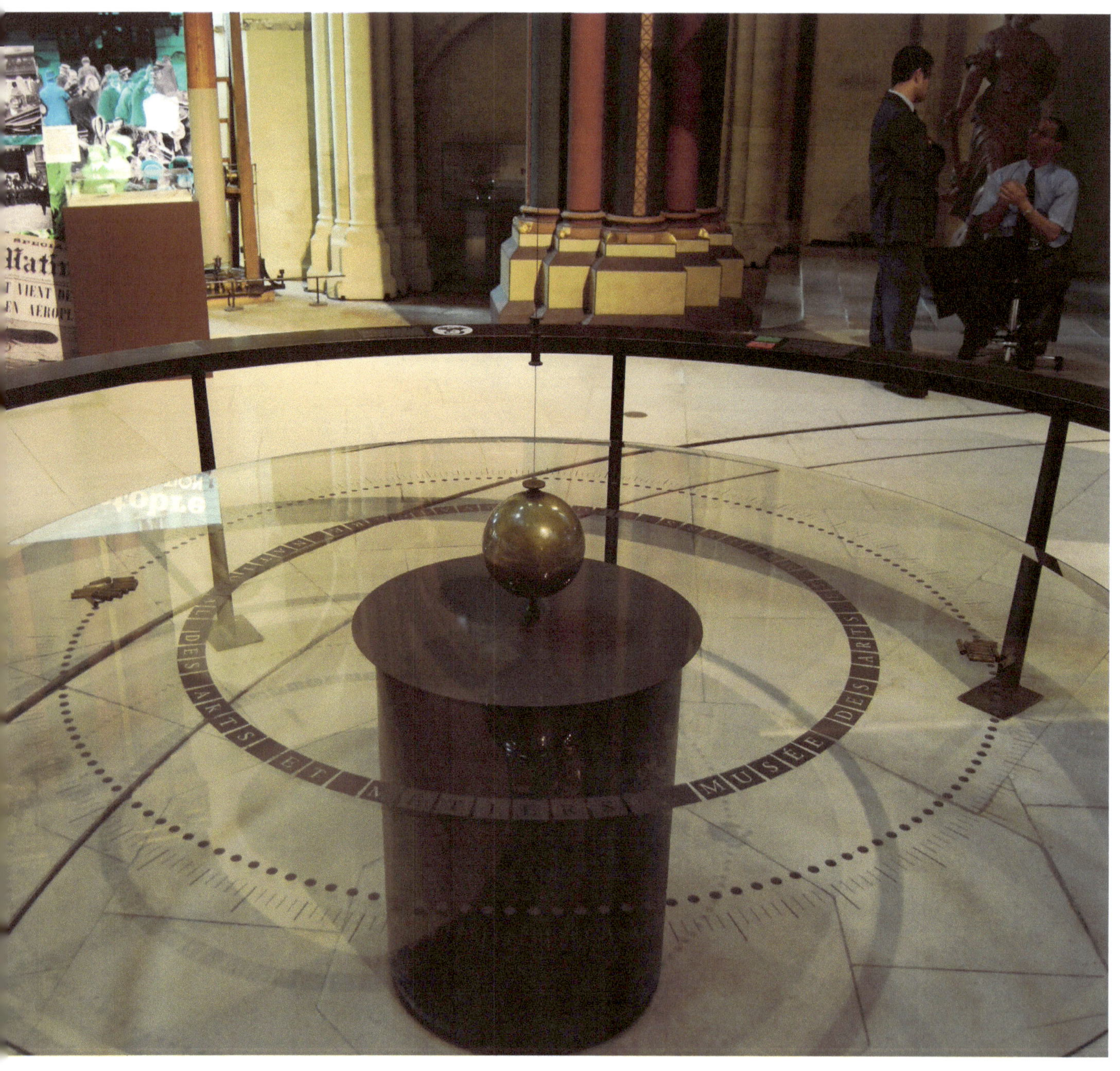

Foucault's Pendulum and two museum guards.

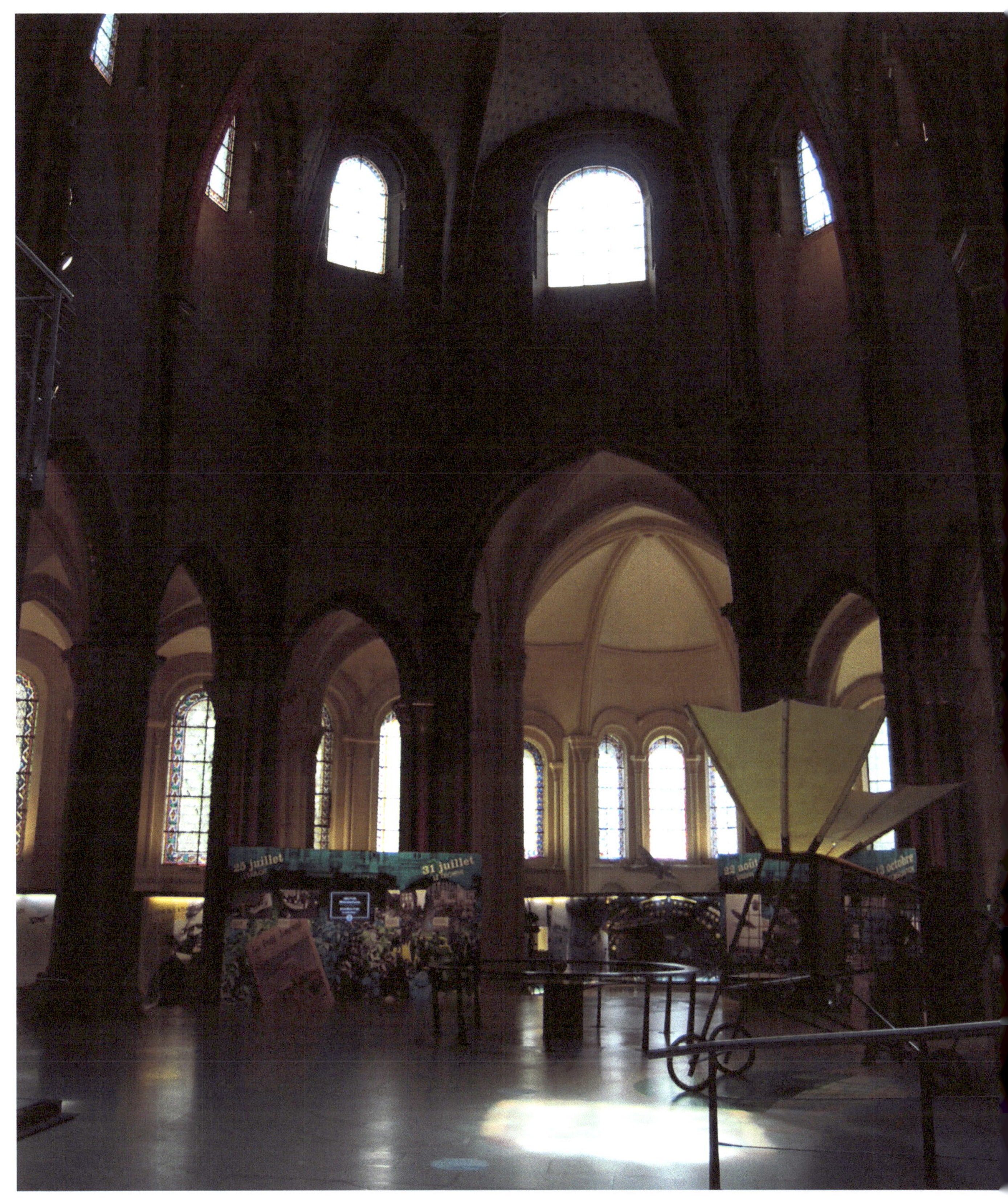
25 juillet
31 juillet
22 août

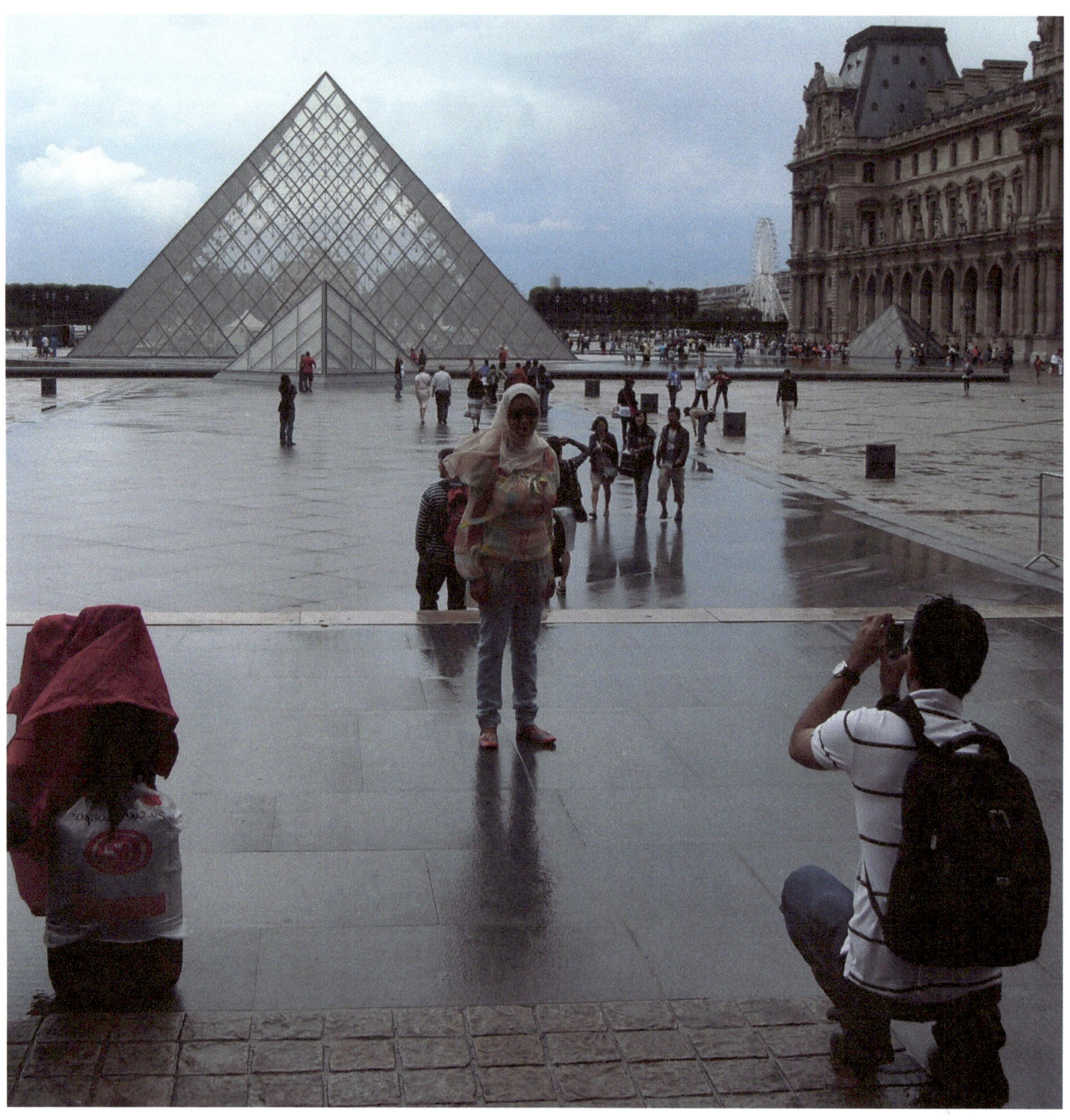

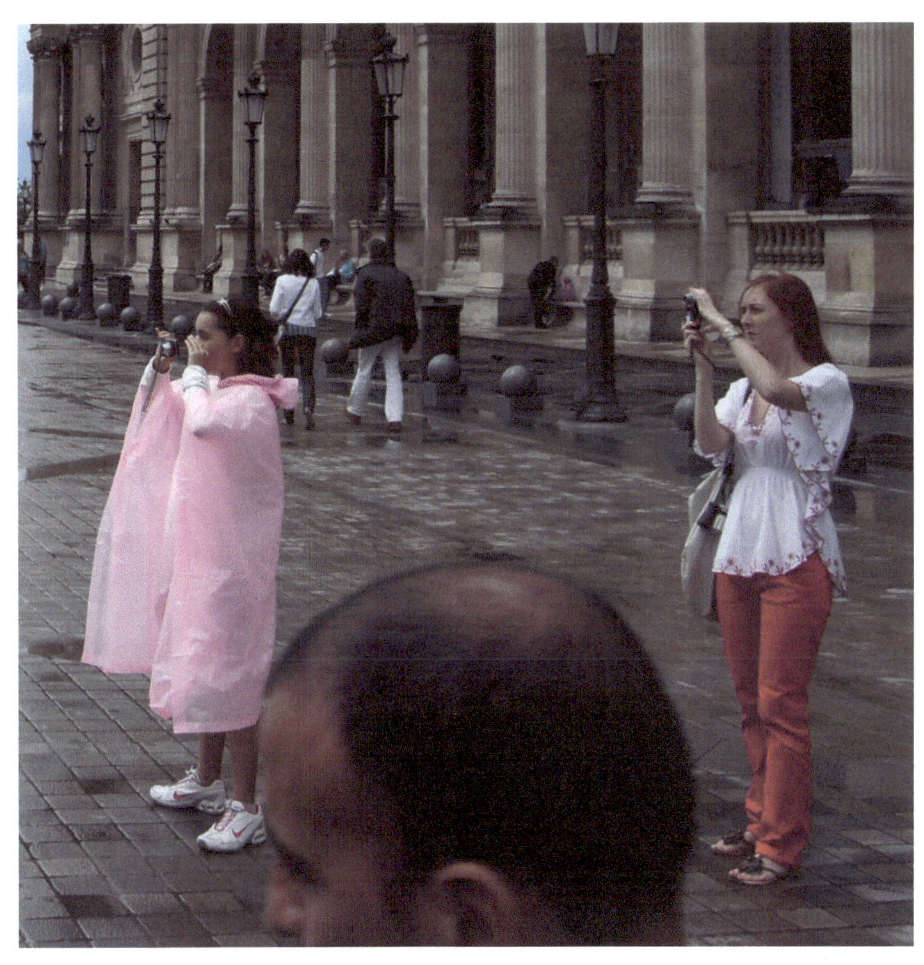

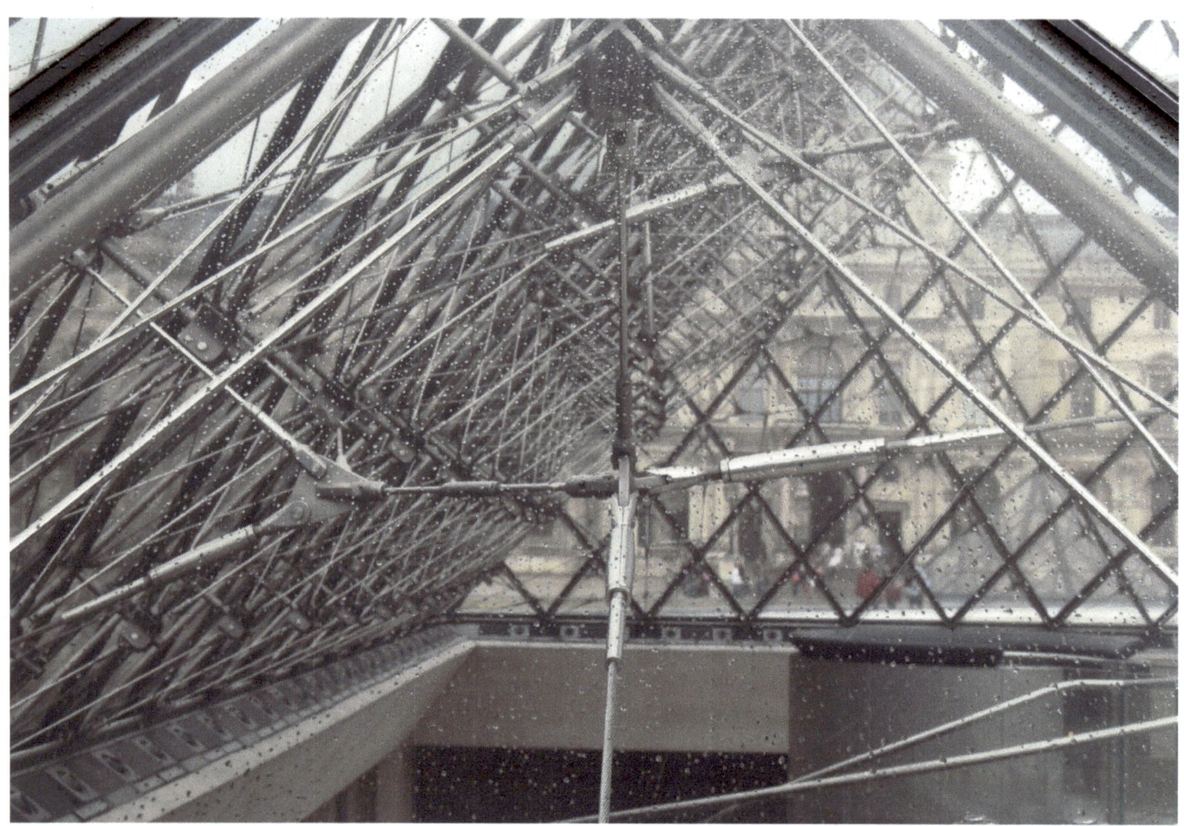

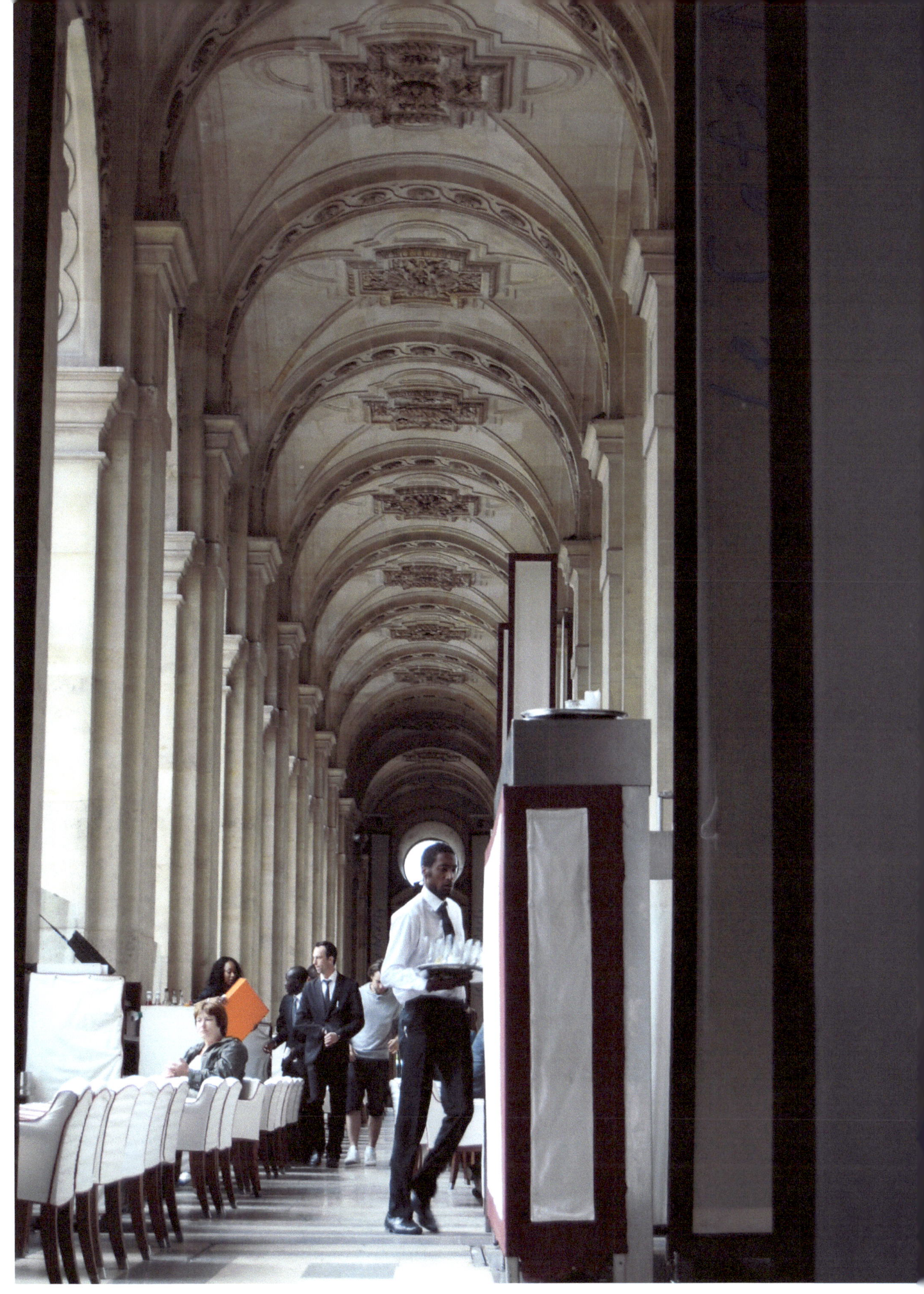

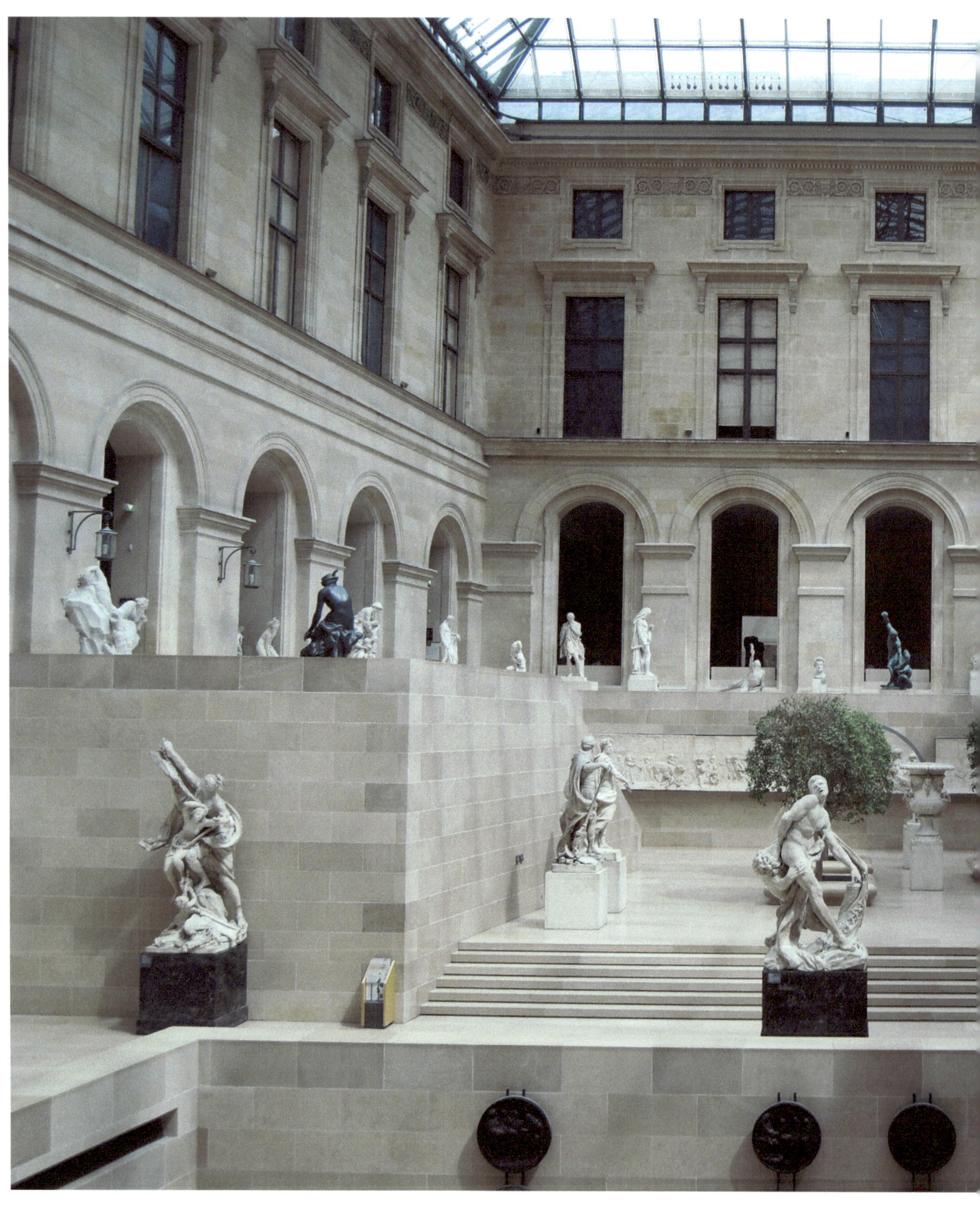

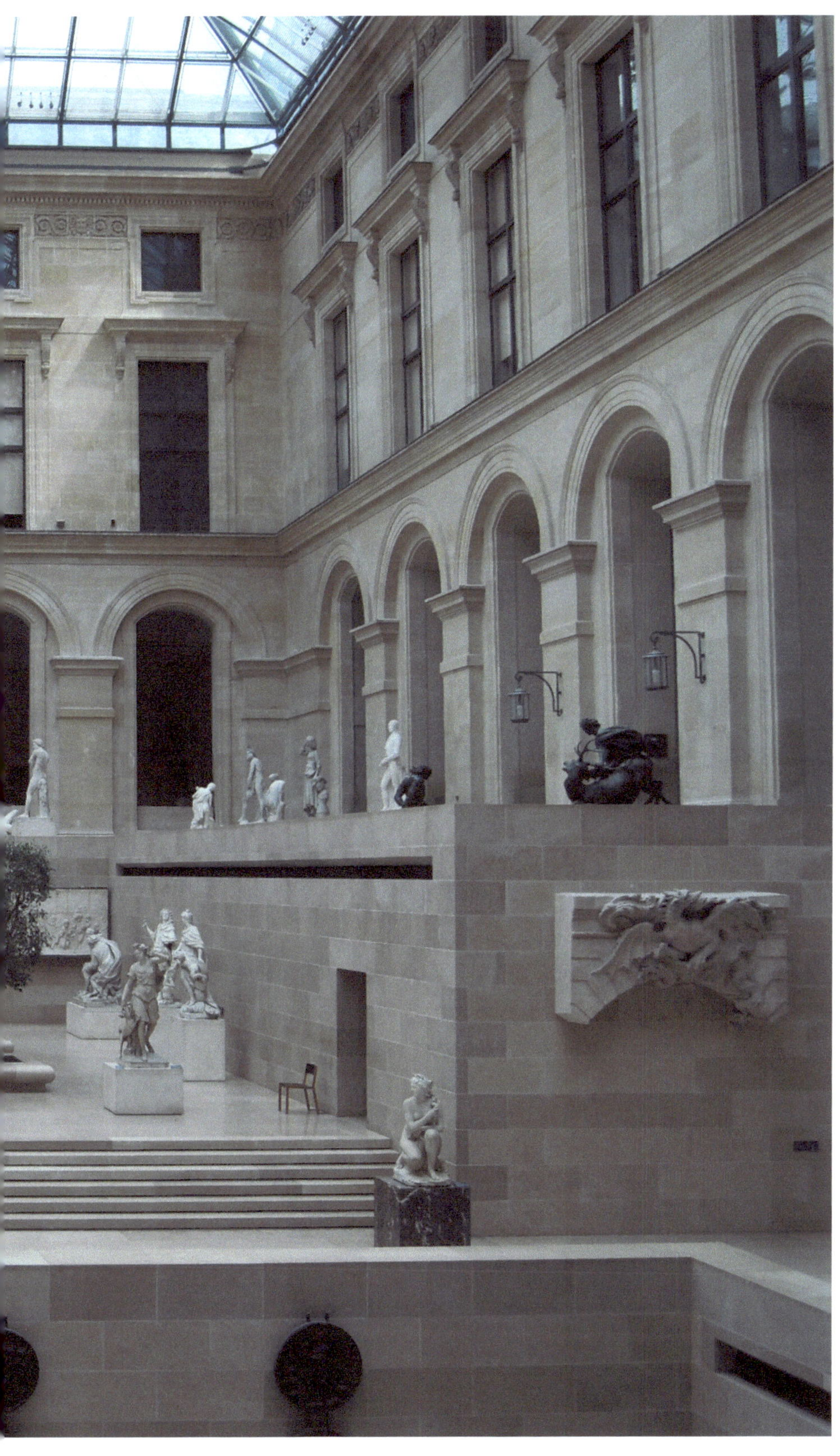

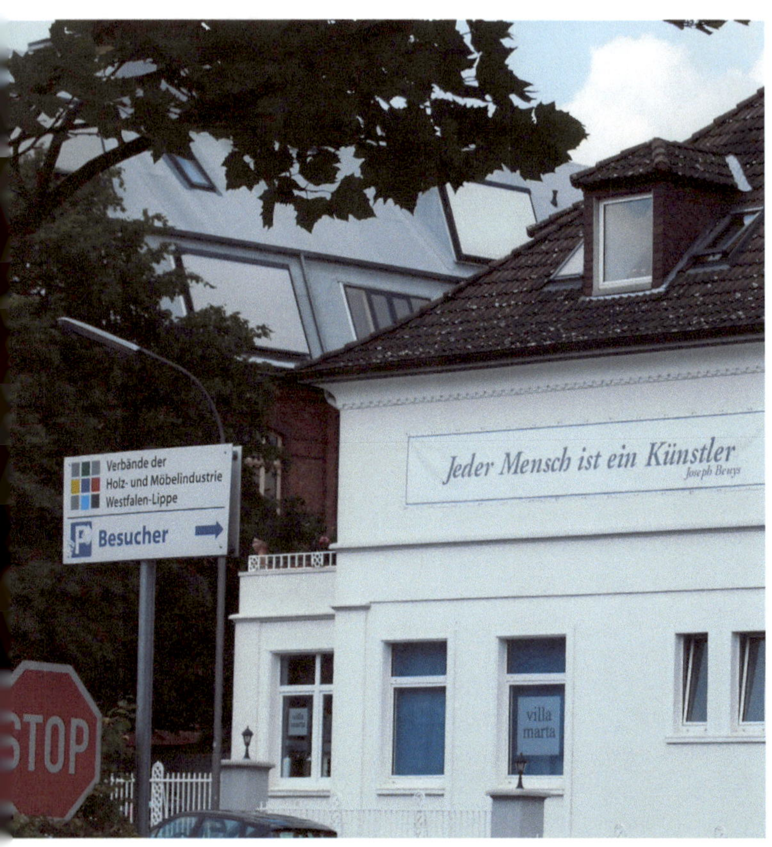
Verbände der
Holz- und Möbelindustrie
Westfalen-Lippe
Besucher
Jeder Mensch ist ein Künstler
Joseph Beuys
STOP
villa
marta

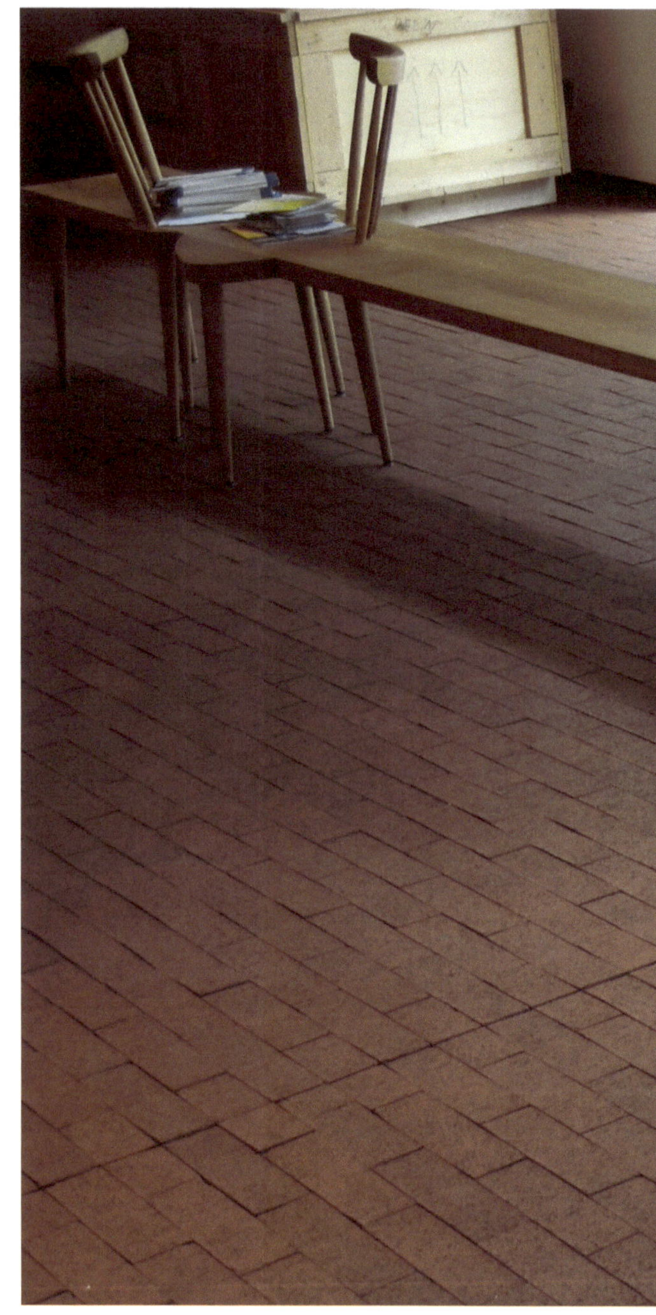

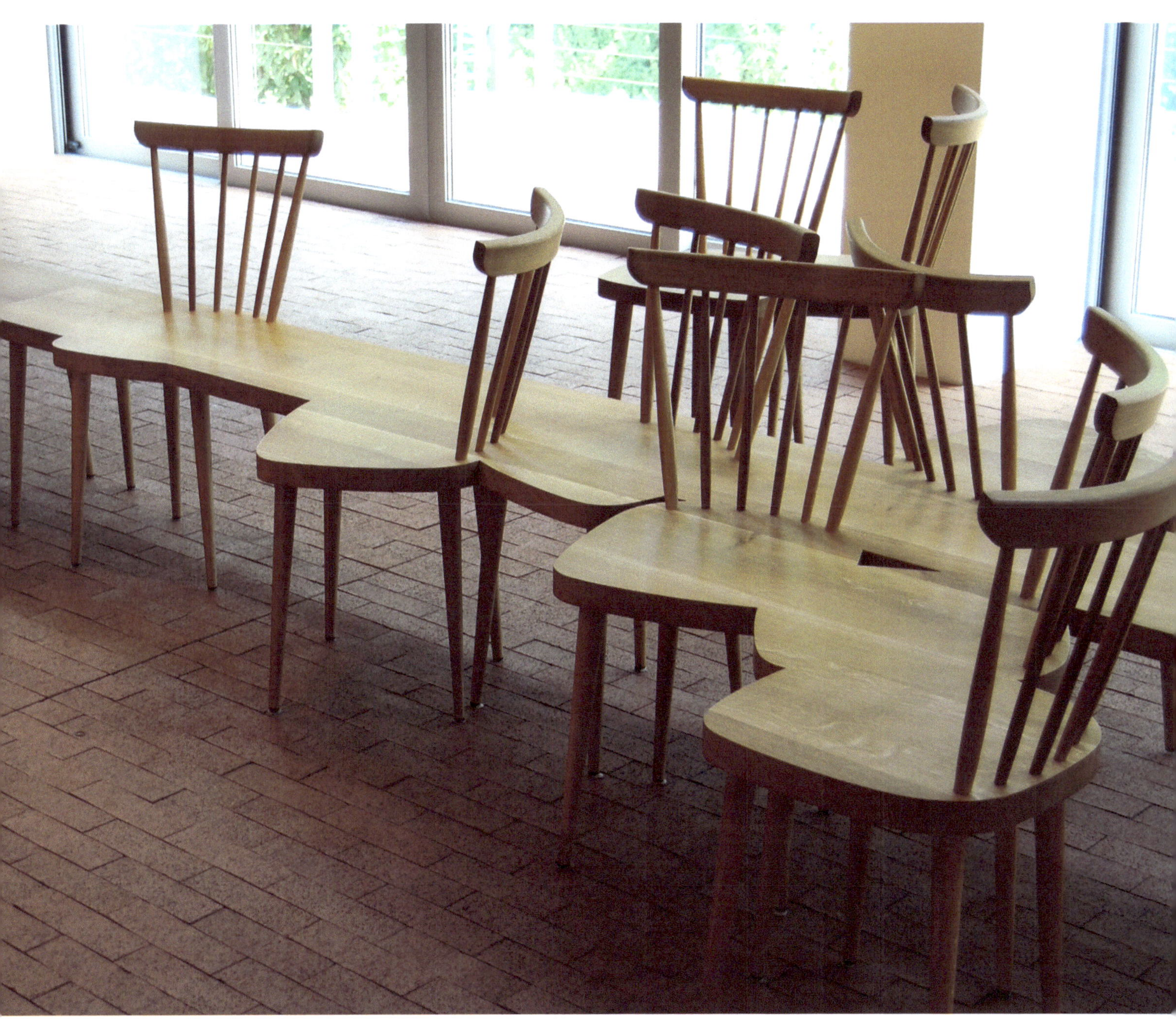

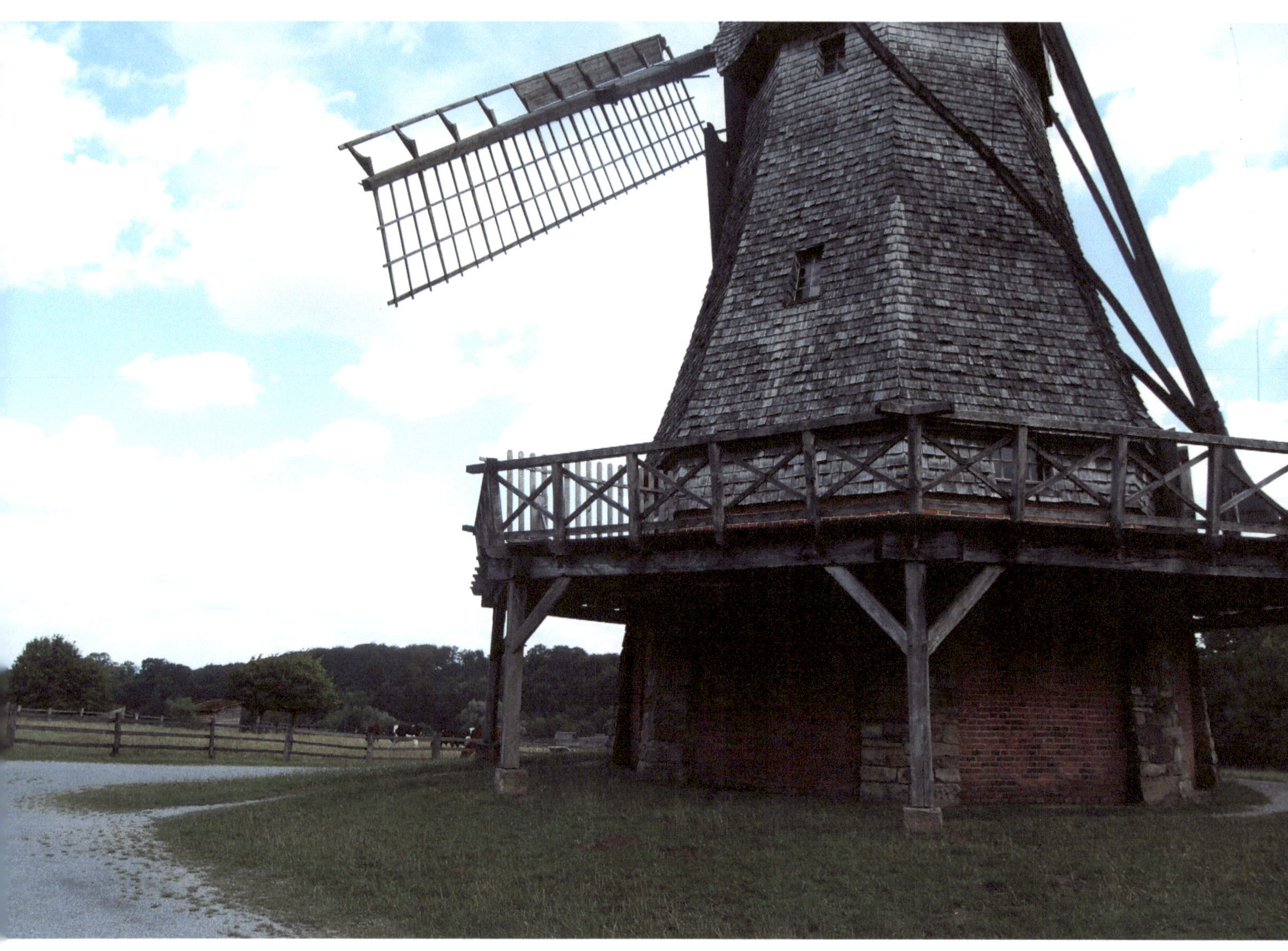

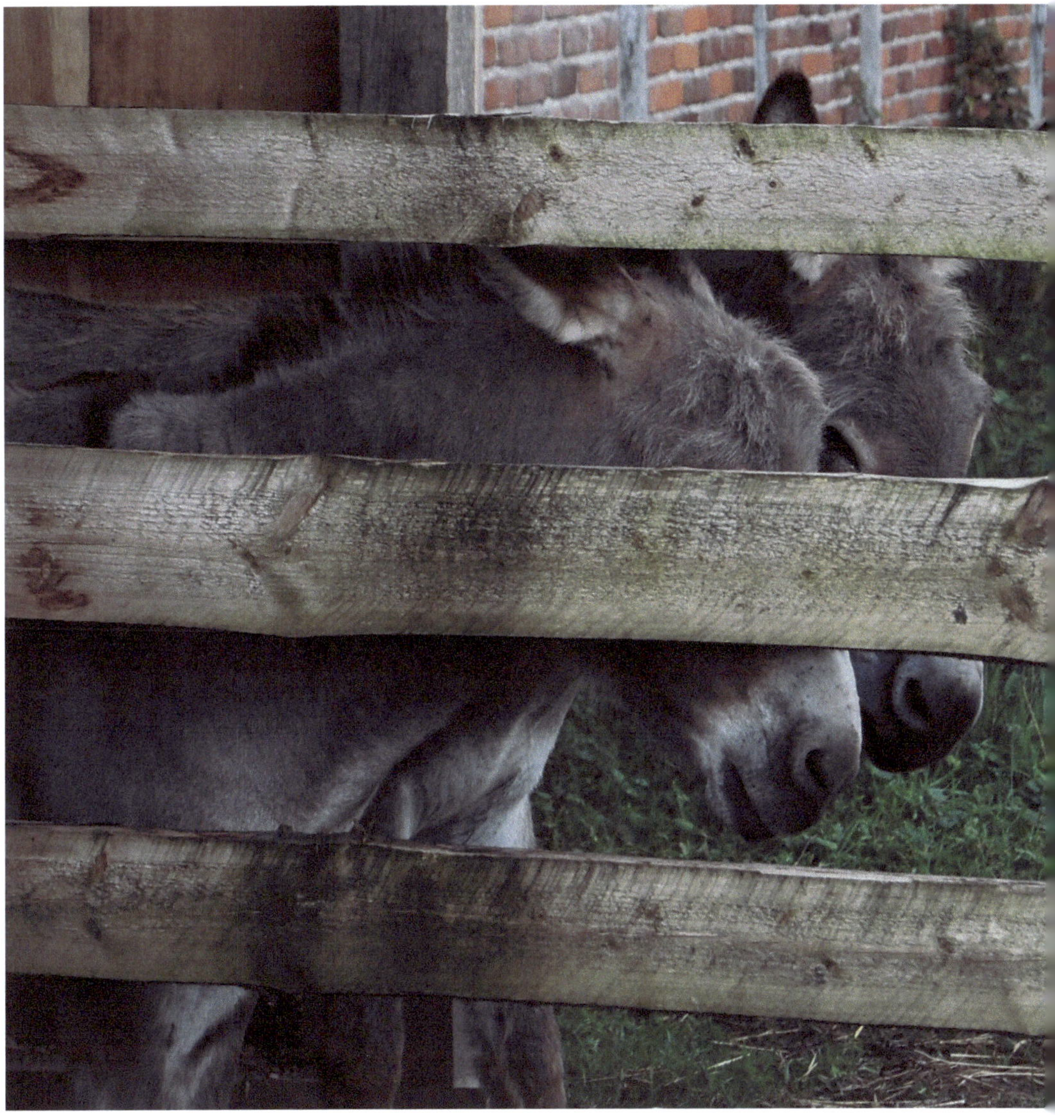

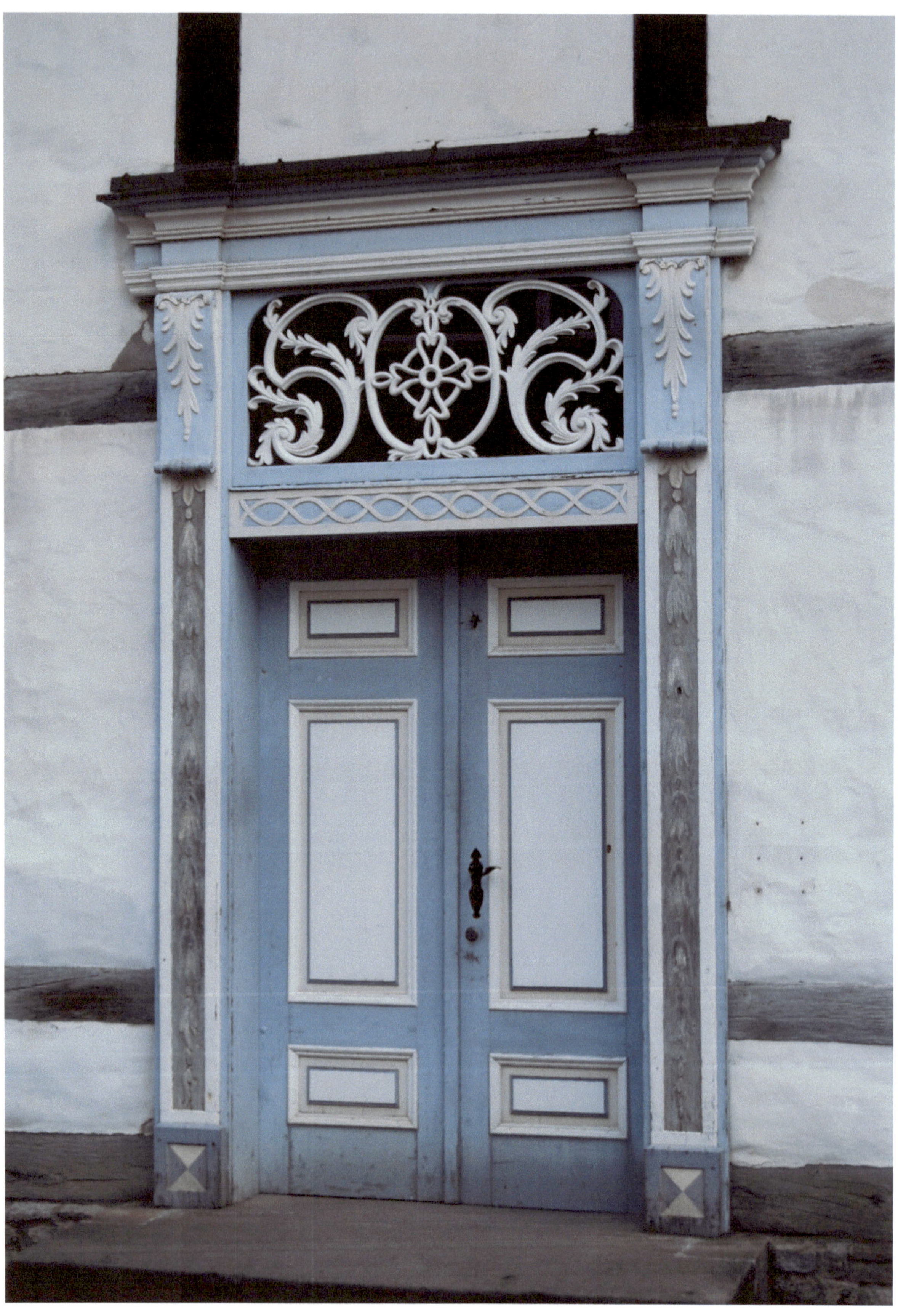

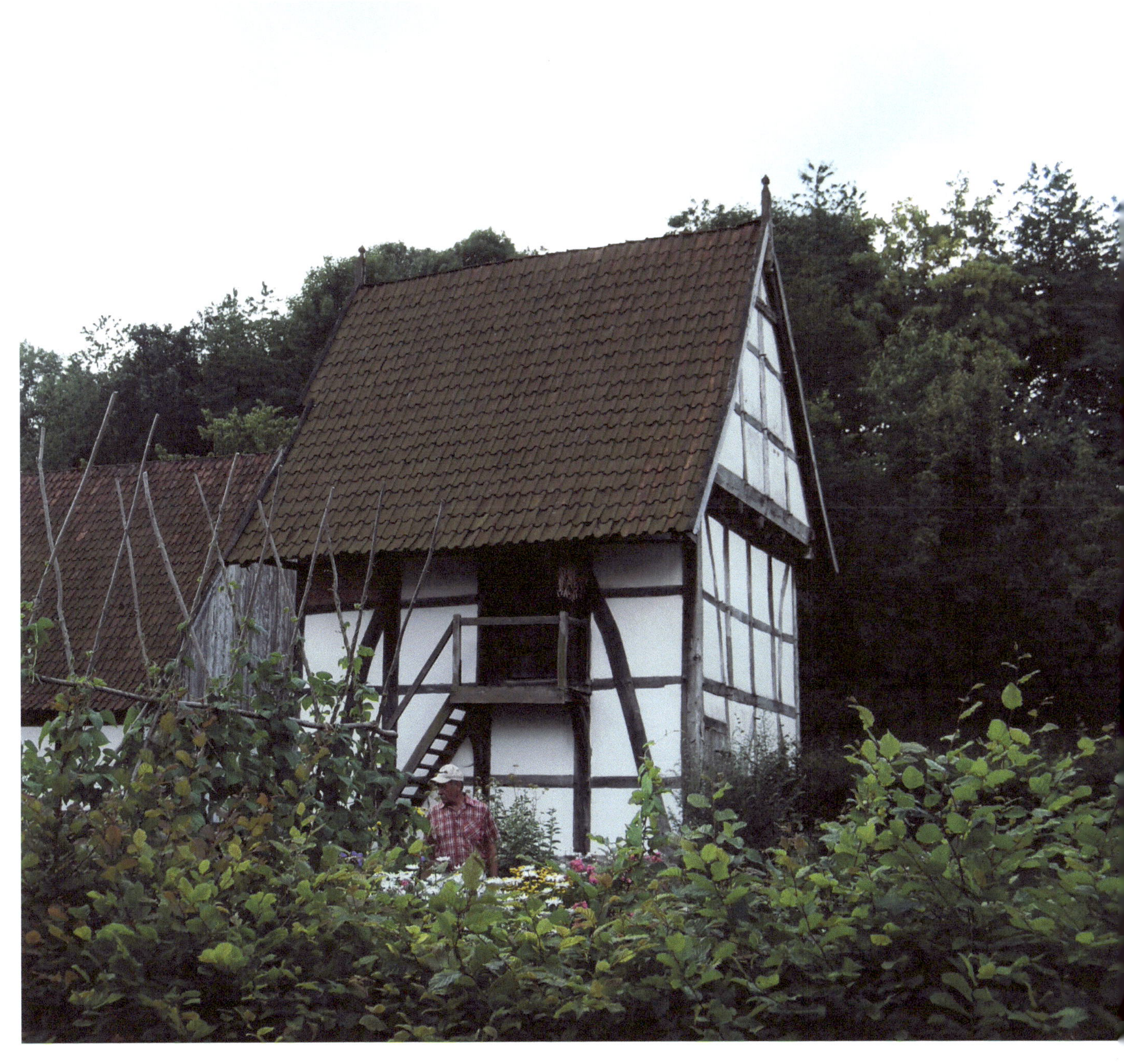

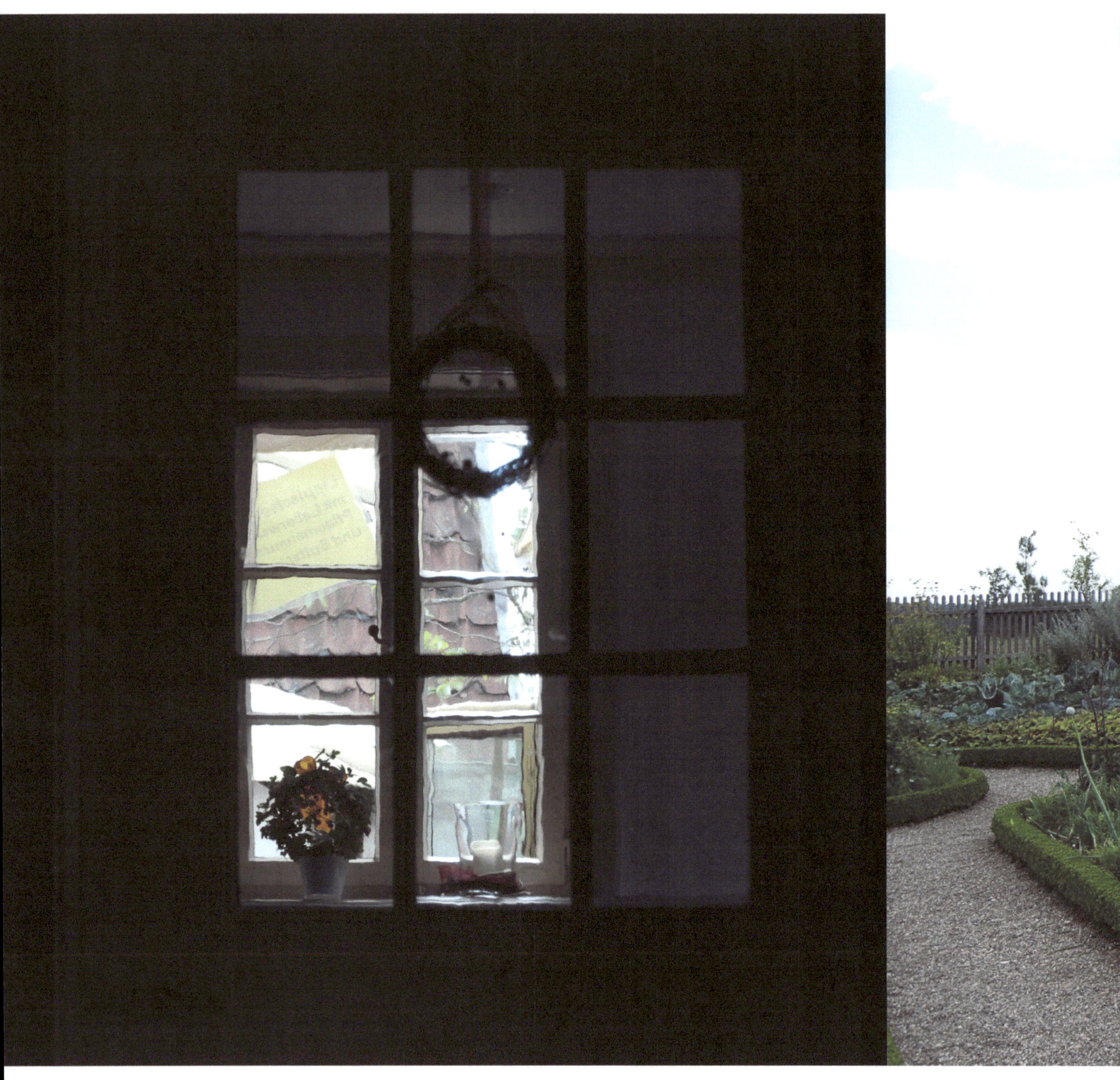

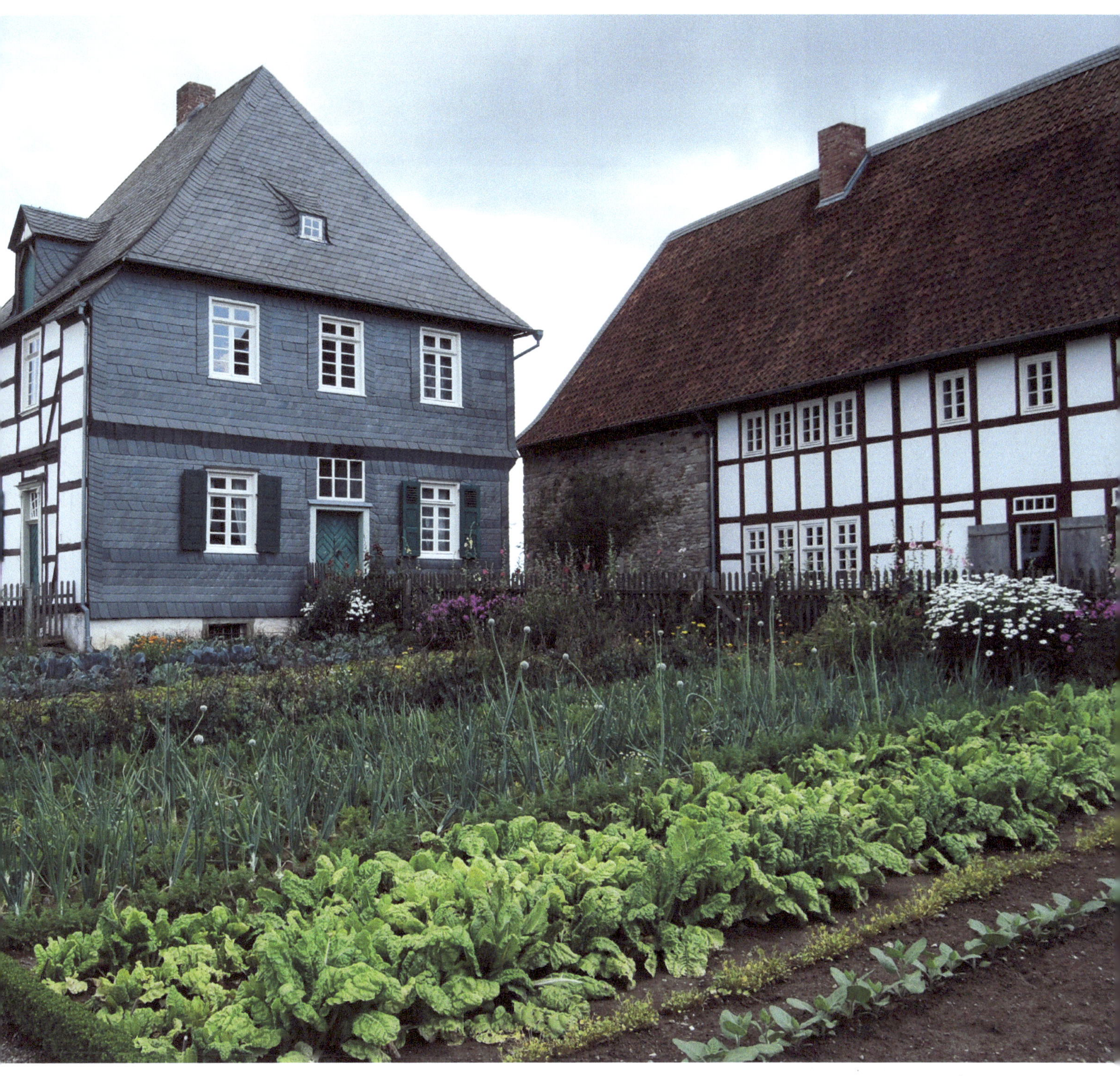

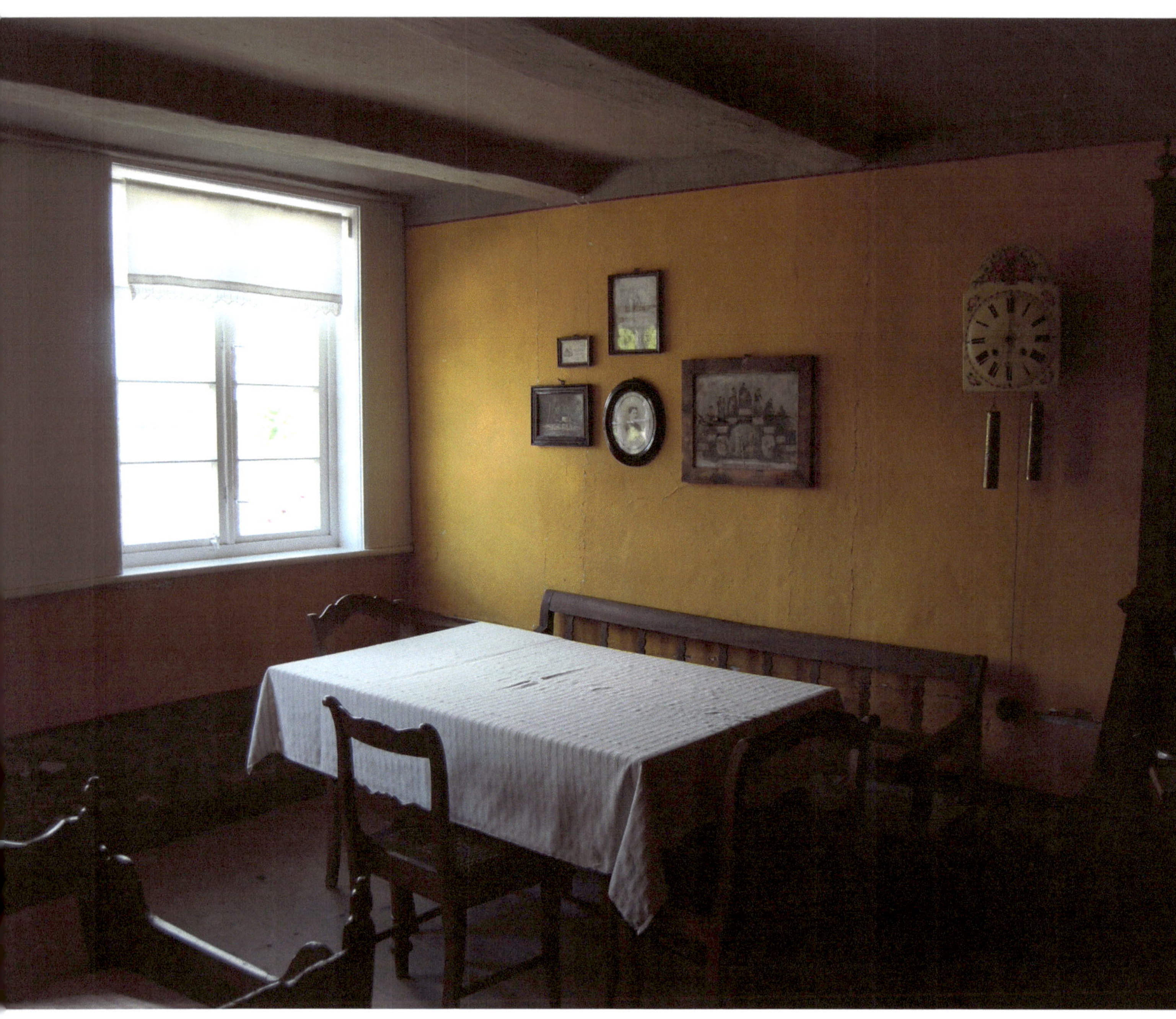

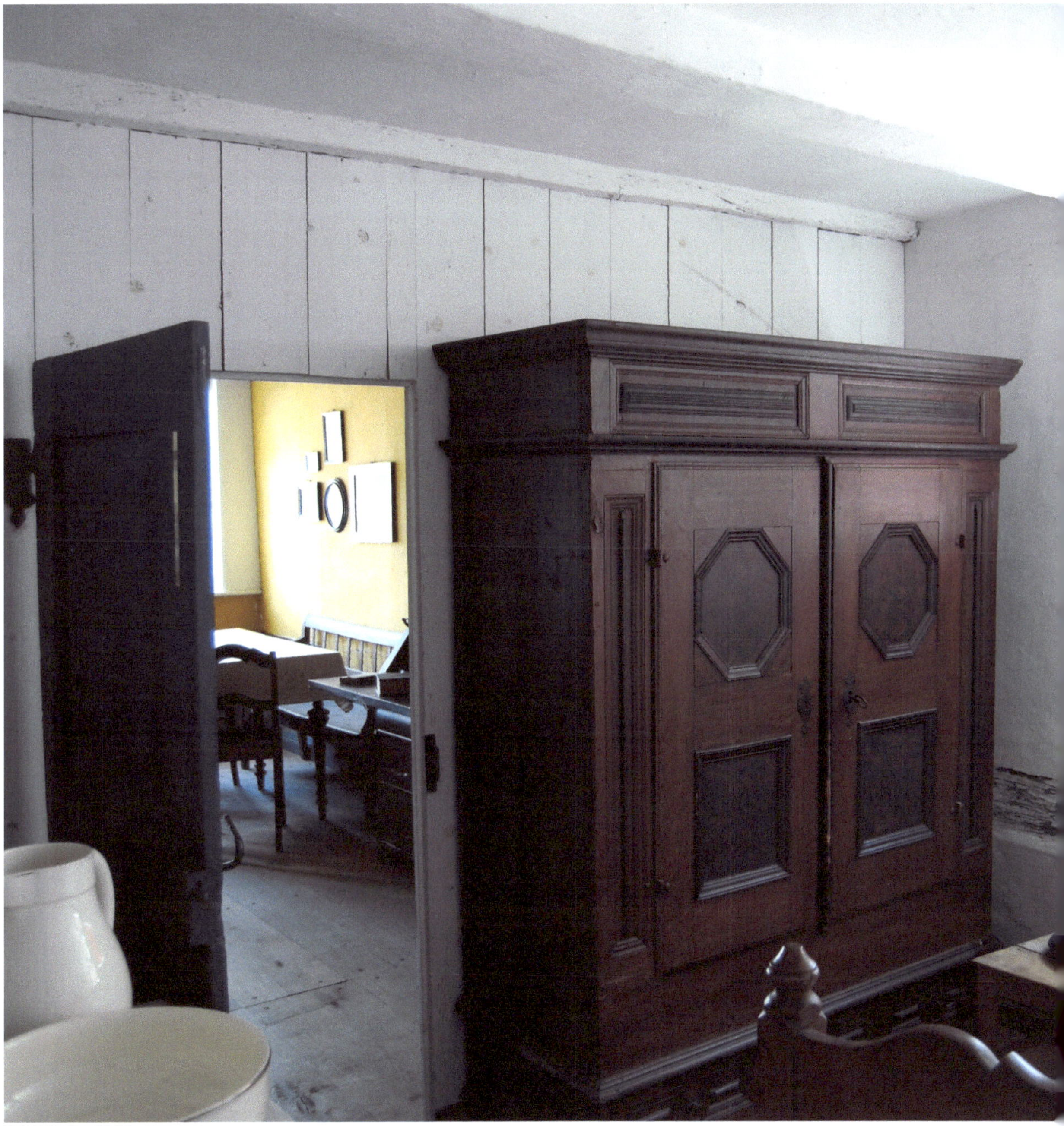

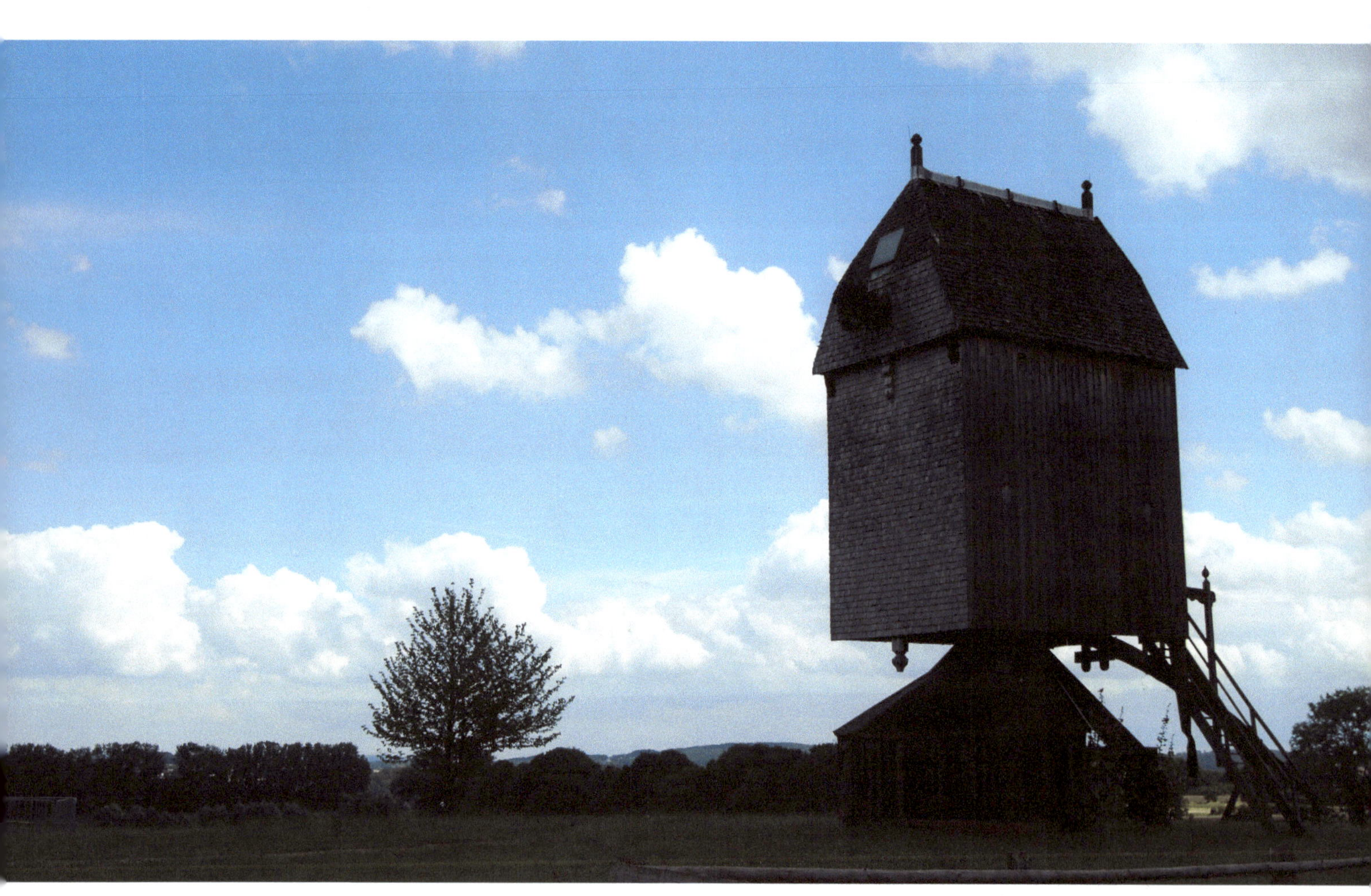

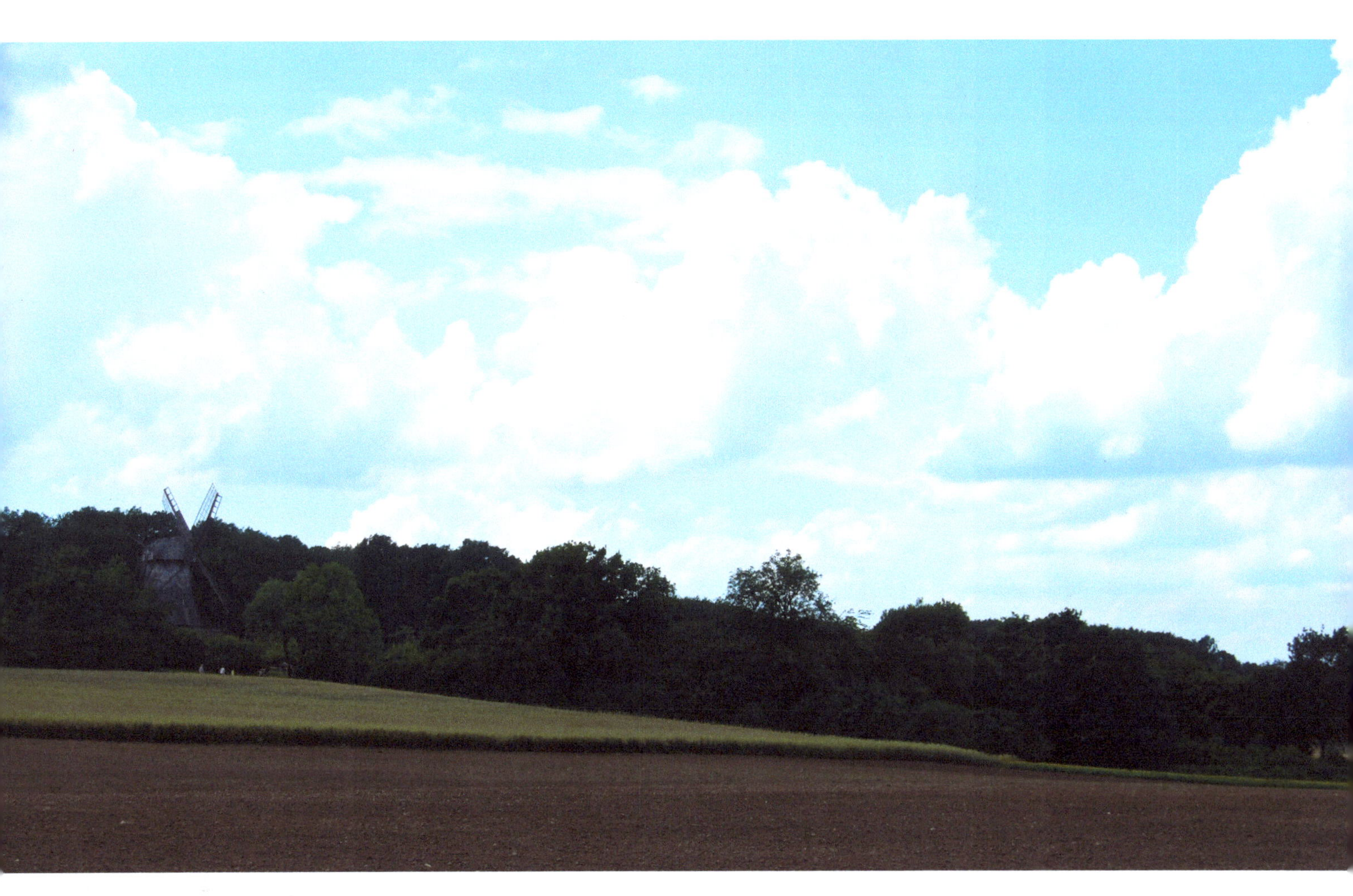

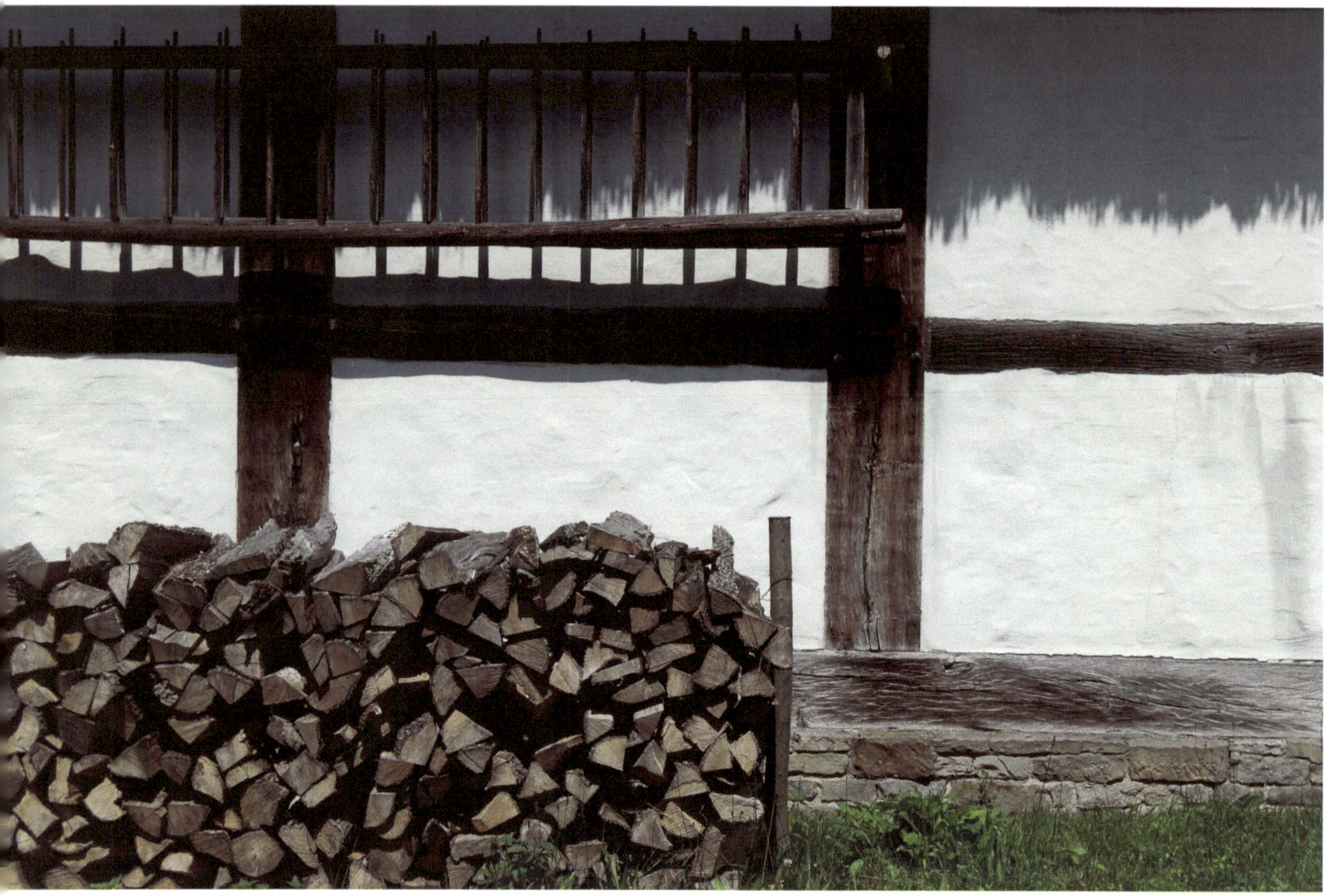

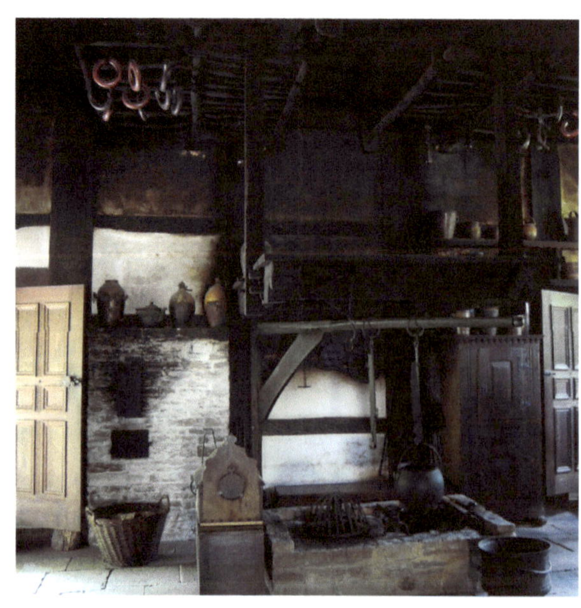

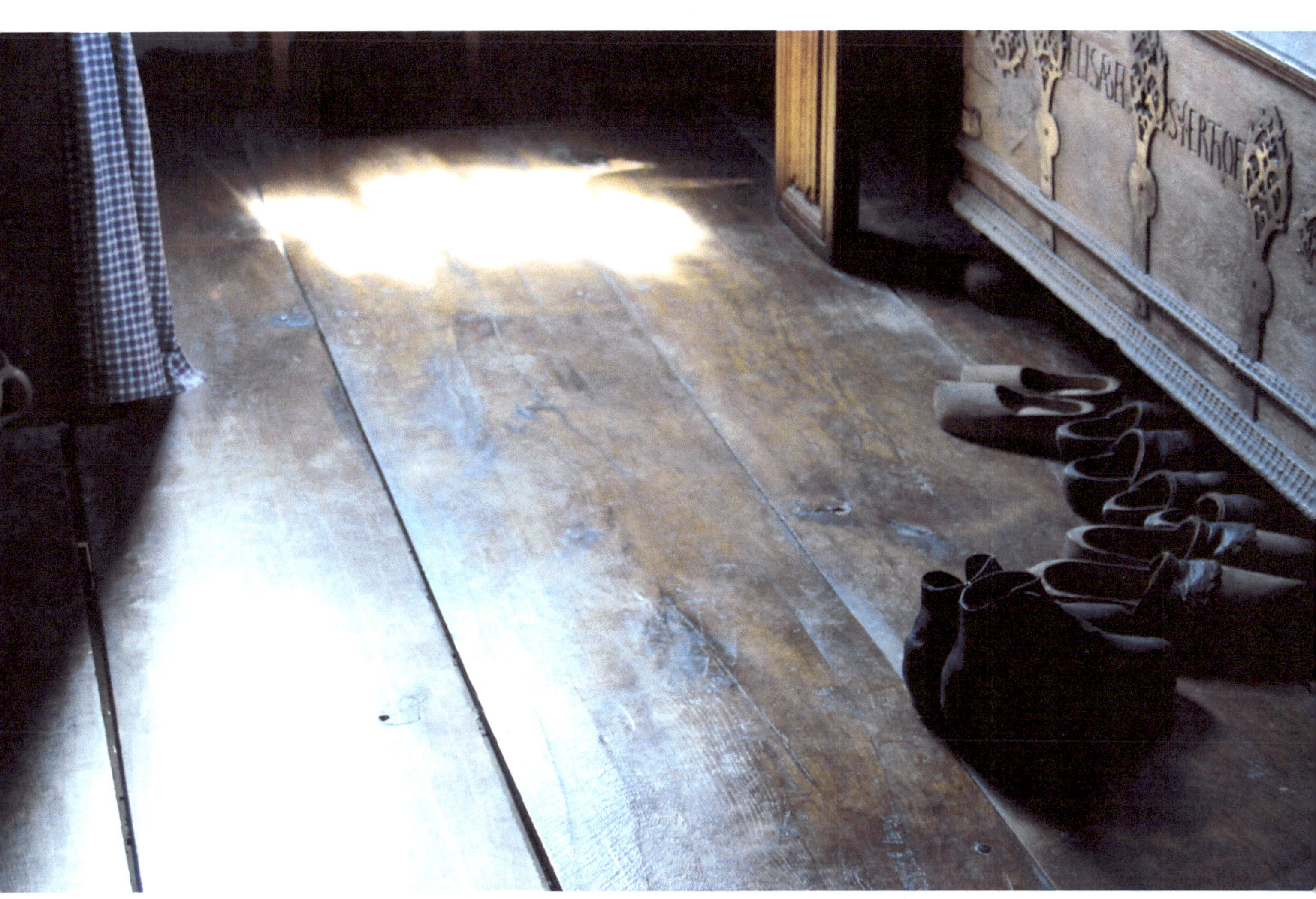

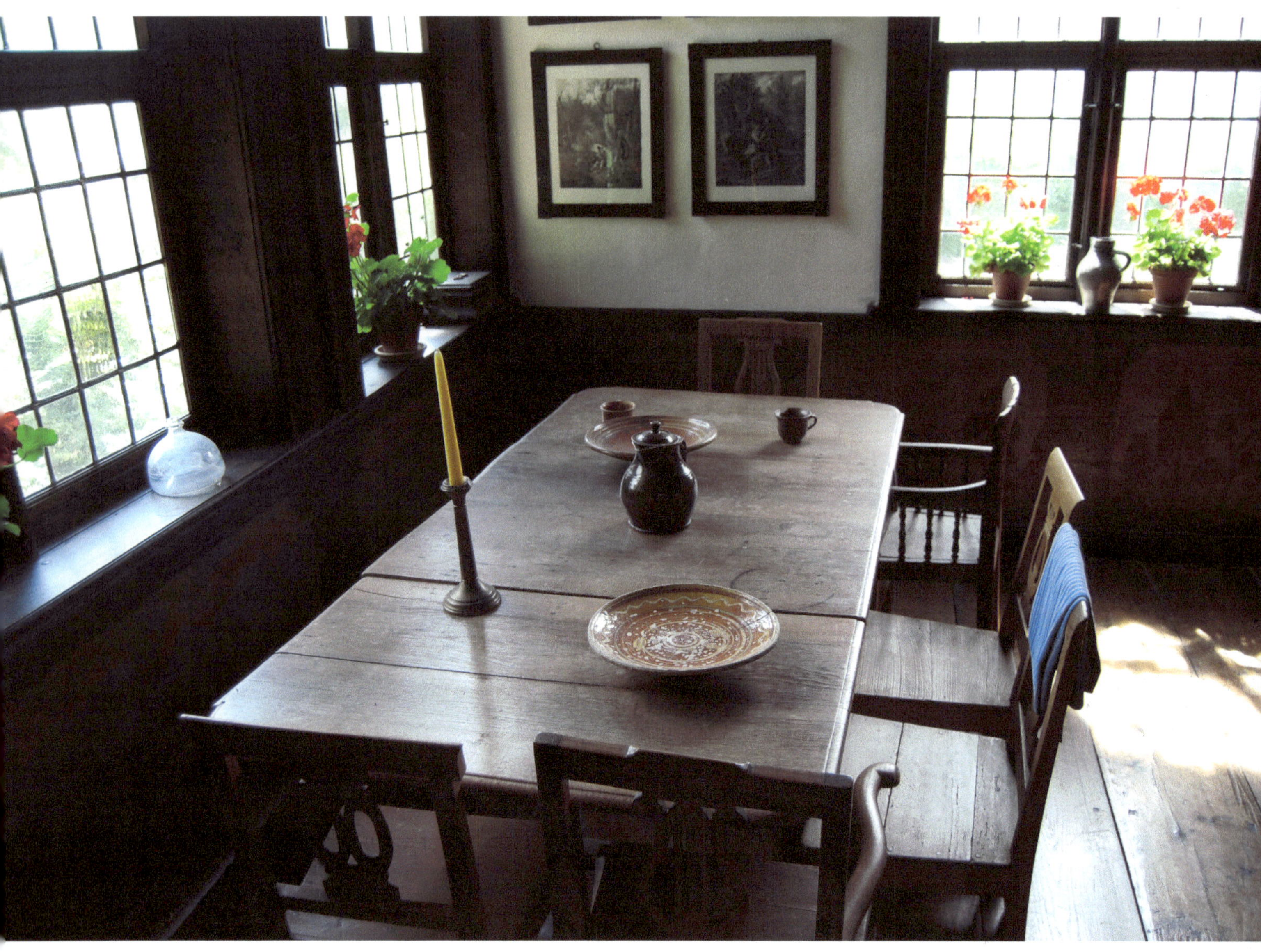

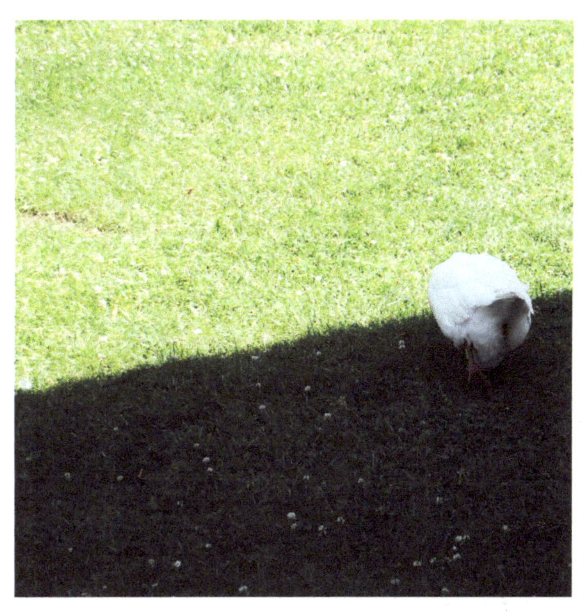

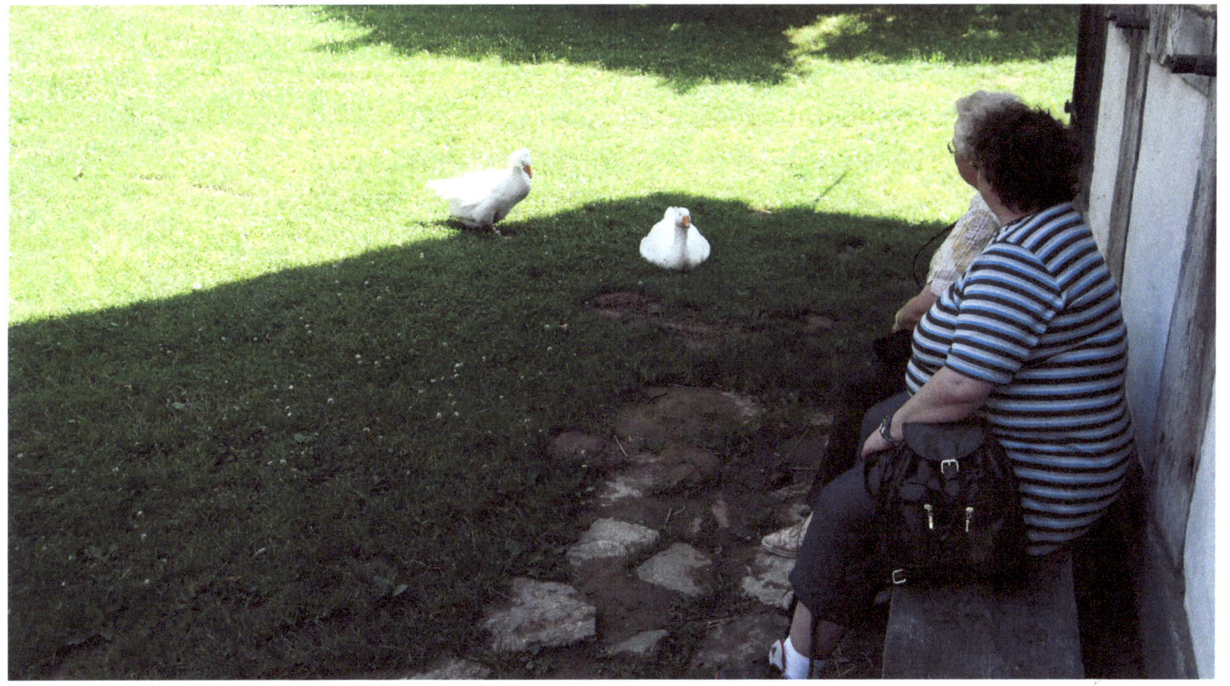

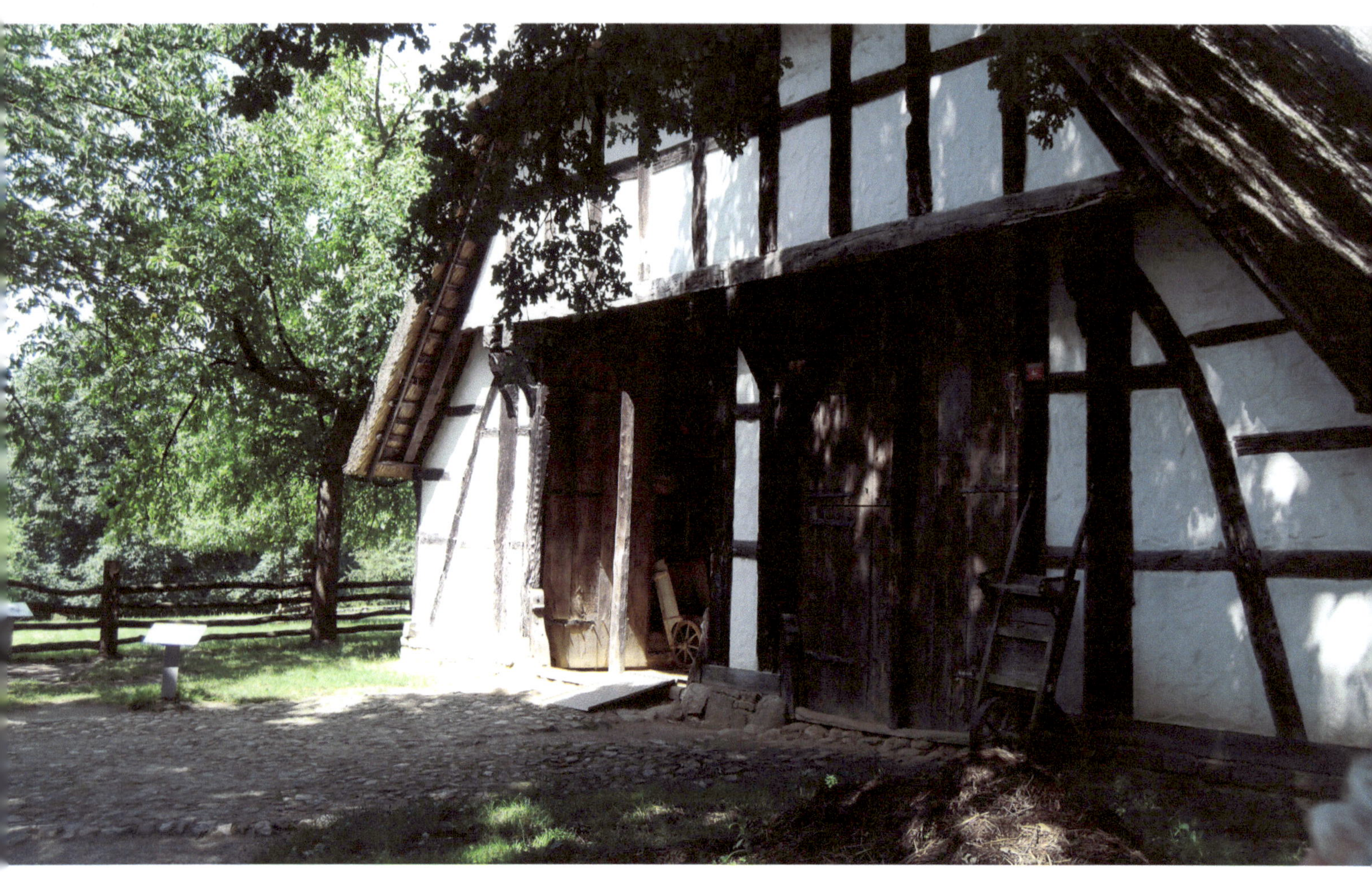

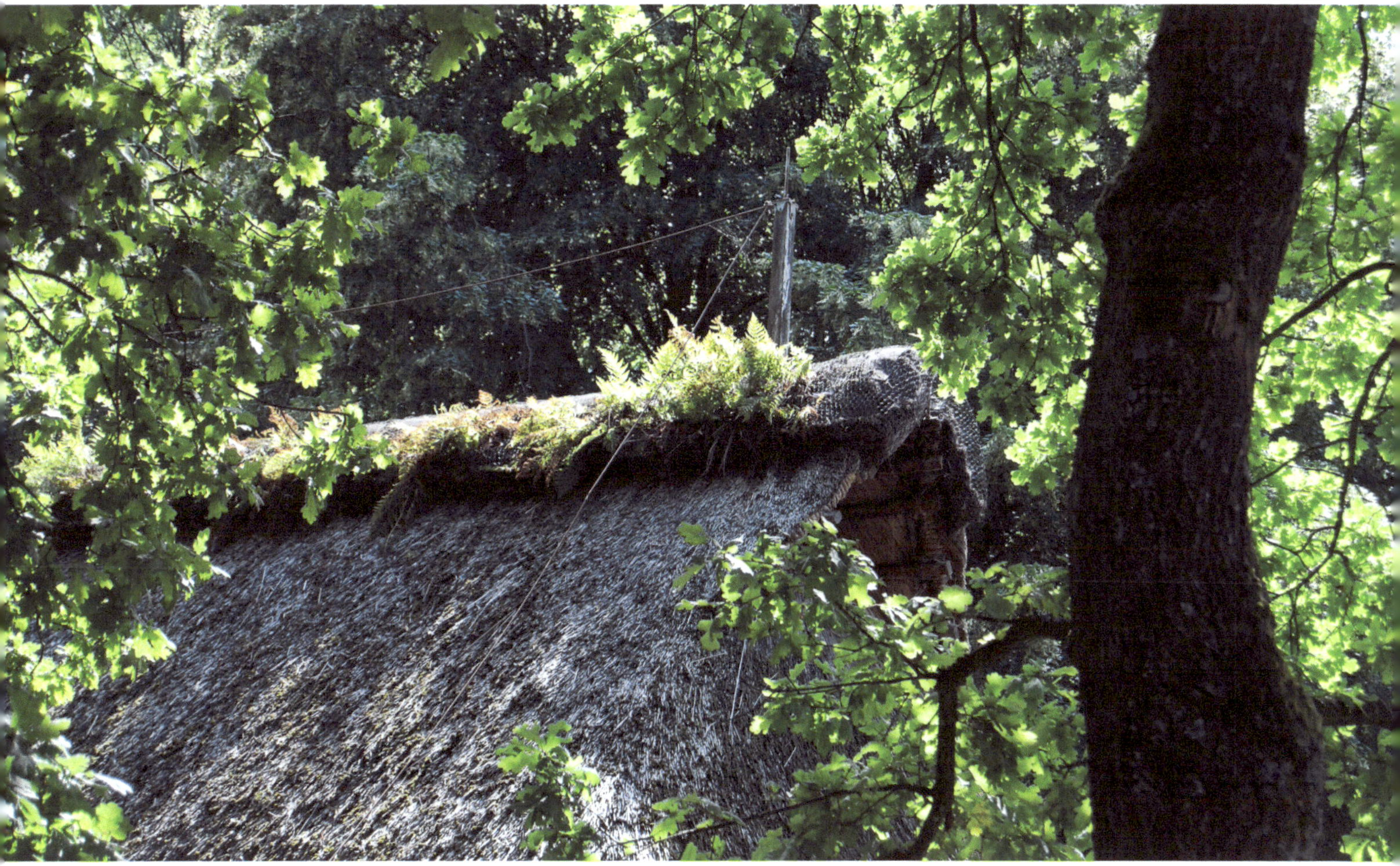

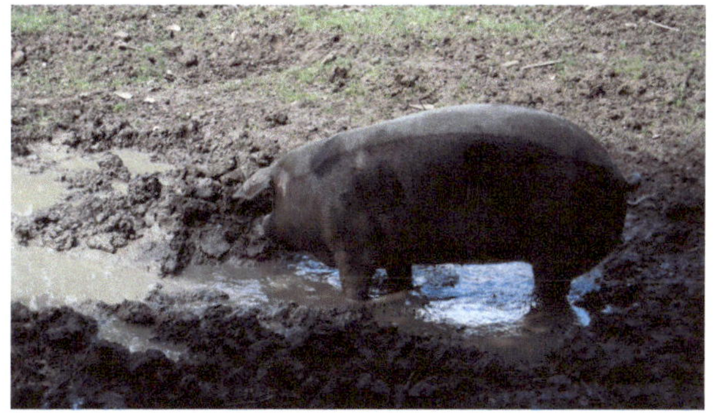

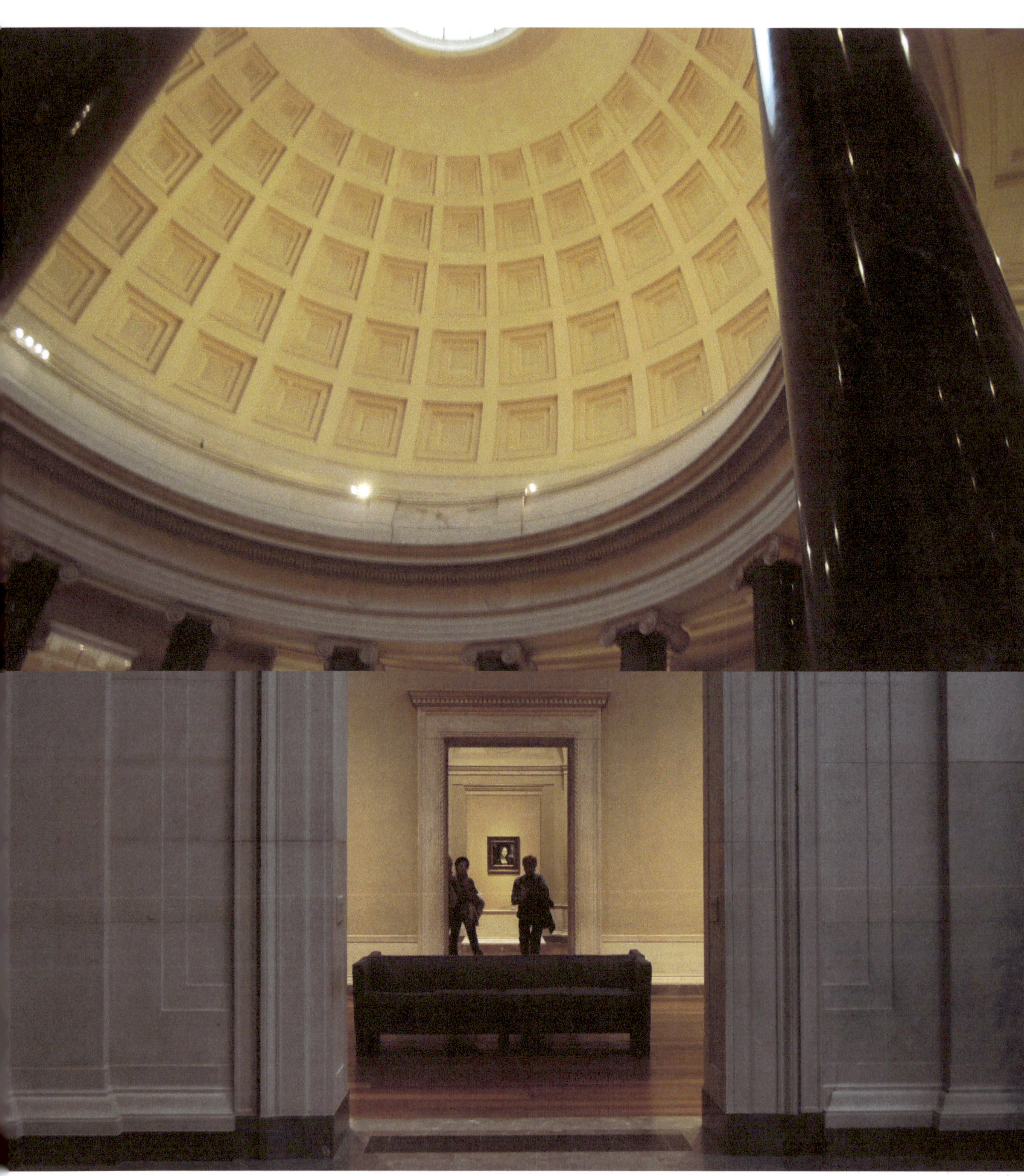

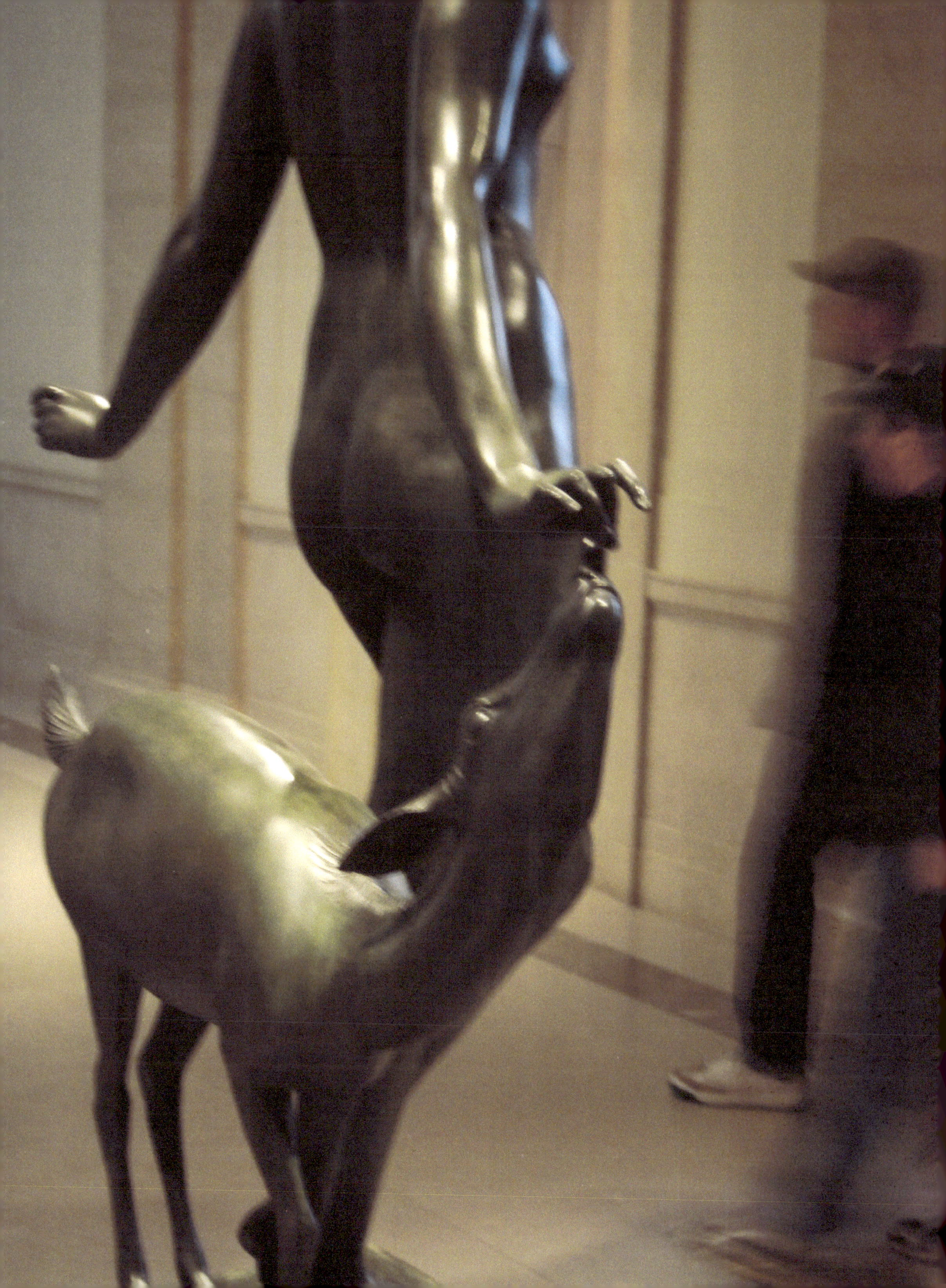

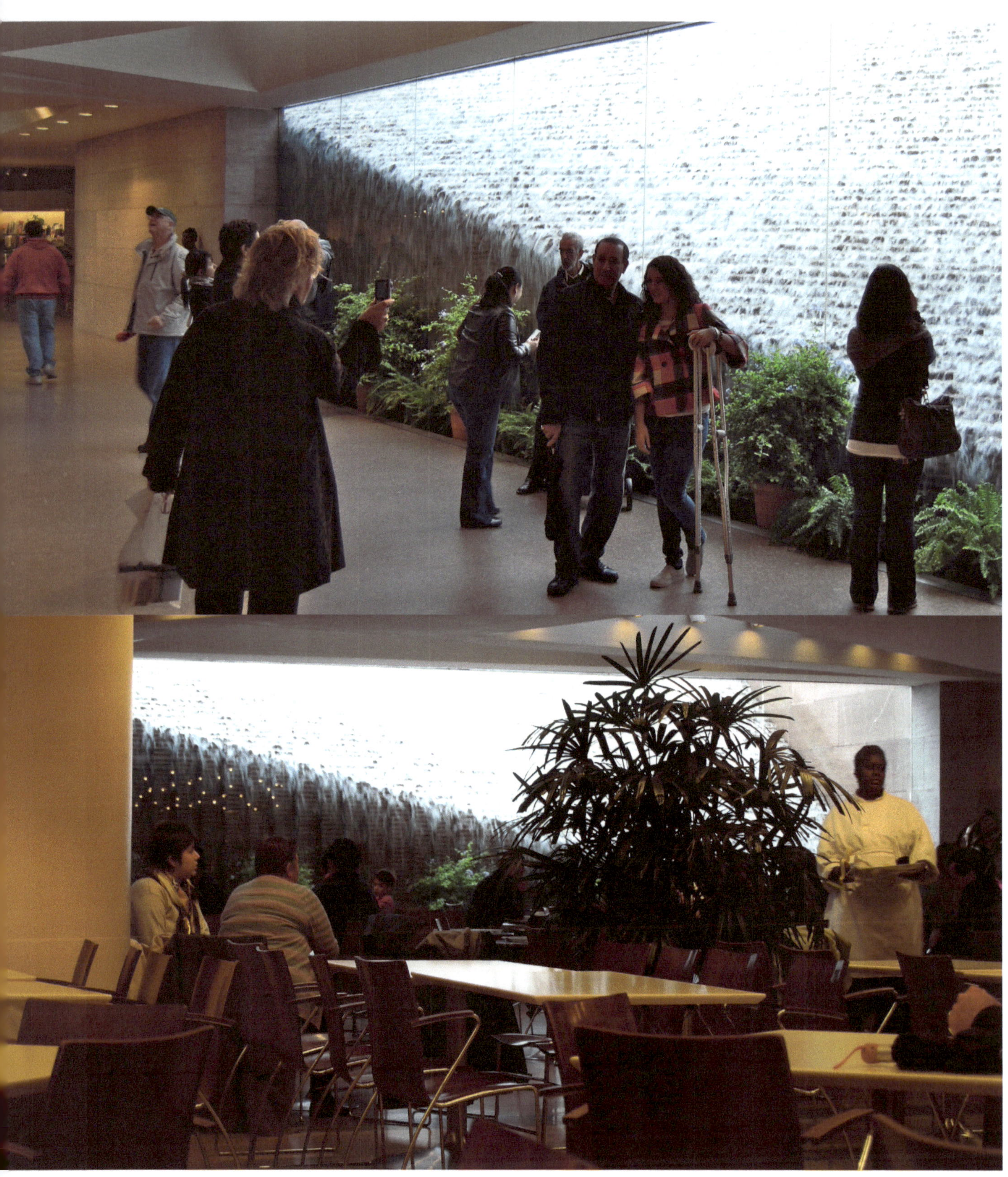

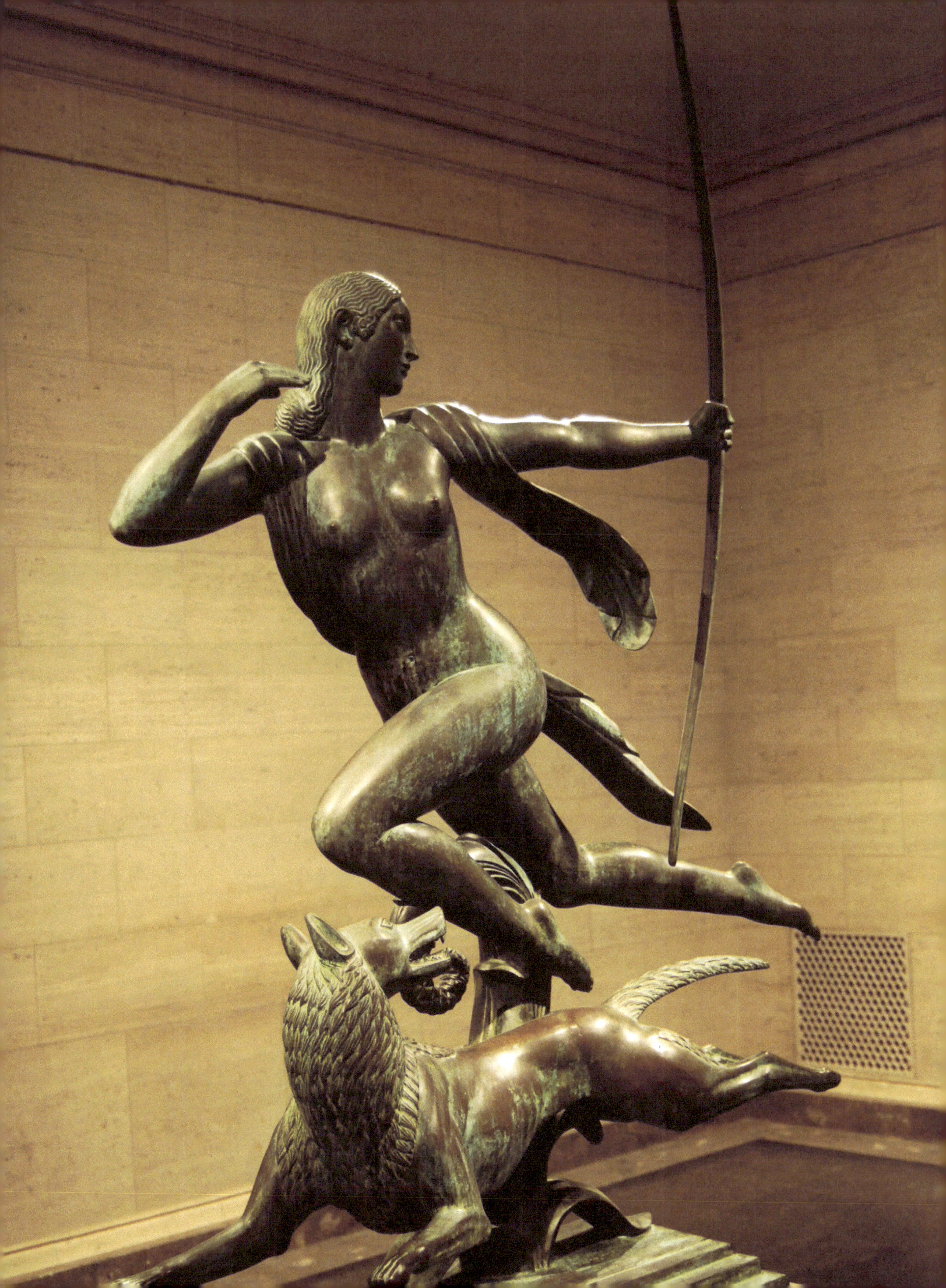

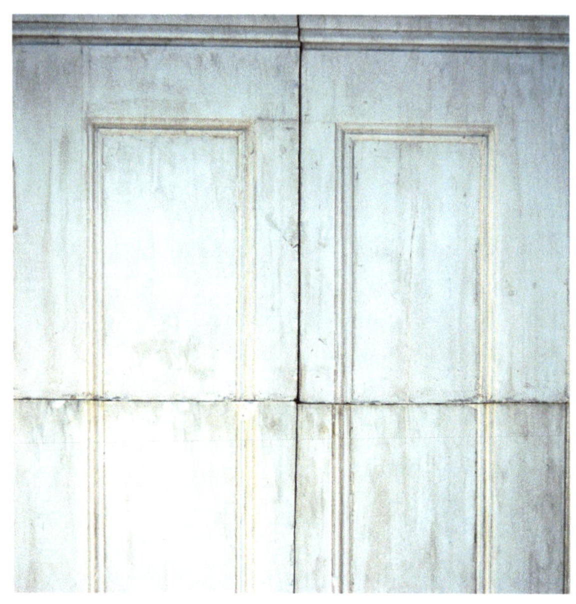

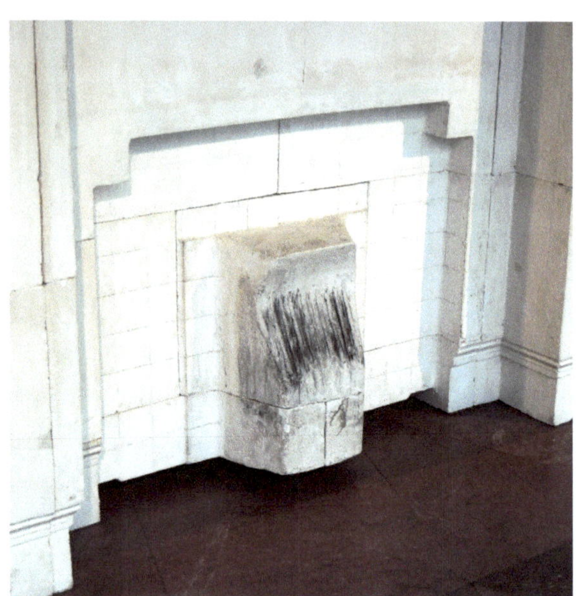

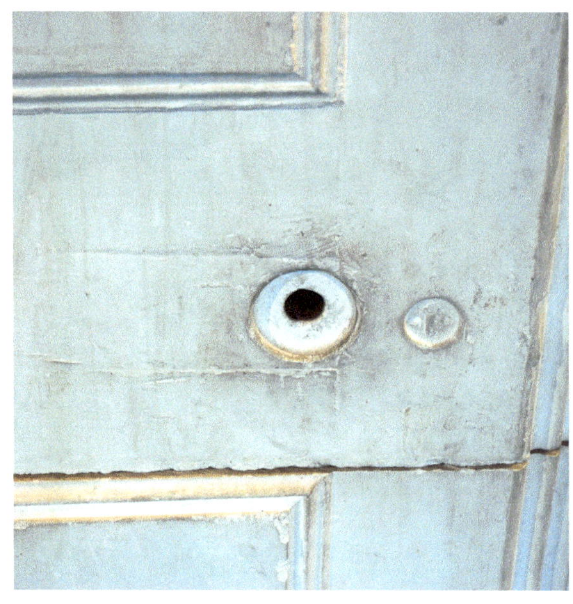

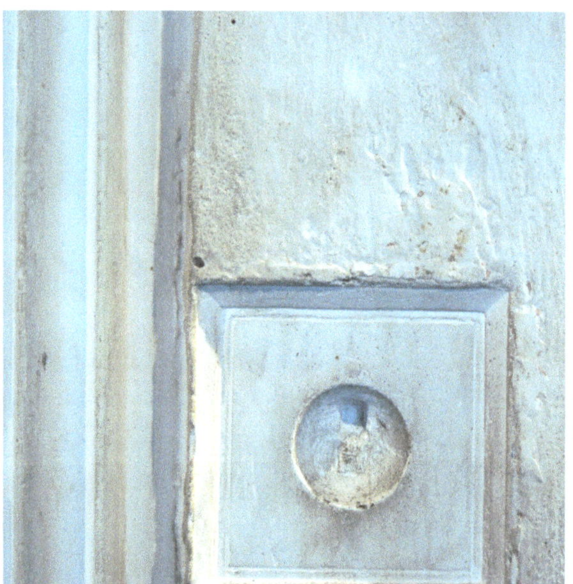

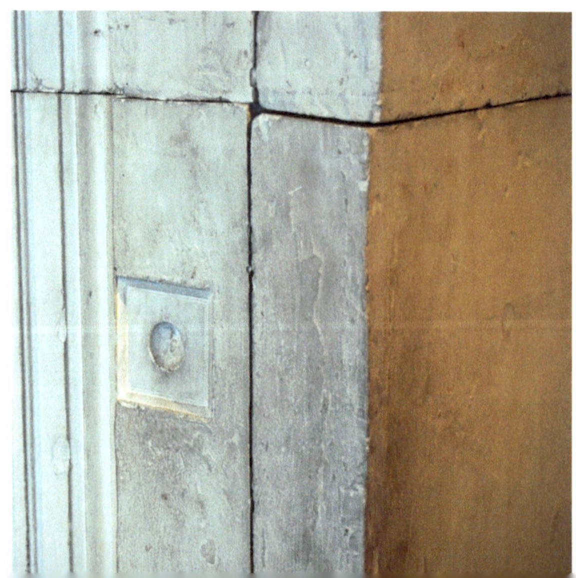

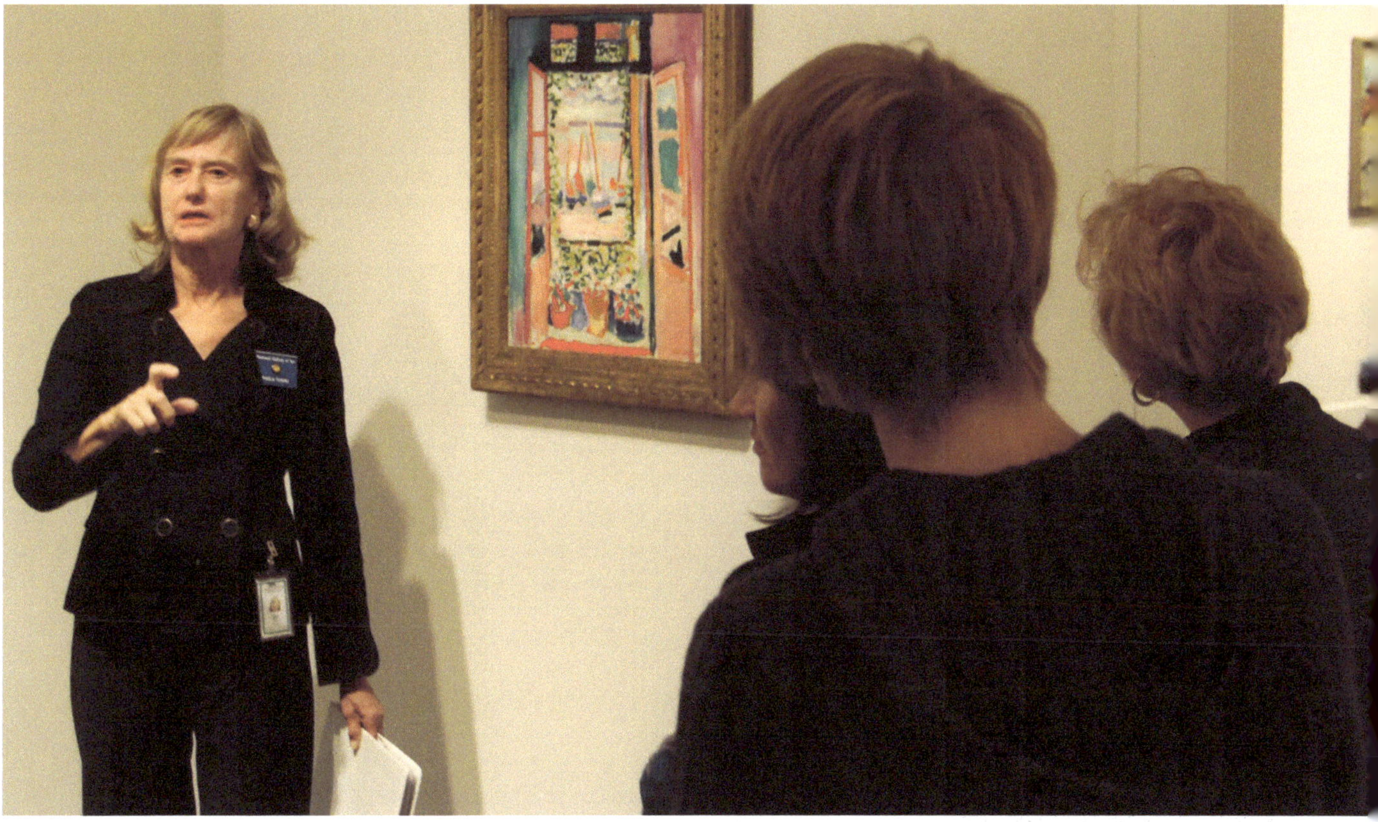

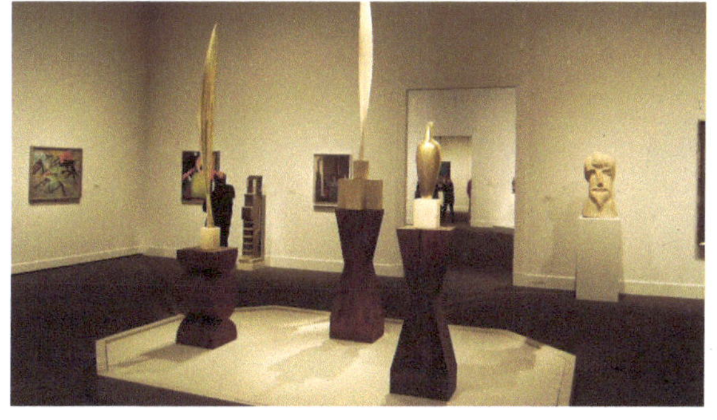

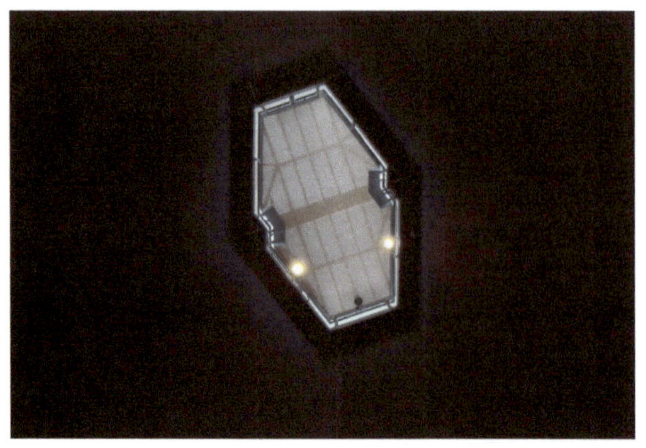

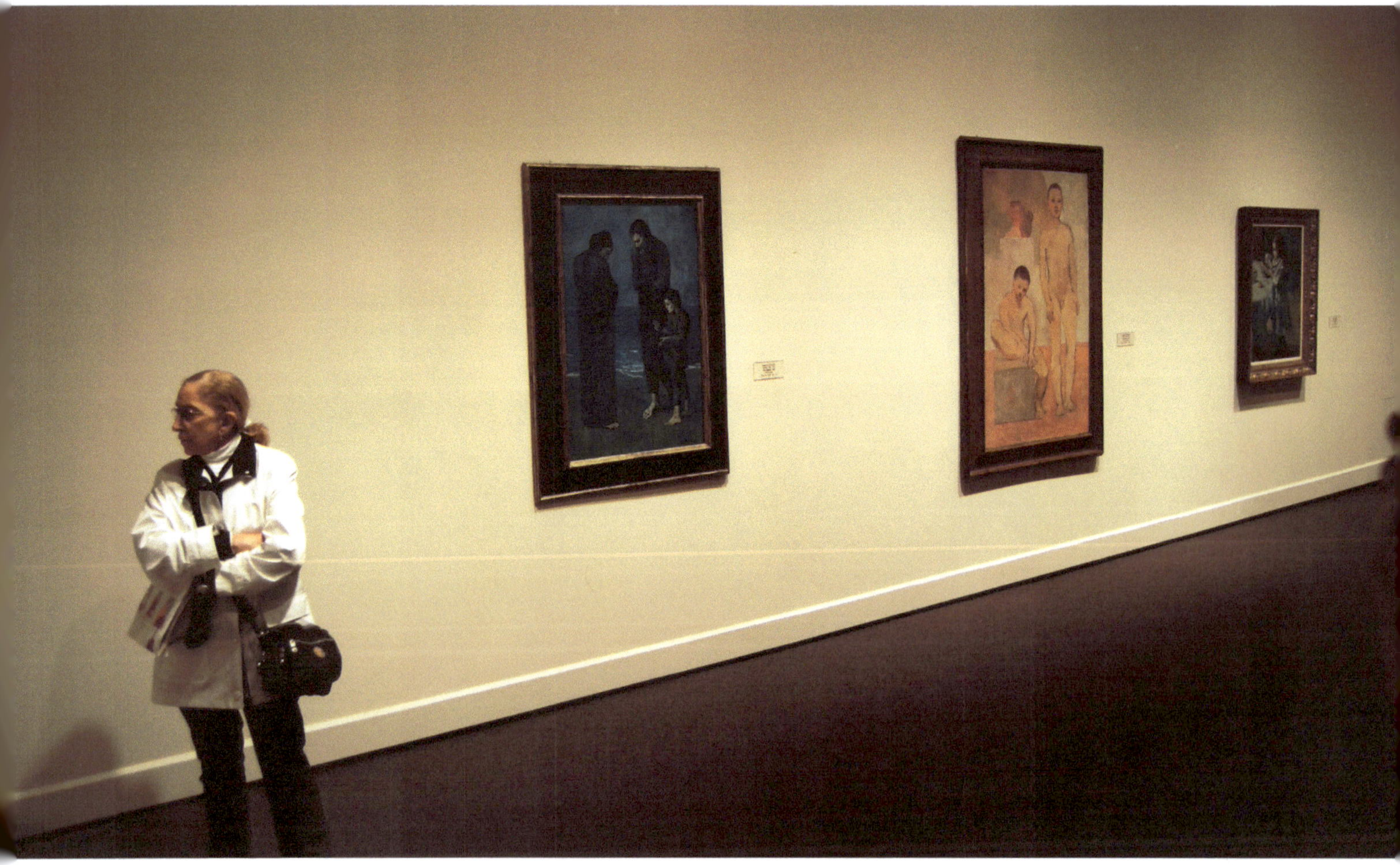

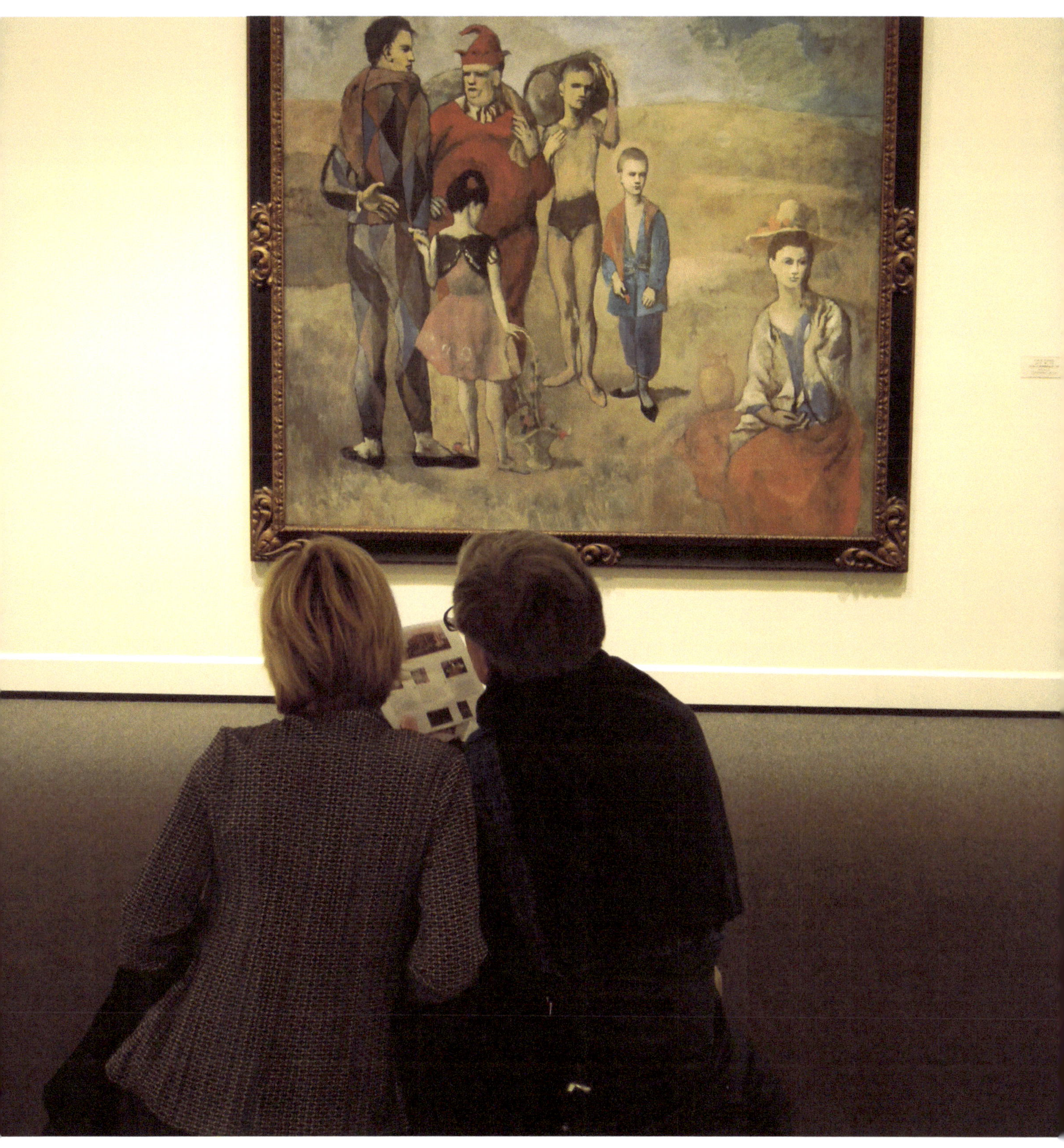

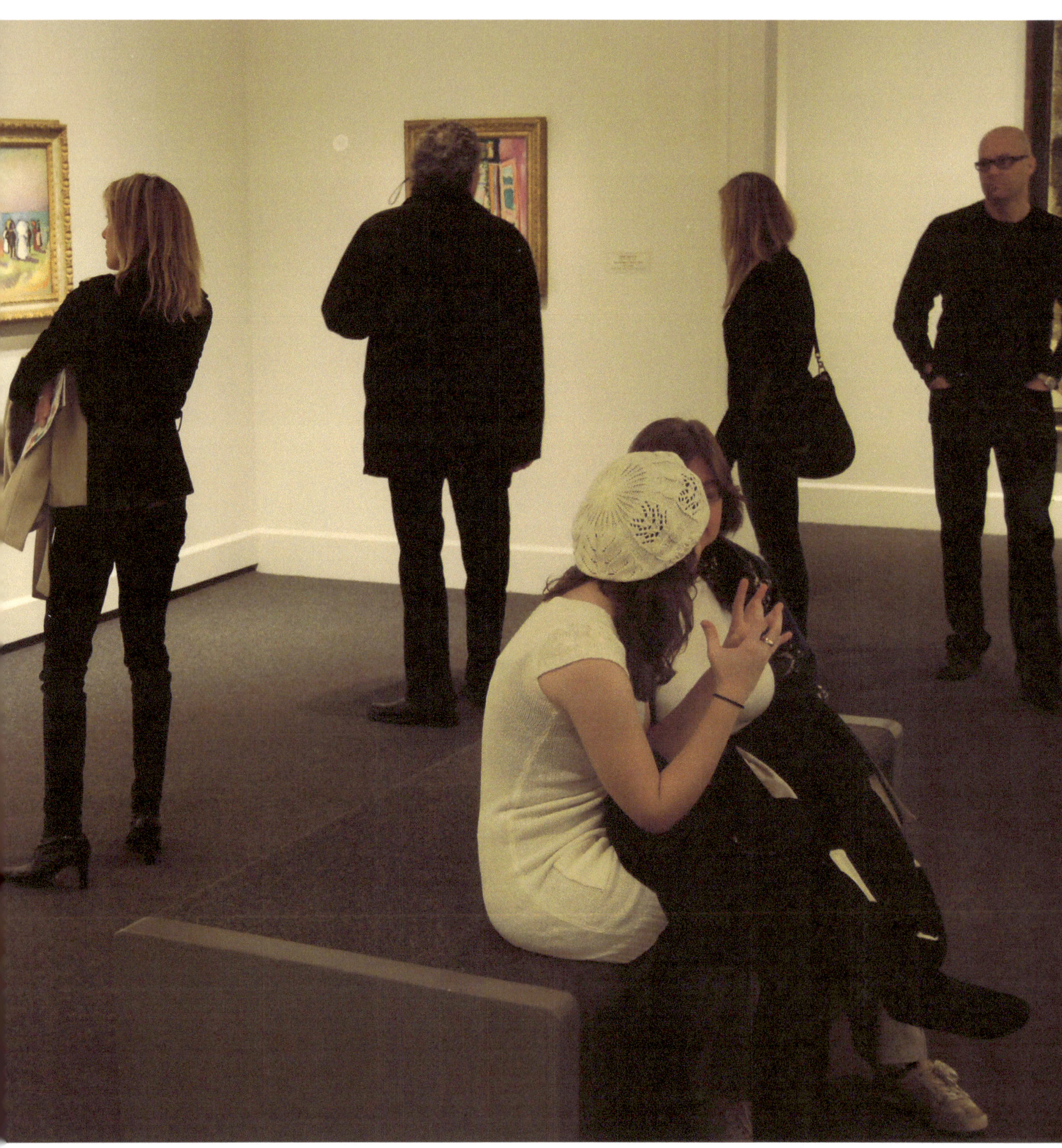

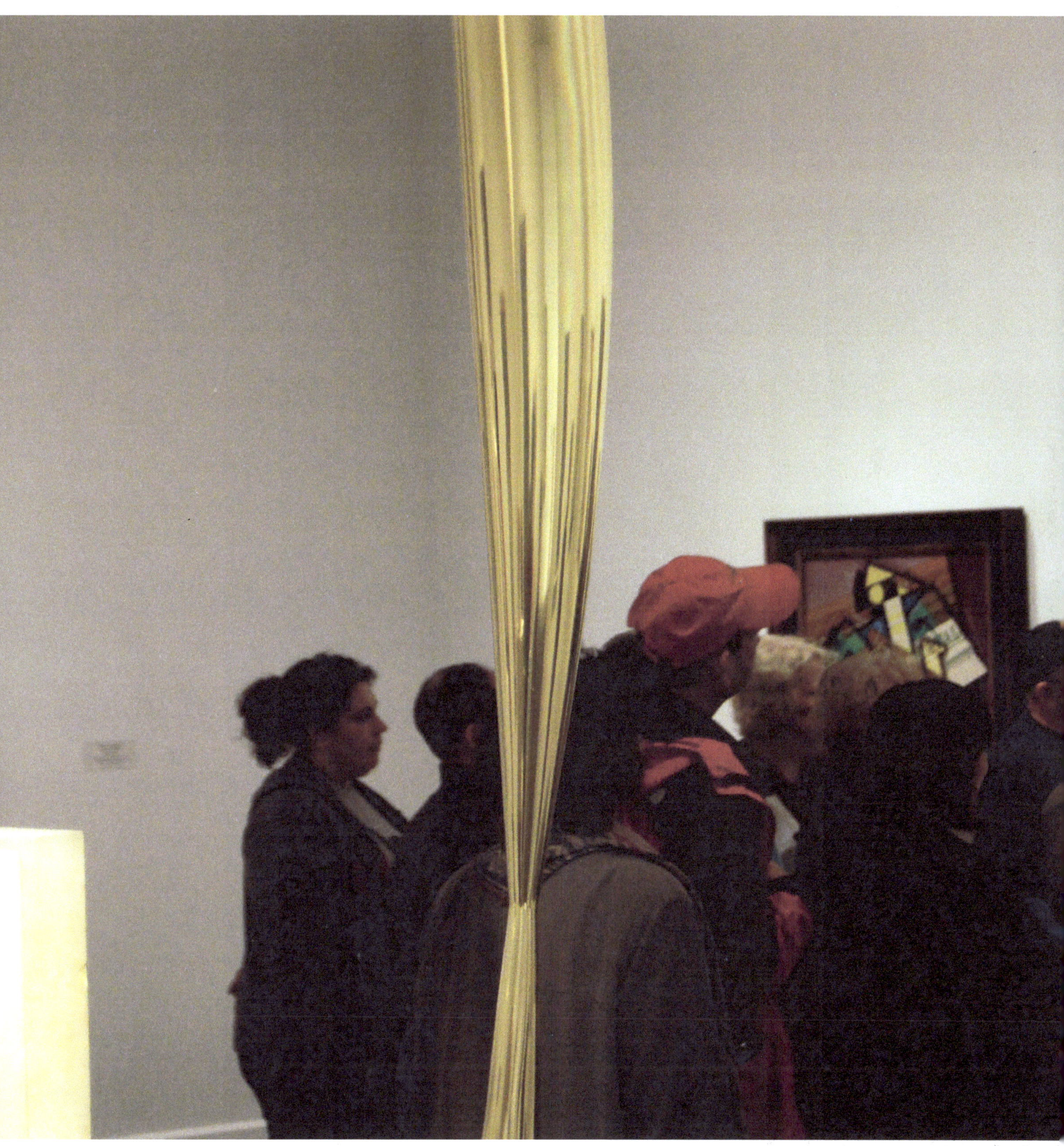

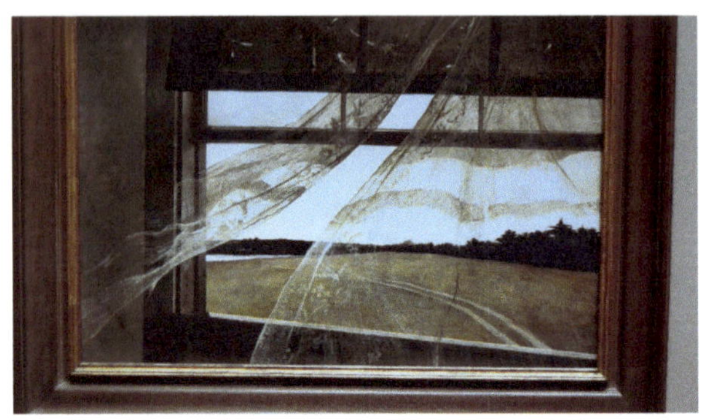

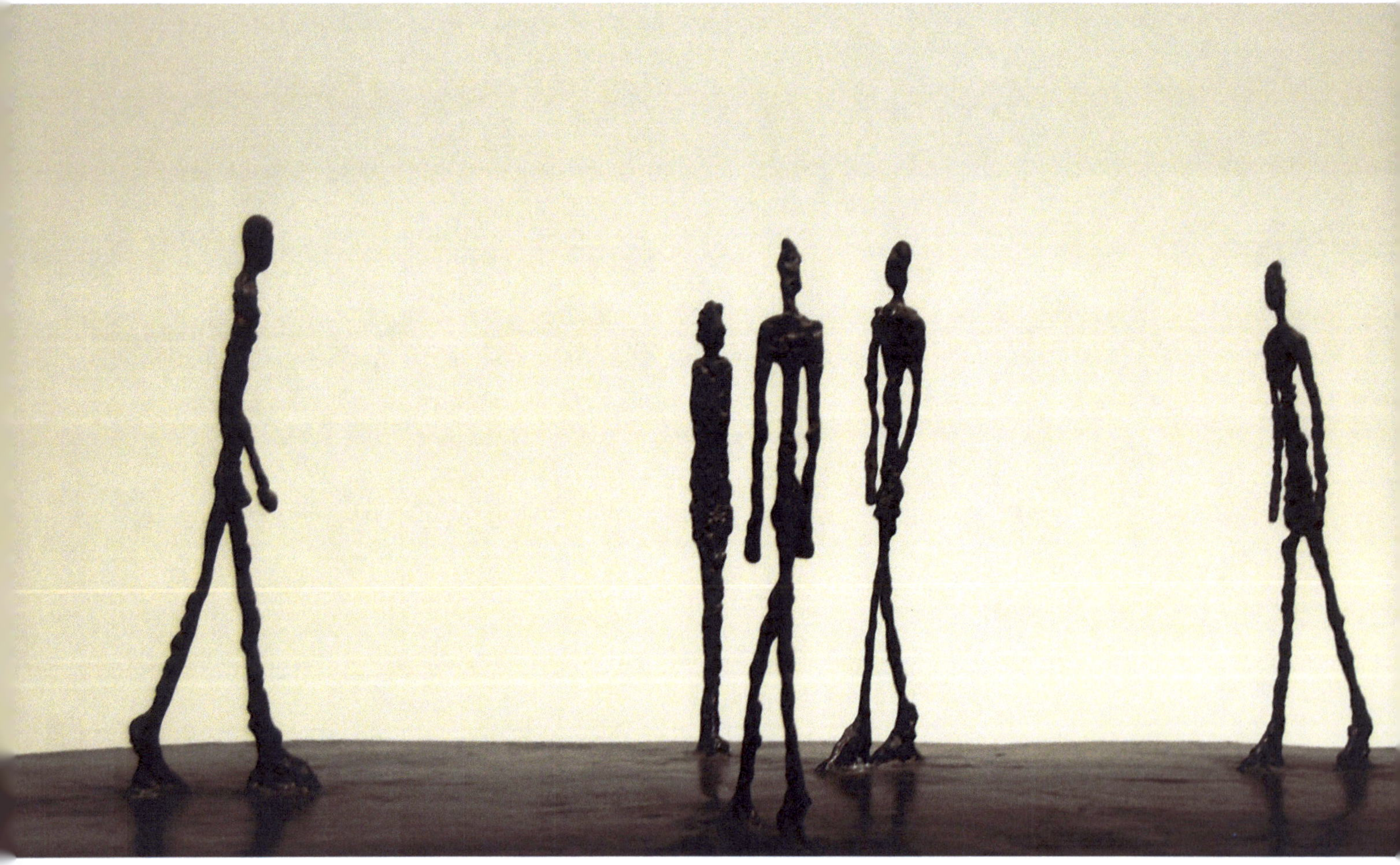

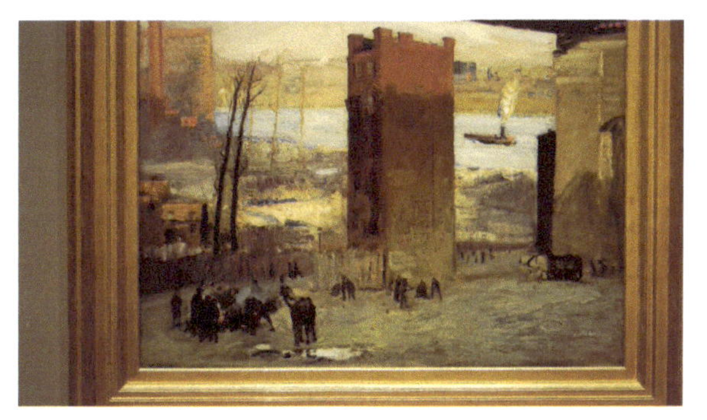

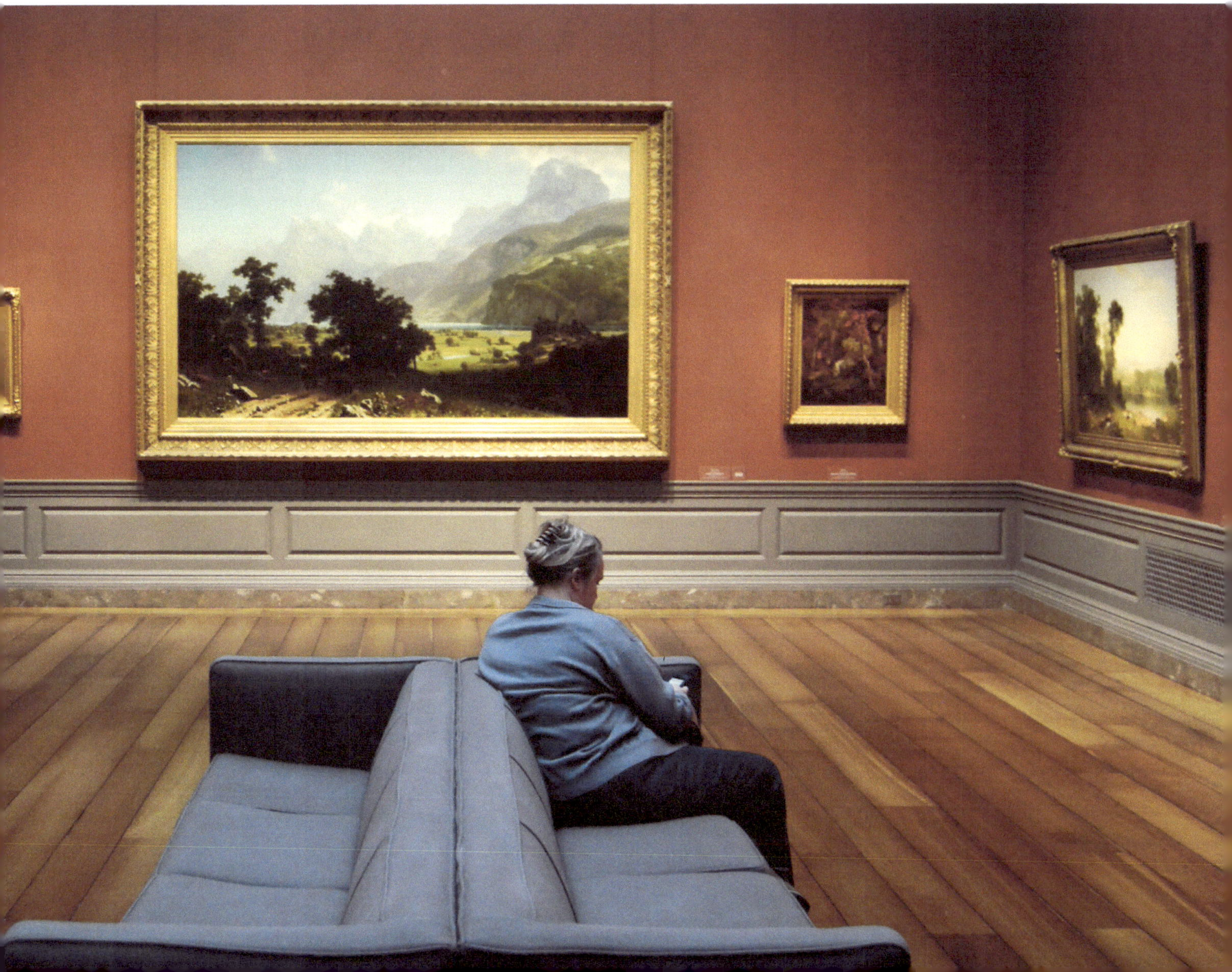

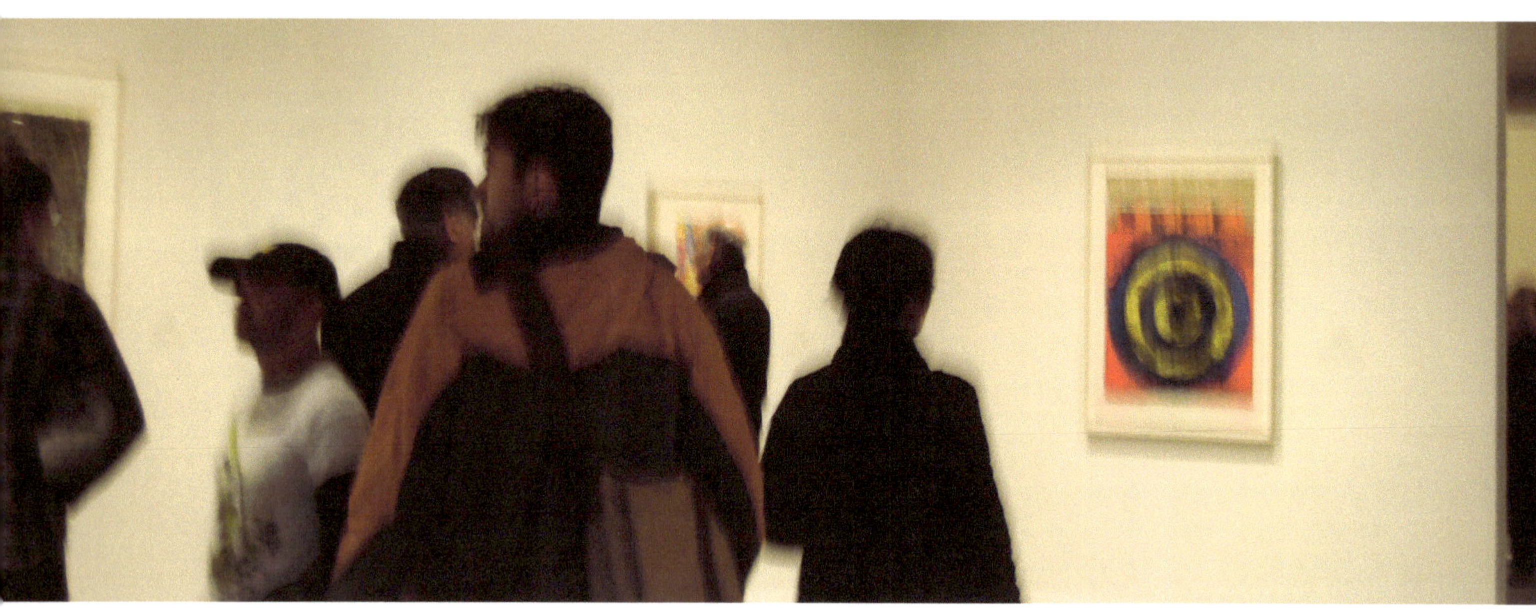

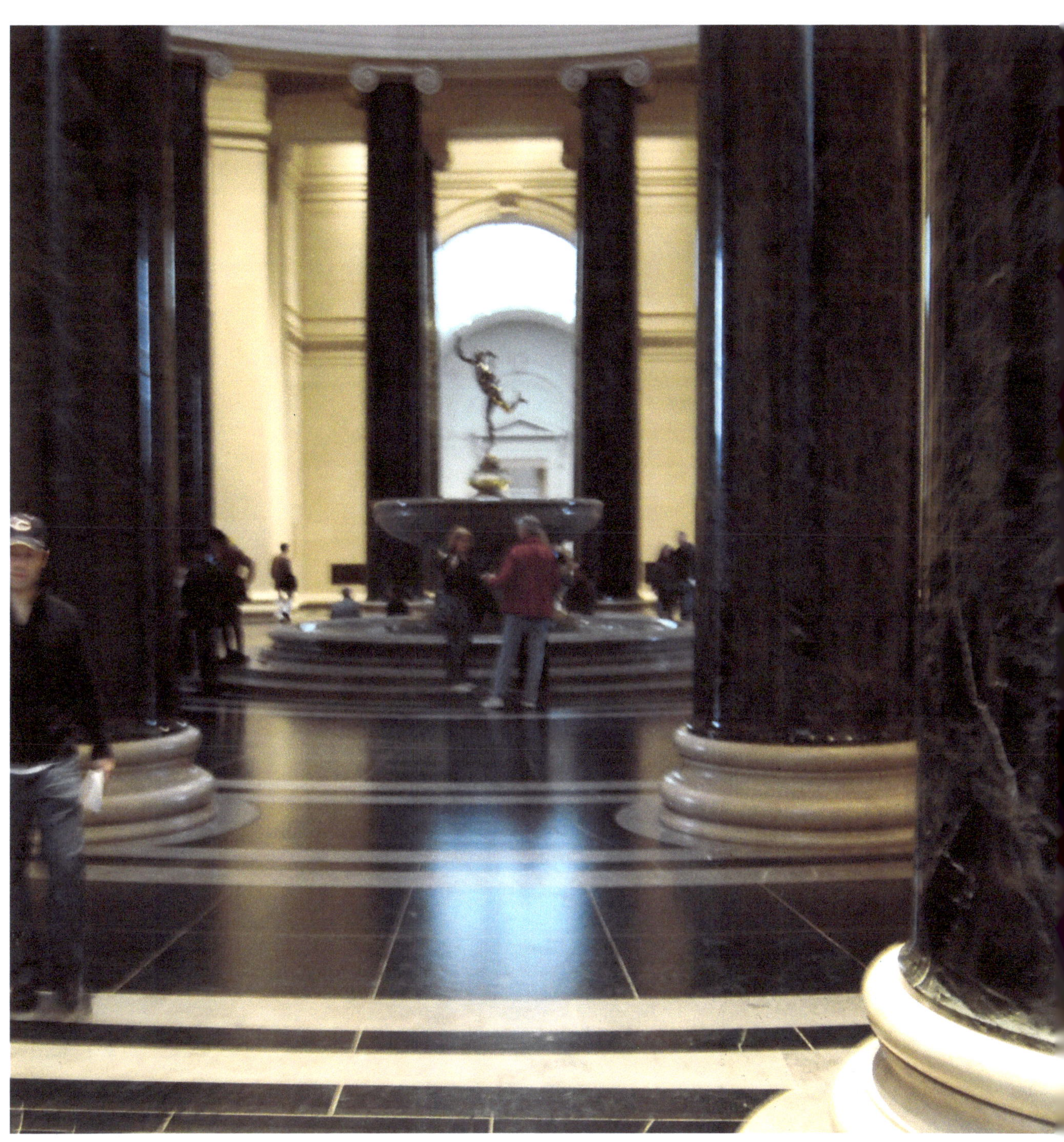

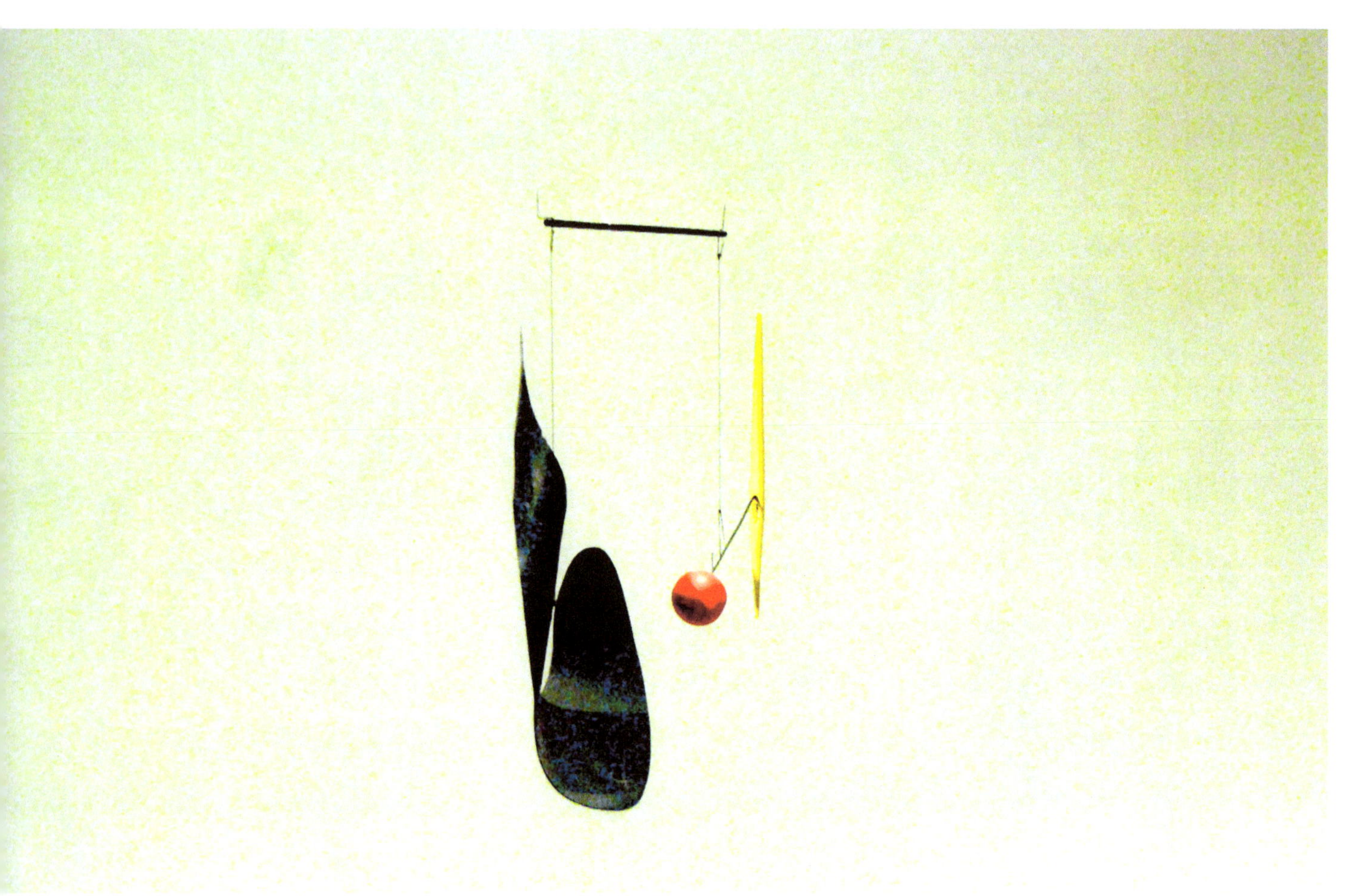

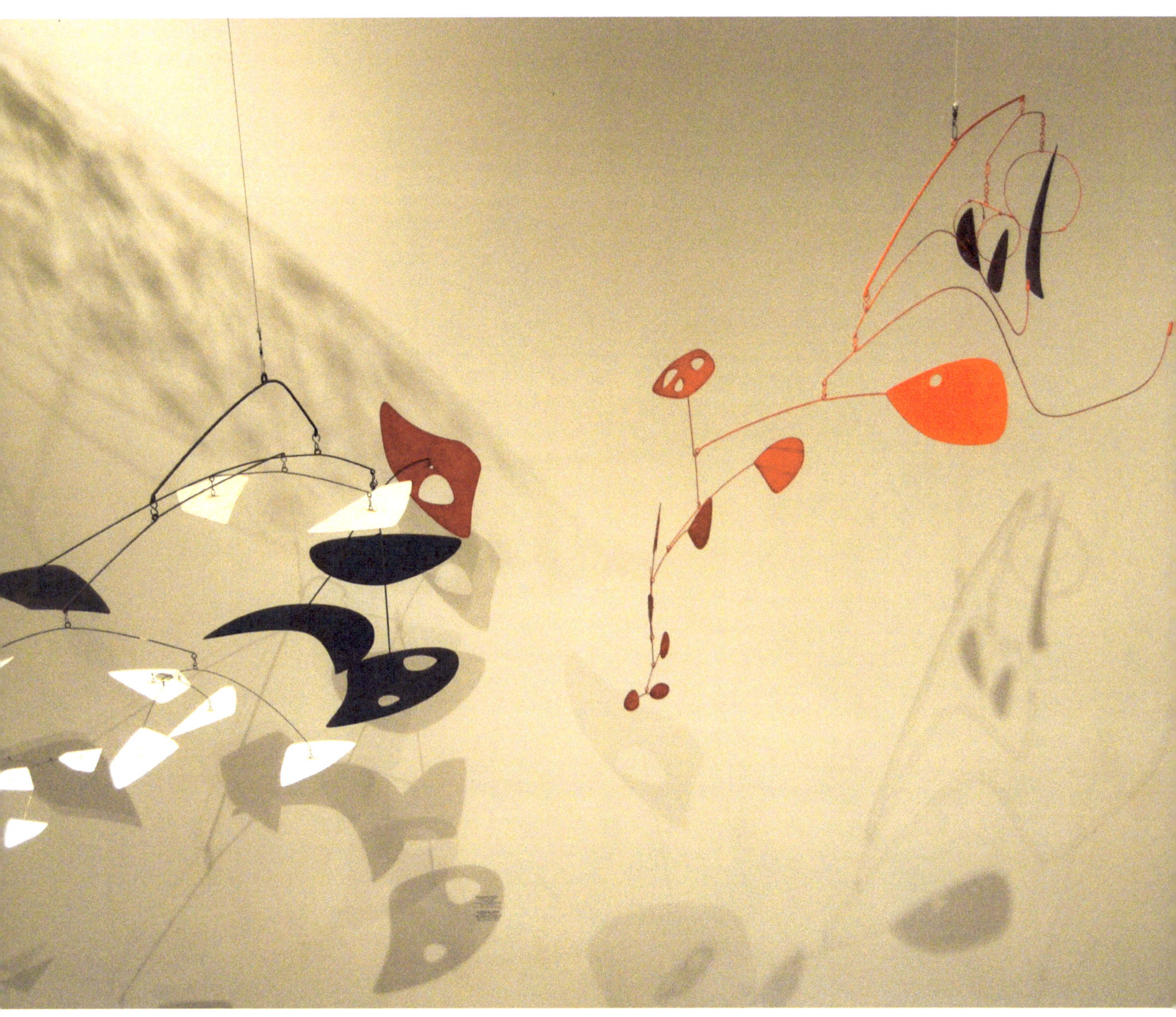

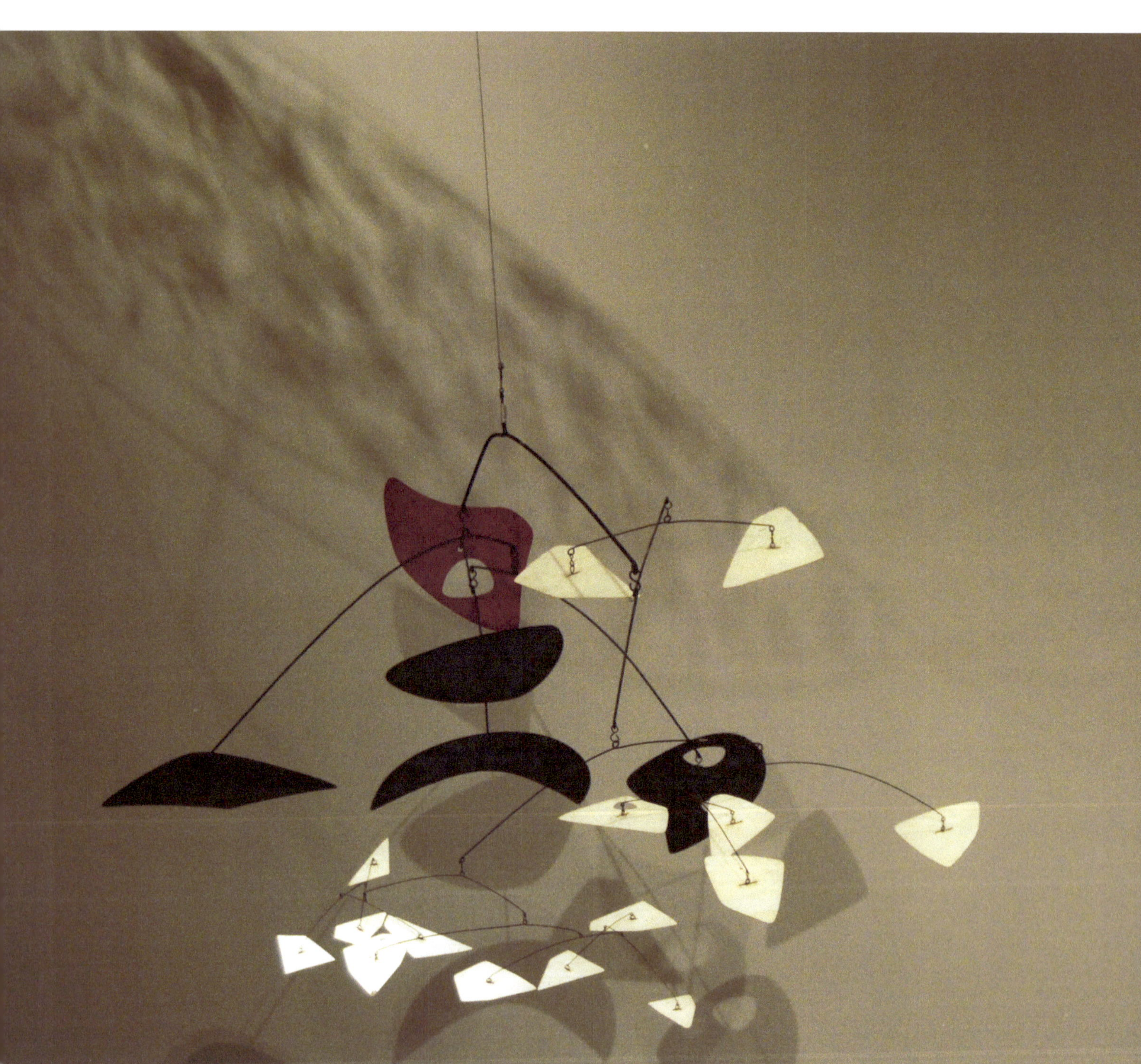

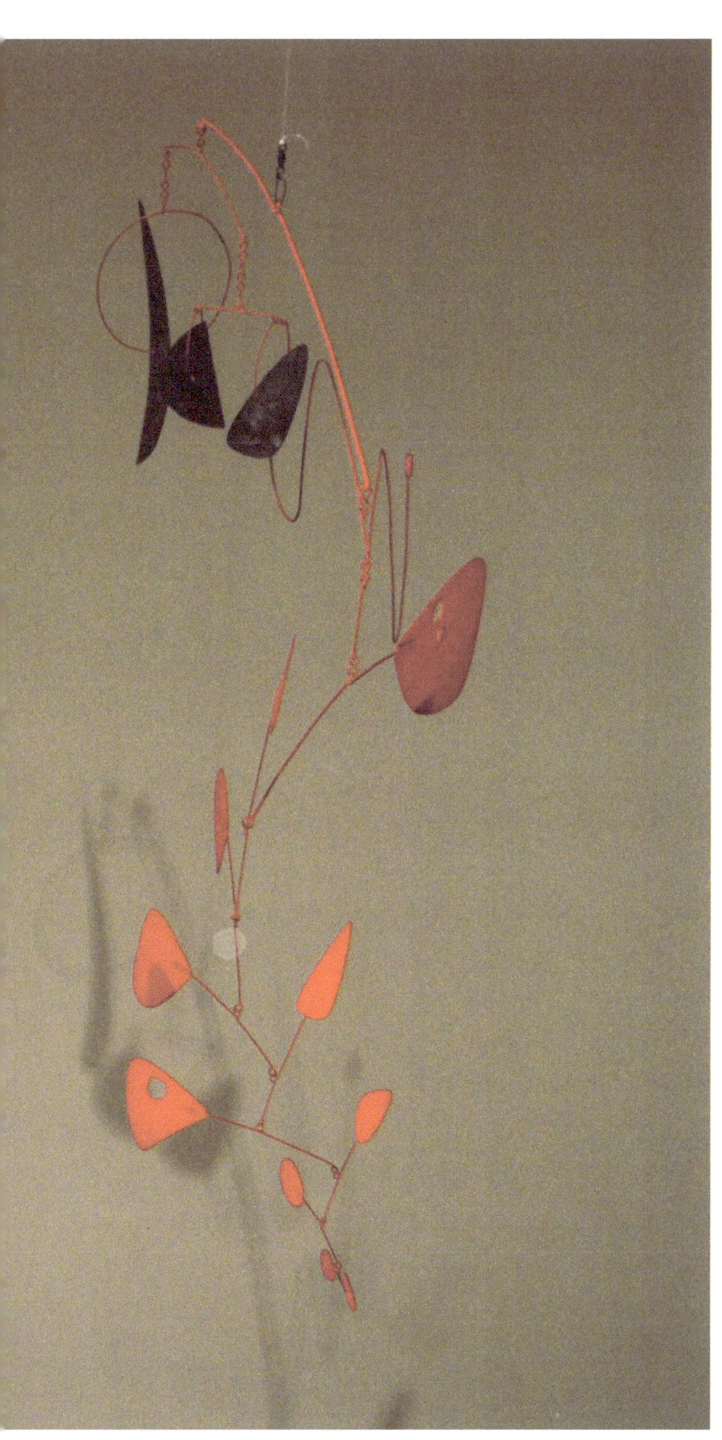

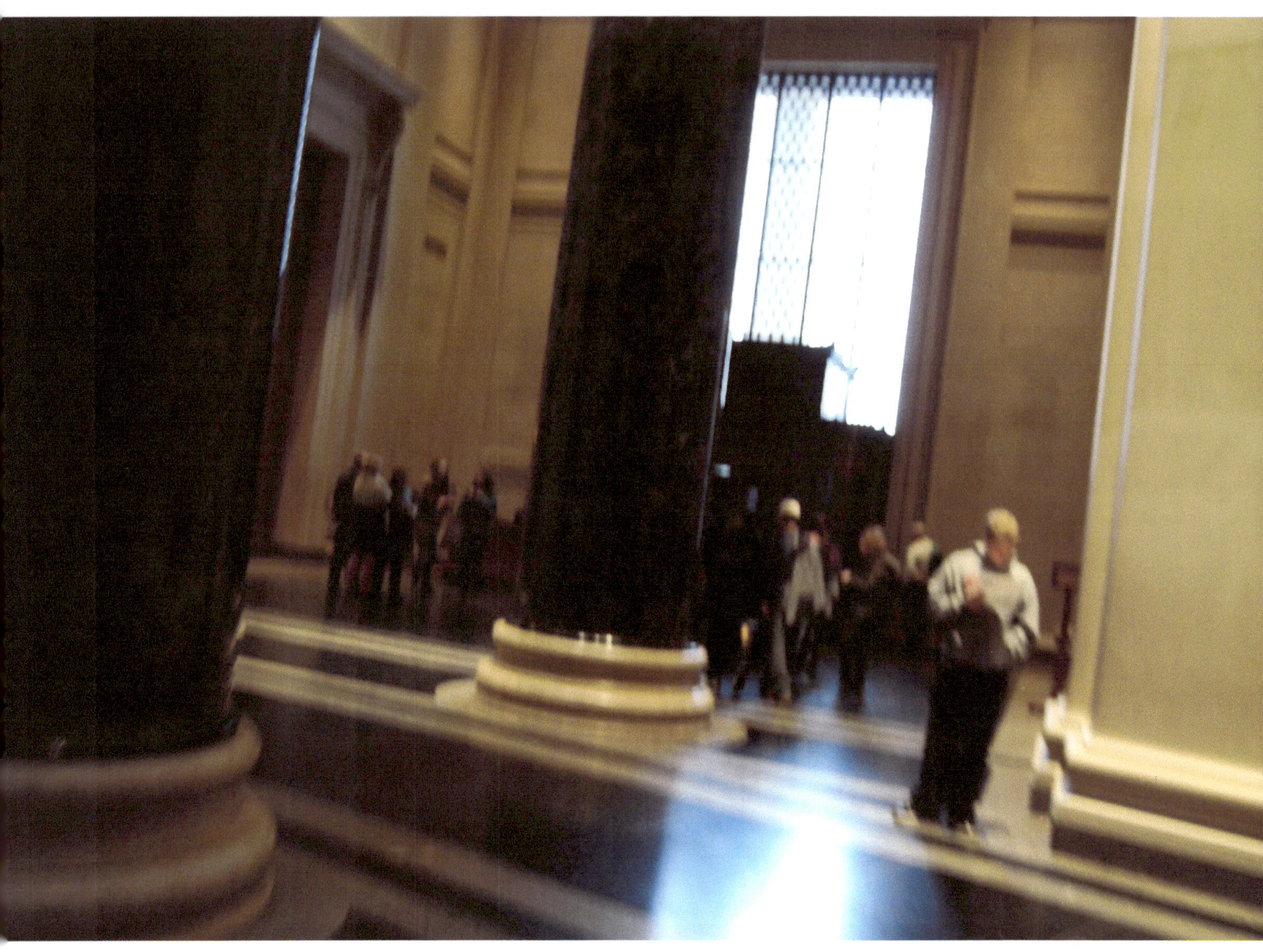

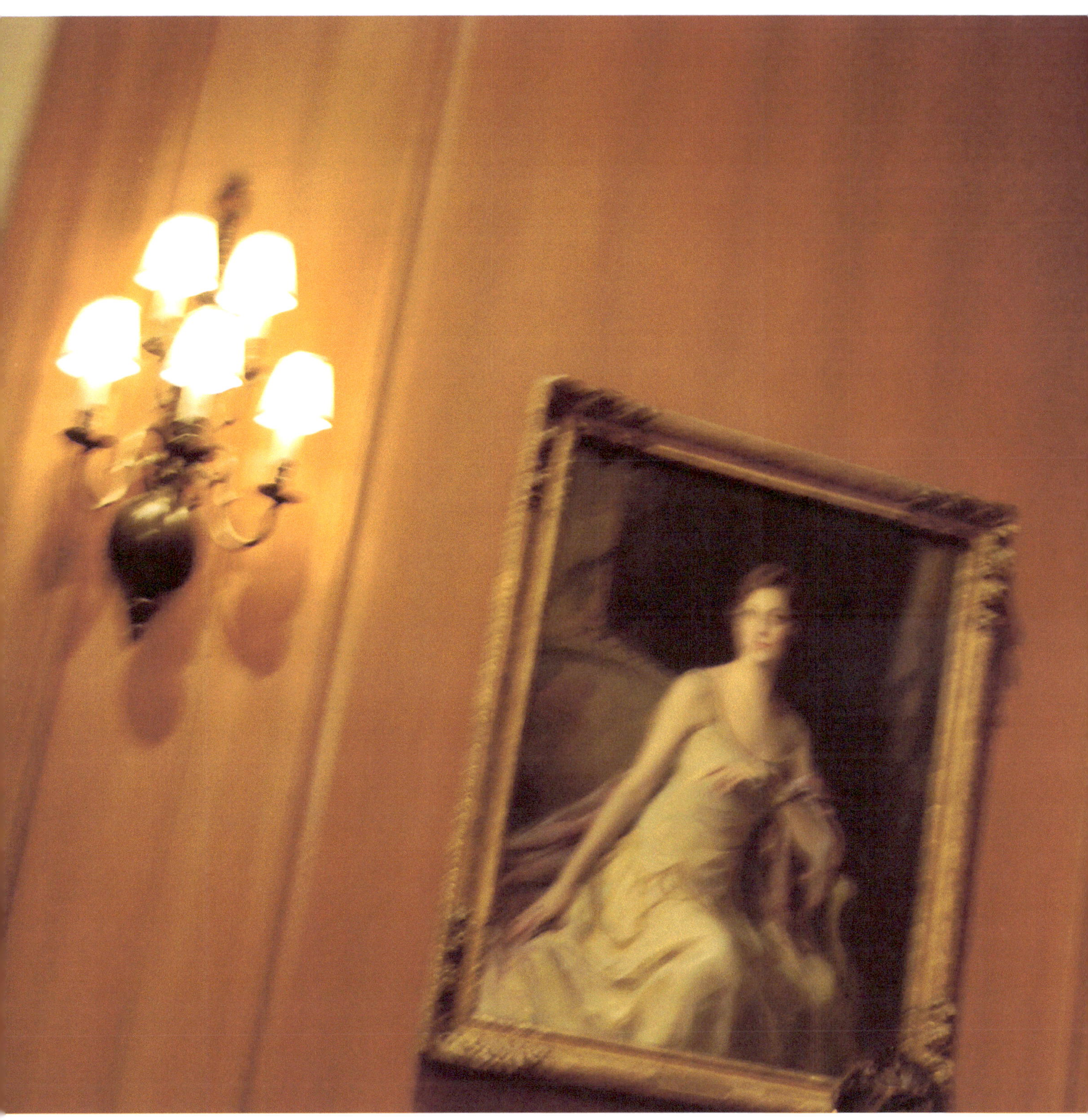

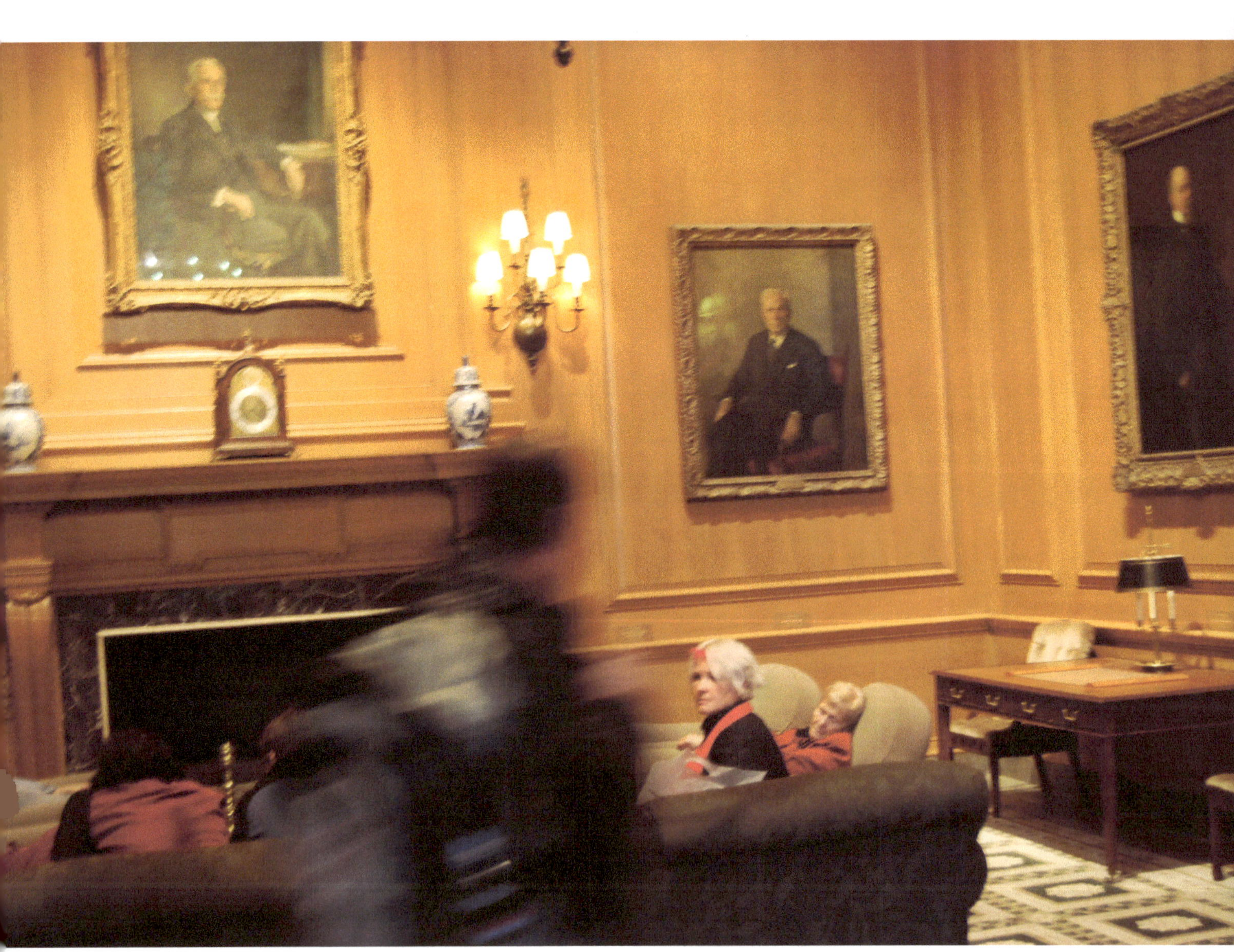

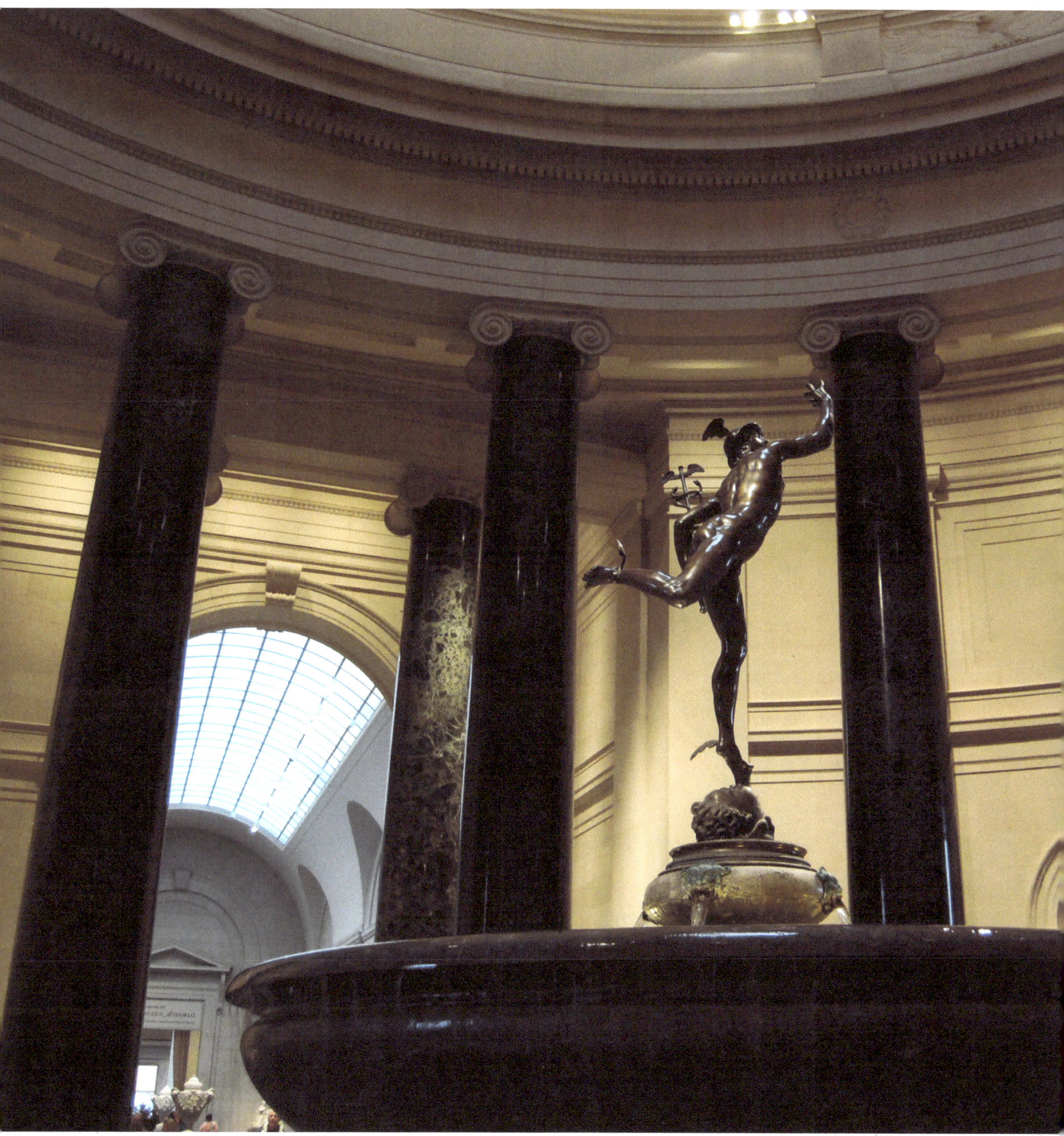

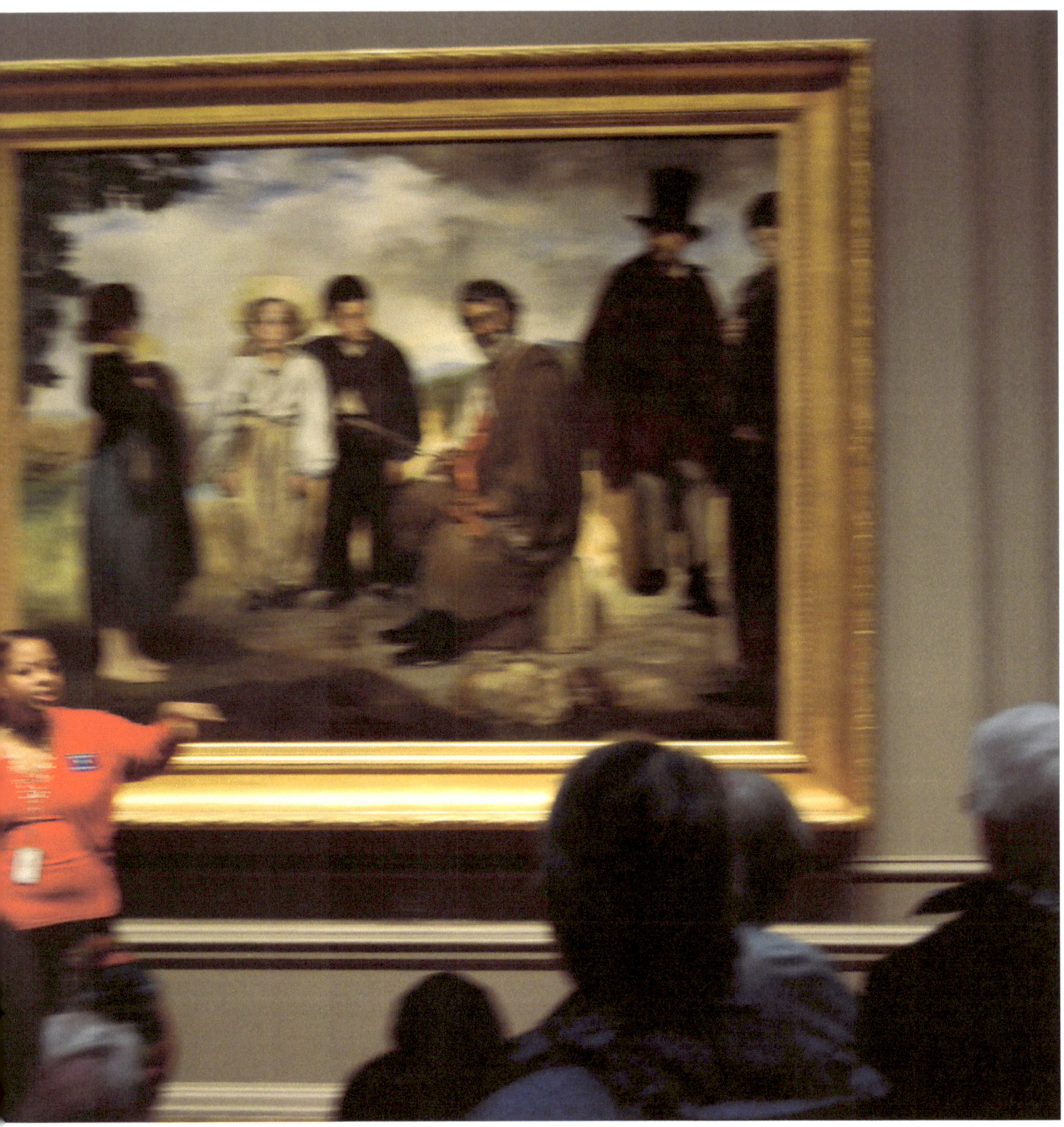

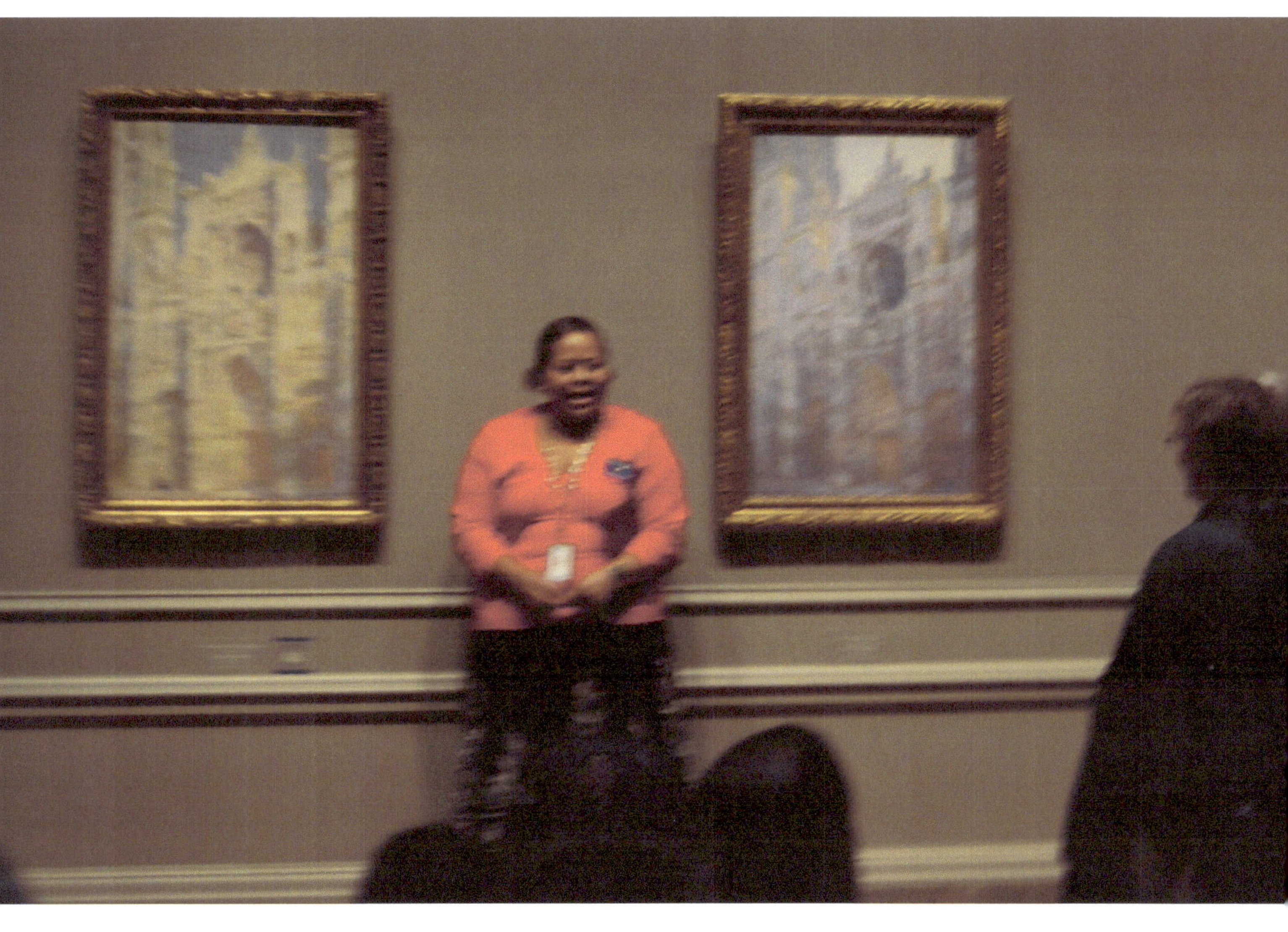

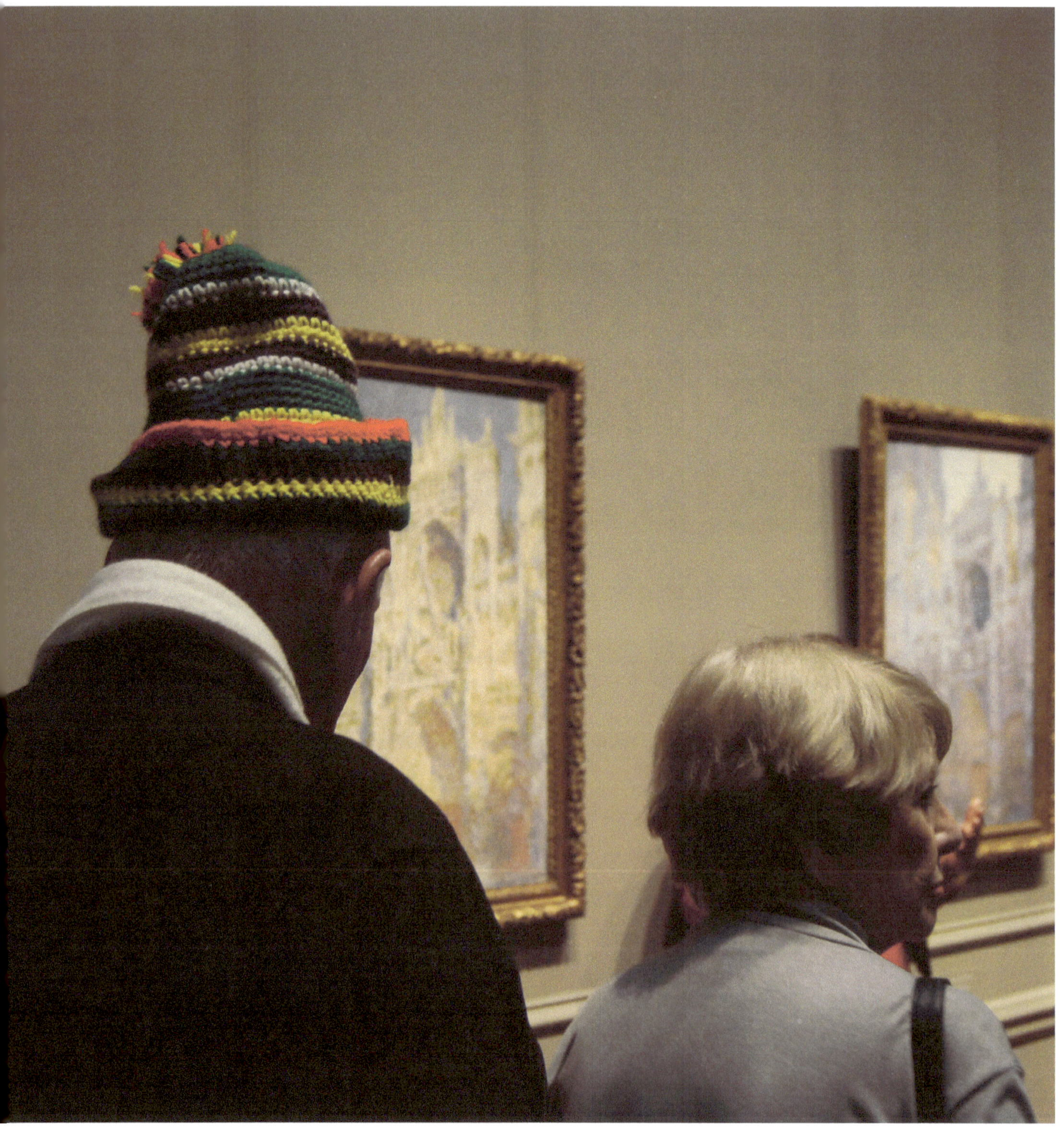

Hat fashion in Washington, DC

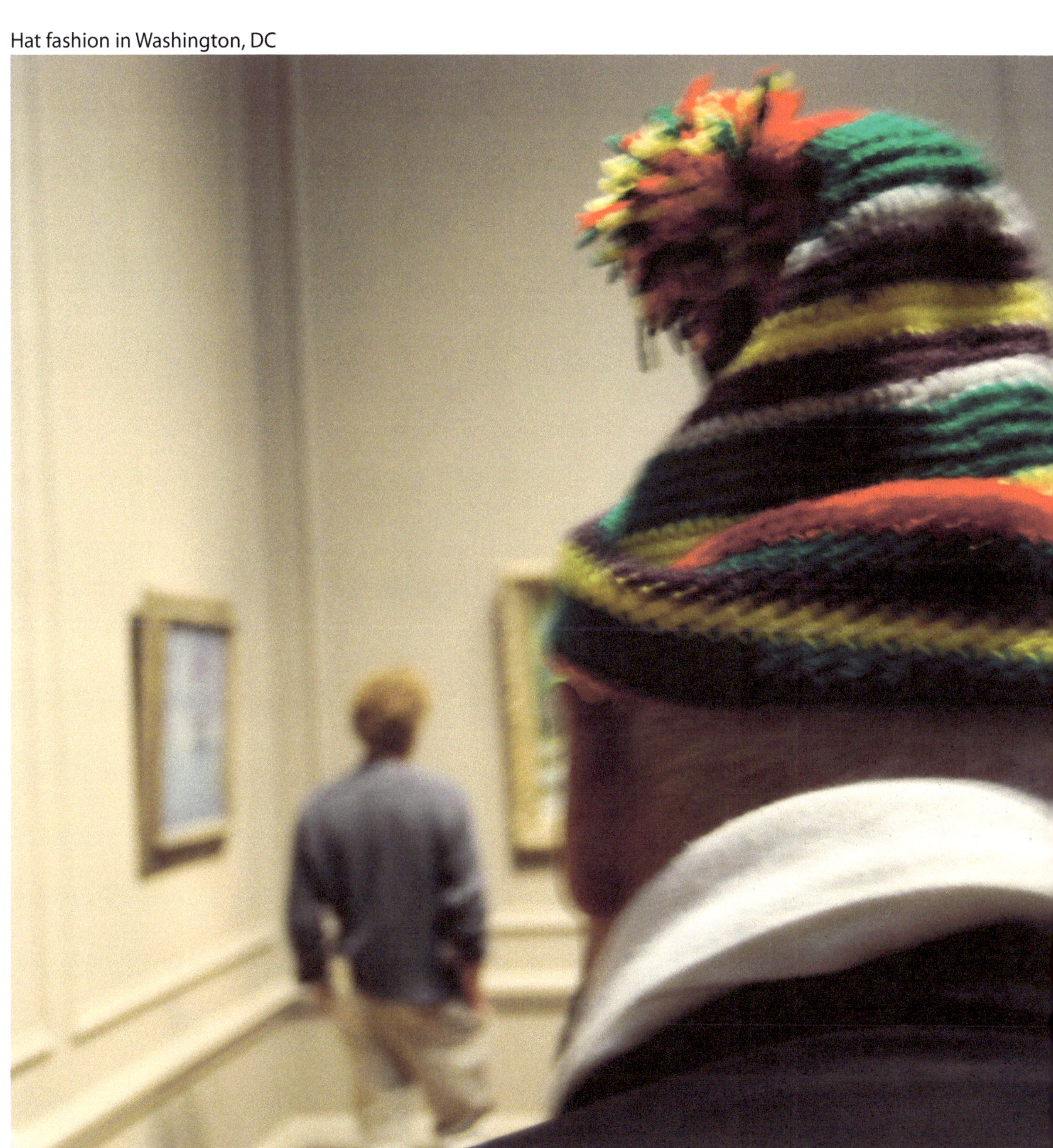

National Gallery of Art in Washington DC

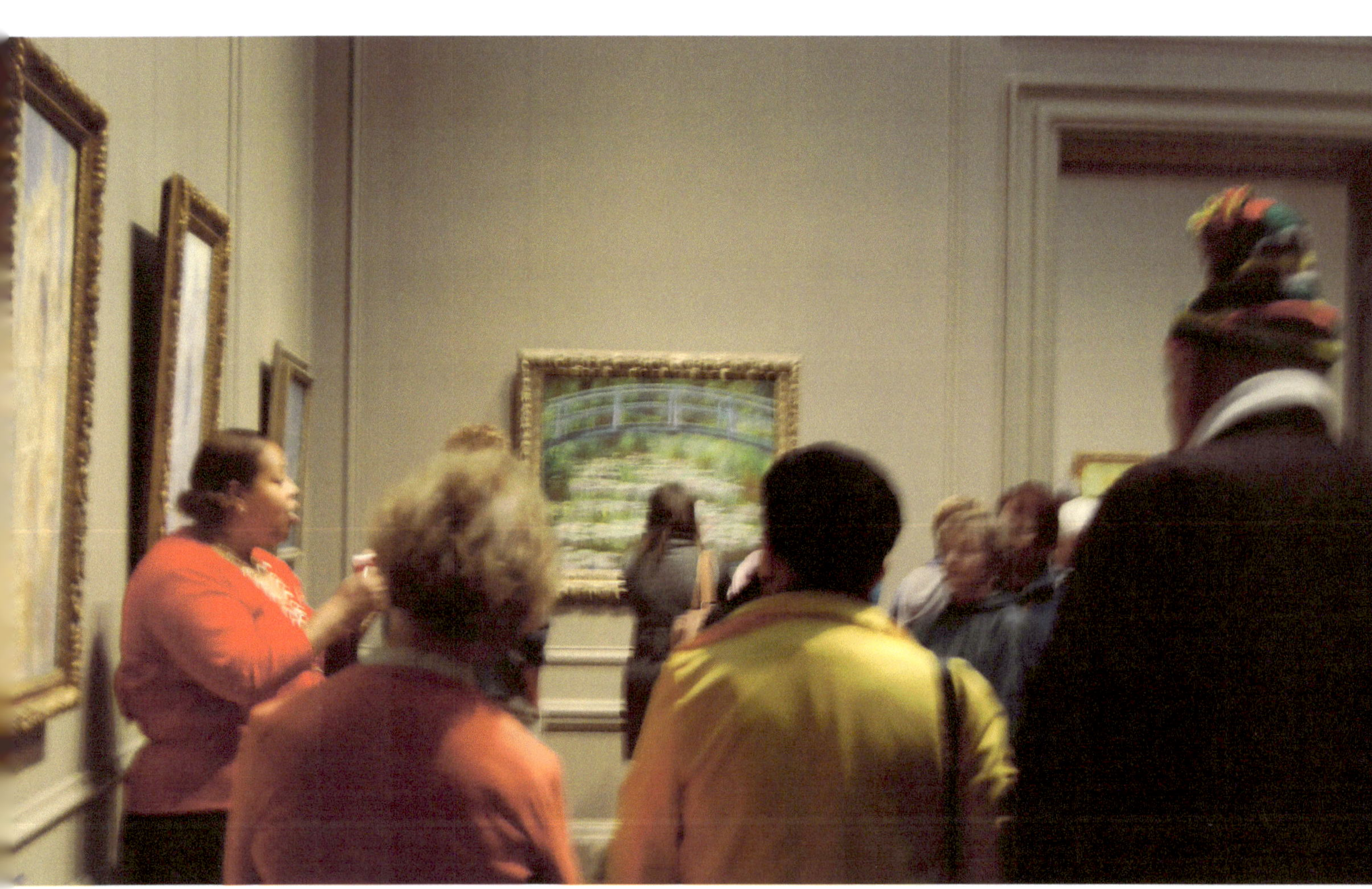

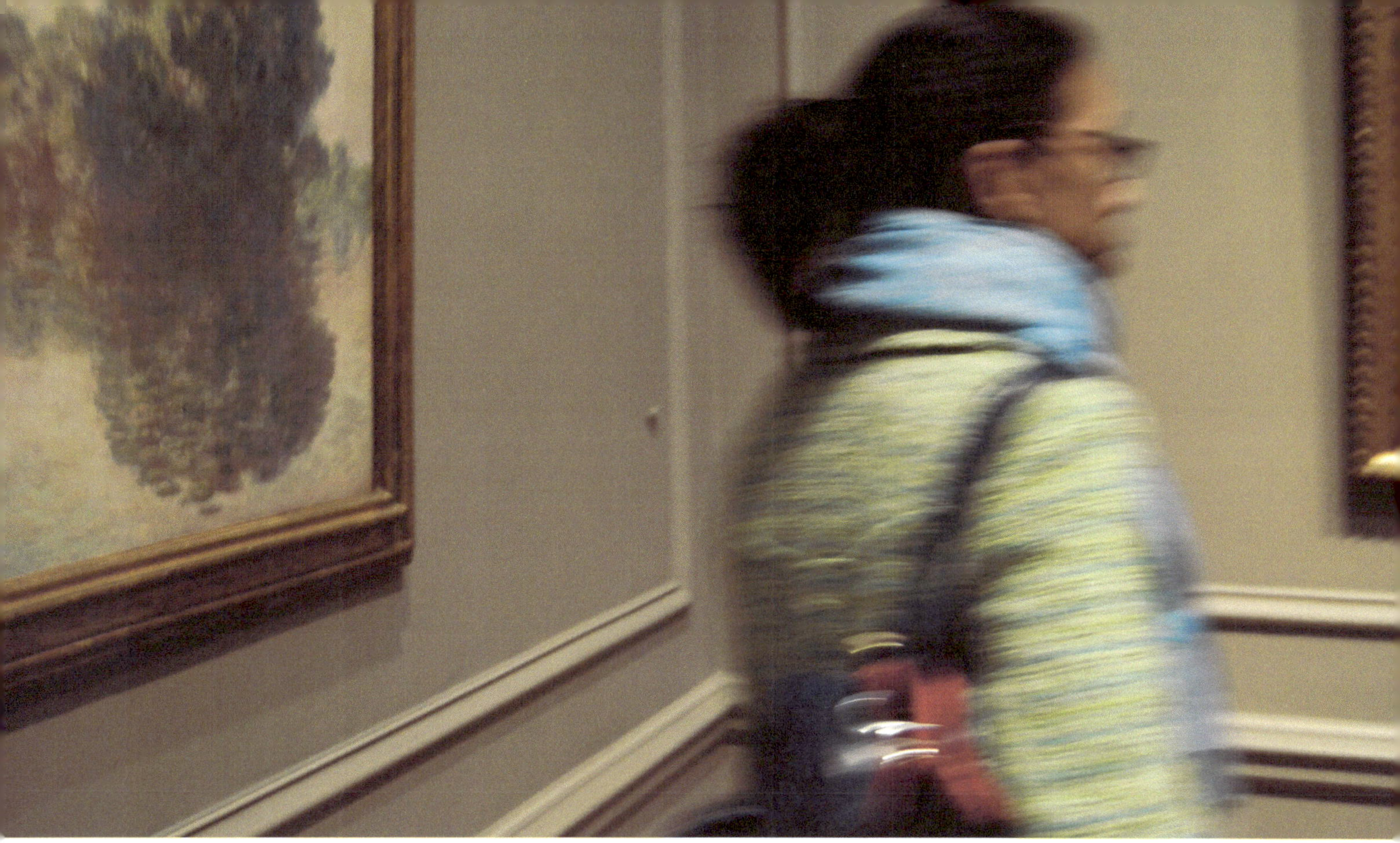

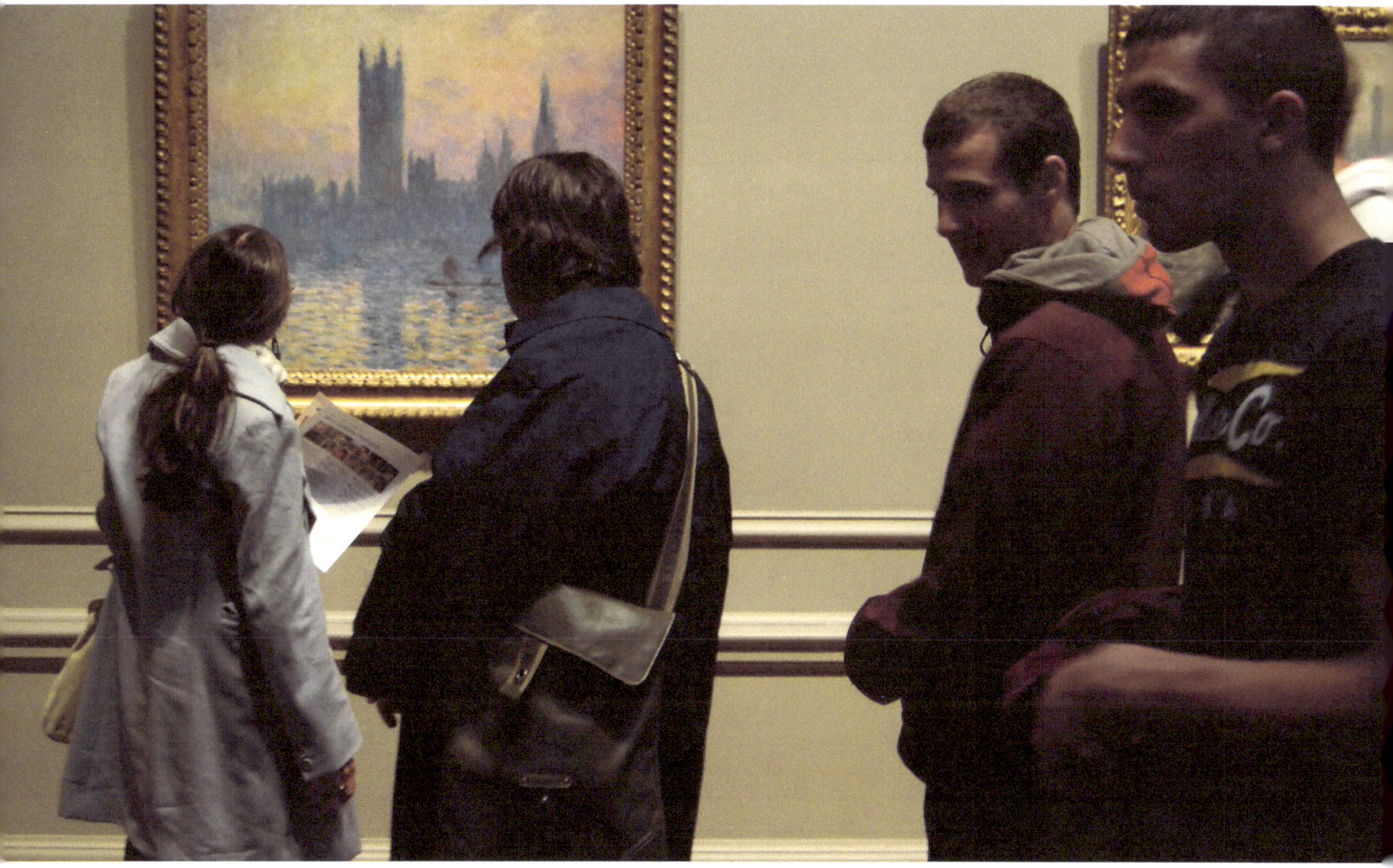

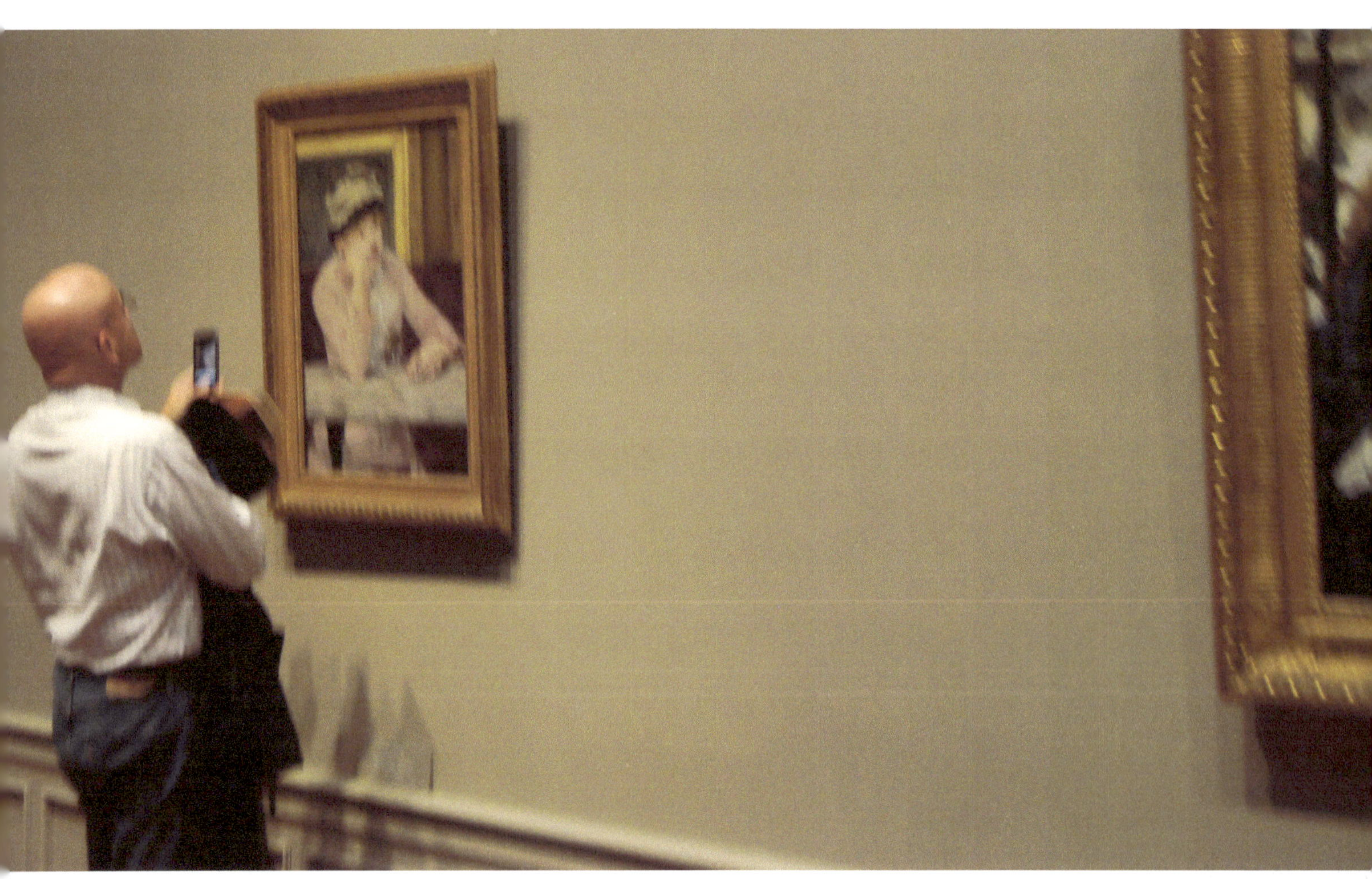

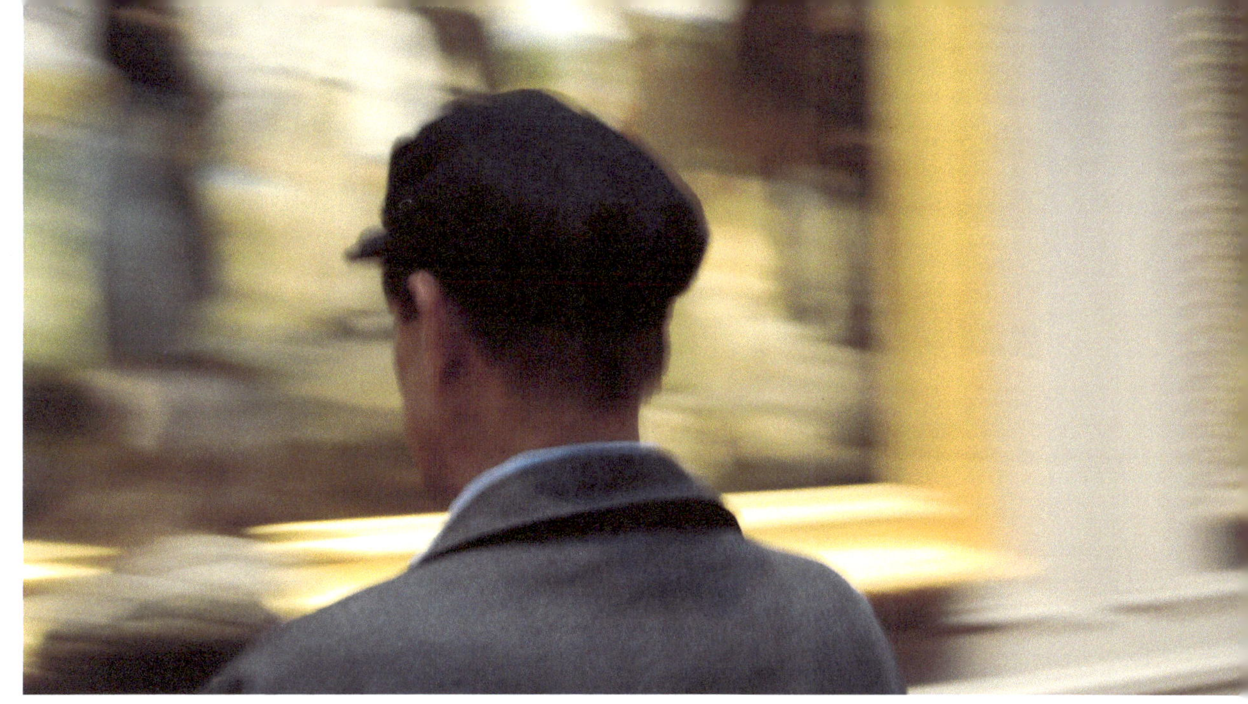

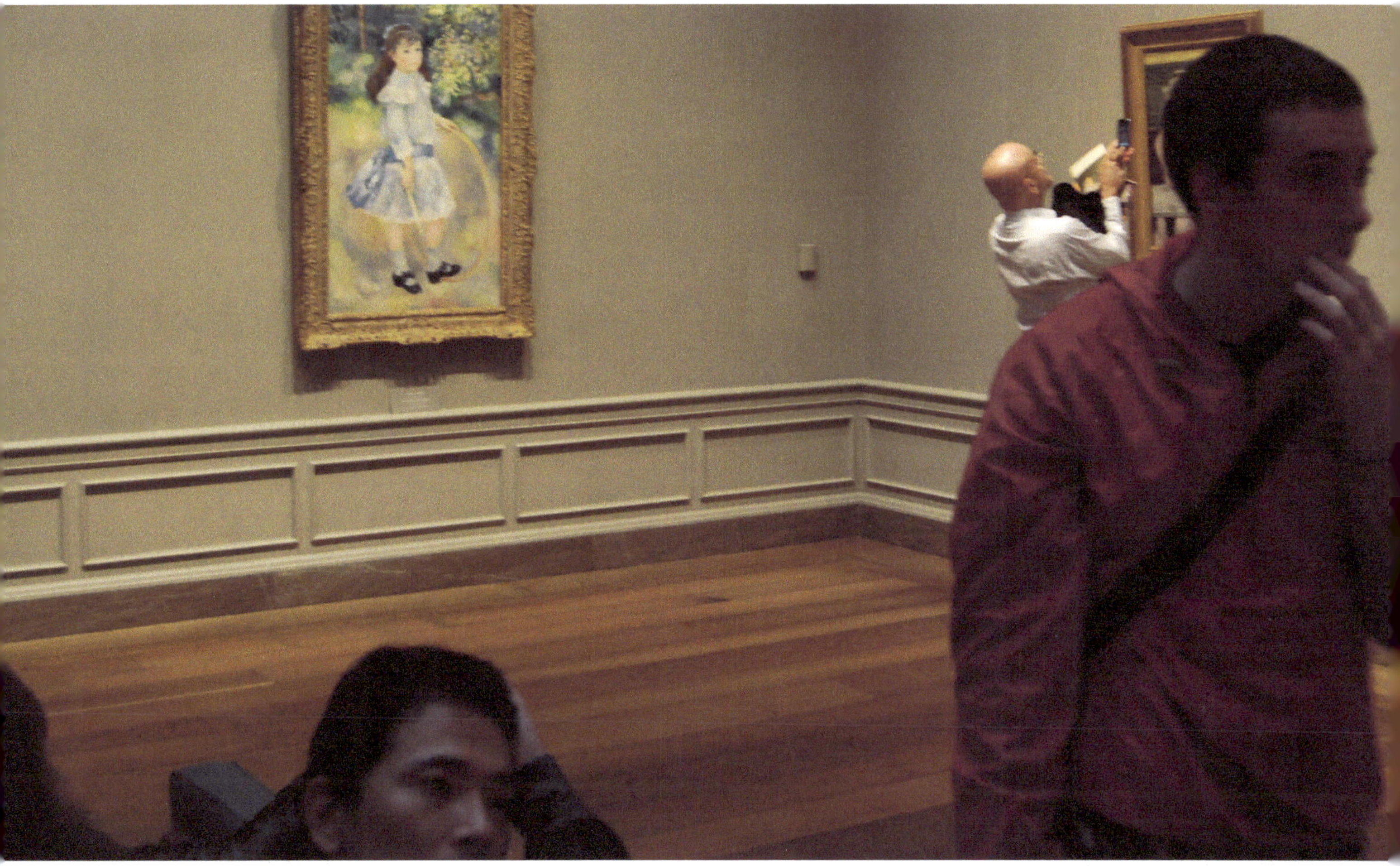

National Gallery of Art in Washington DC

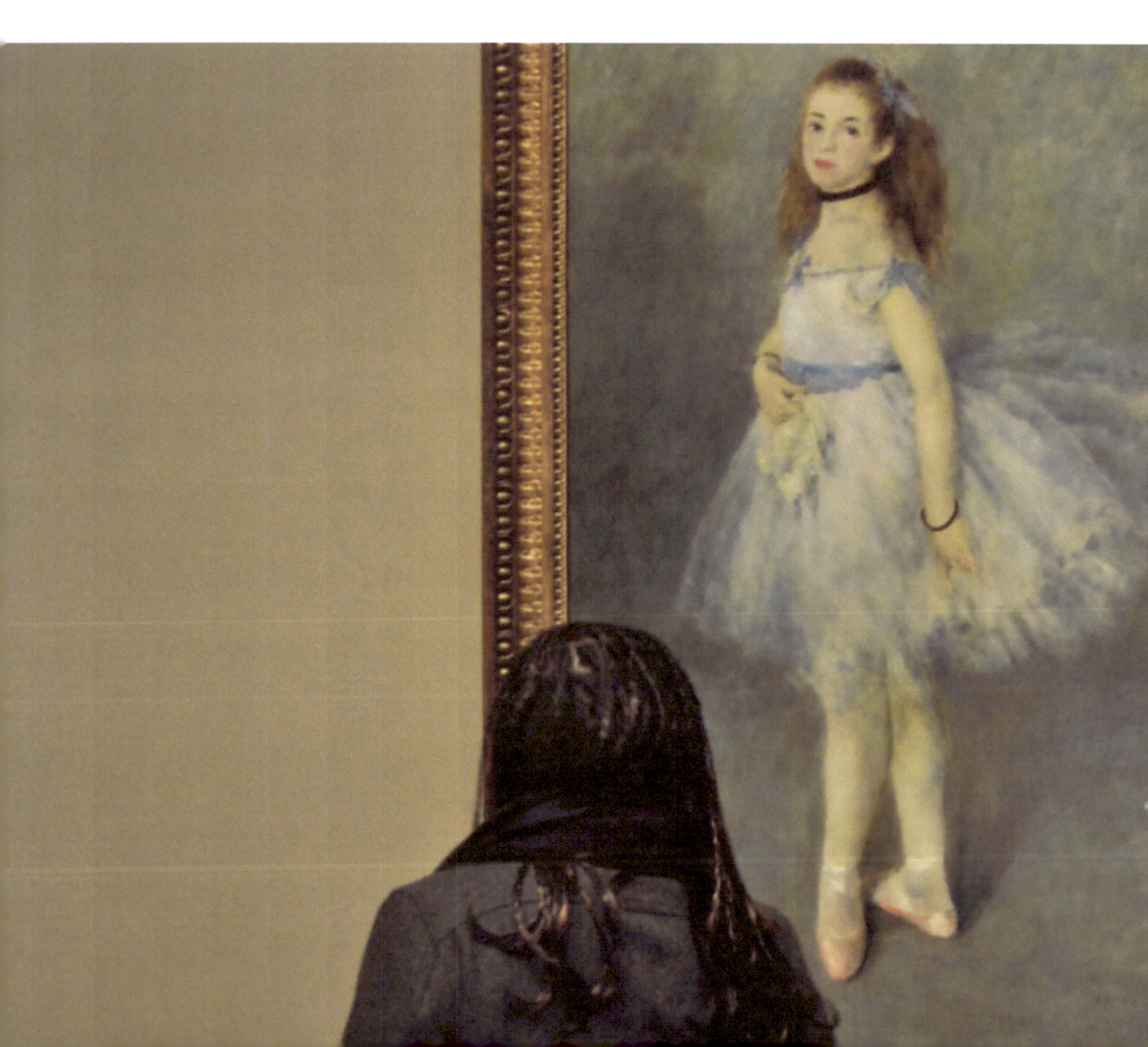

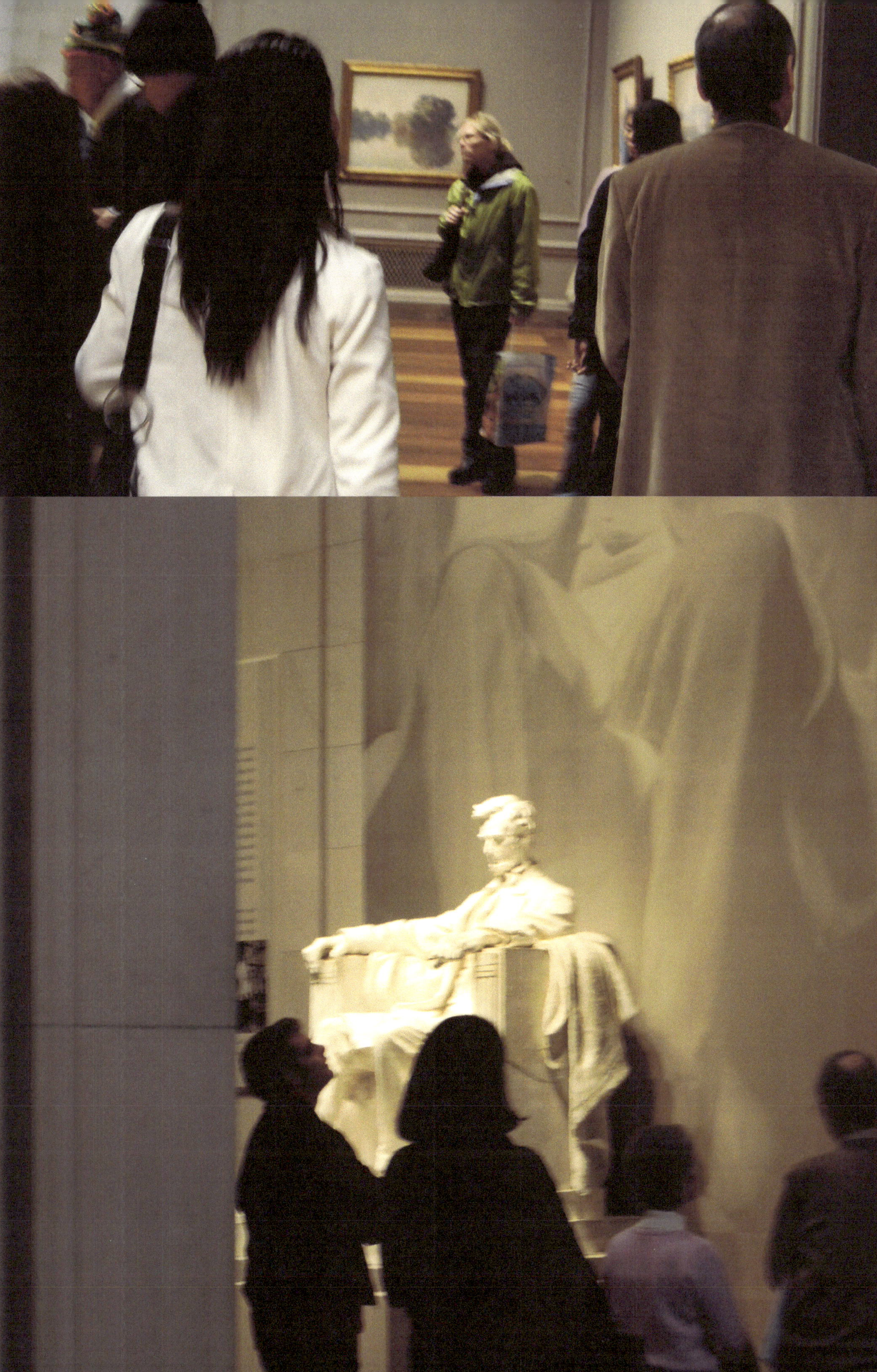

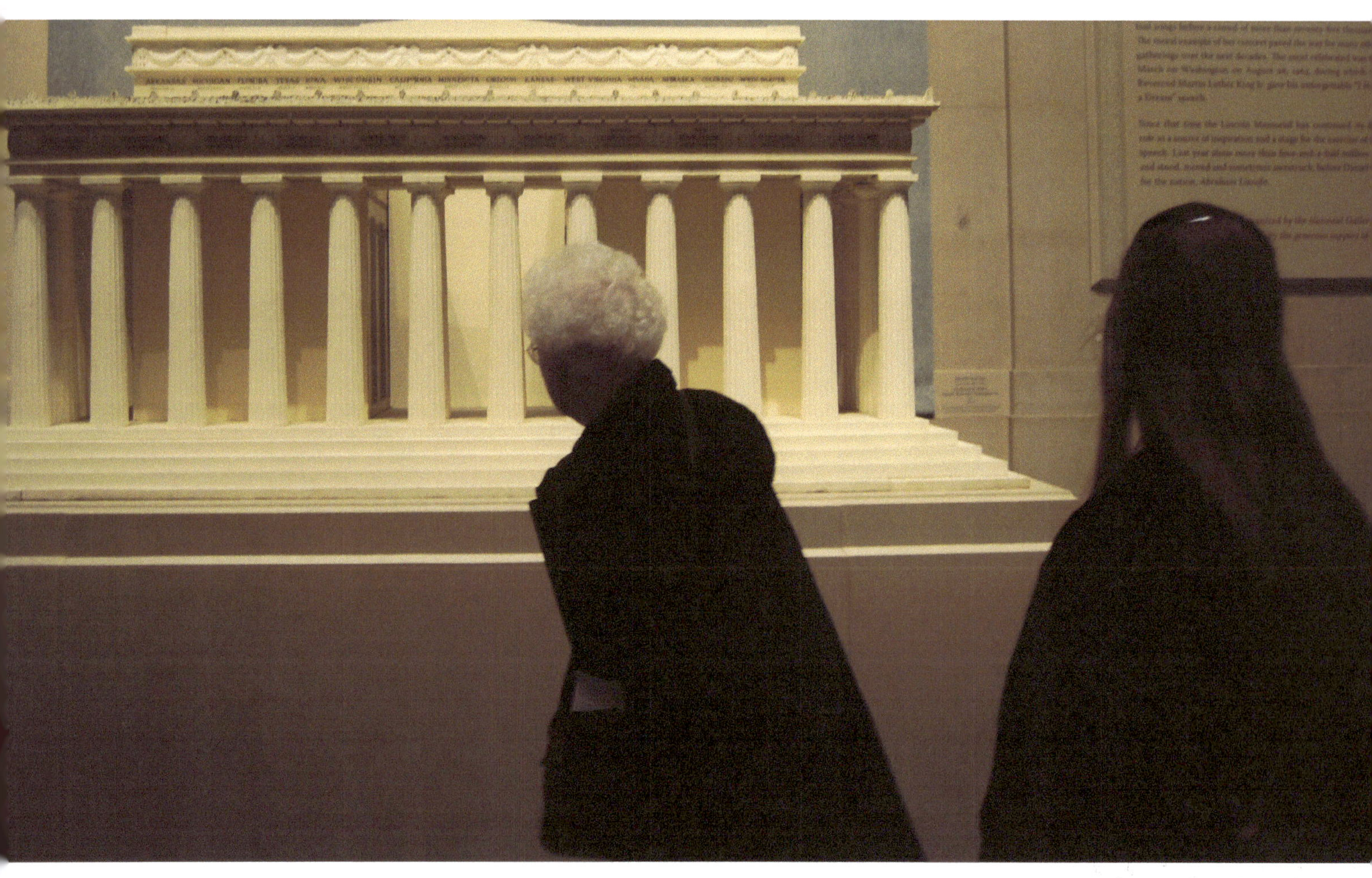

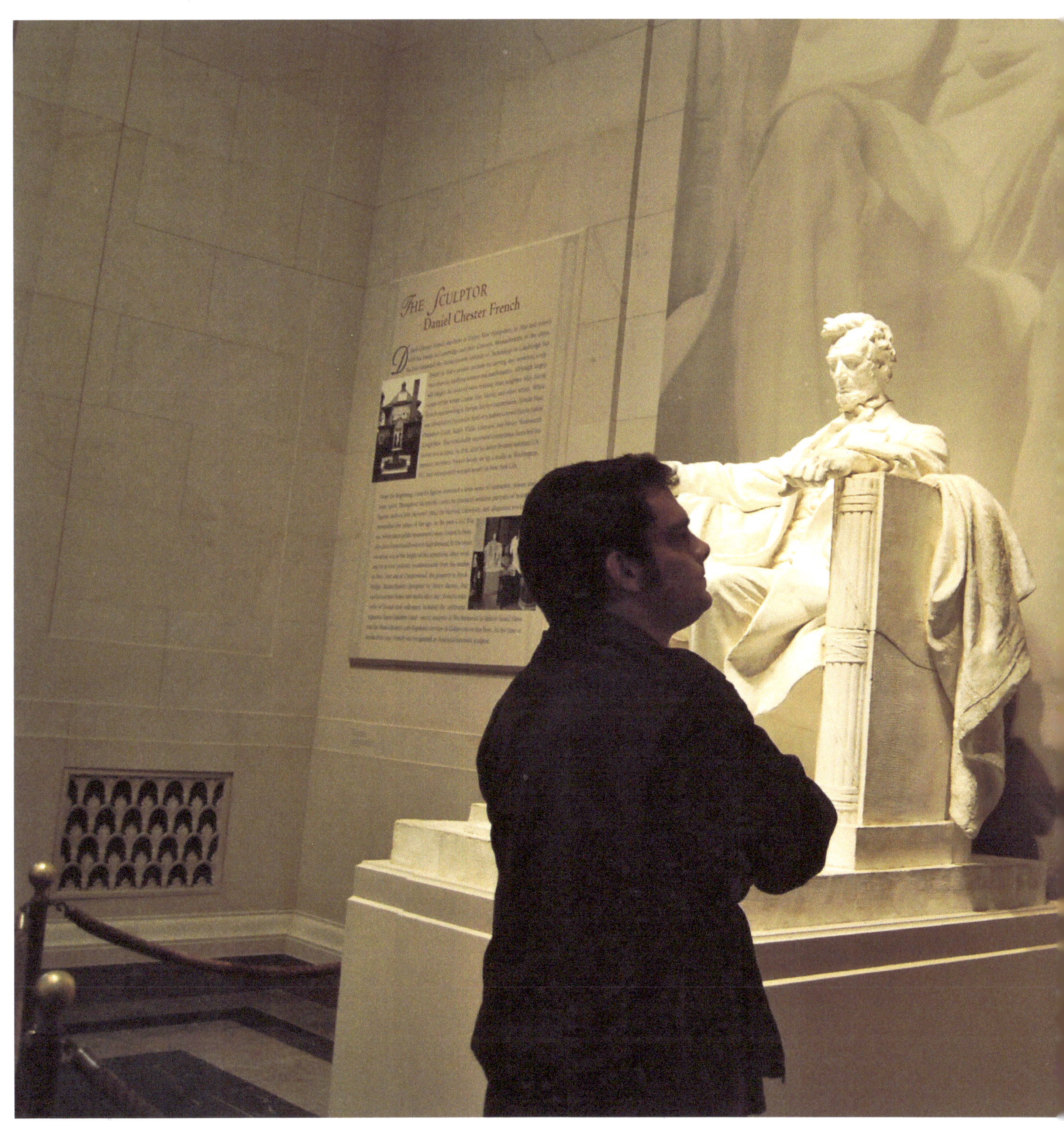
THE SCULPTOR
Daniel Chester French

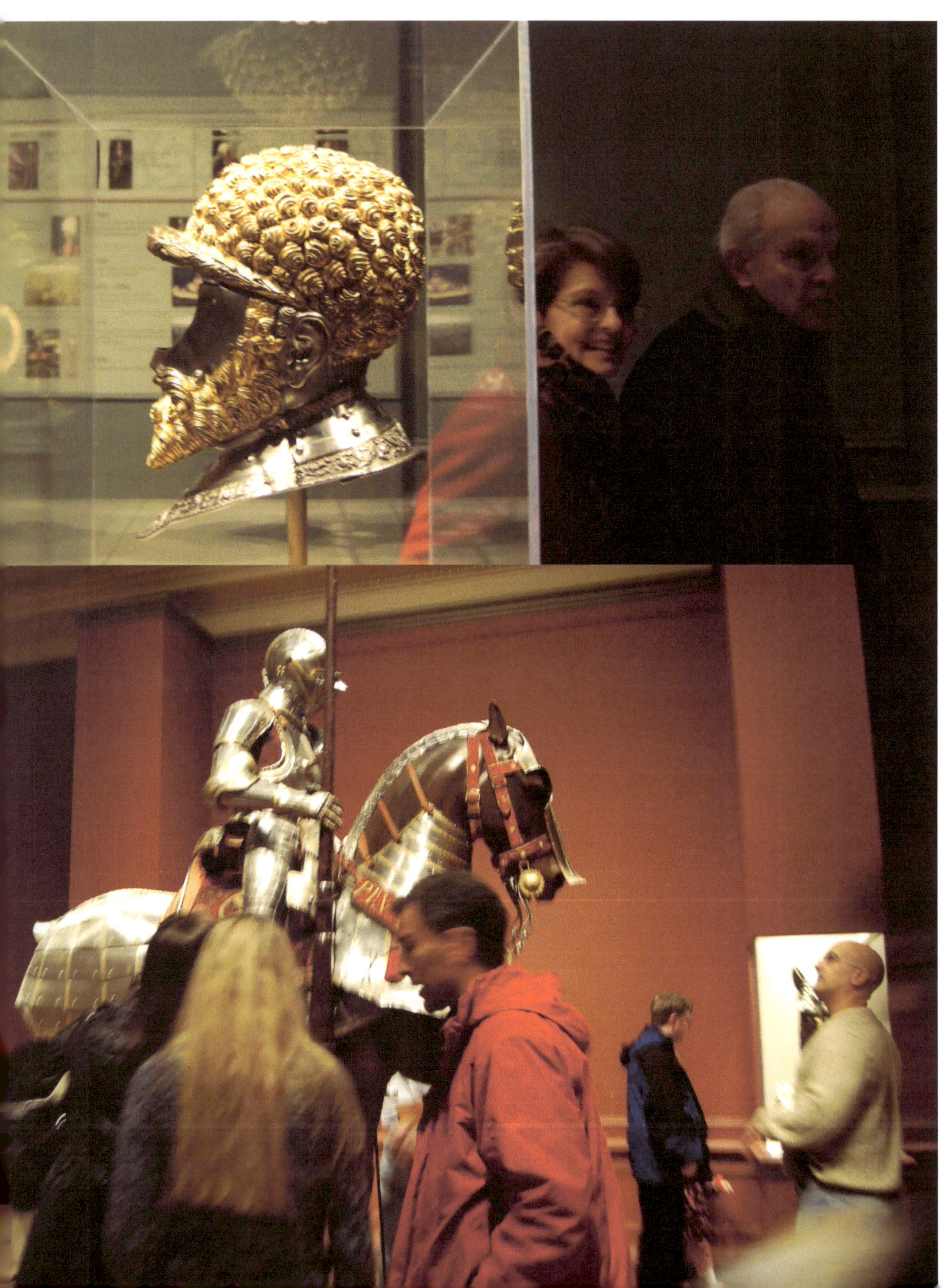

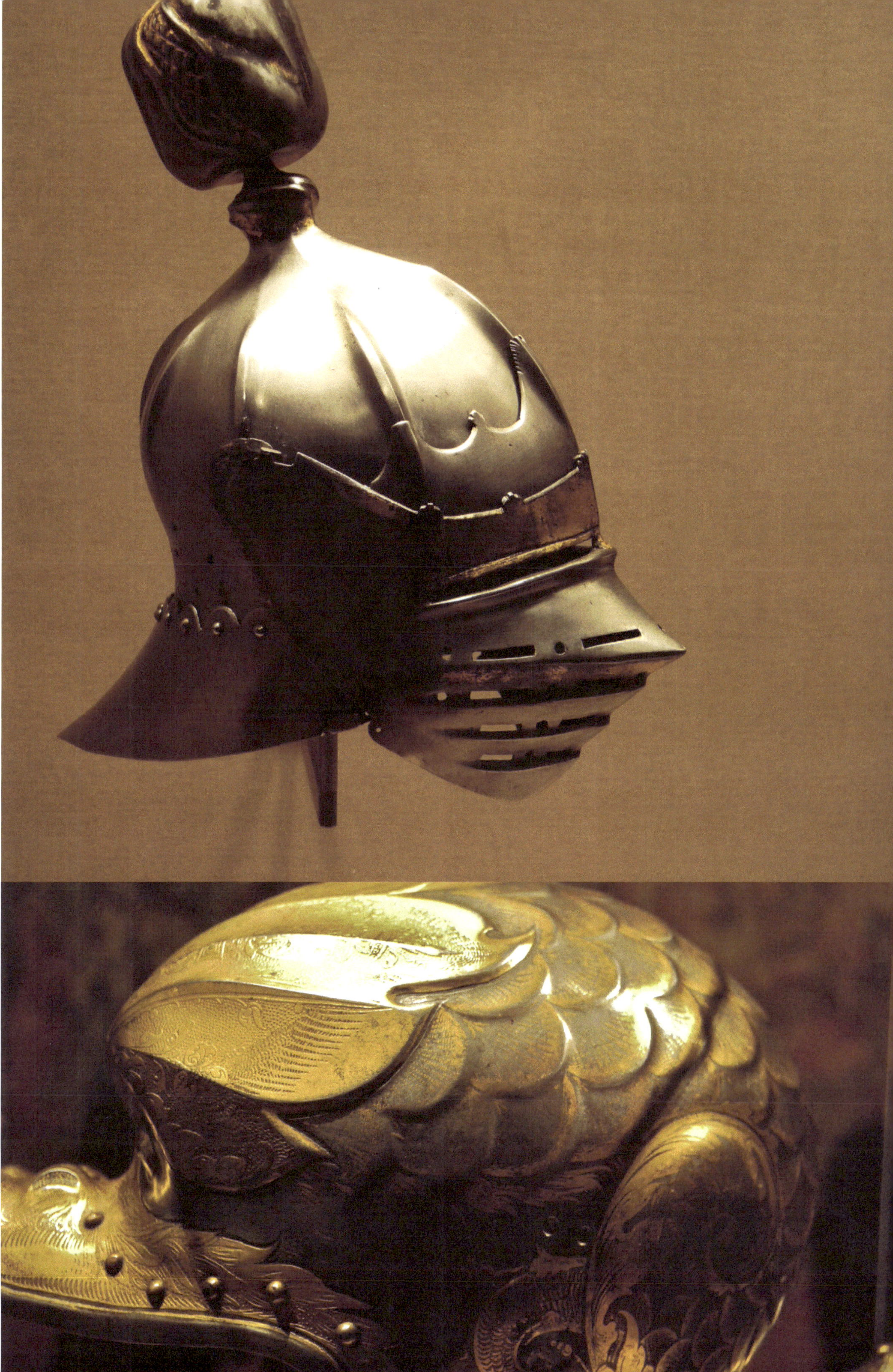

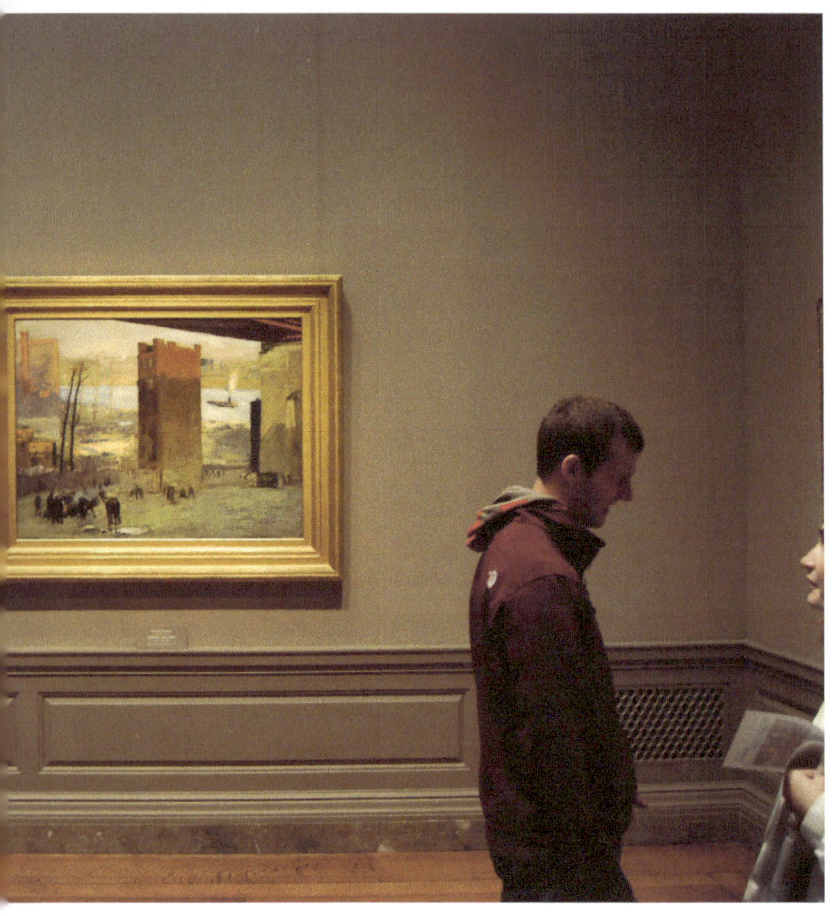

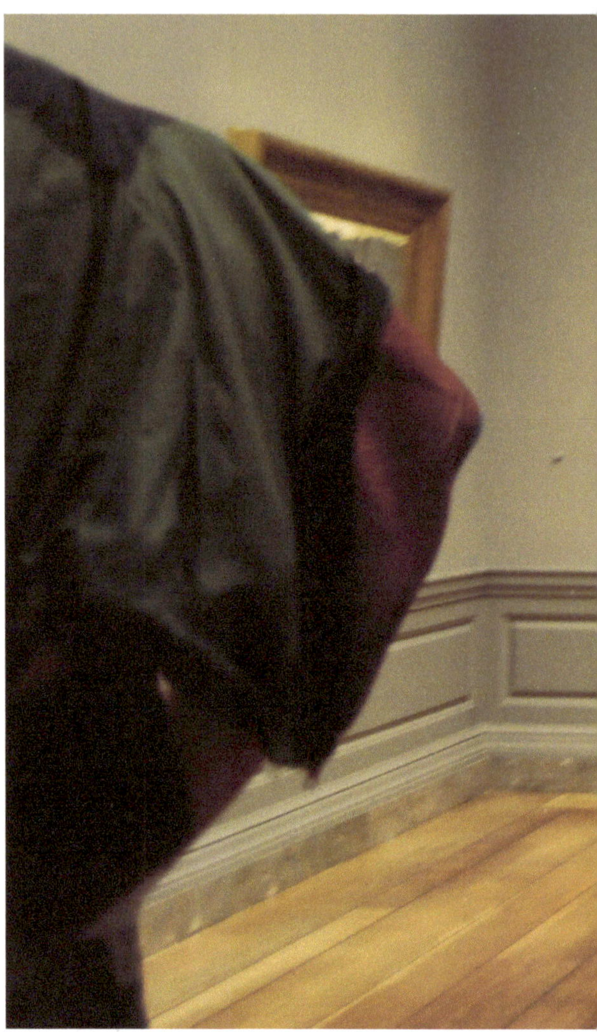

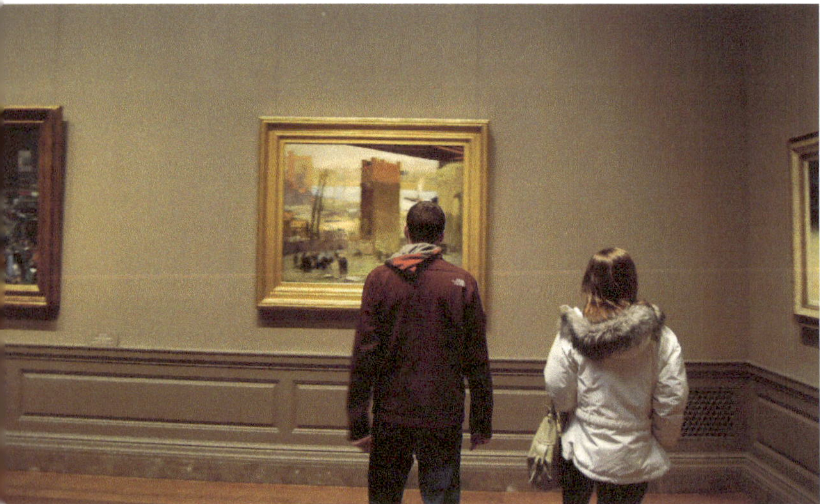

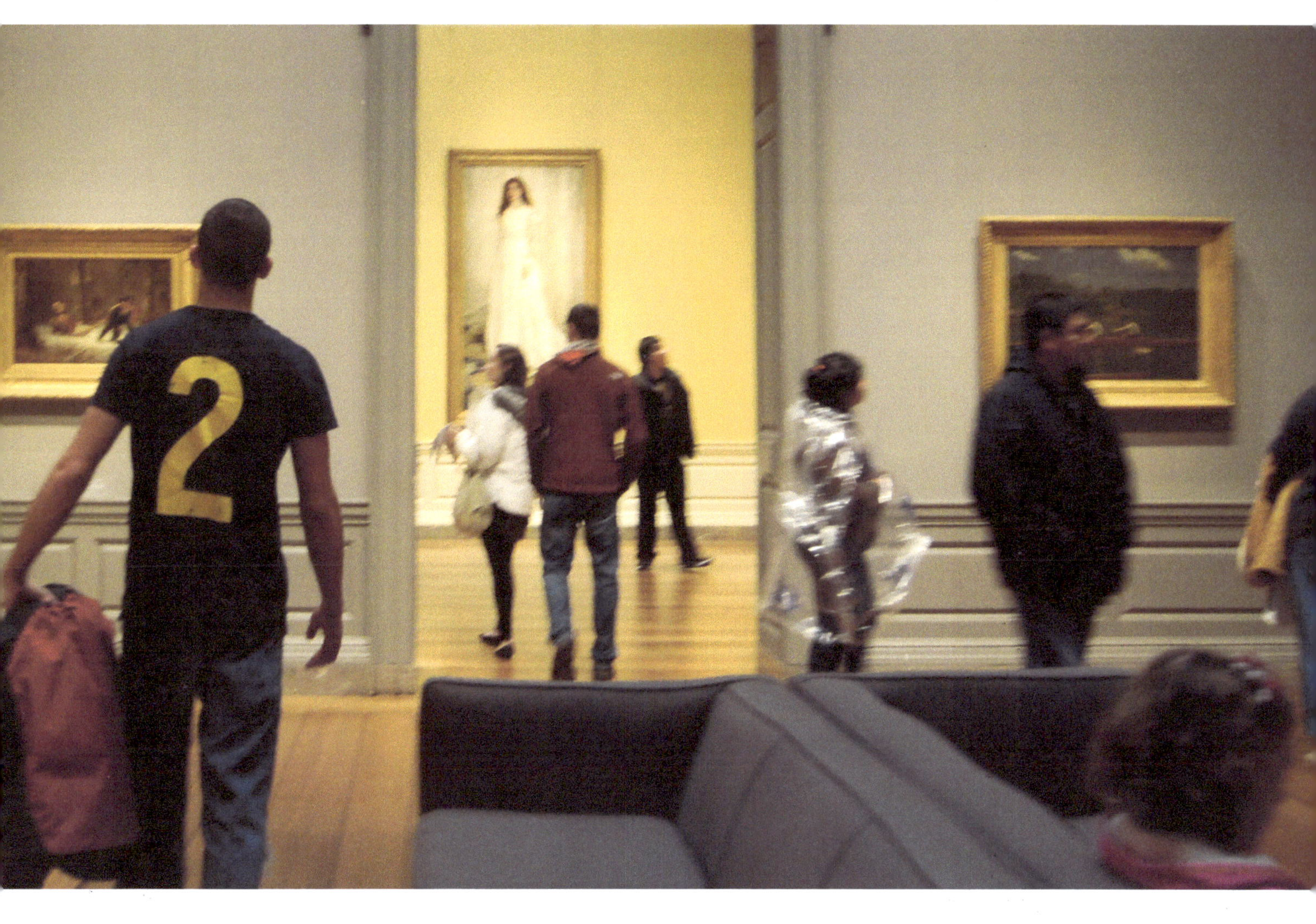
2

National Gallery of Art in Washington DC

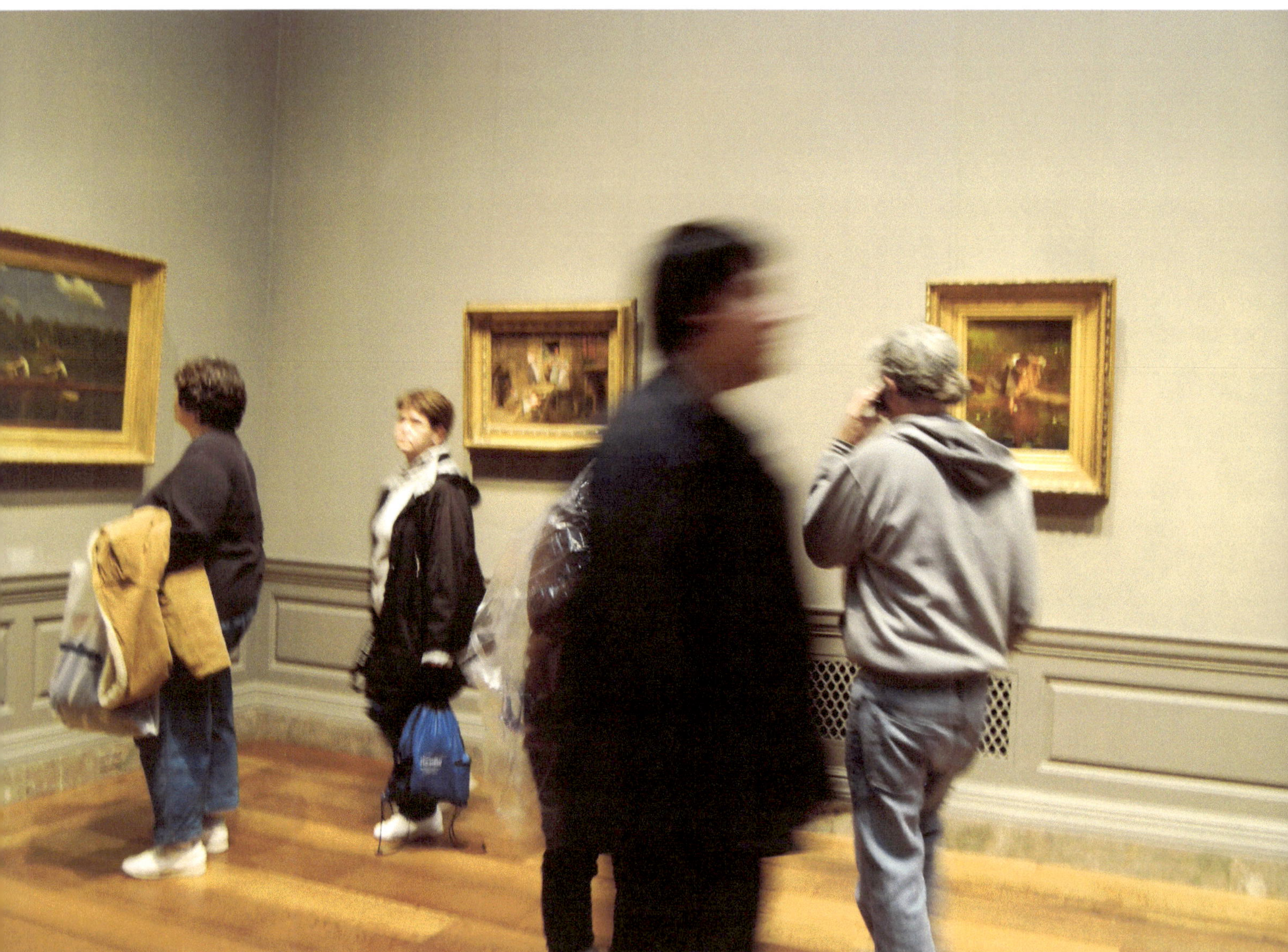

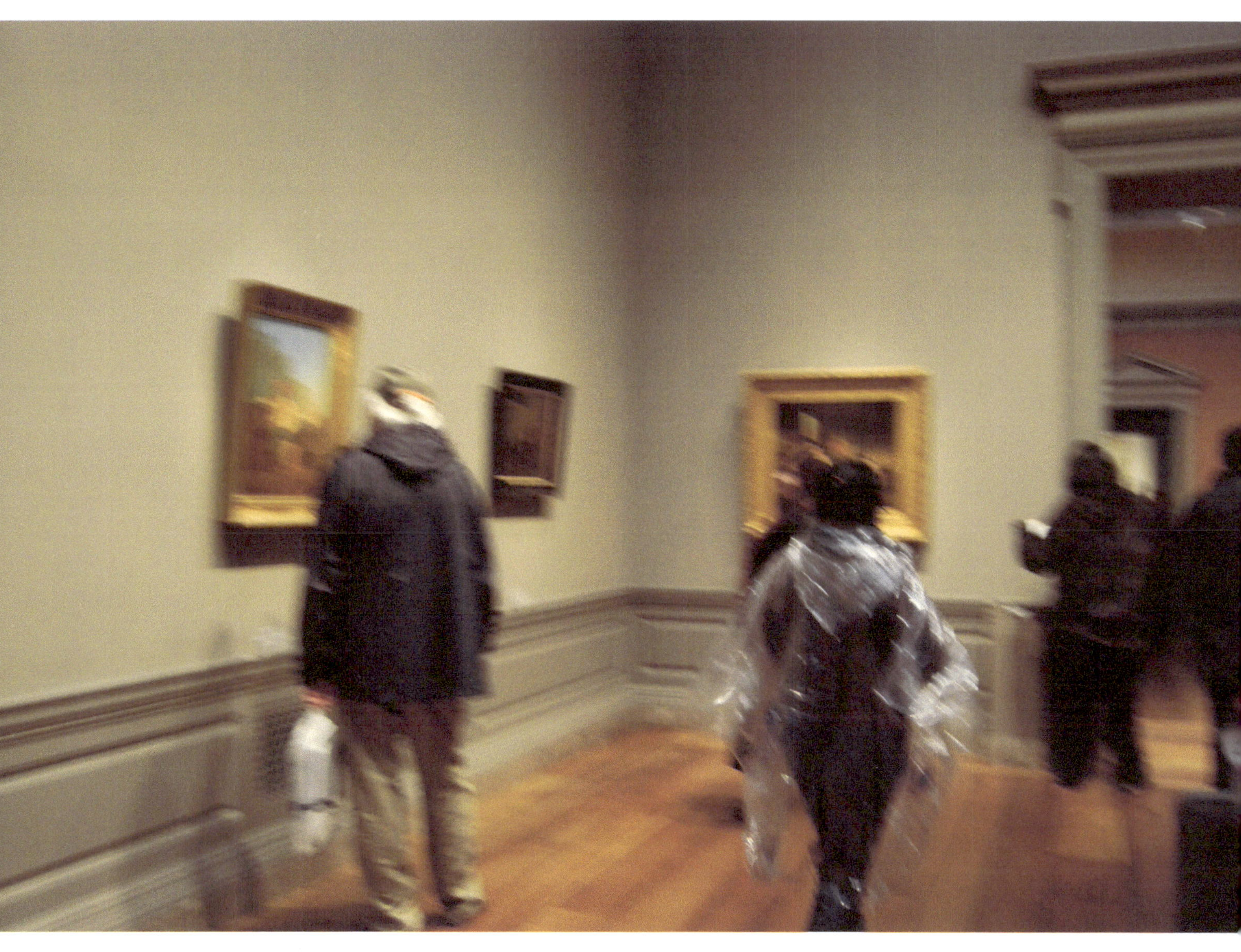

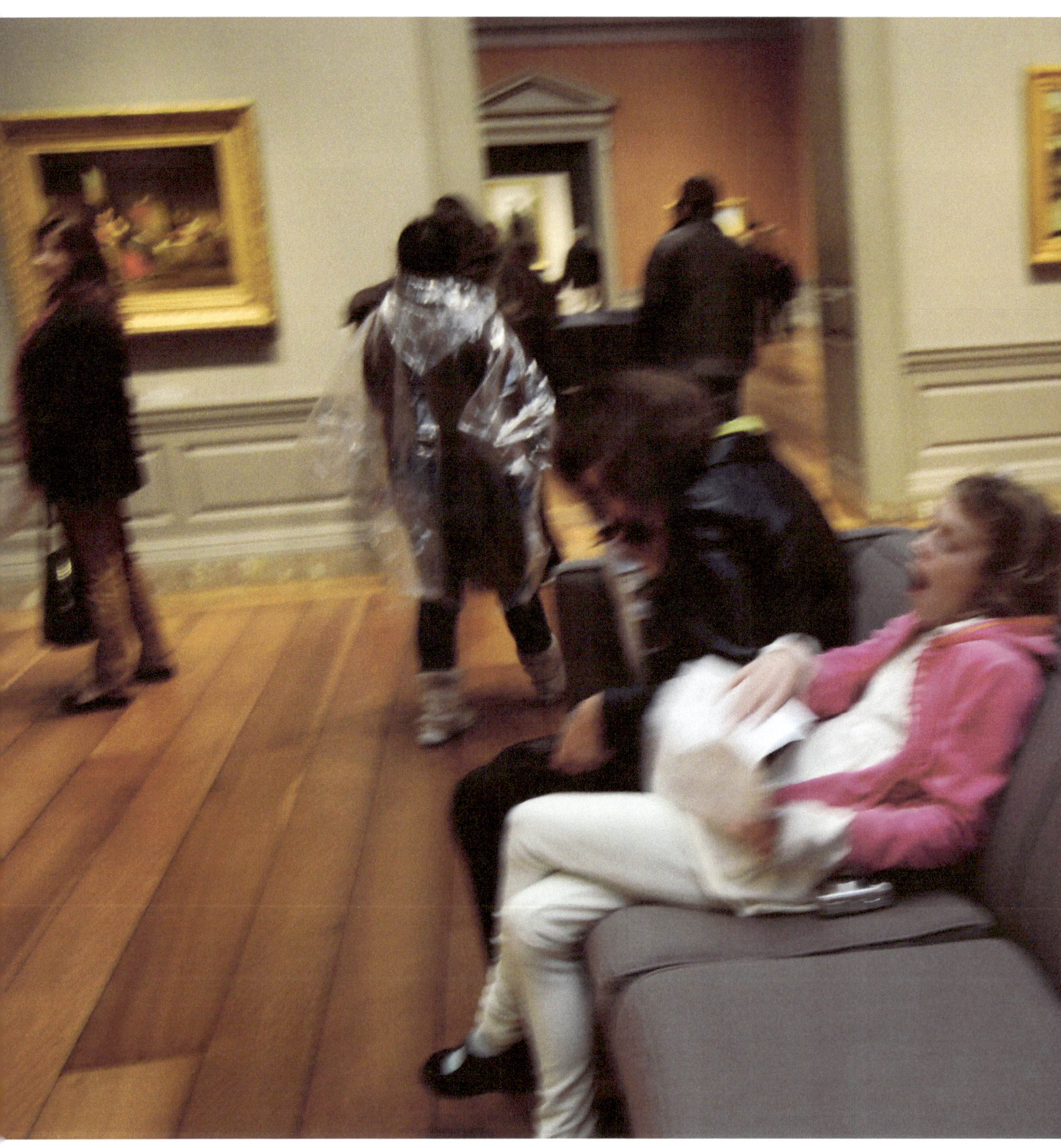

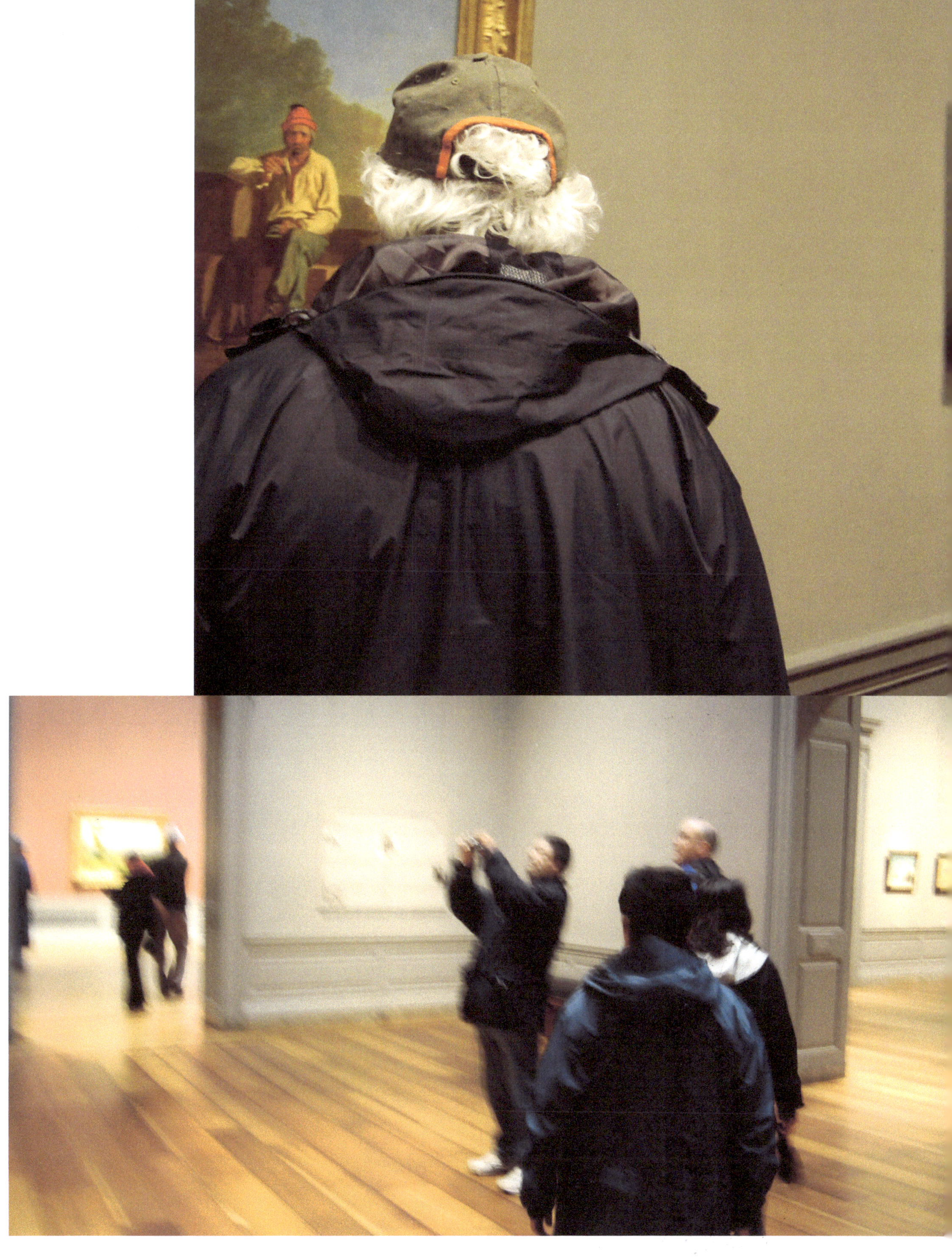

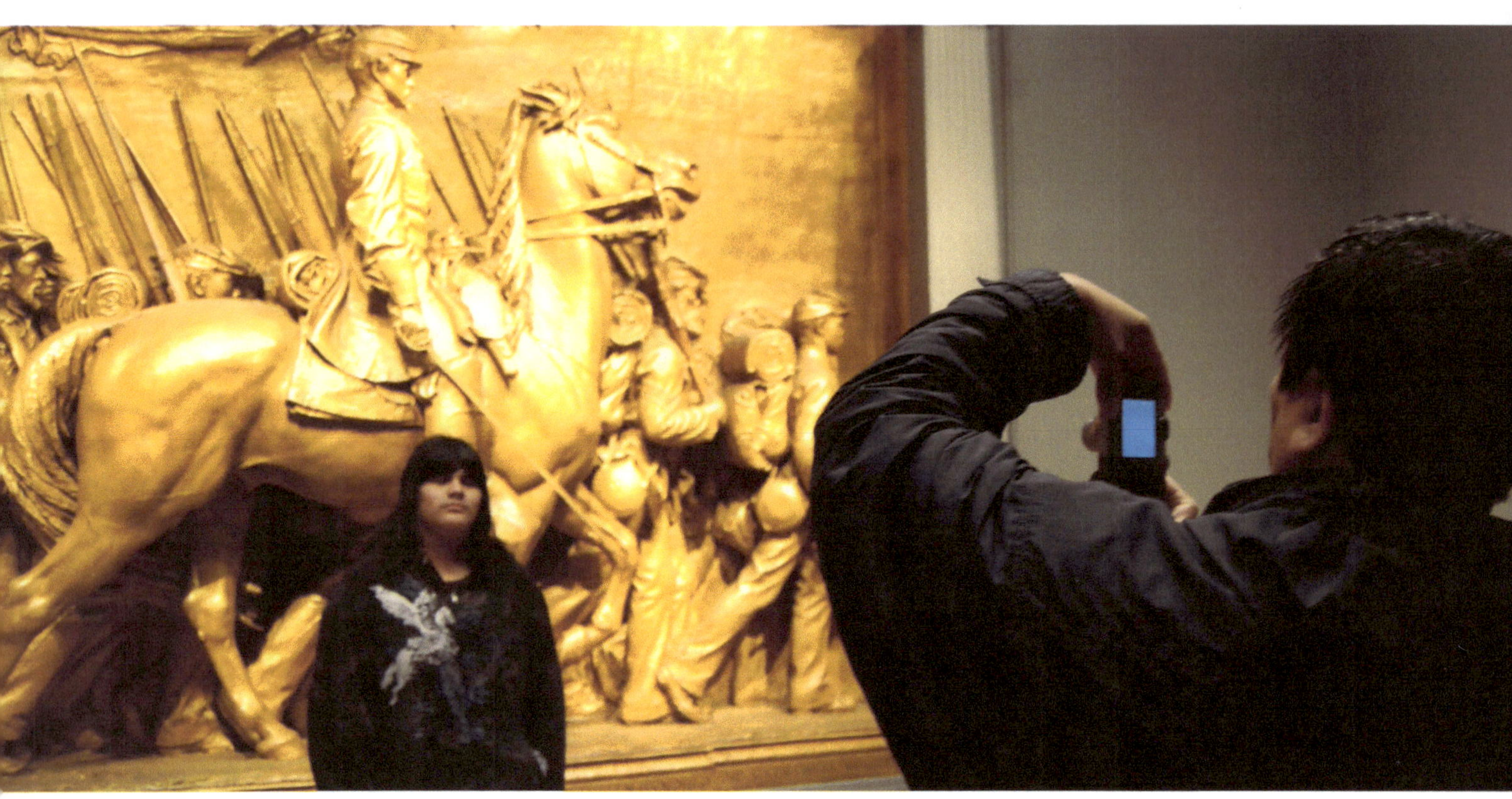

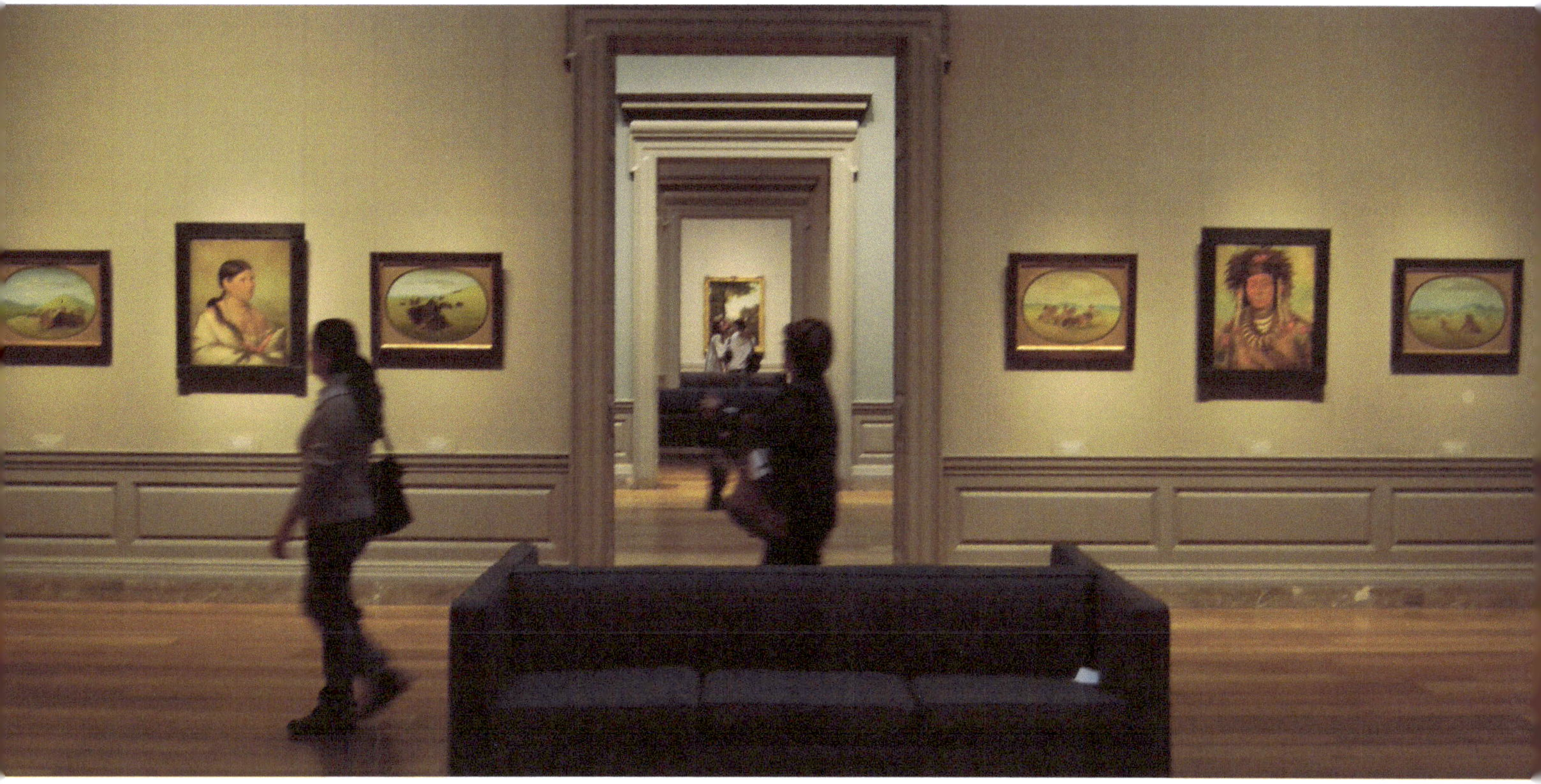

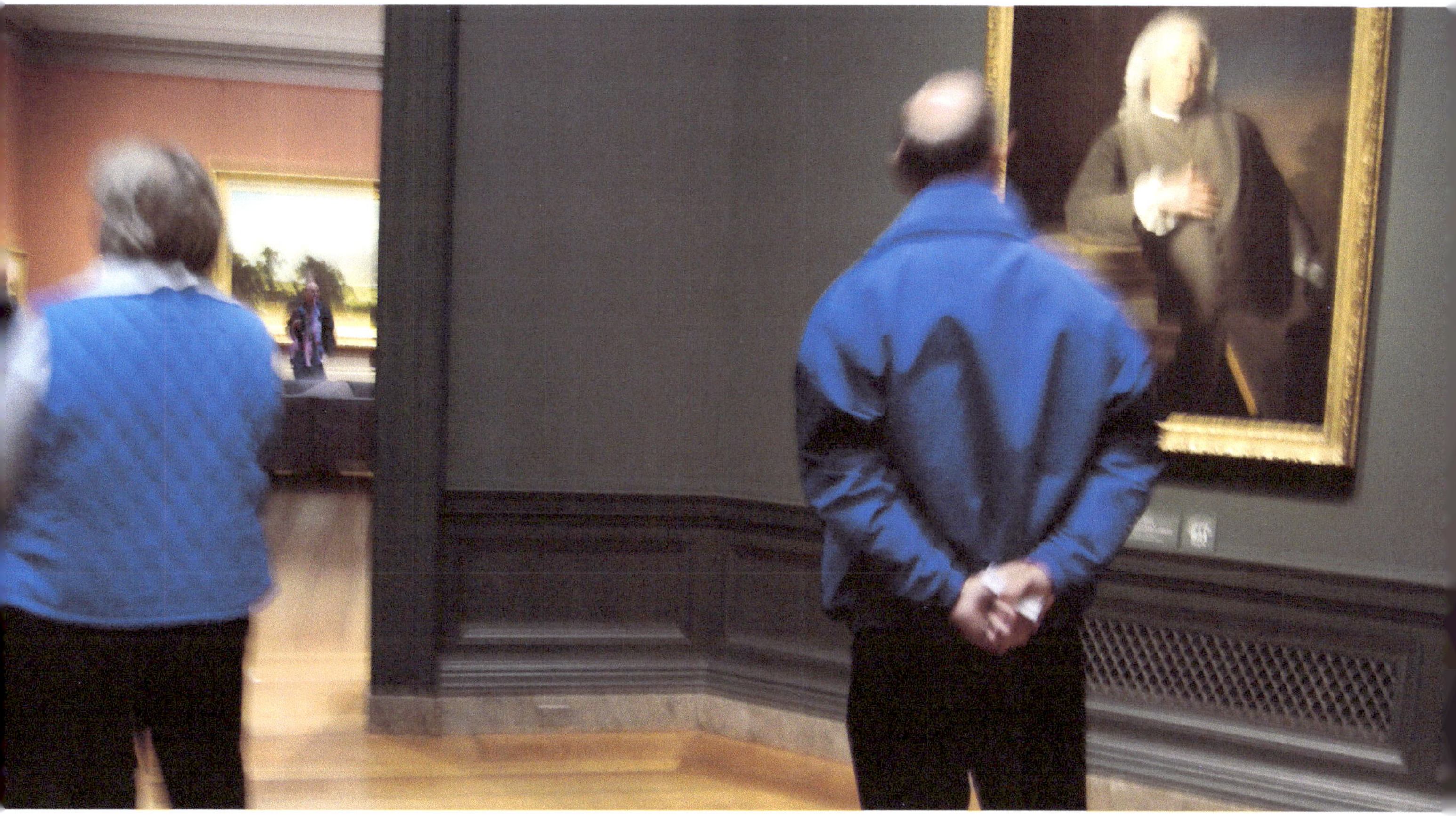

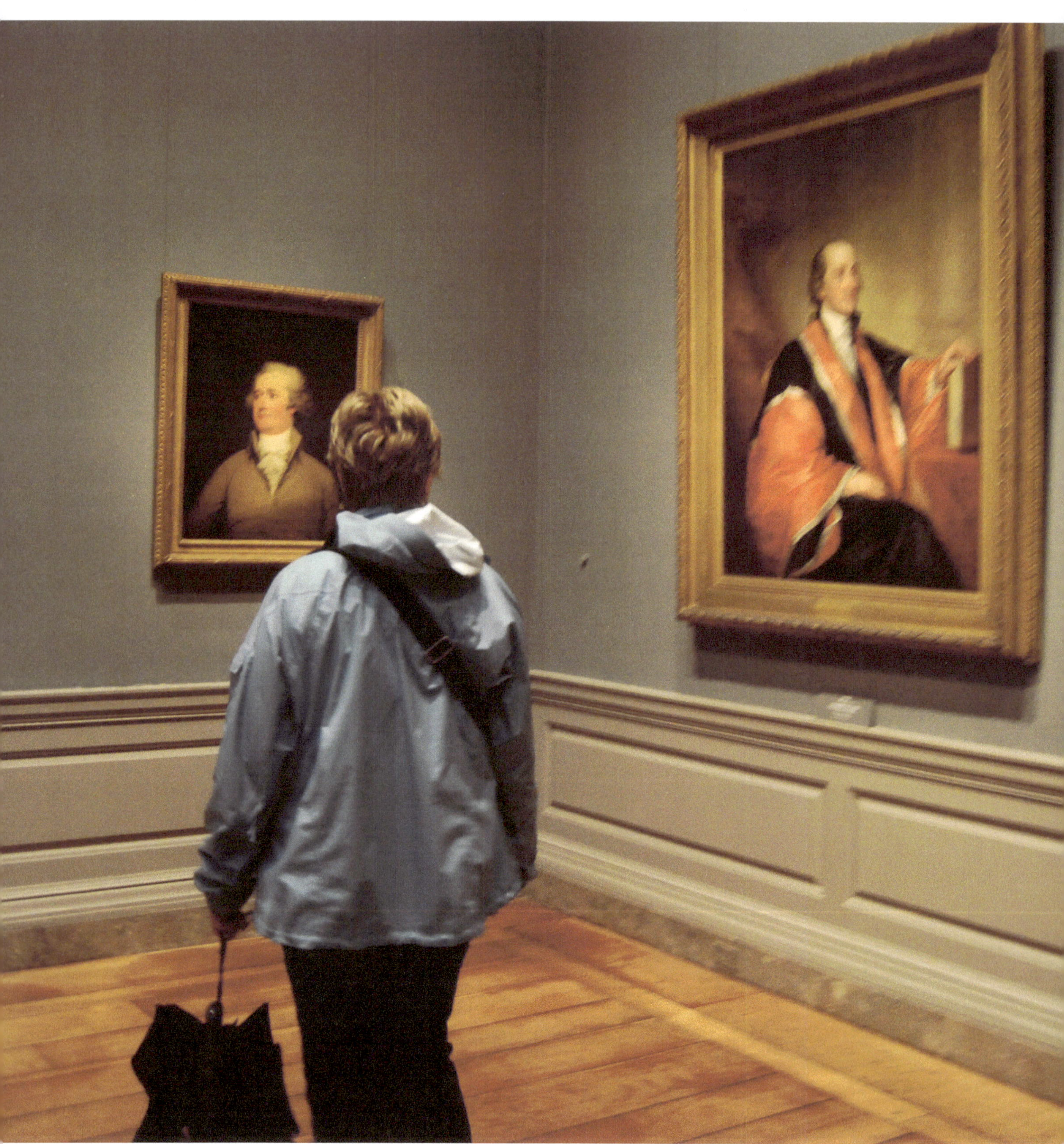

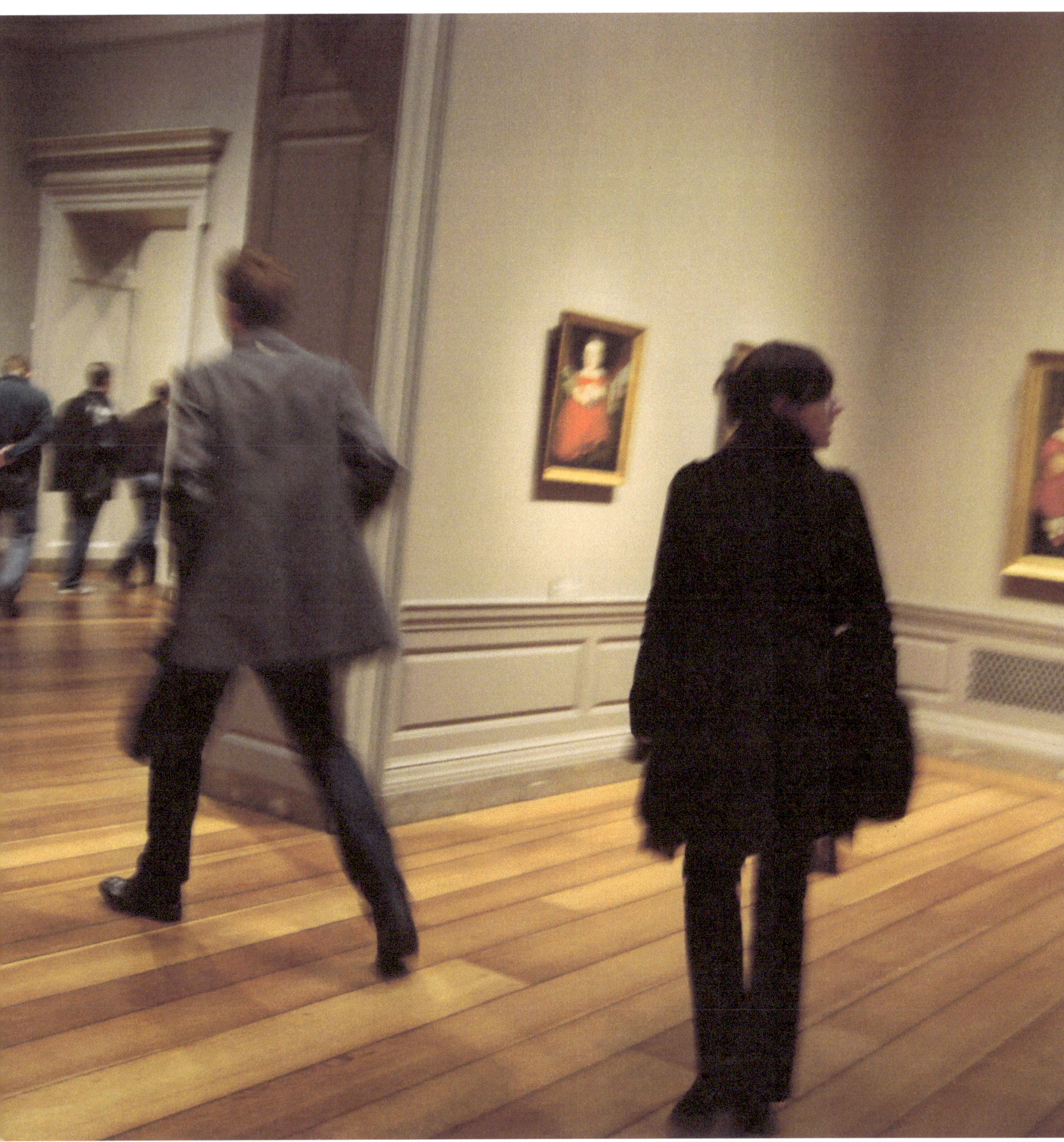

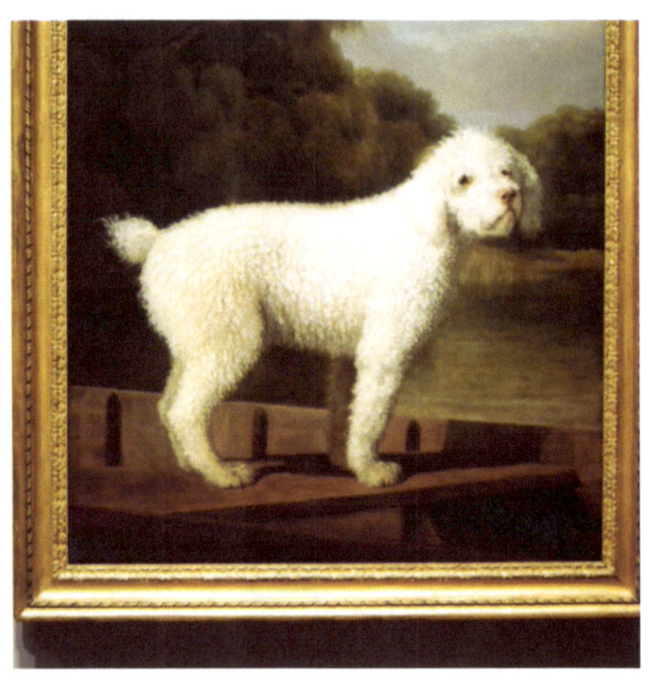

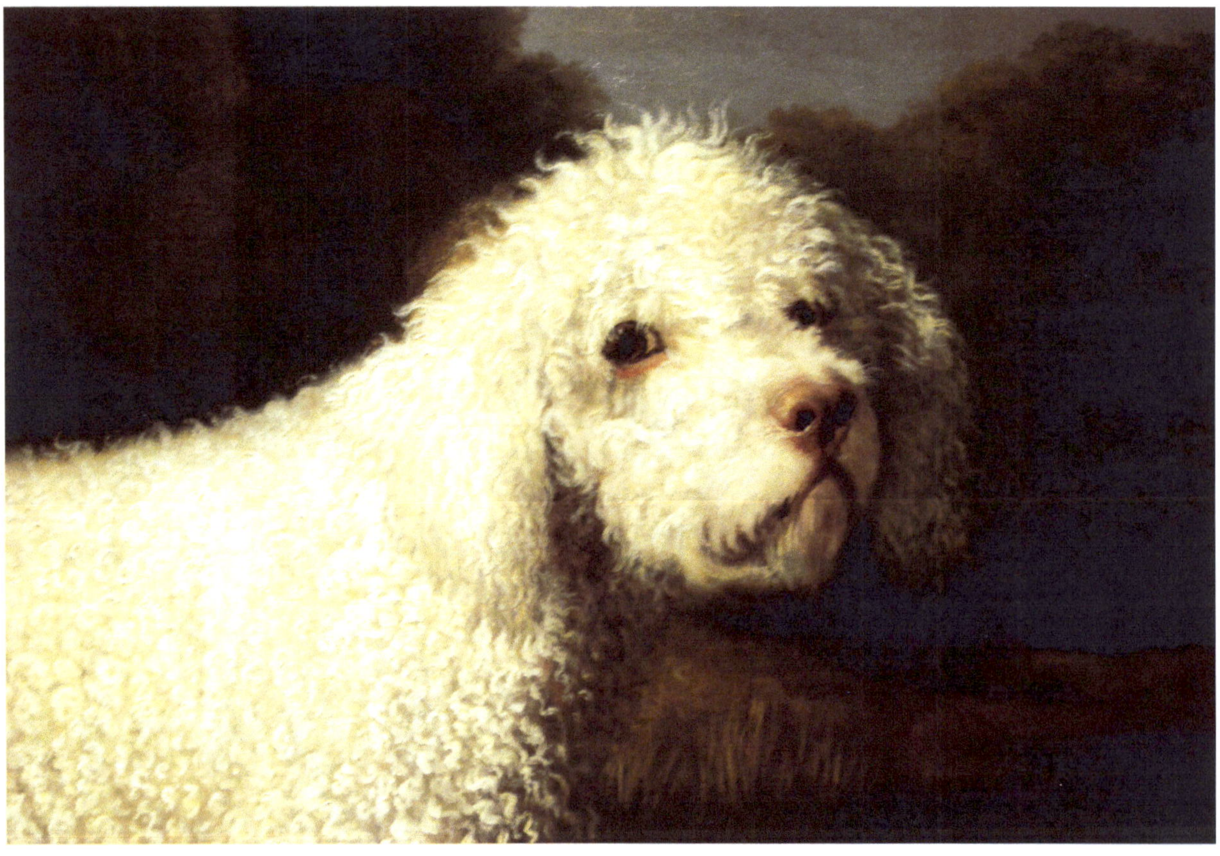

George Stubbs
White Poodle in a Punt, c. 1780

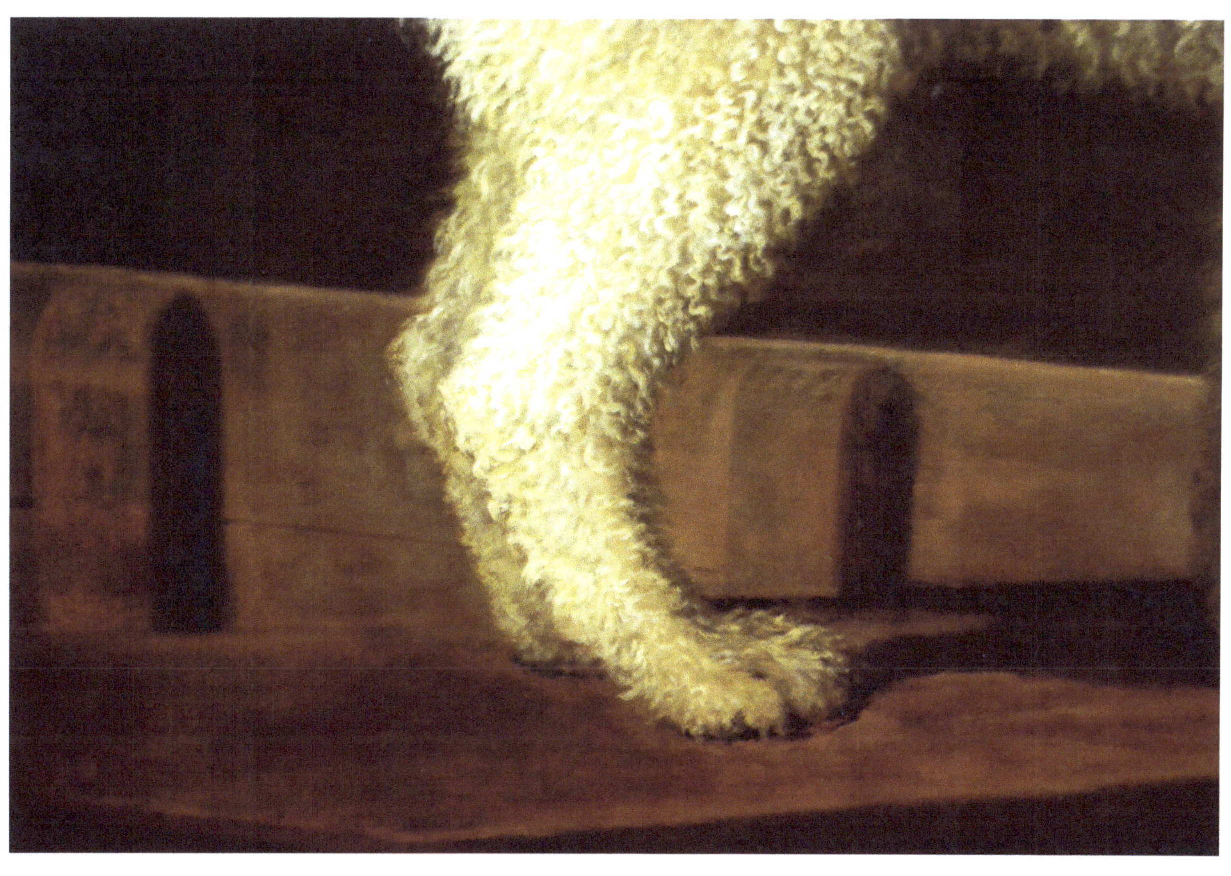

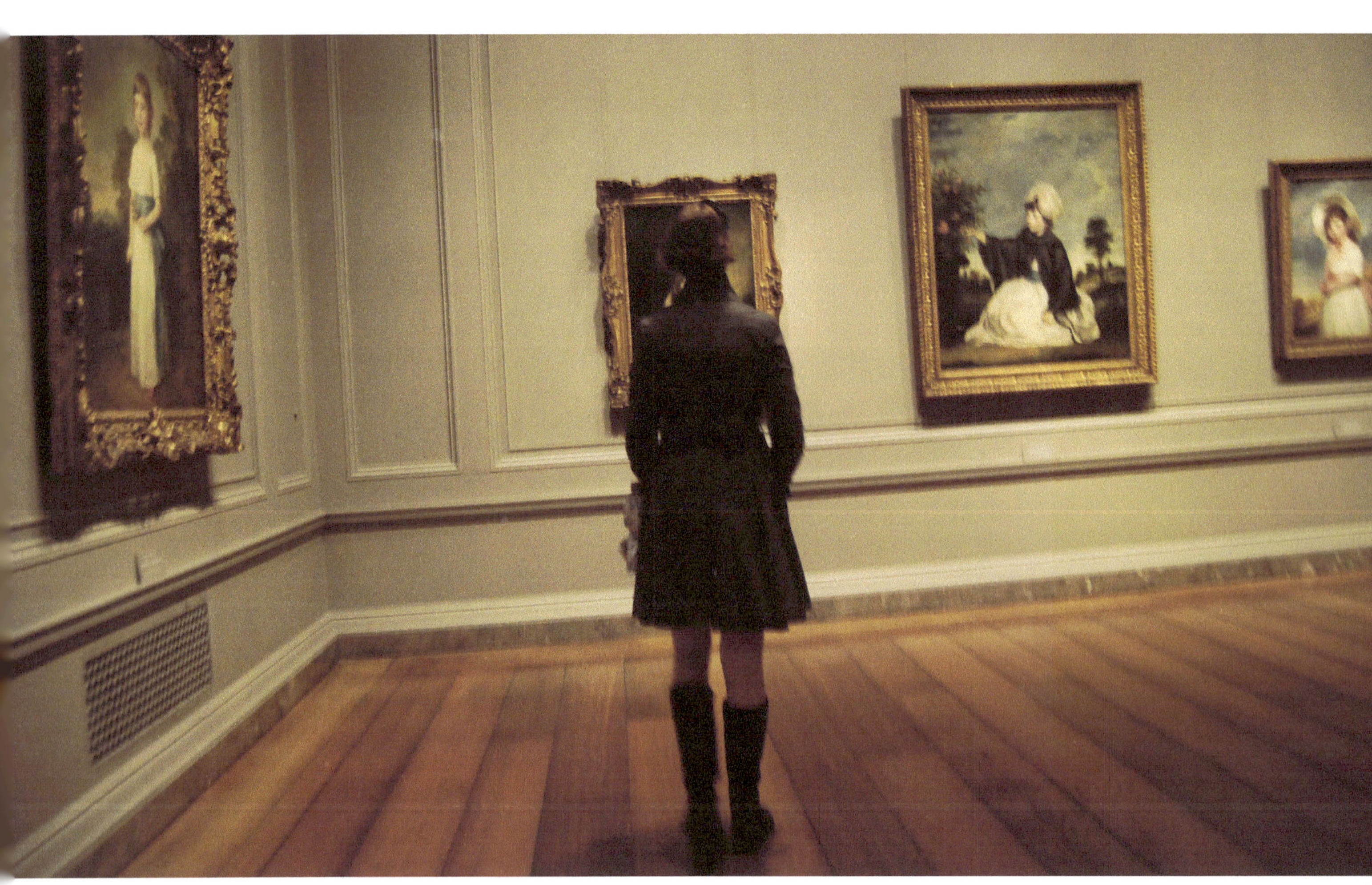

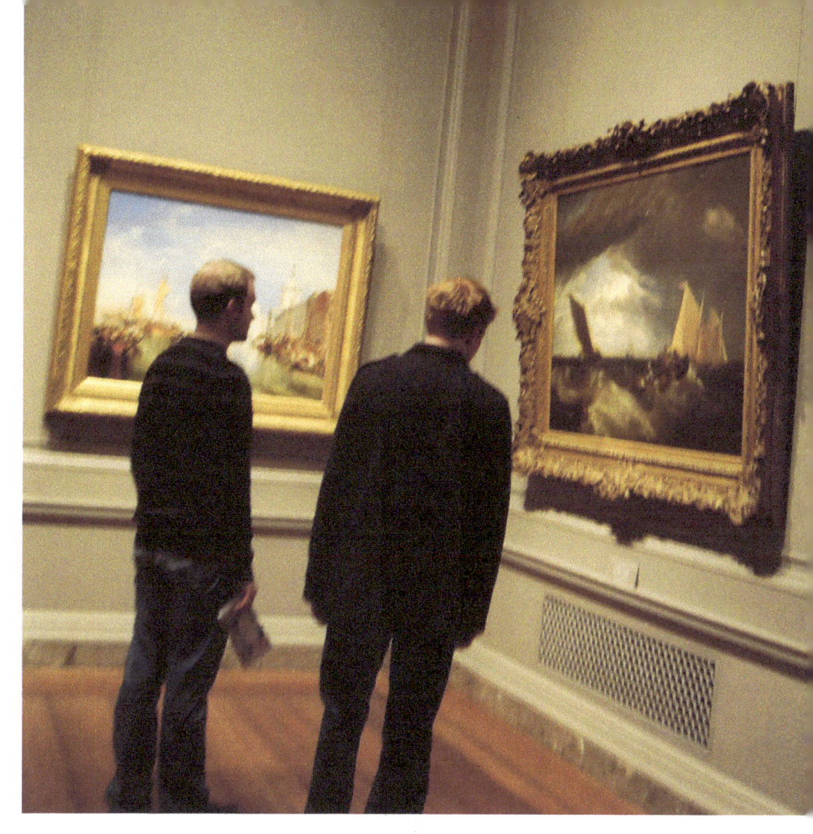

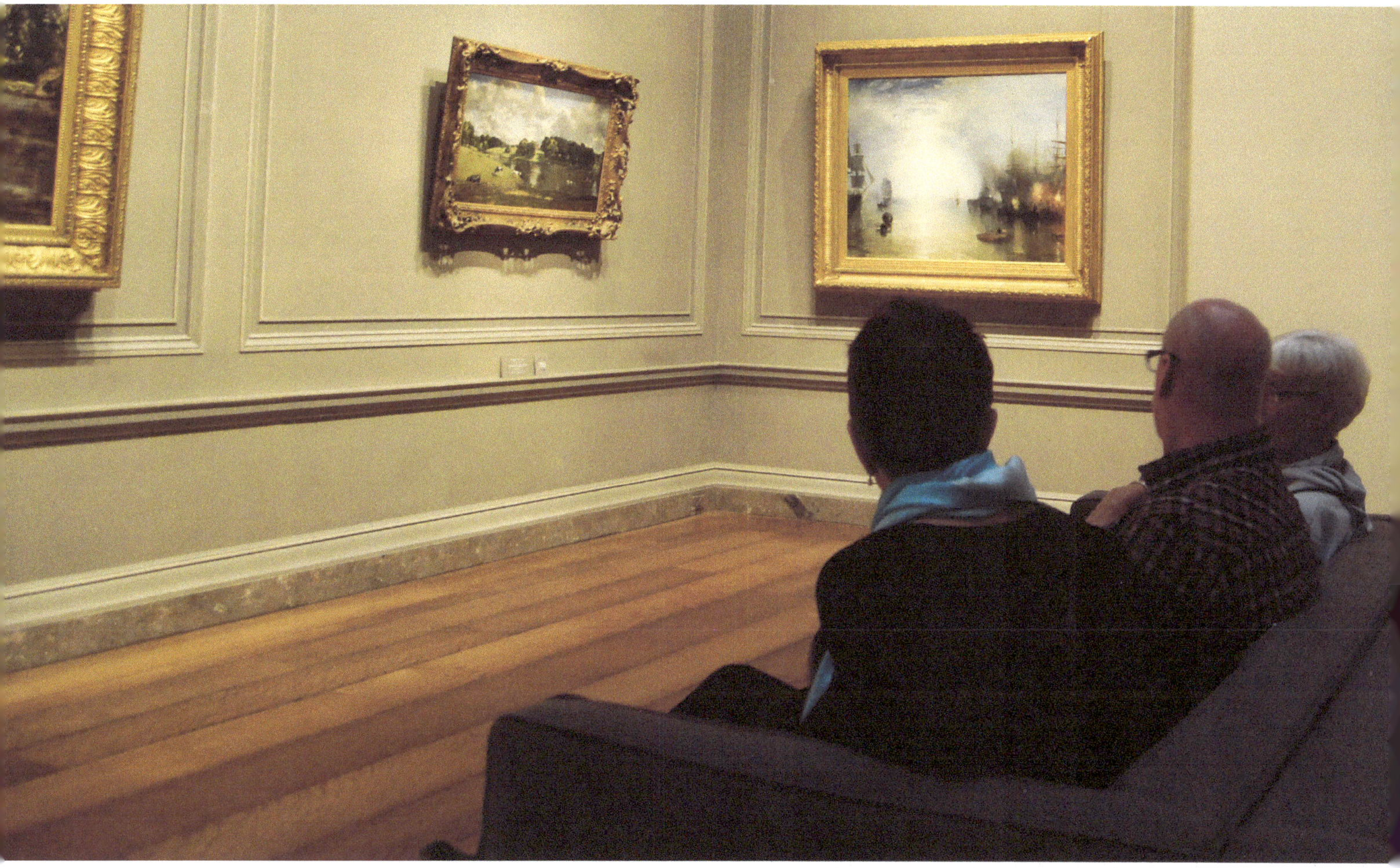

National Gallery of Art in Washington DC

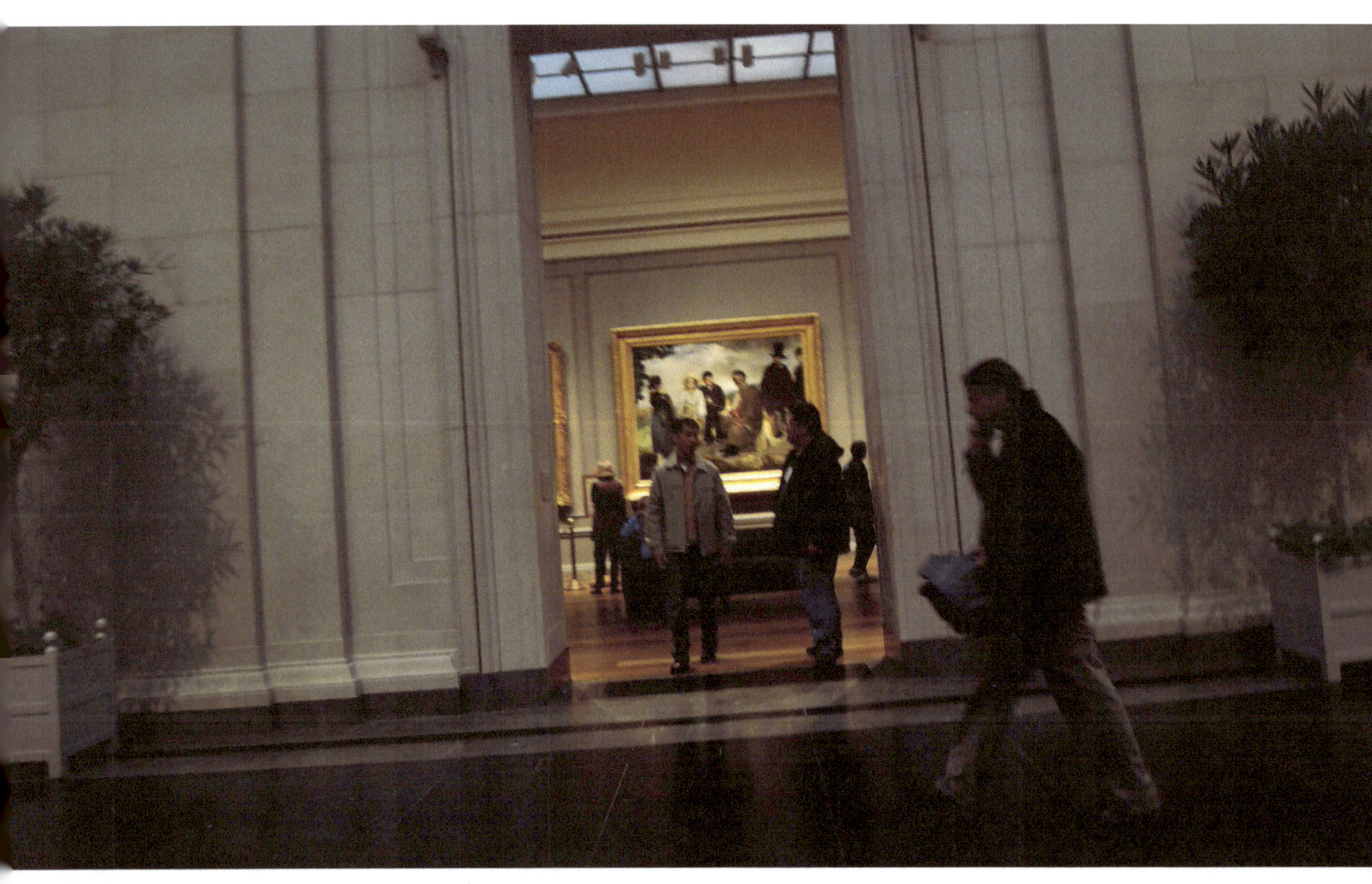

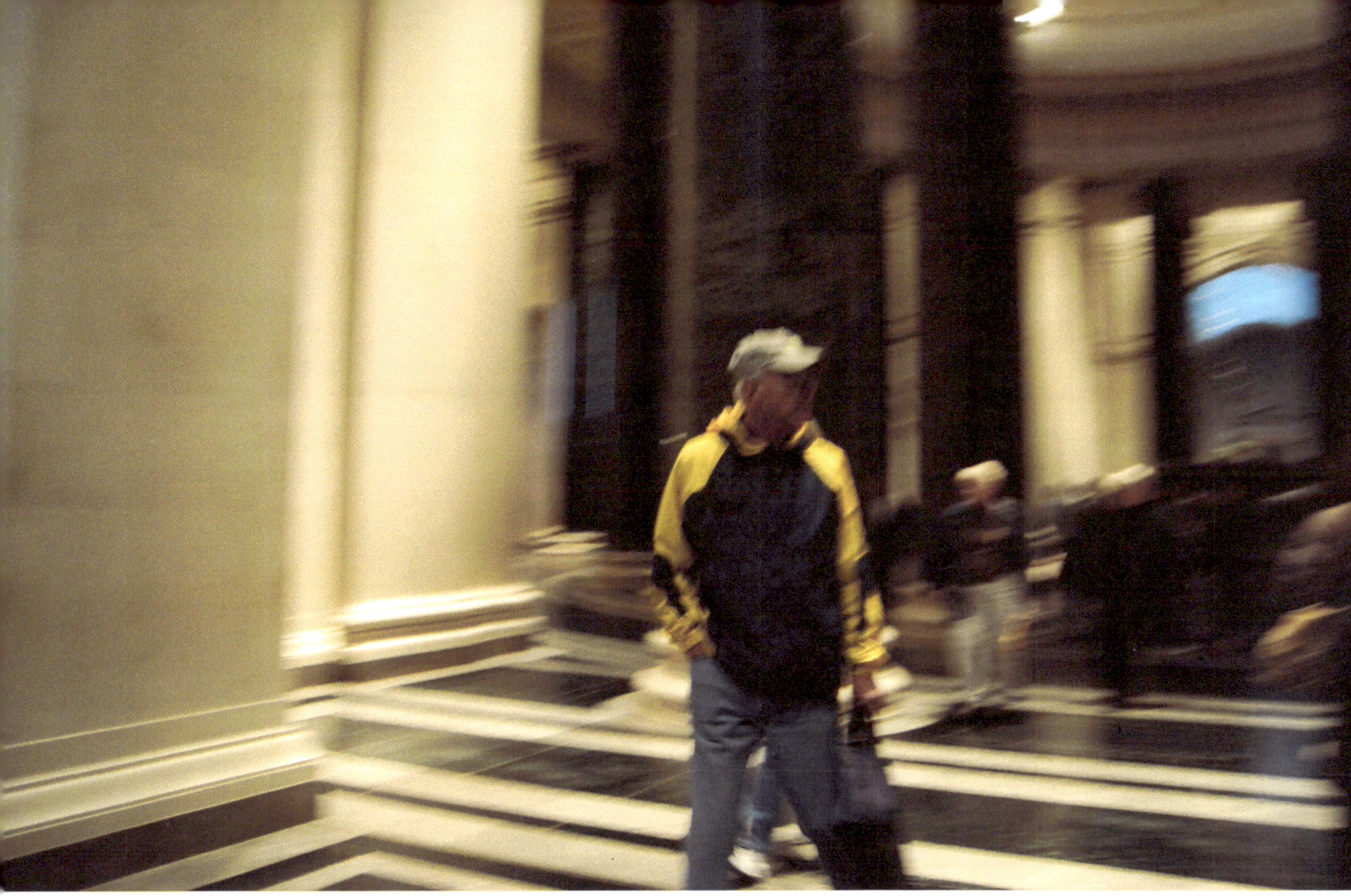

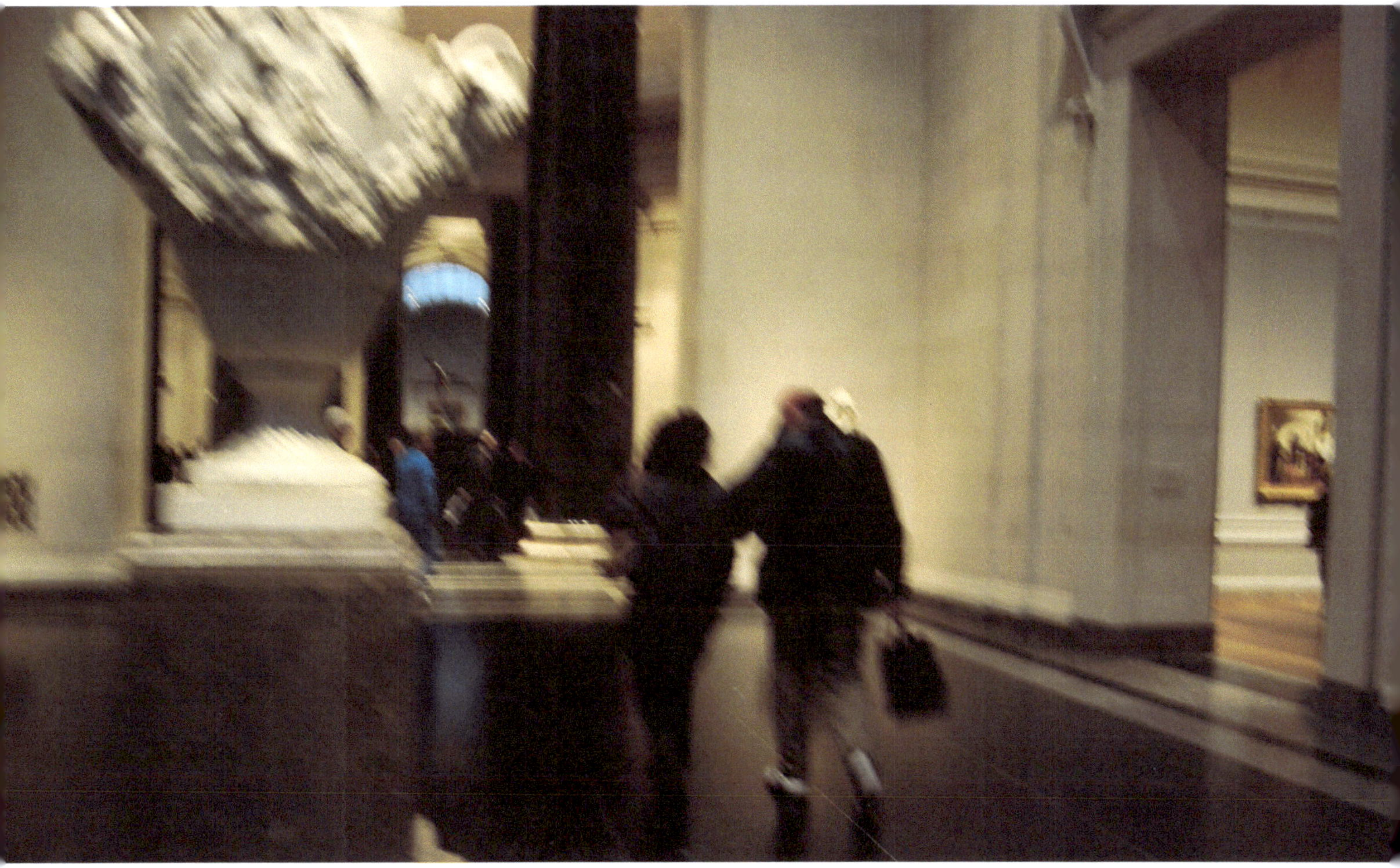

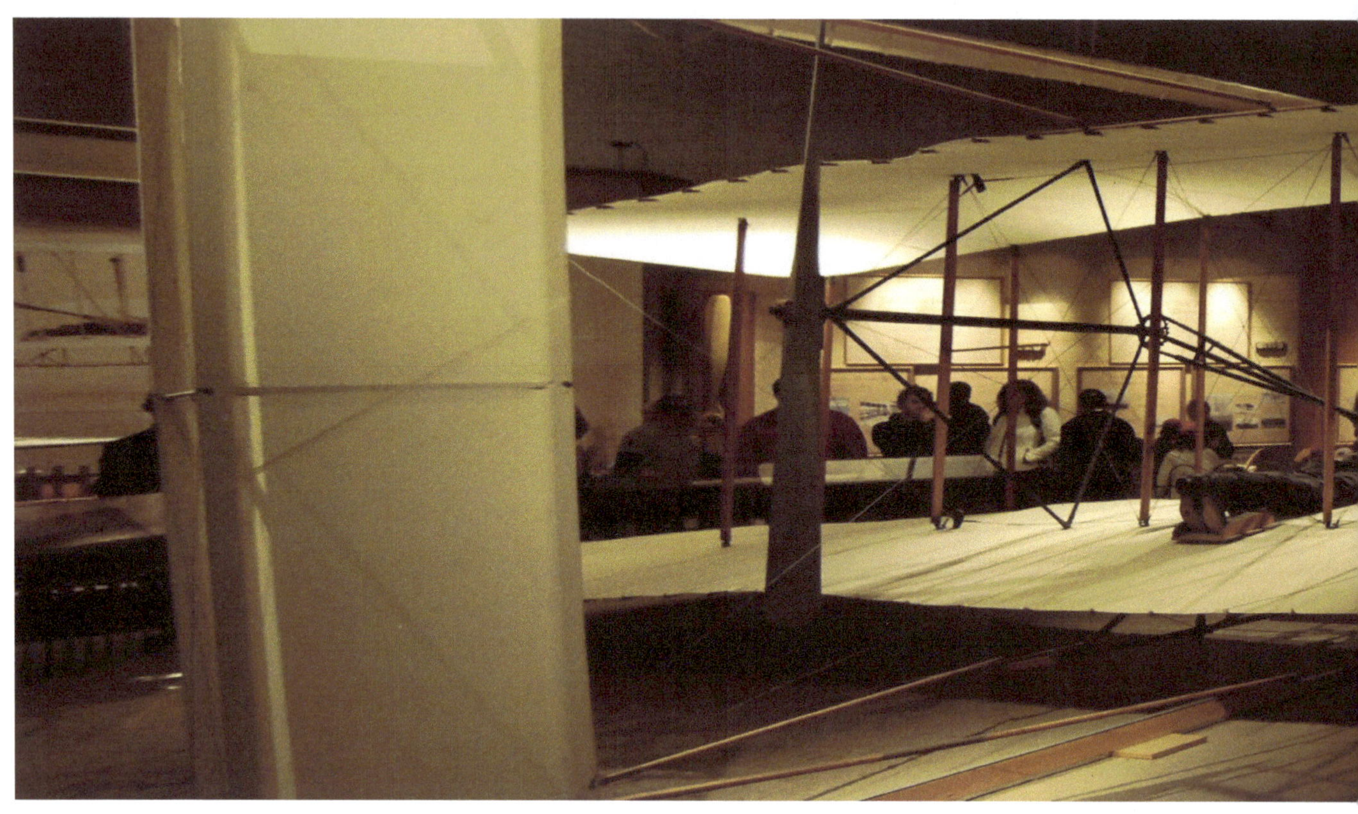

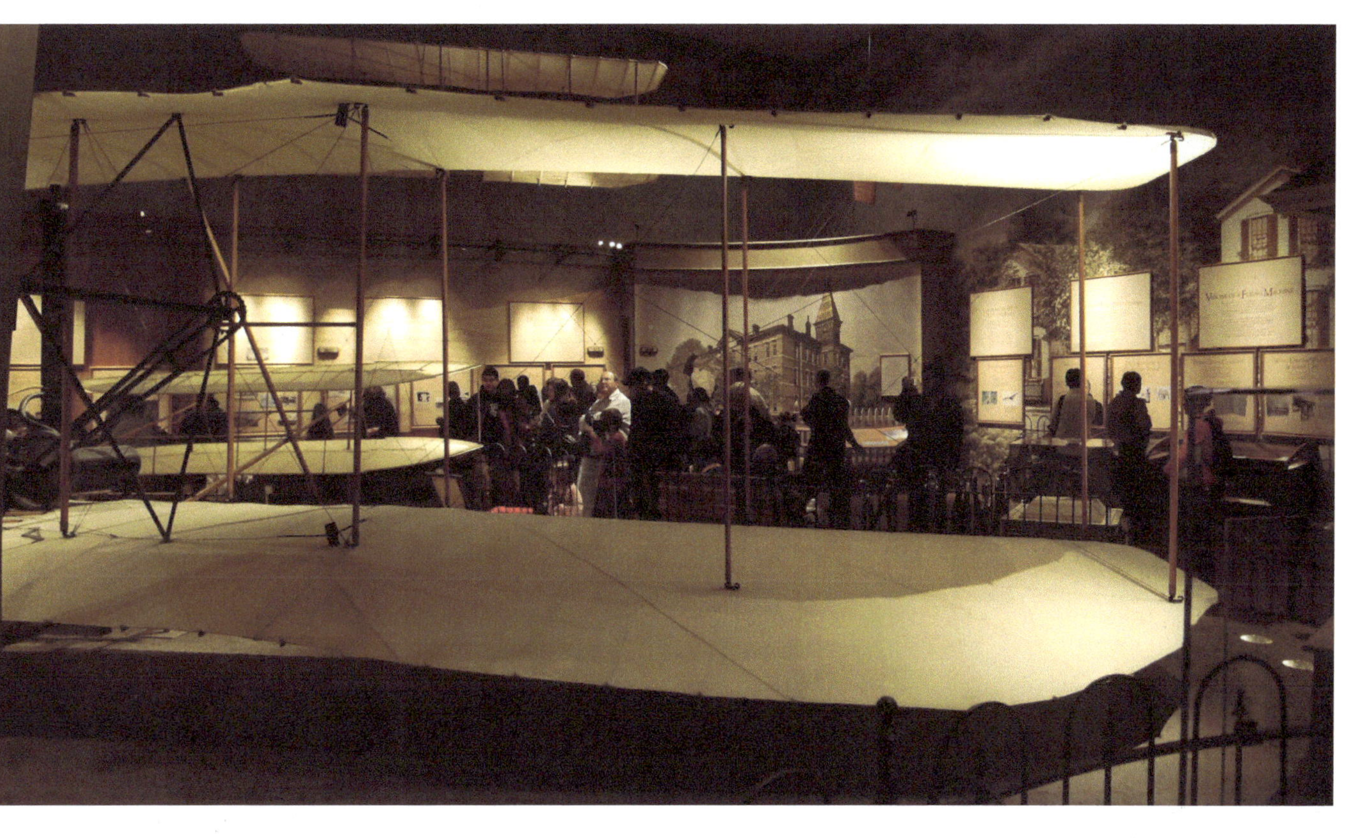

National Building Museum in Washington DC

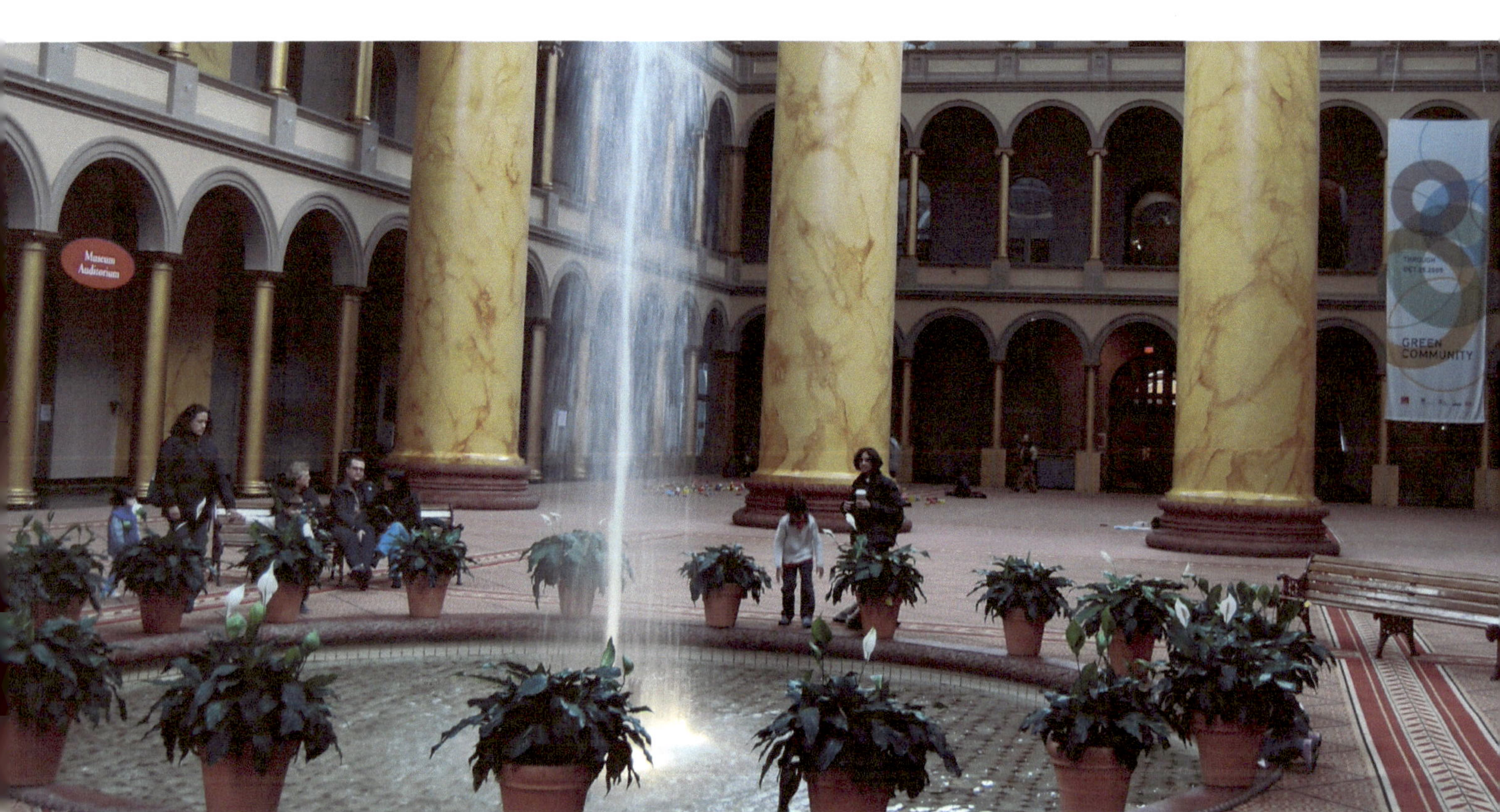

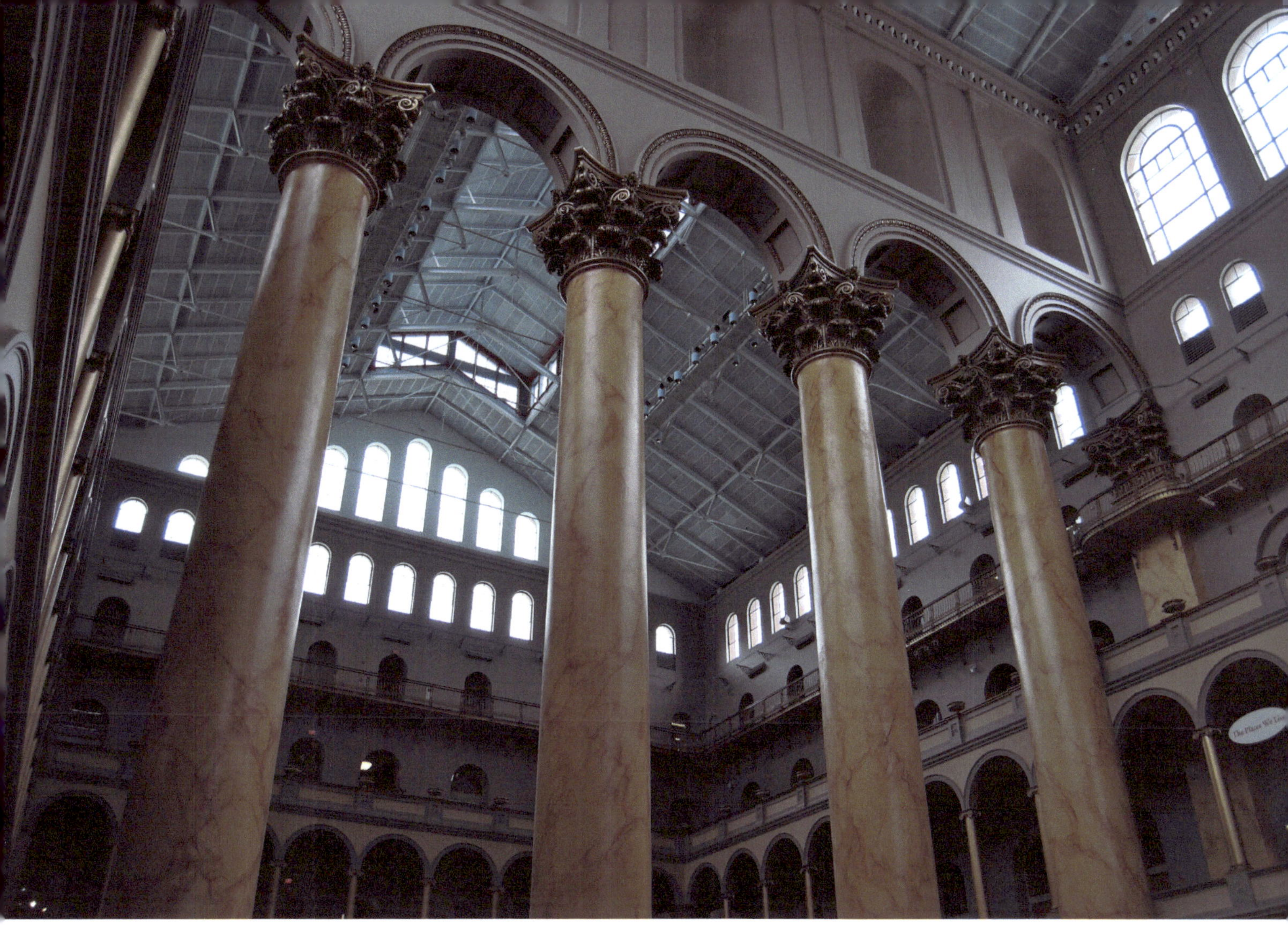

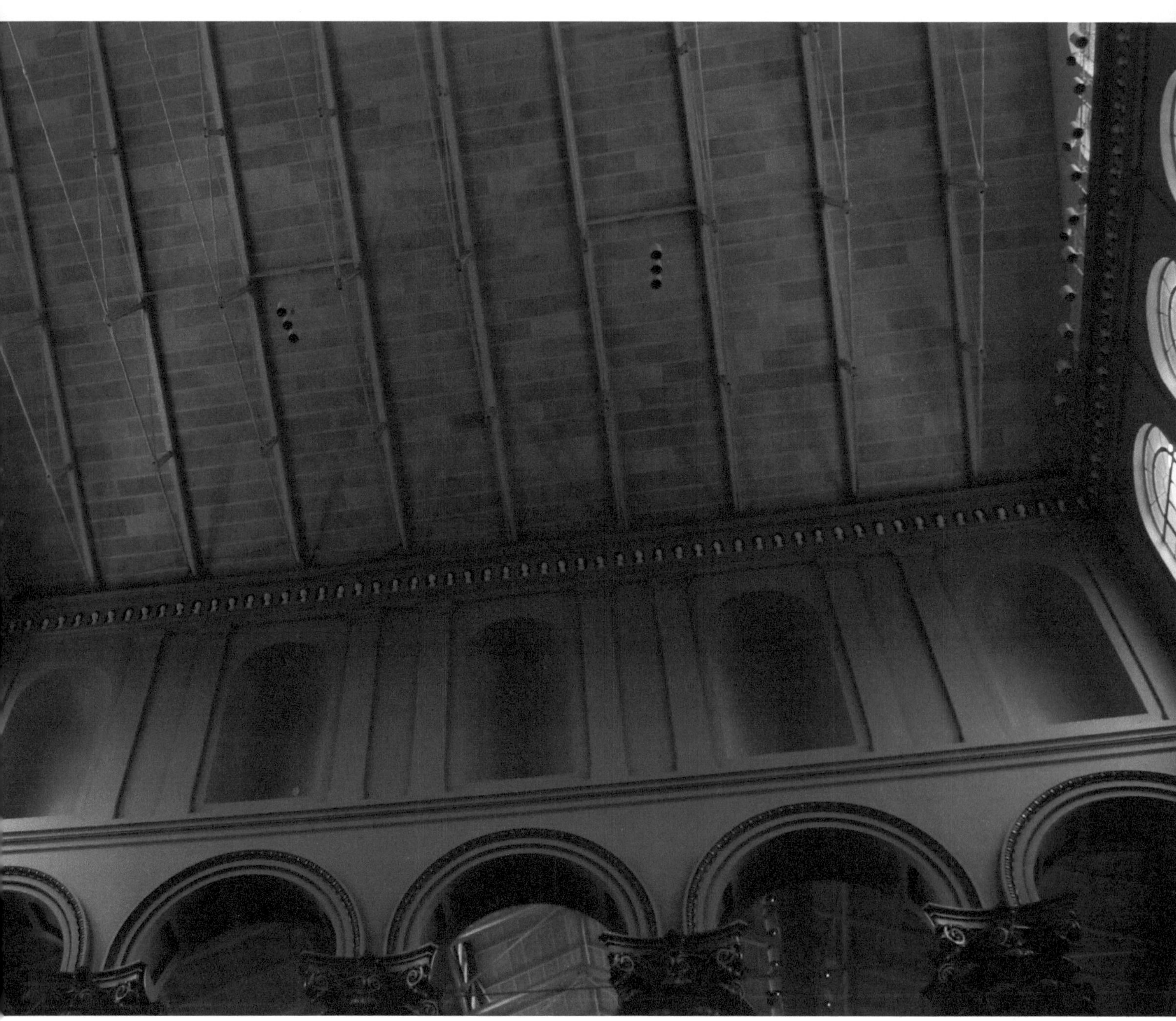

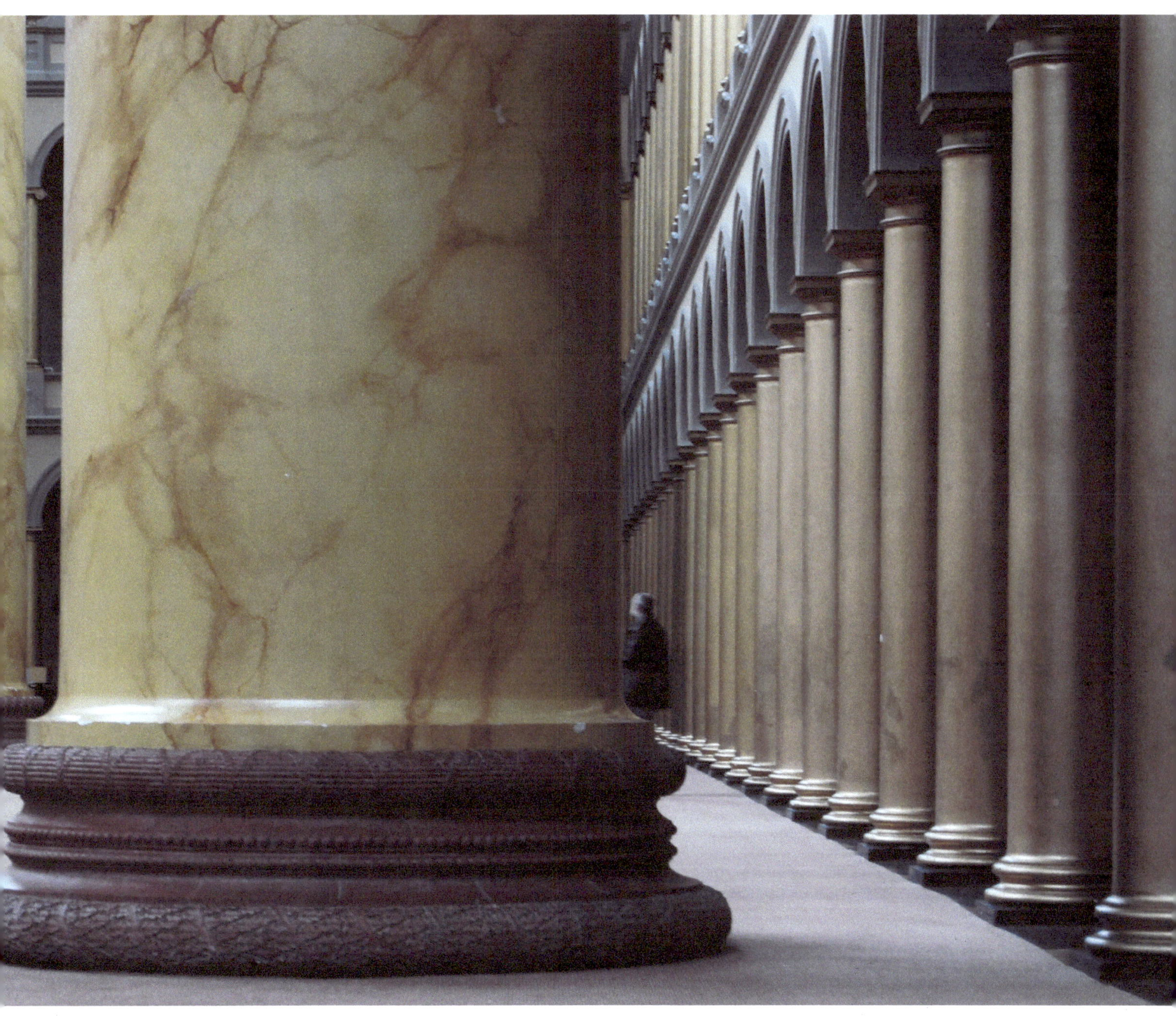

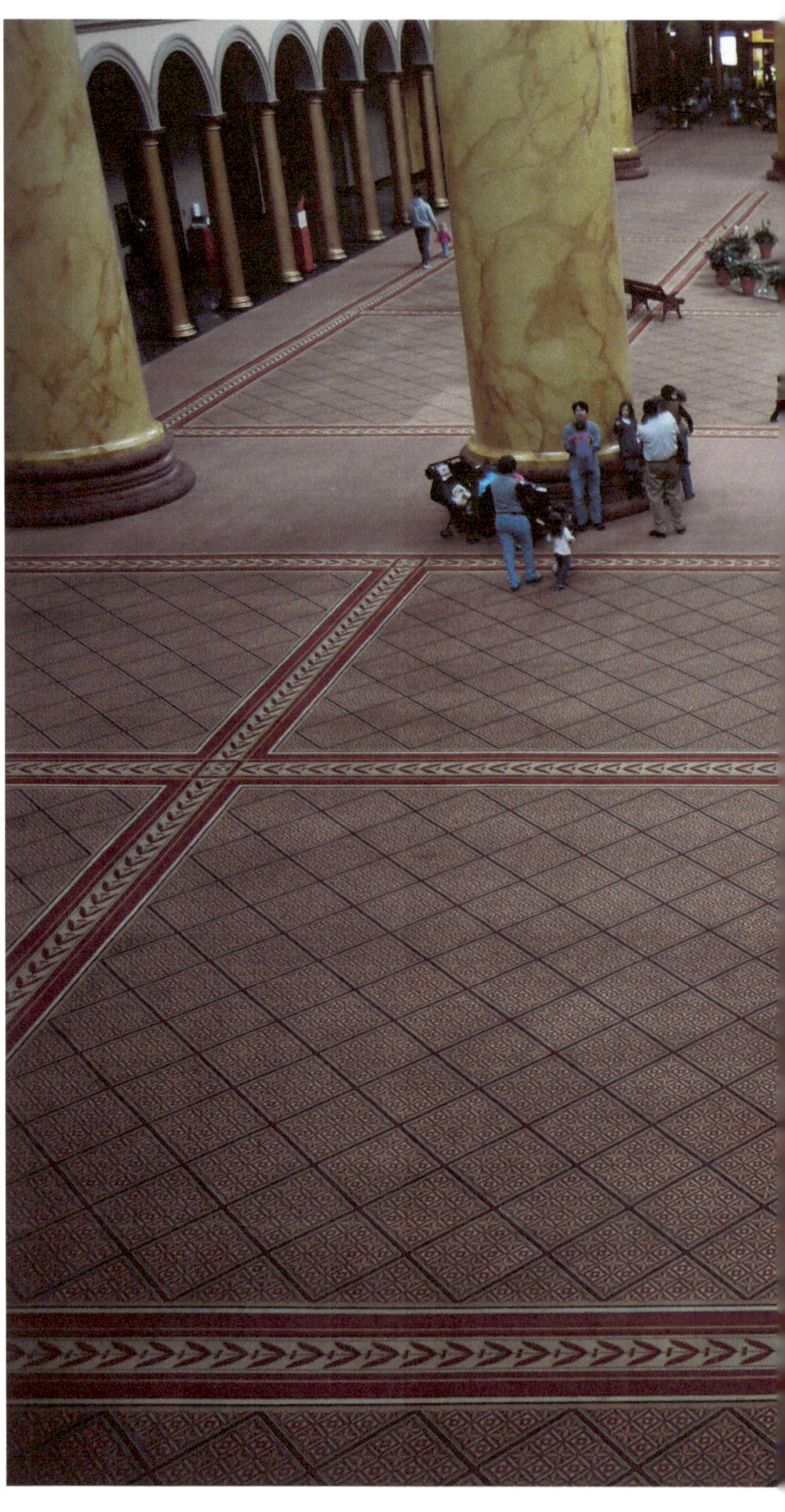

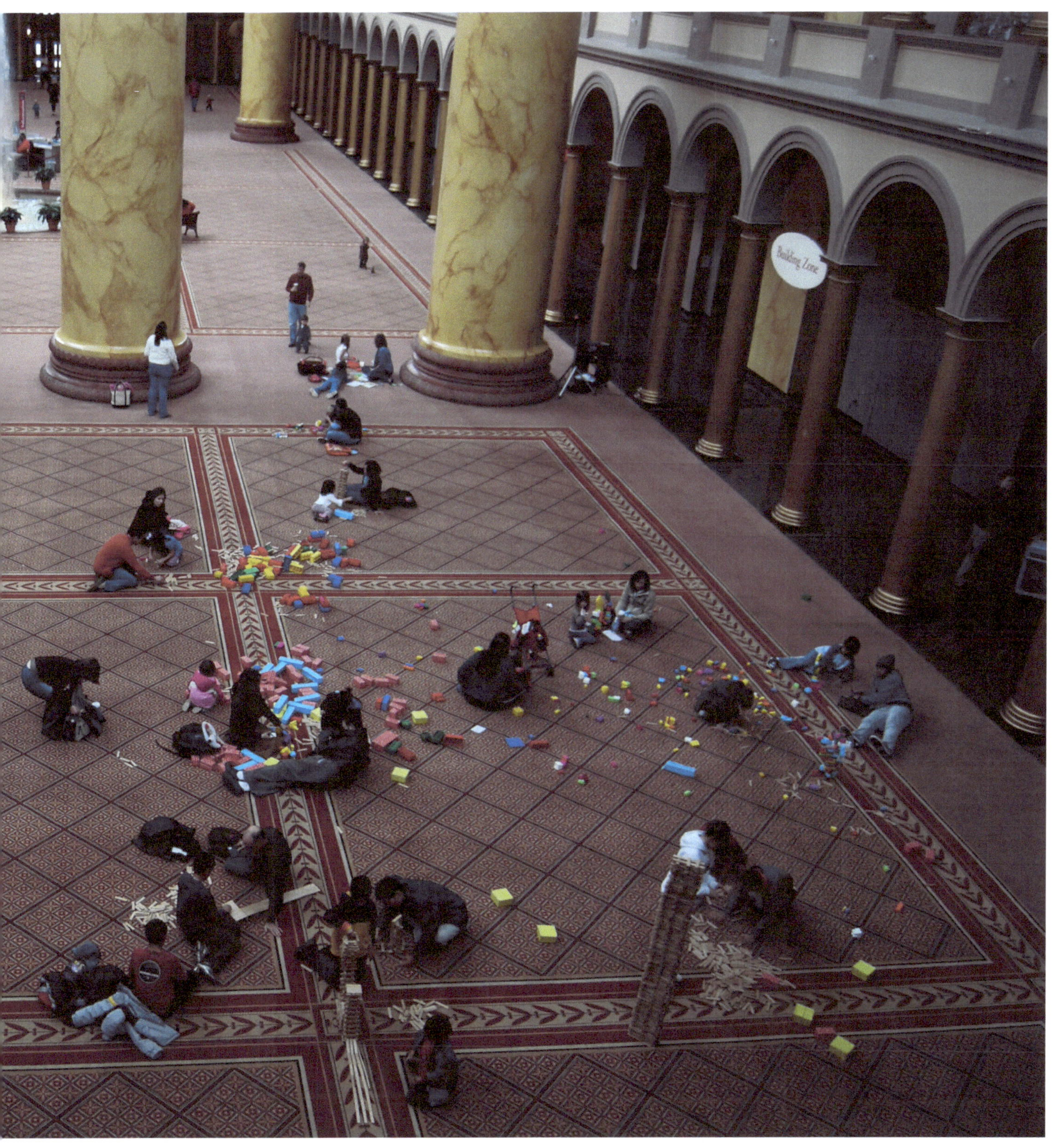
Building Zone

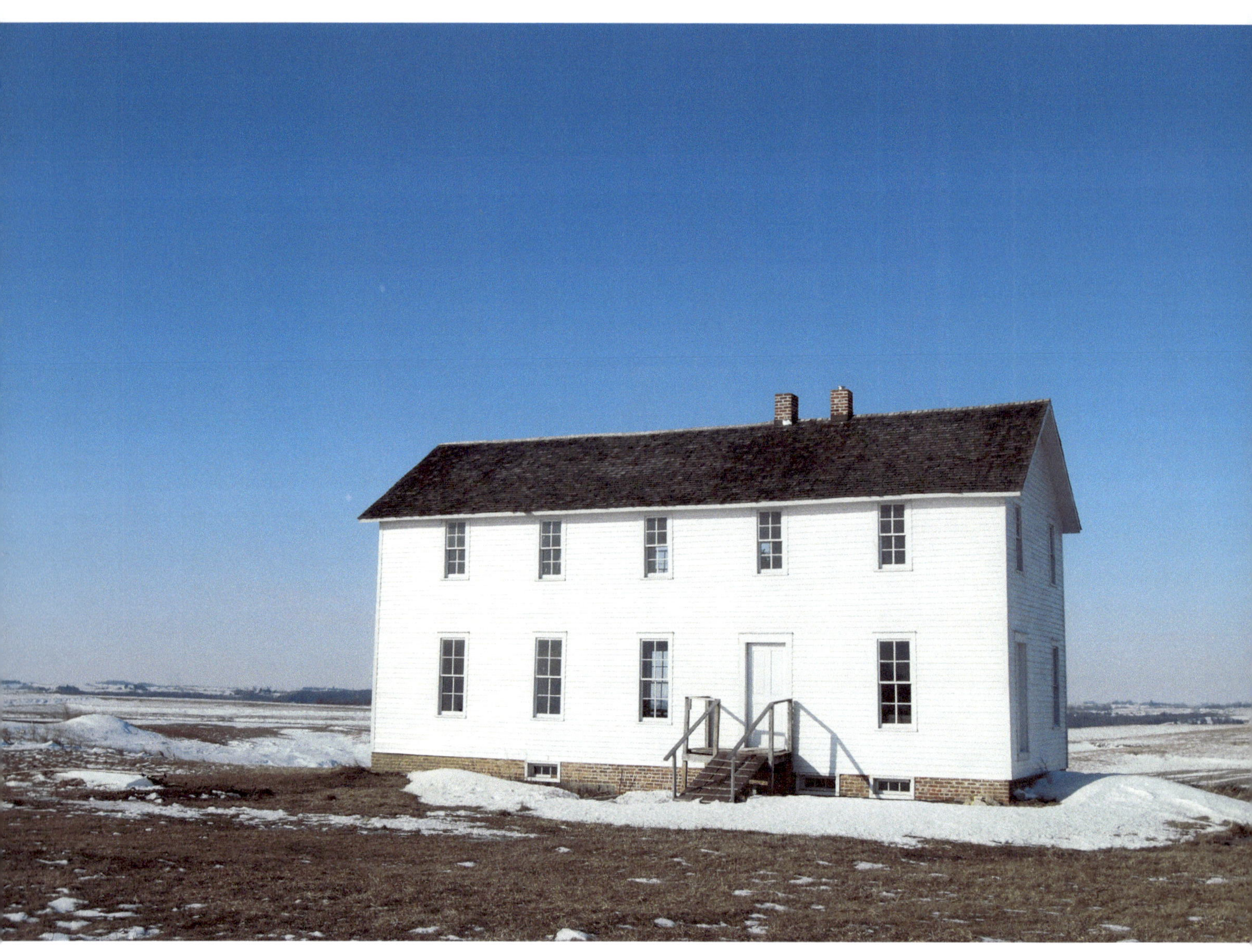

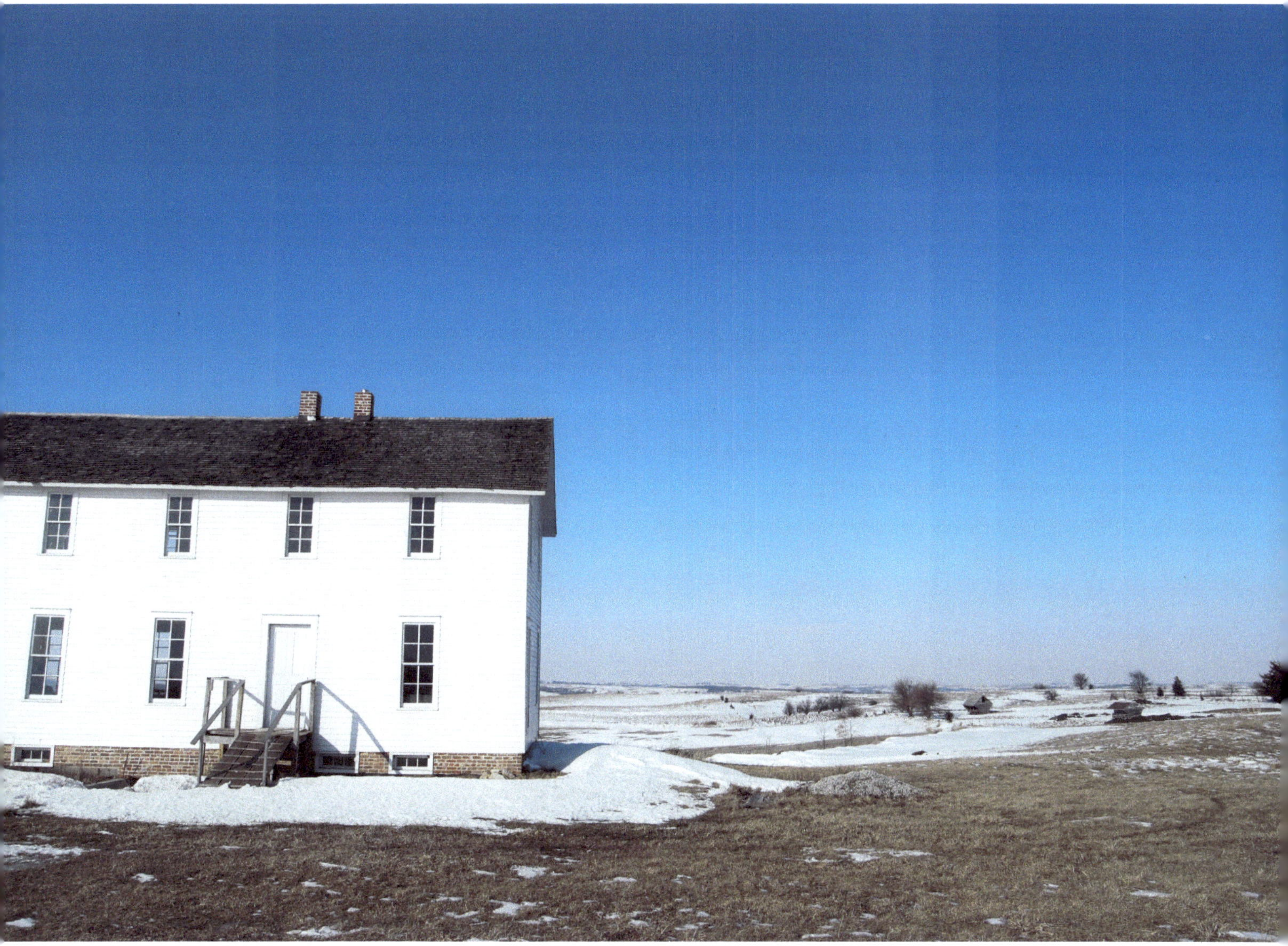

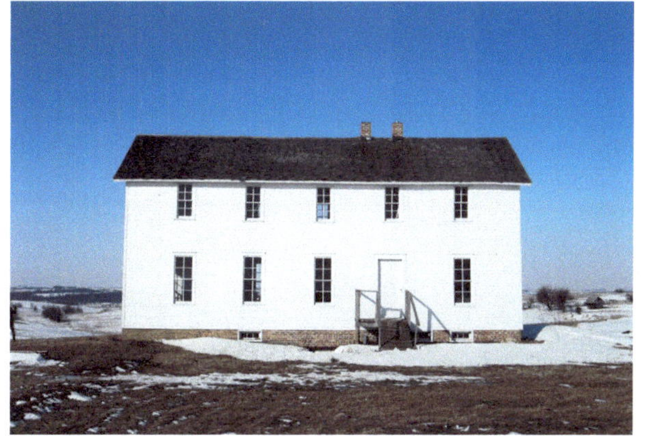

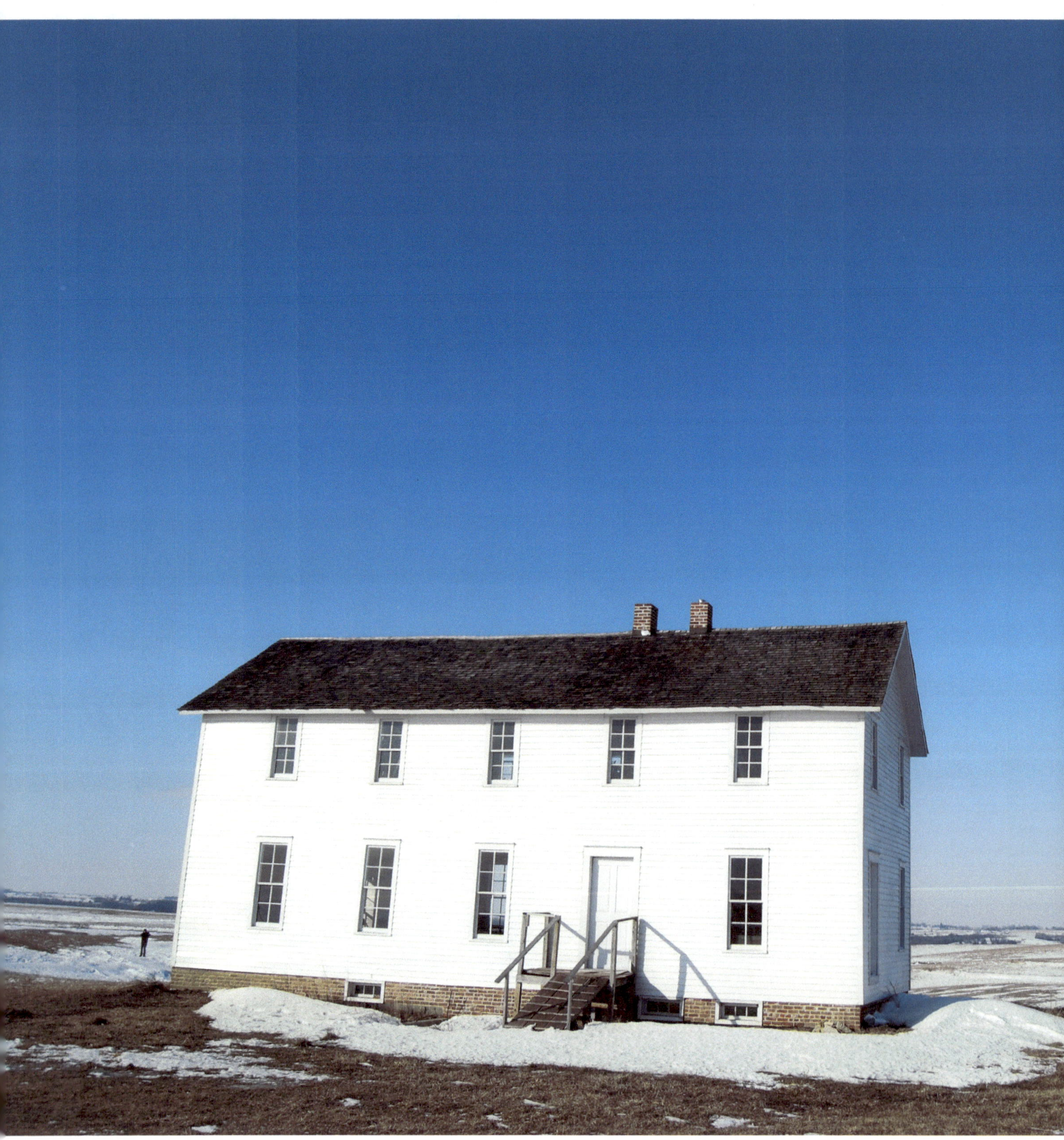

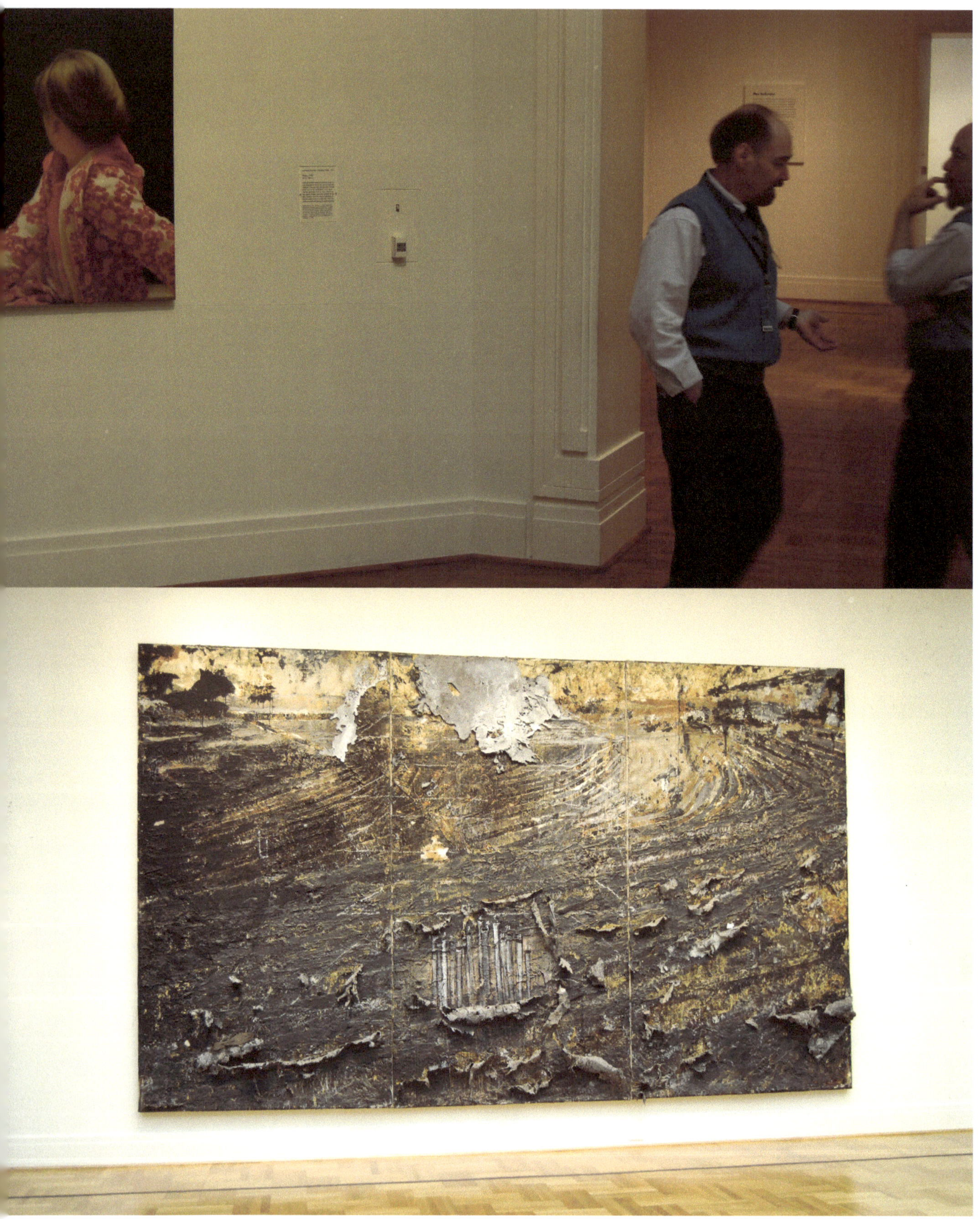

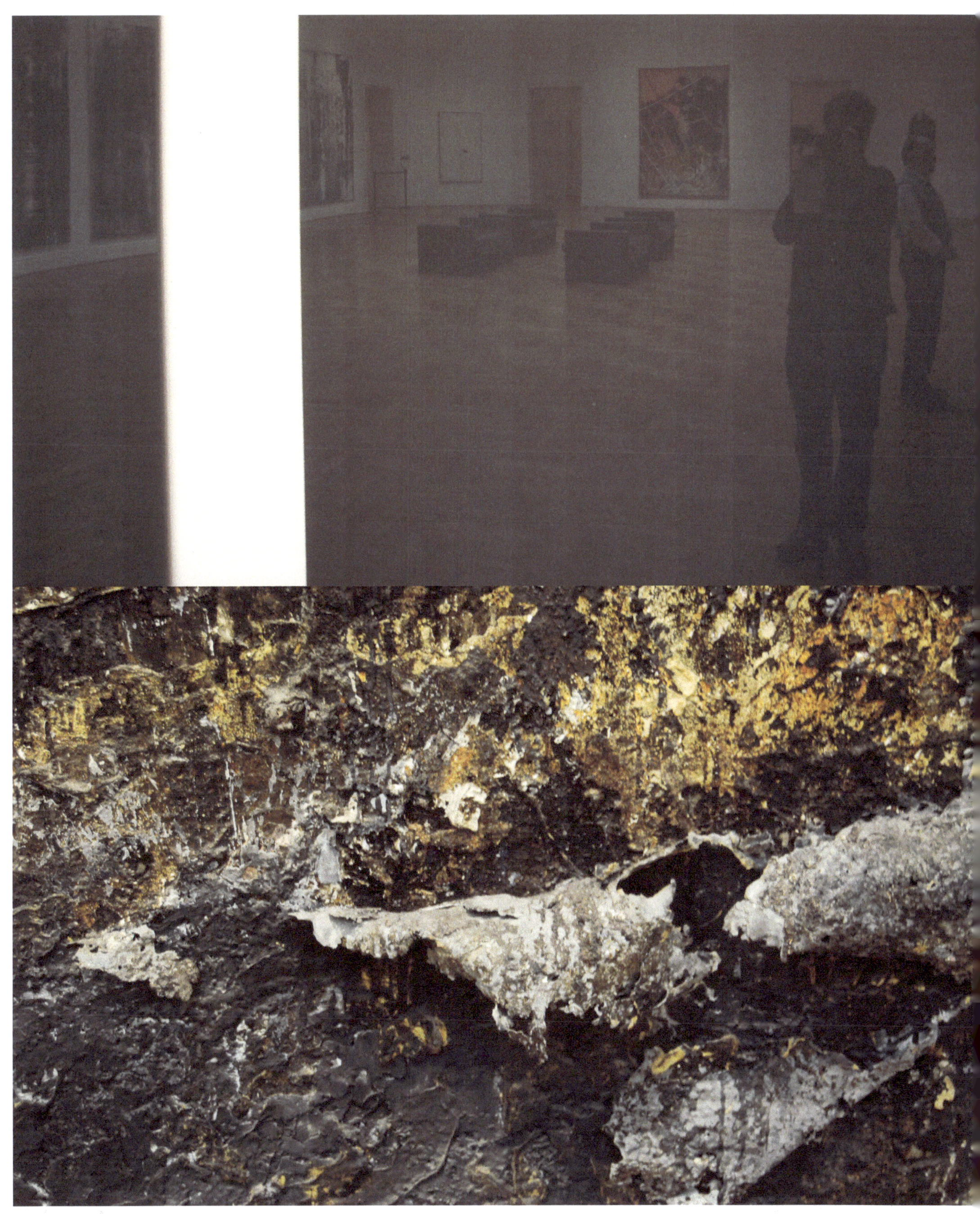

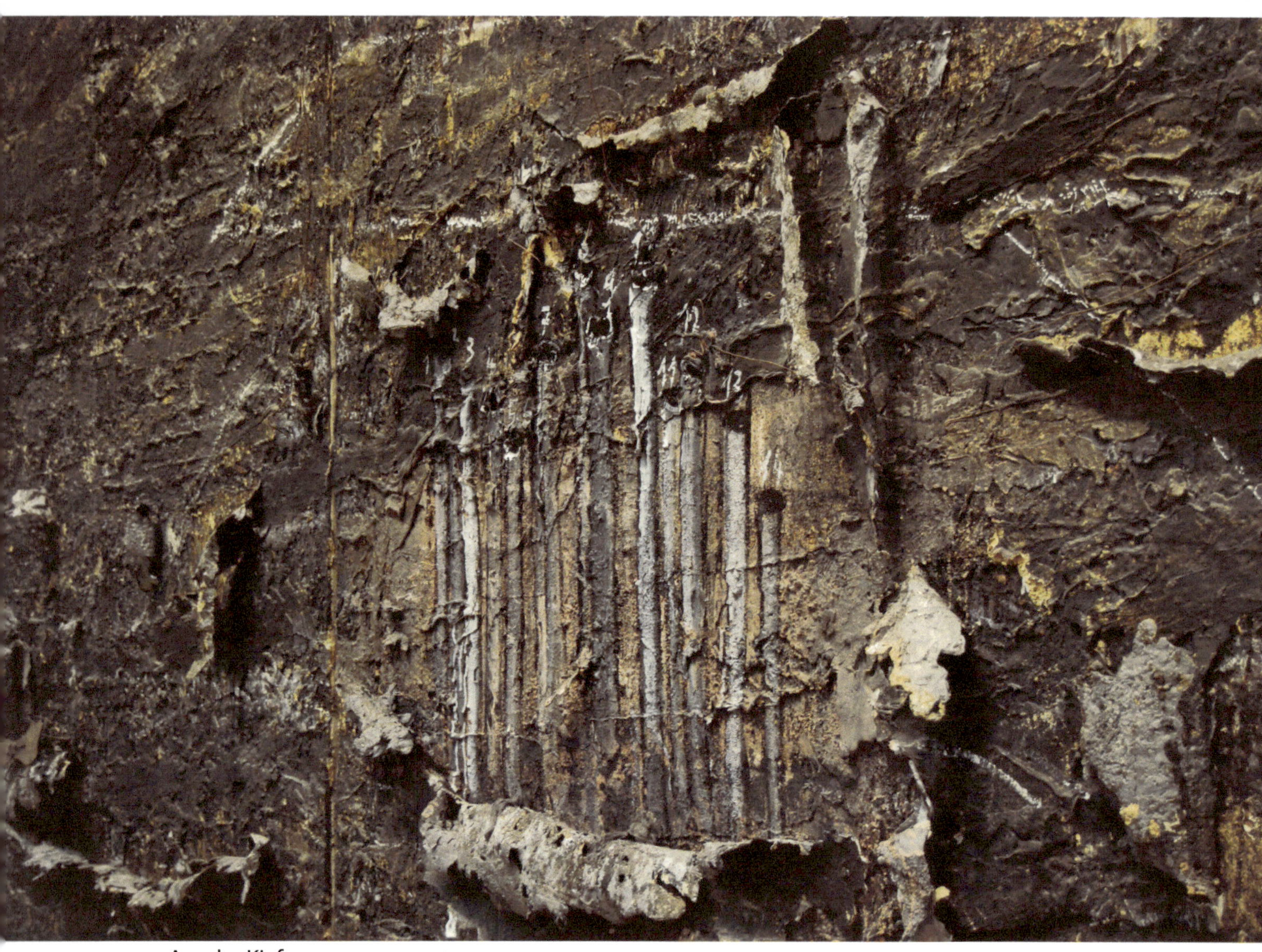

Anselm Kiefer
Burning Rods, 1984-1987

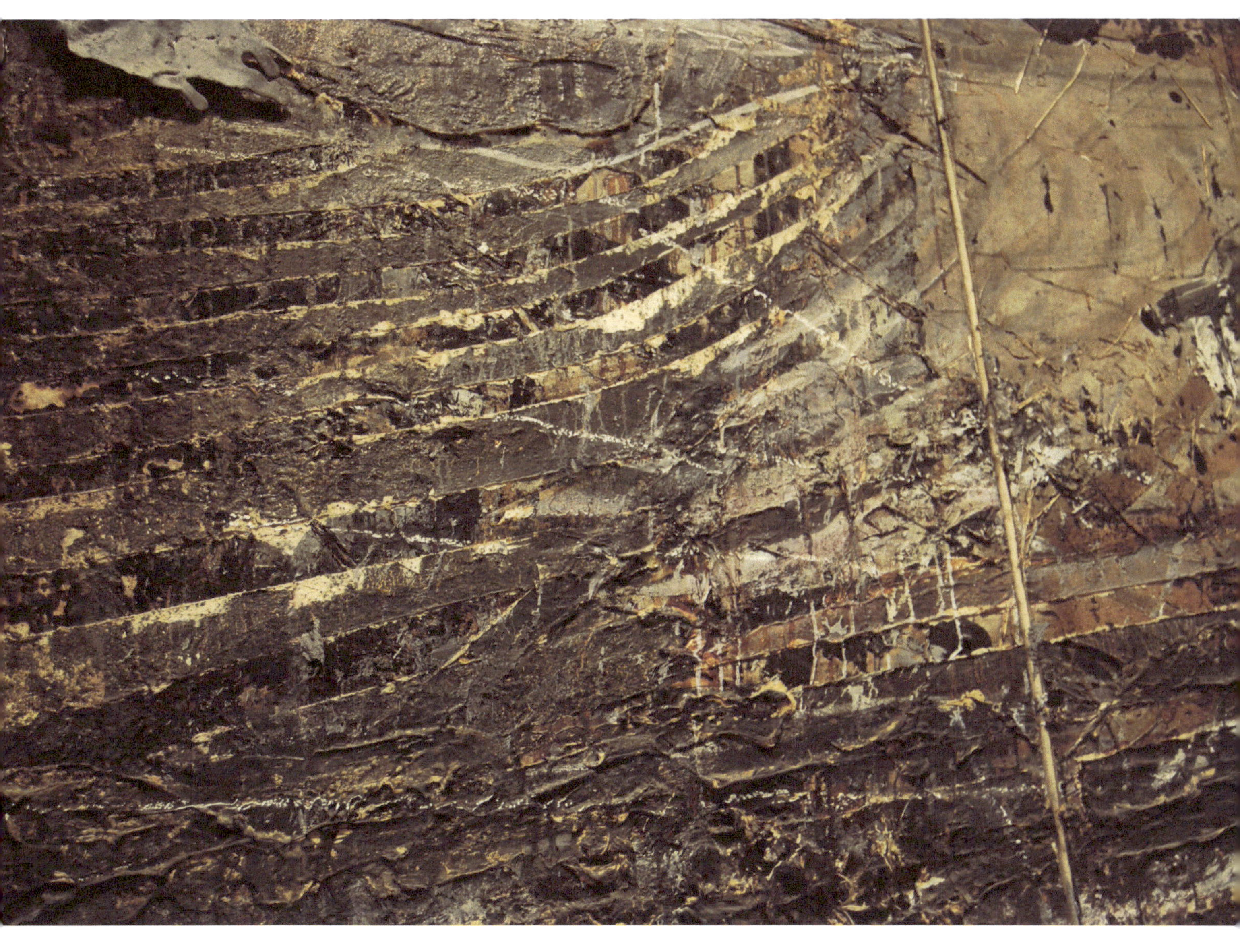

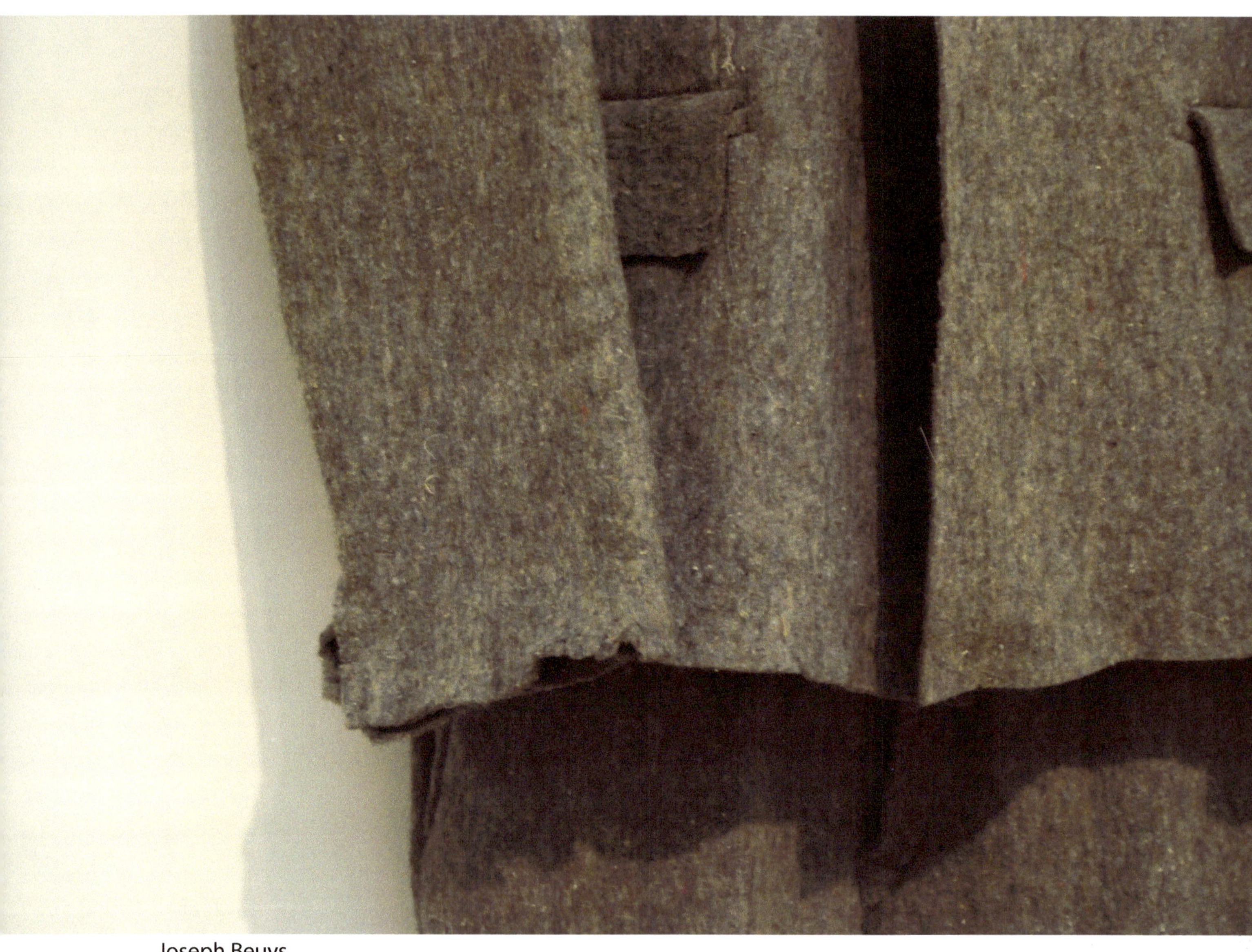

Joseph Beuys
Felt Suit, 1970

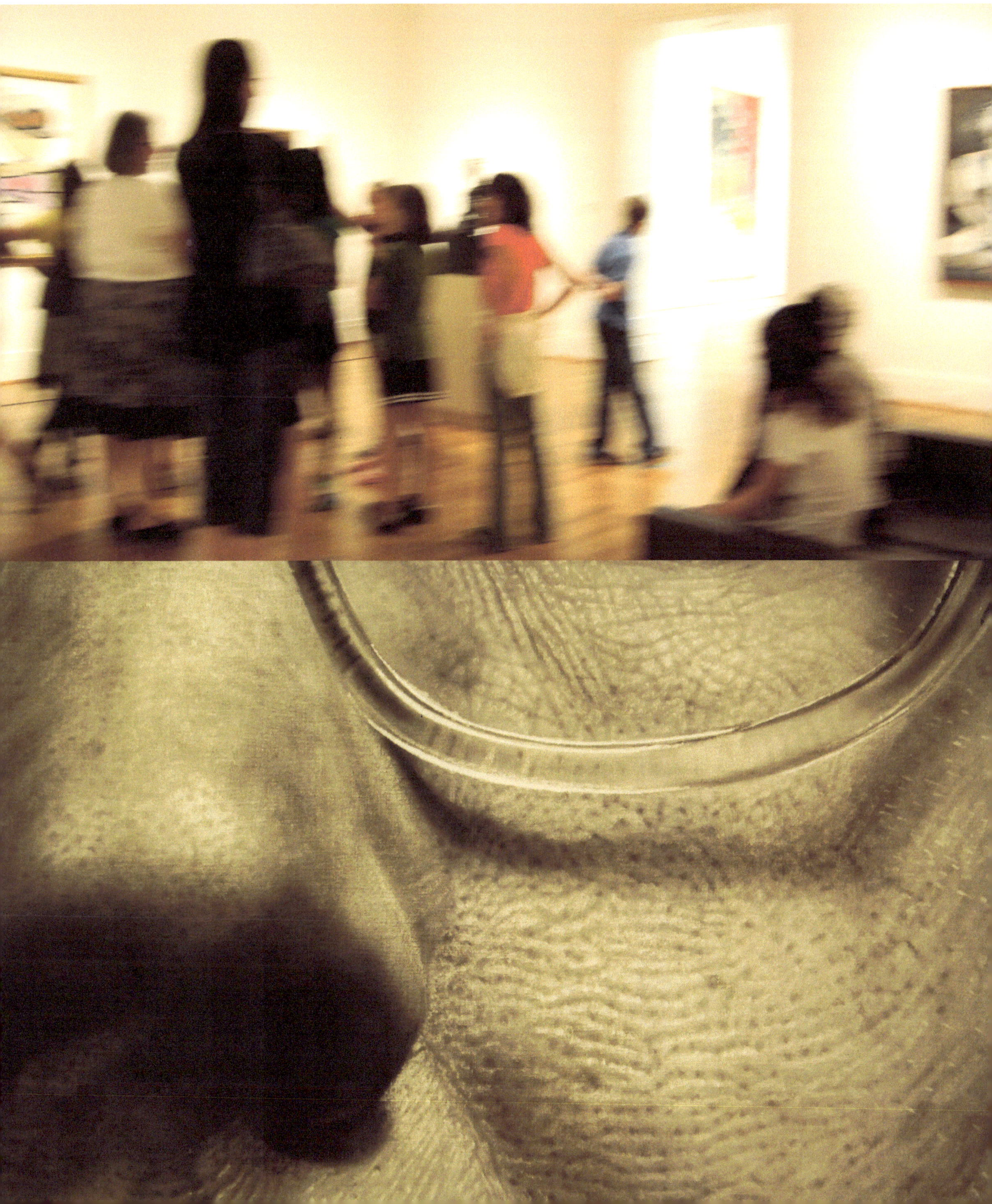

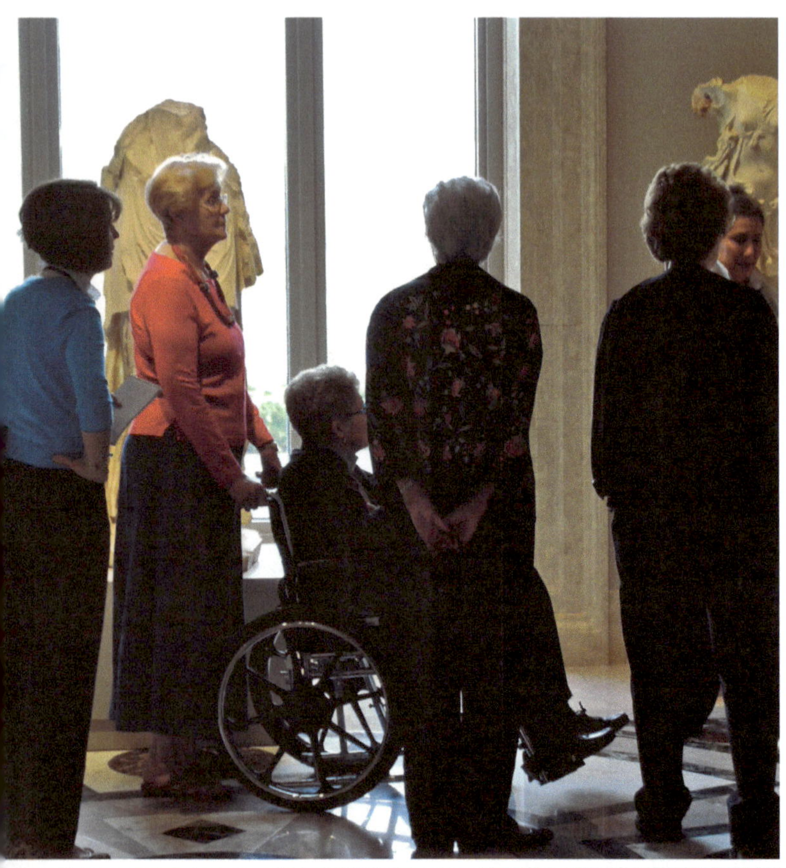

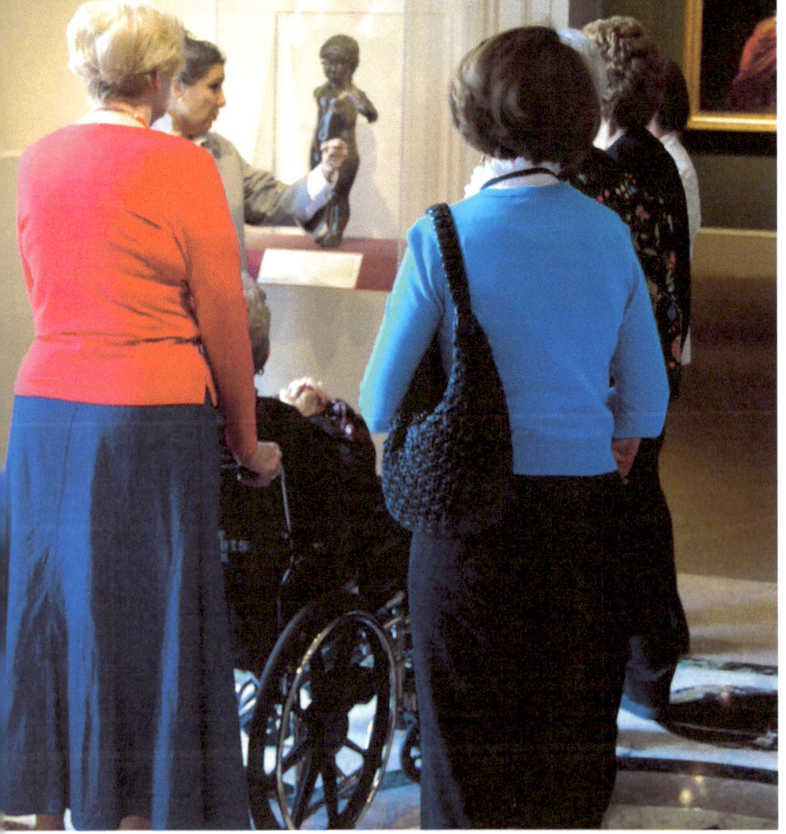

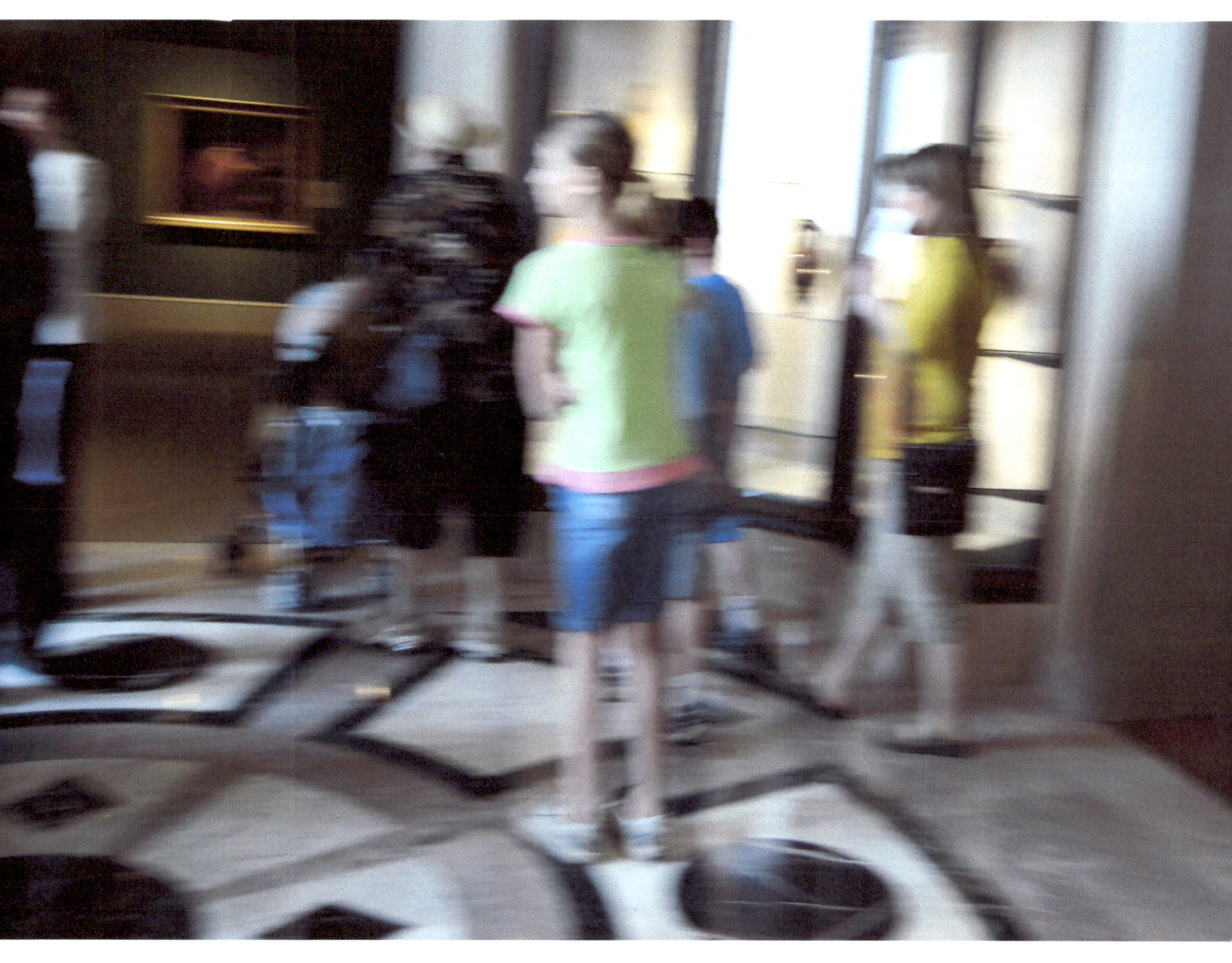

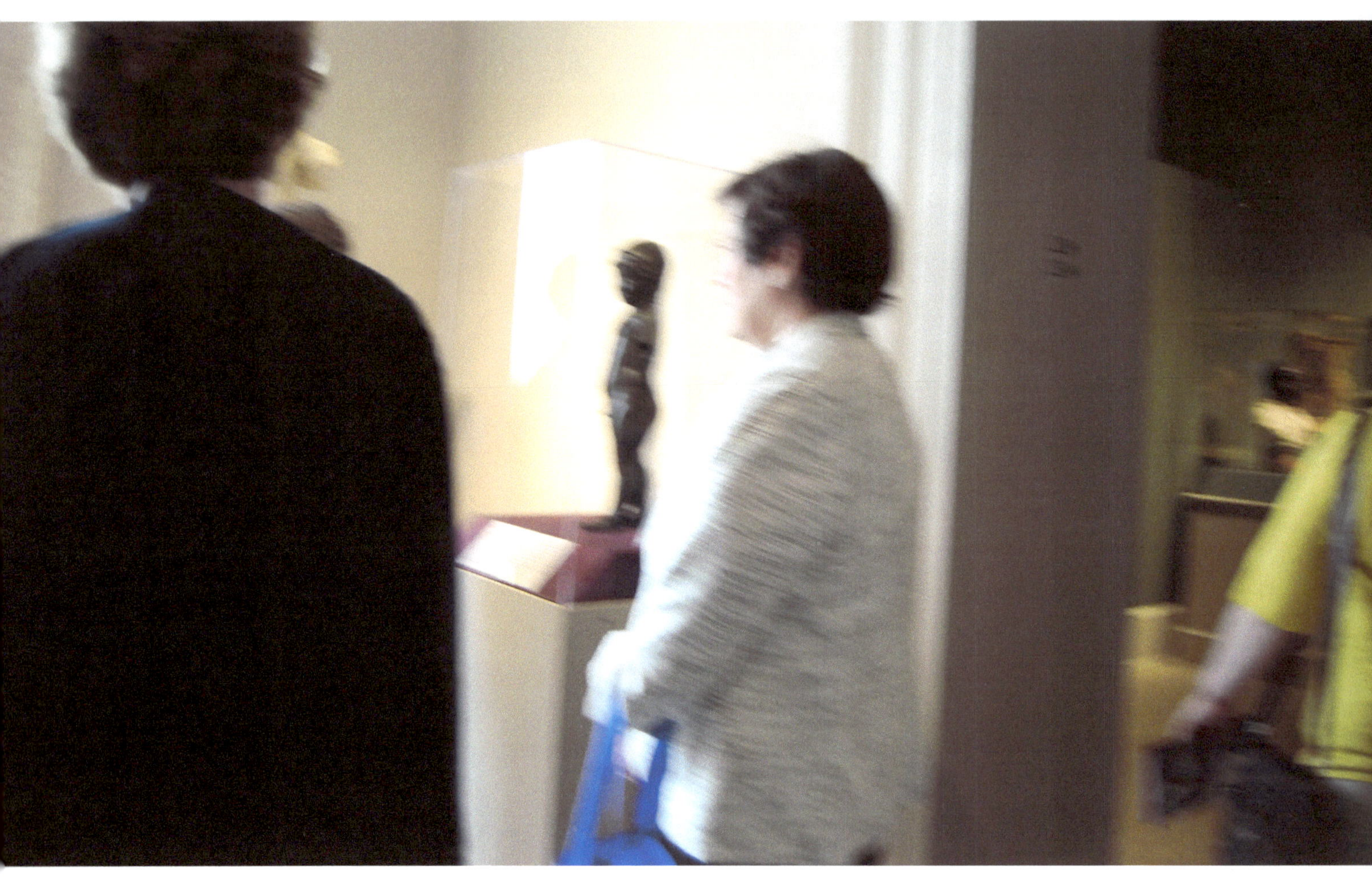

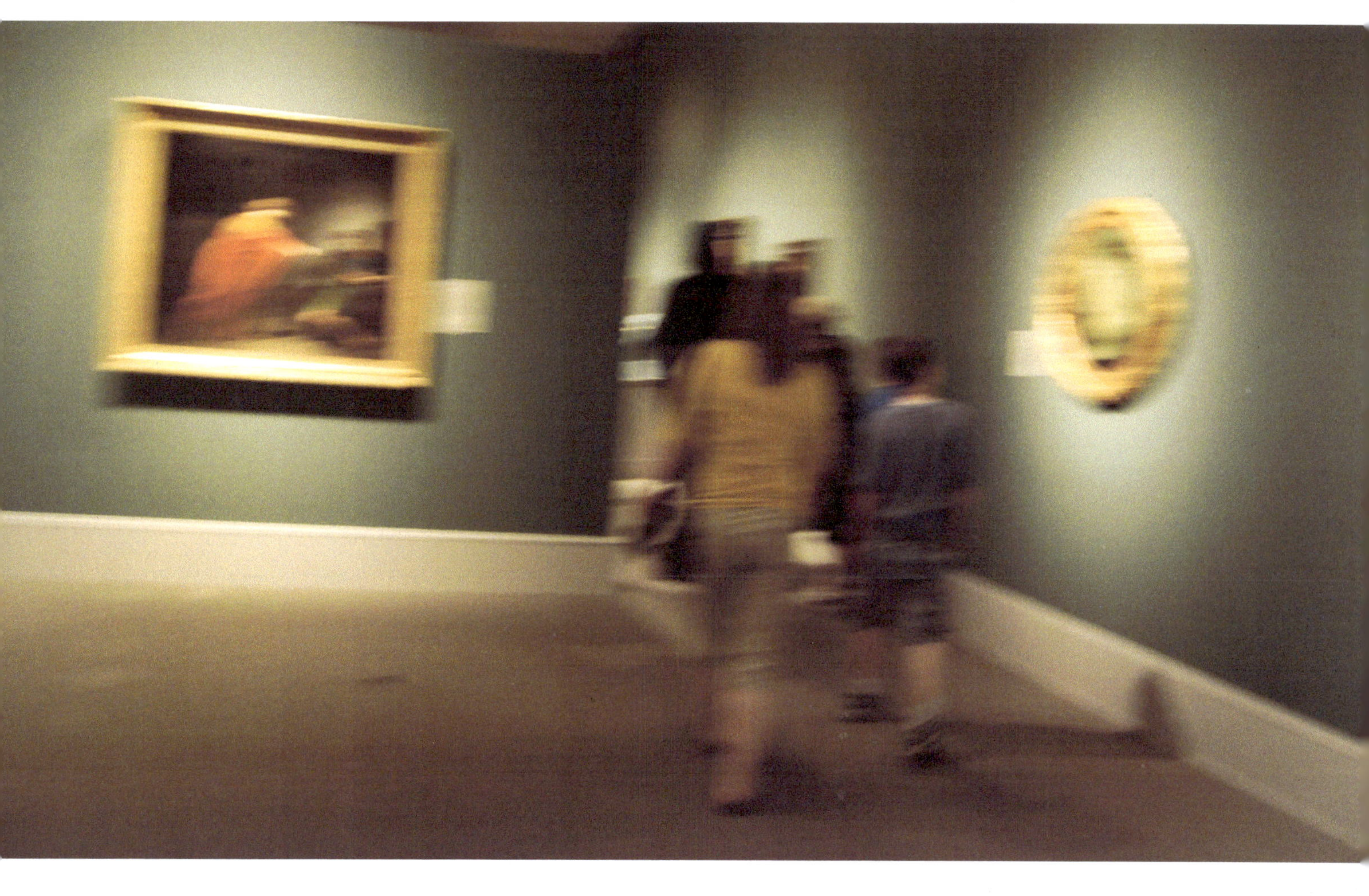

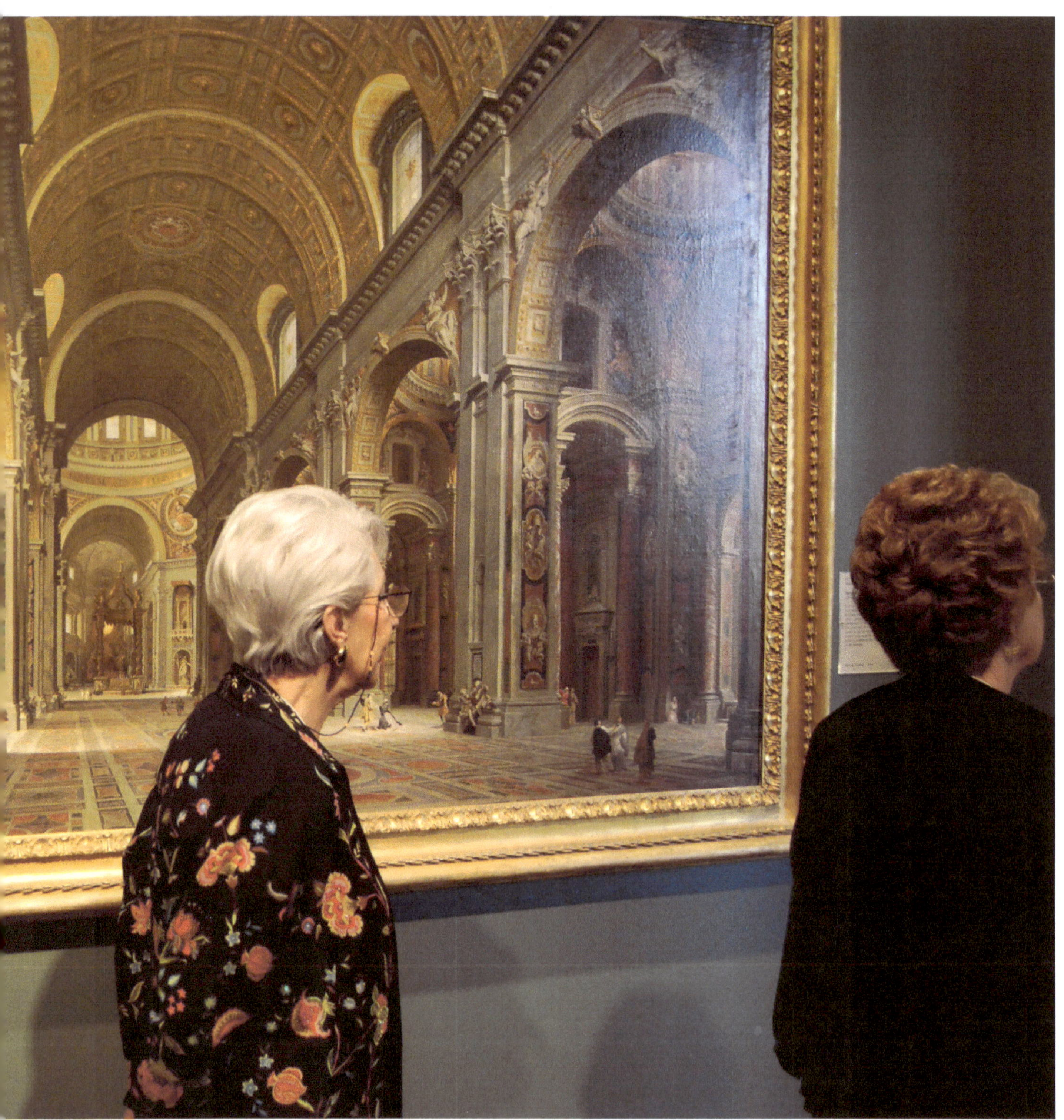

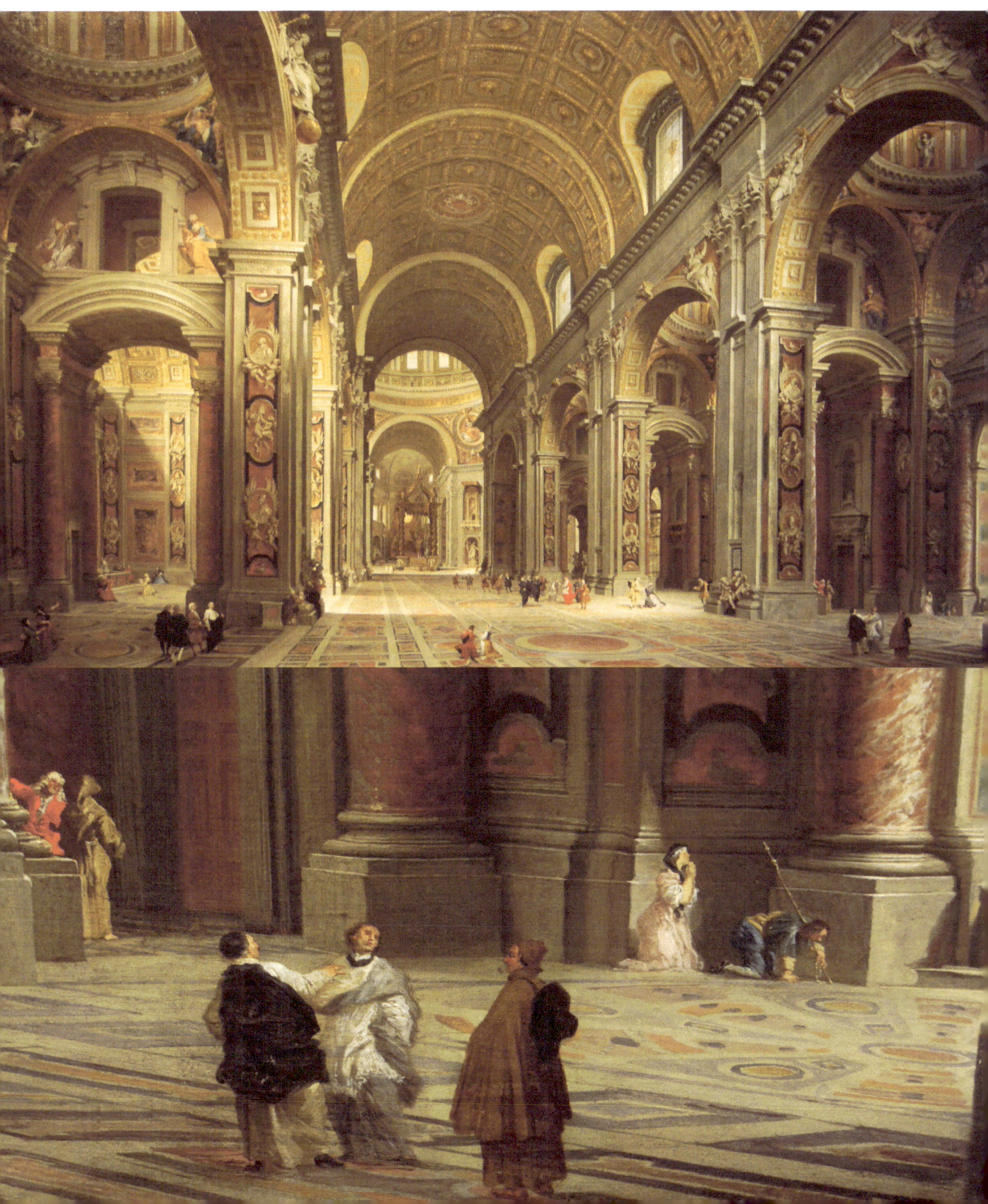

Saint Louis Art Museum

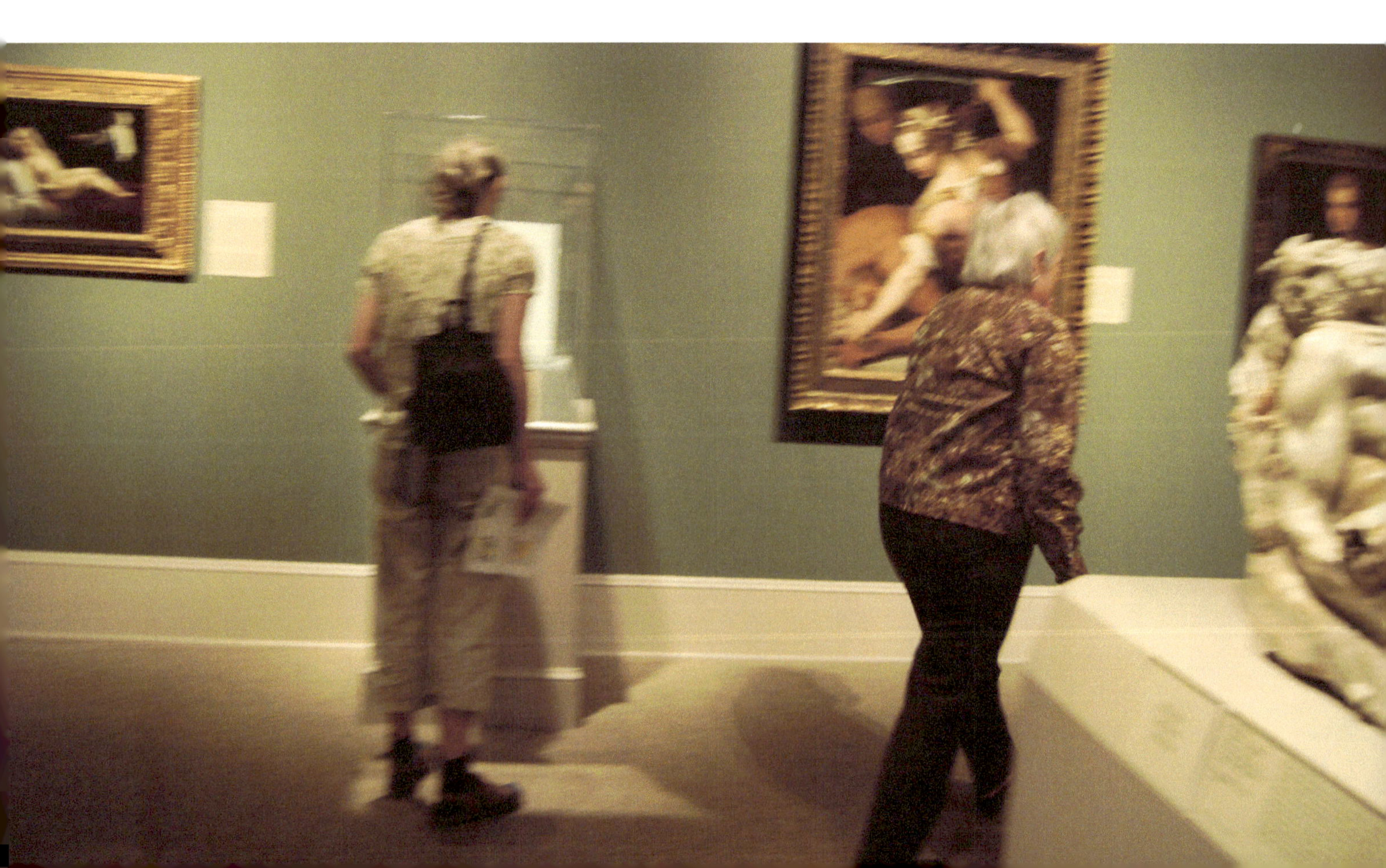

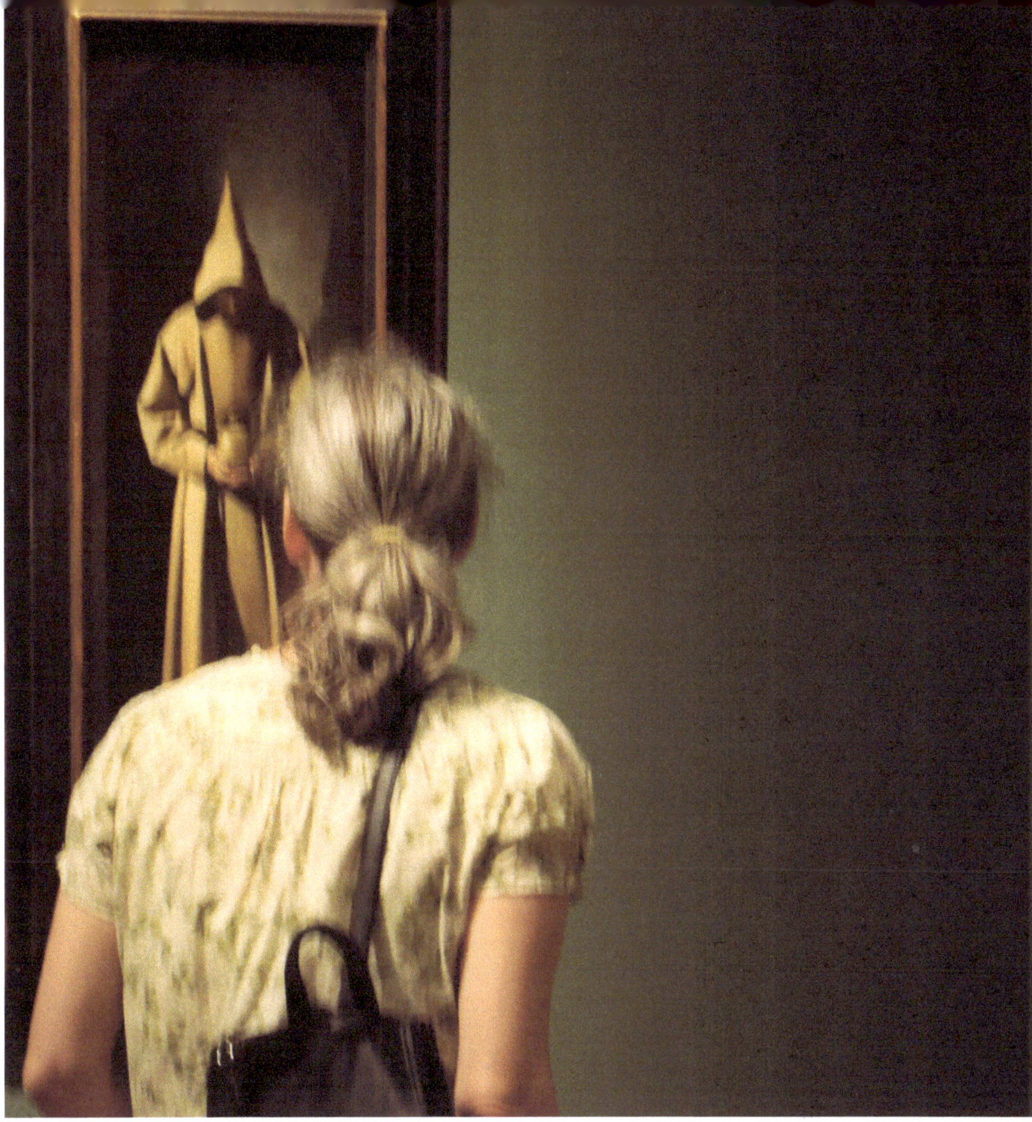

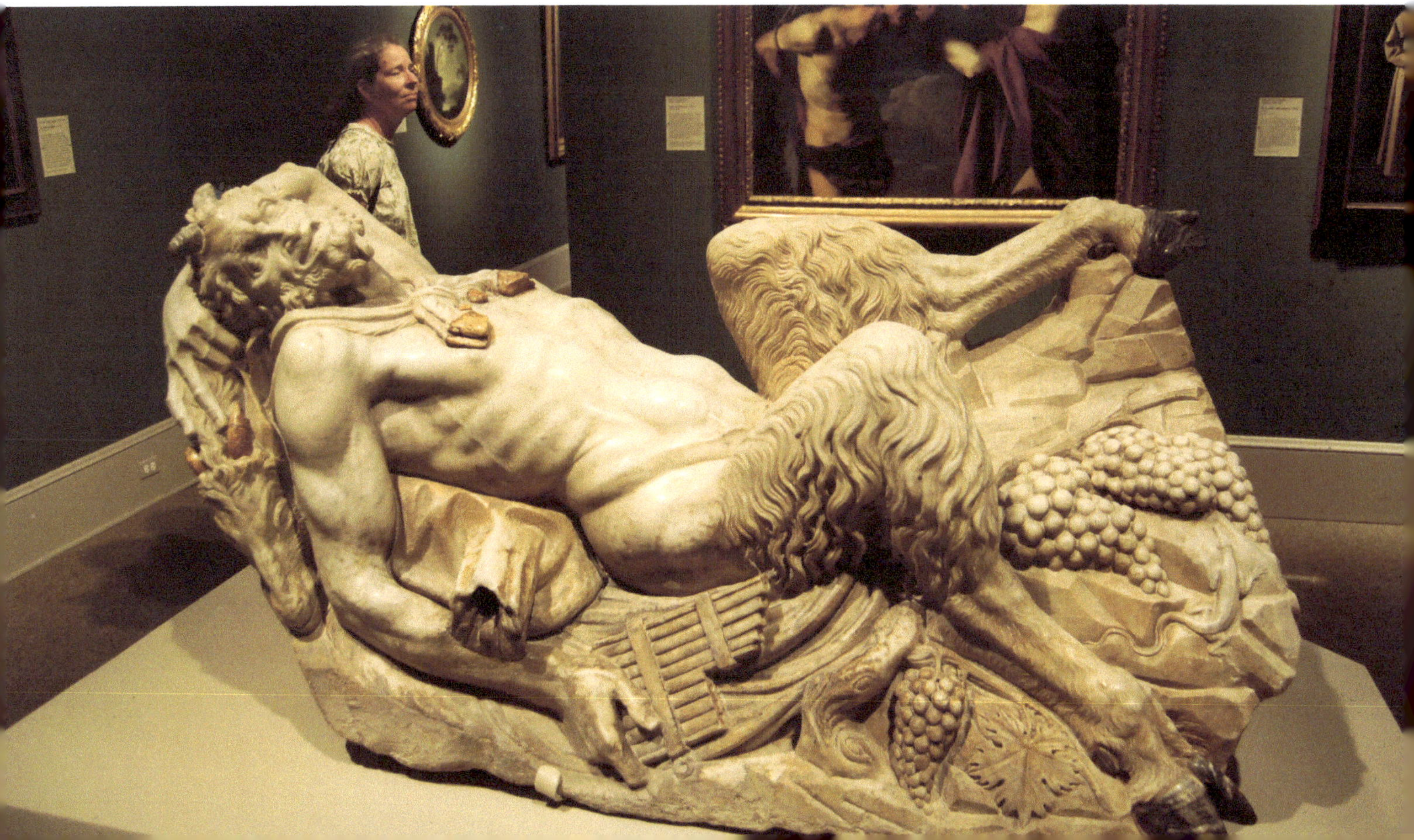

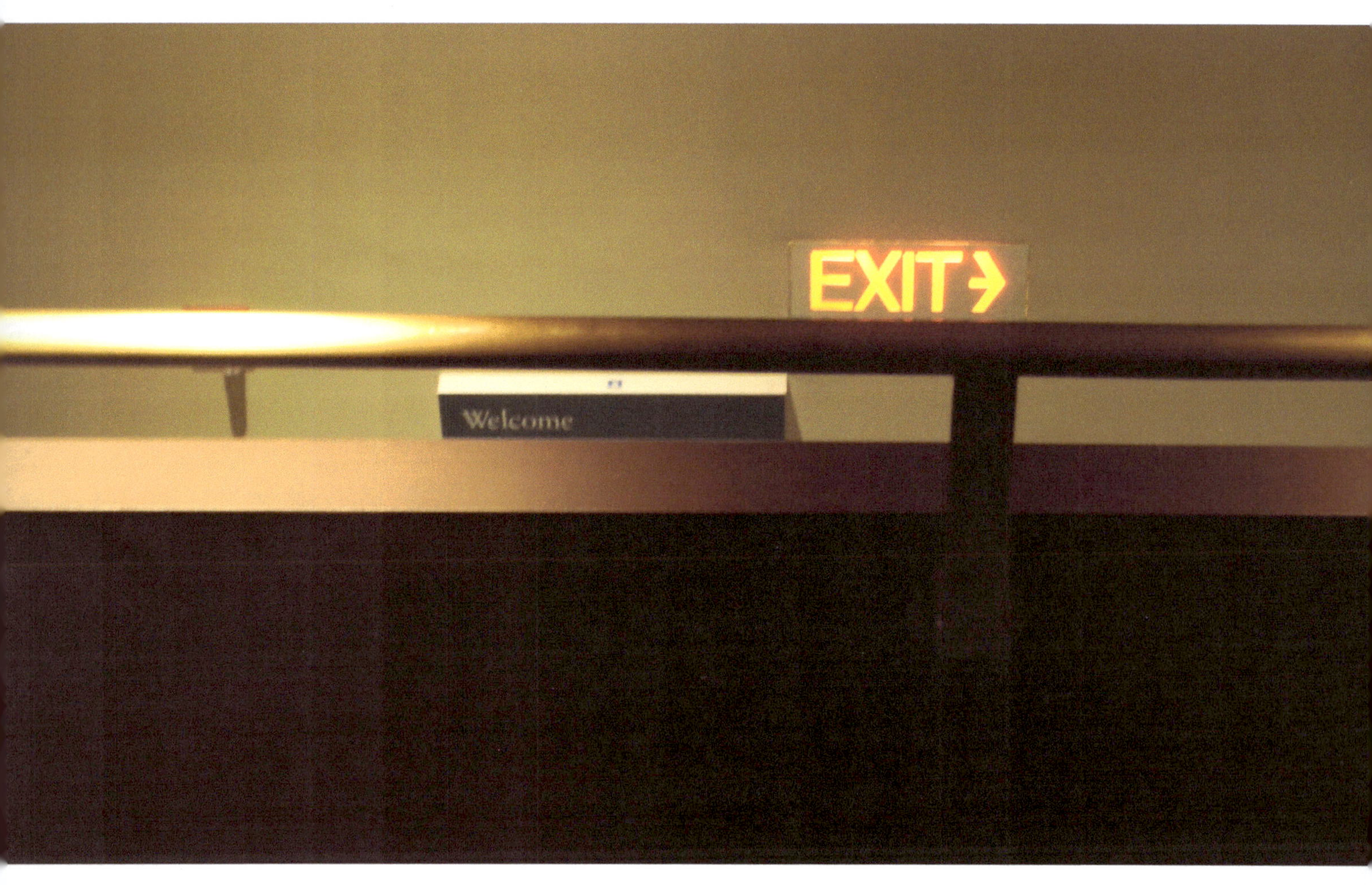
EXIT
Welcome

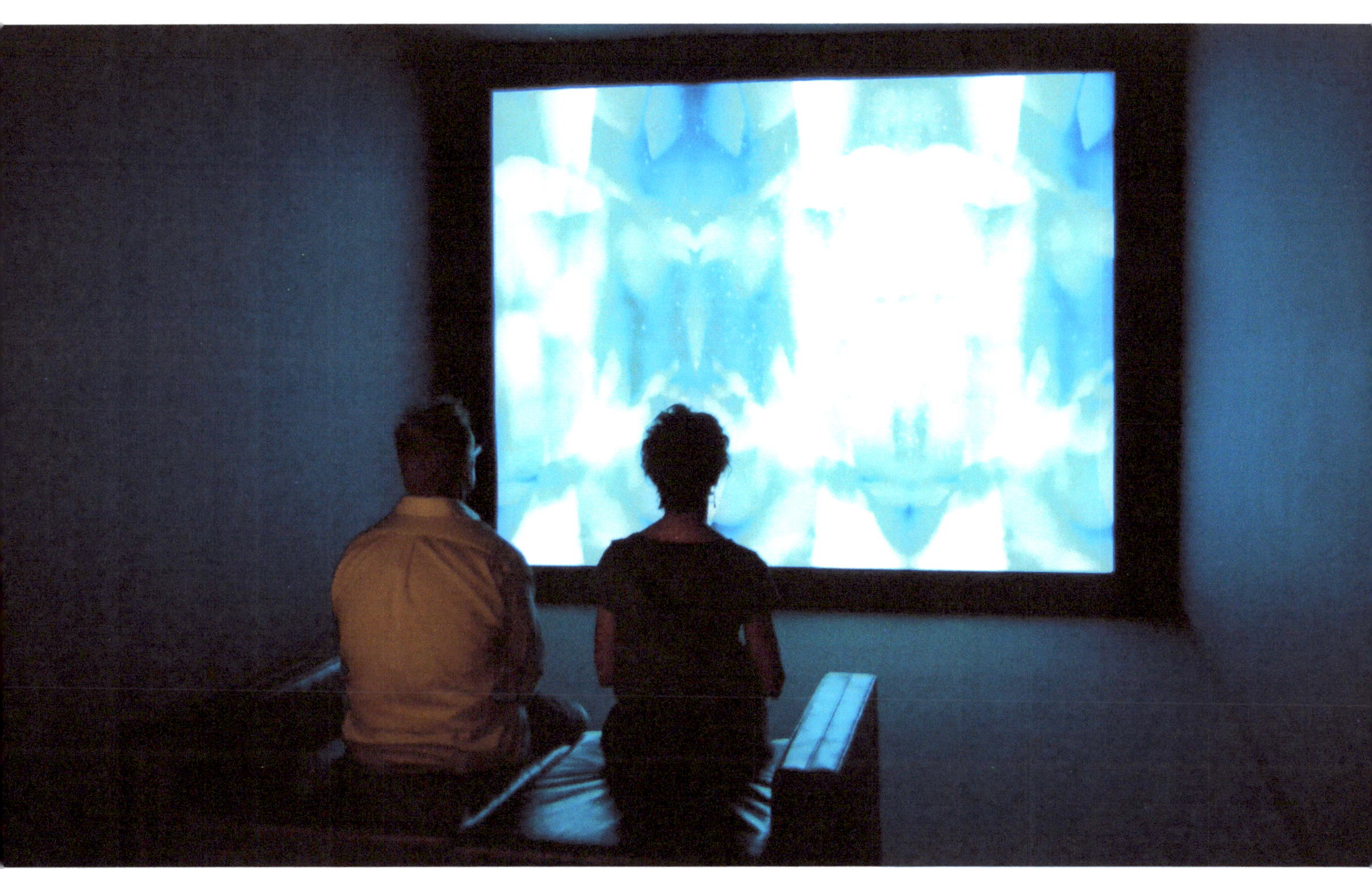

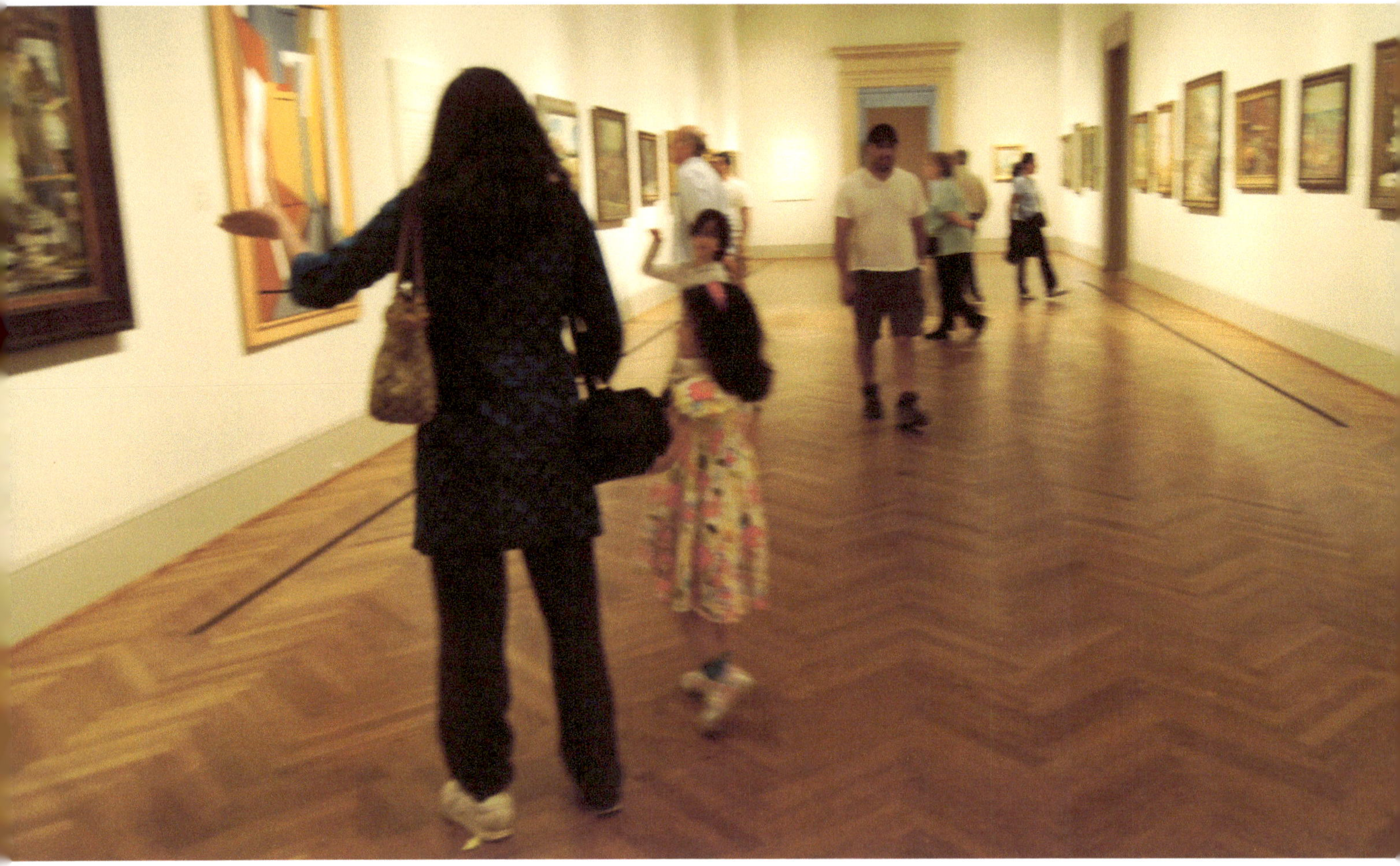

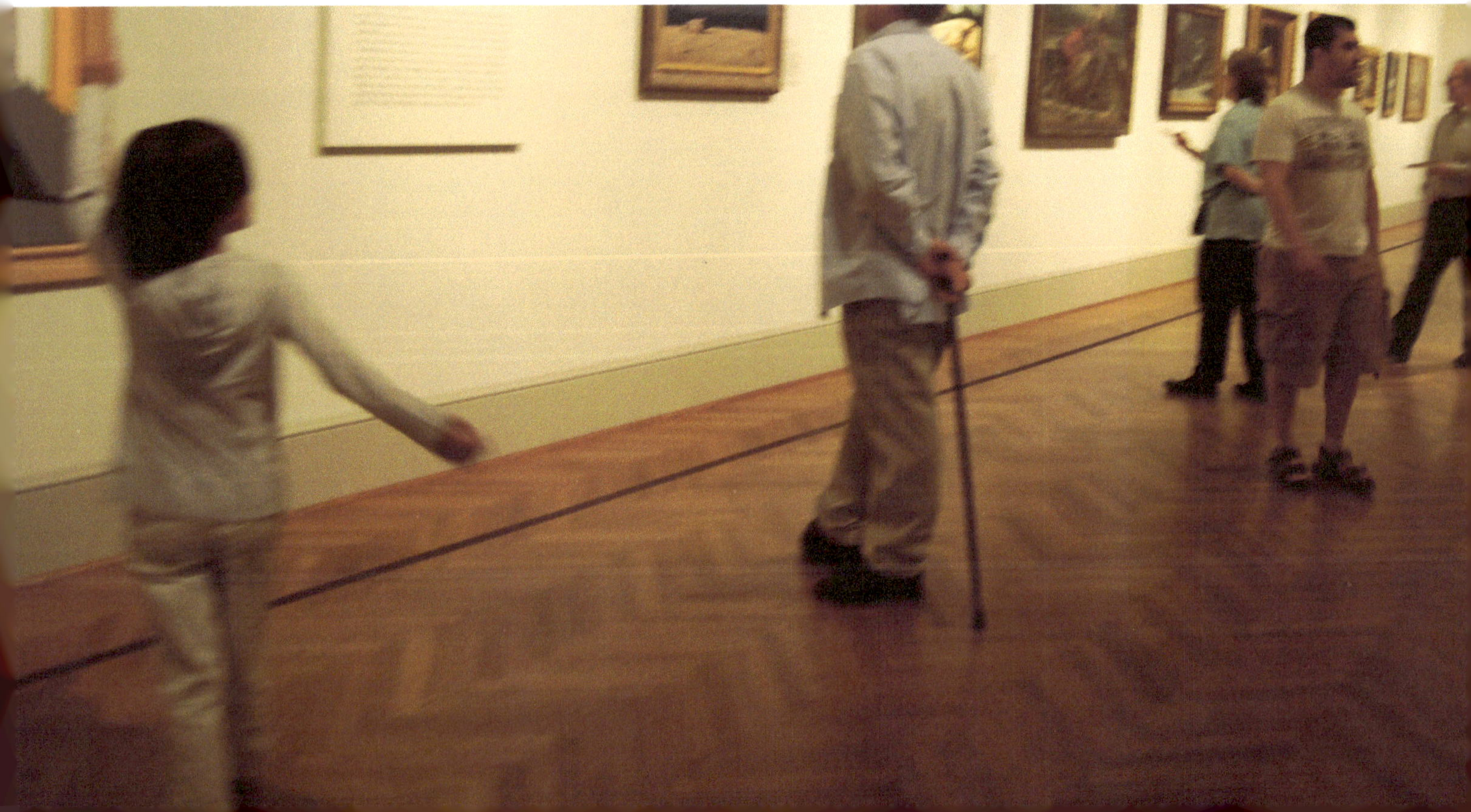

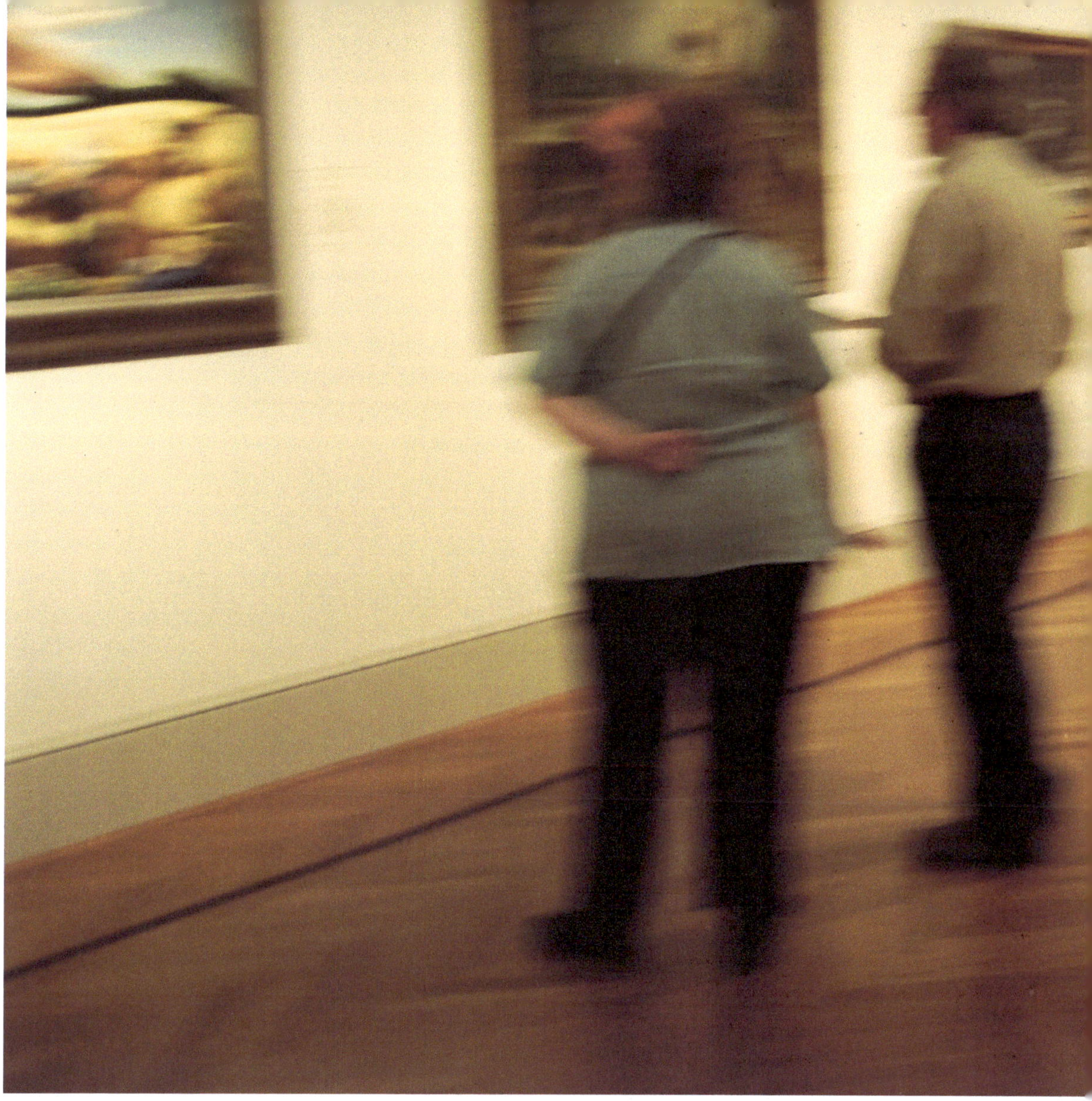

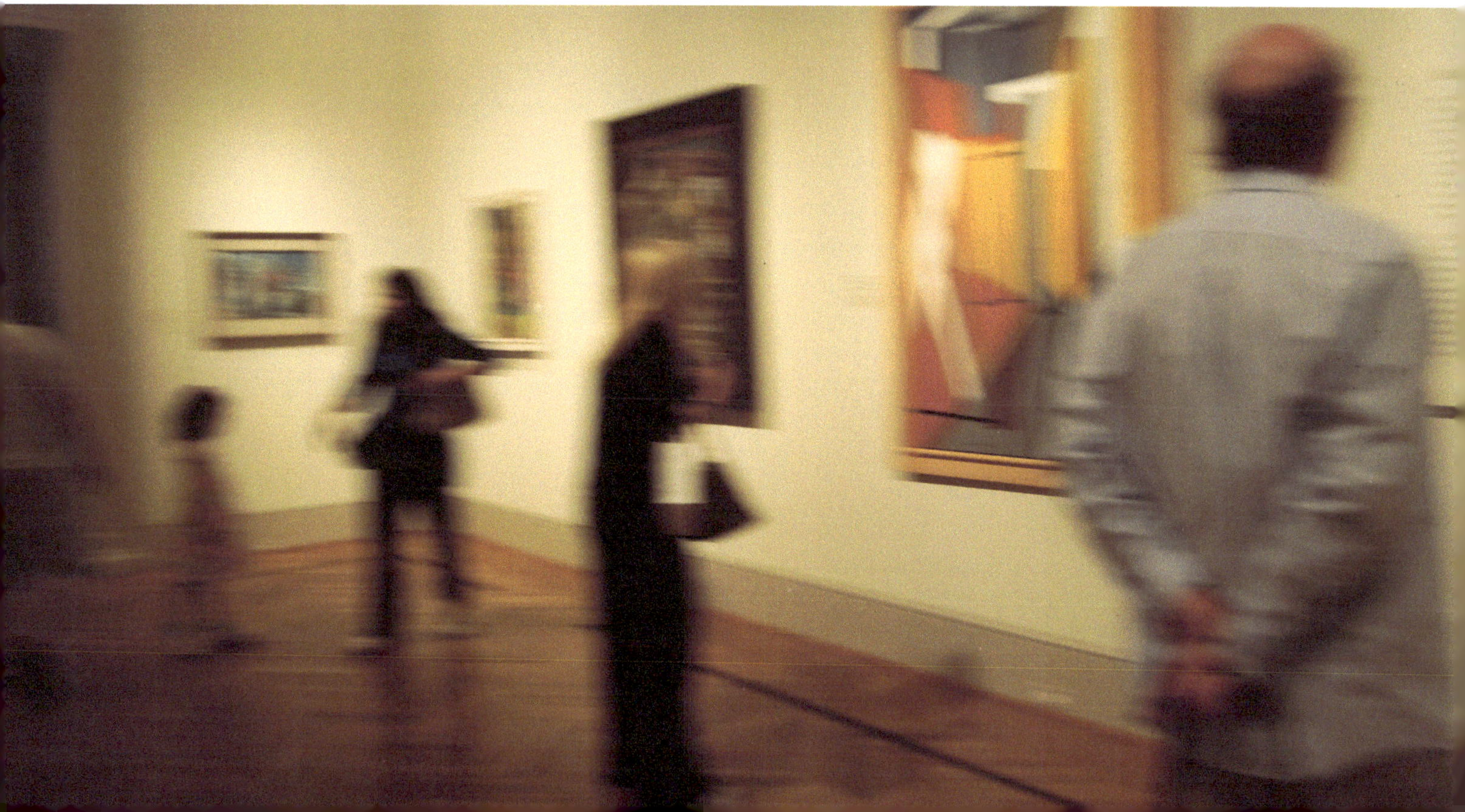

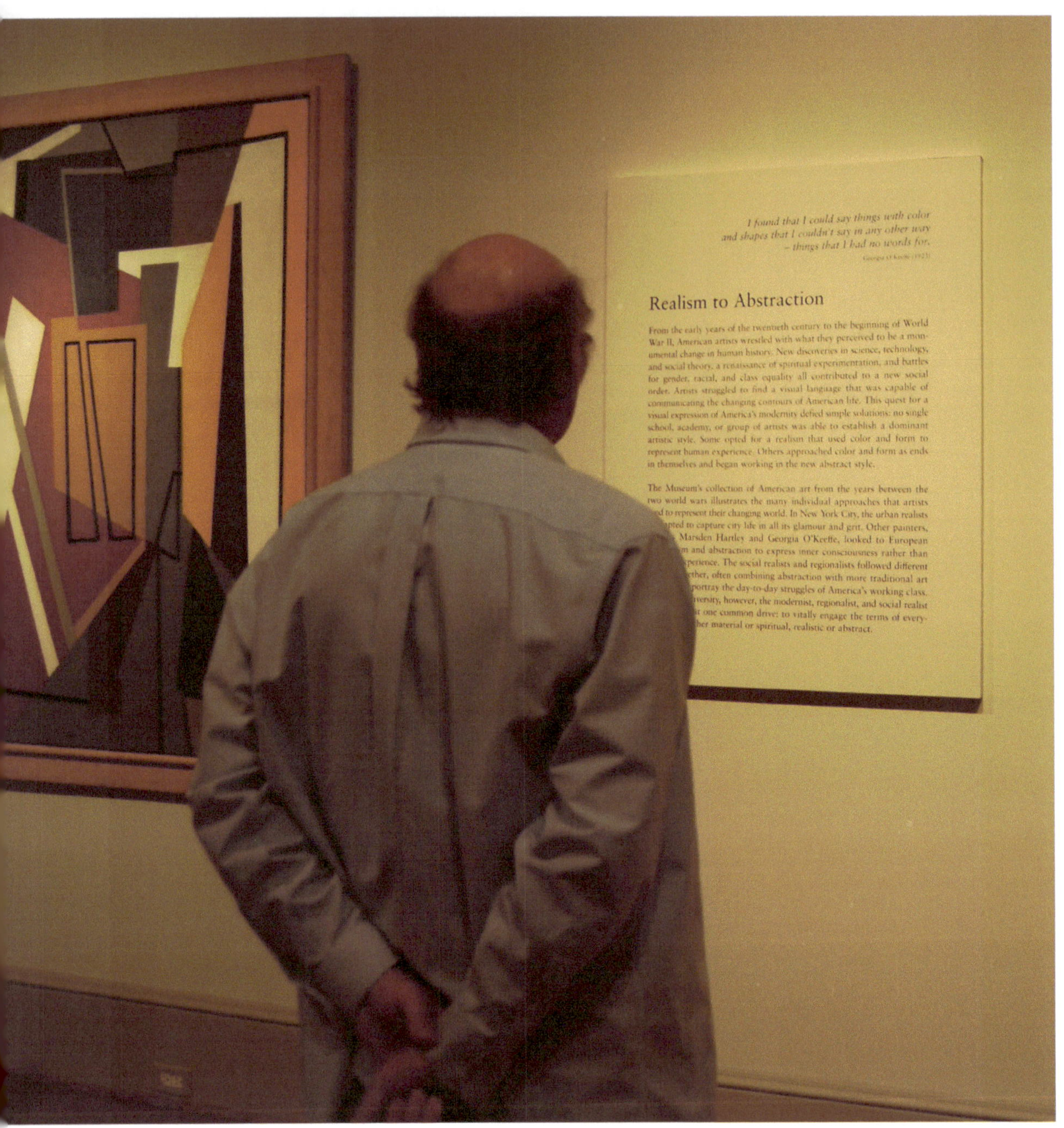
I found that I could say things with color
and shapes that I couldn't say in any other way
– things that I had no words for.
Realism to Abstraction
From the early years of the twentieth century to the beginning of World War II, American artists wrestled with what they perceived to be a monumental change in human history. New discoveries in science, technology, and social theory, a renaissance of spiritual experimentation, and battles for gender, racial, and class equality all contributed to a new social order. Artists struggled to find a visual language that was capable of communicating the changing contours of American life. This quest for a visual expression of America's modernity defied simple solutions: no single school, academy, or group of artists was able to establish a dominant artistic style. Some opted for a realism that used color and form to represent human experience. Others approached color and form as ends in themselves and began working in the new abstract style.
The Museum's collection of American art from the years between the two world wars illustrates the many individual approaches that artists
to represent their changing world. In New York City, the urban realists
to capture city life in all its glamour and grit. Other painters,
Marsden Hartley and Georgia O'Keeffe, looked to European
and abstraction to express inner consciousness rather than
The social realists and regionalists followed different
often combining abstraction with more traditional art
portray the day-to-day struggles of America's working class.
however, the modernist, regionalist, and social realist
one common drive: to vitally engage the terms of every-
material or spiritual, realistic or abstract.

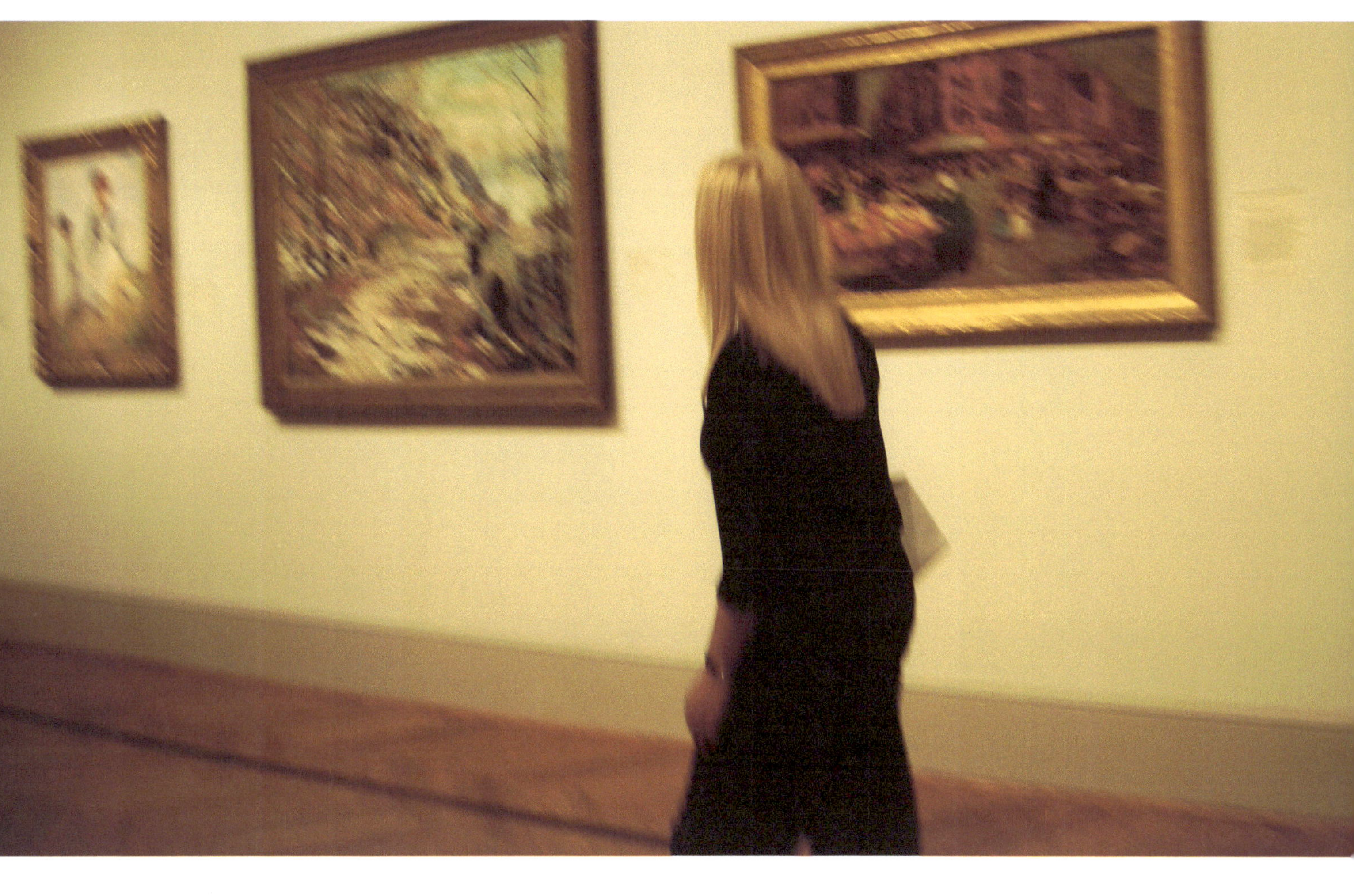

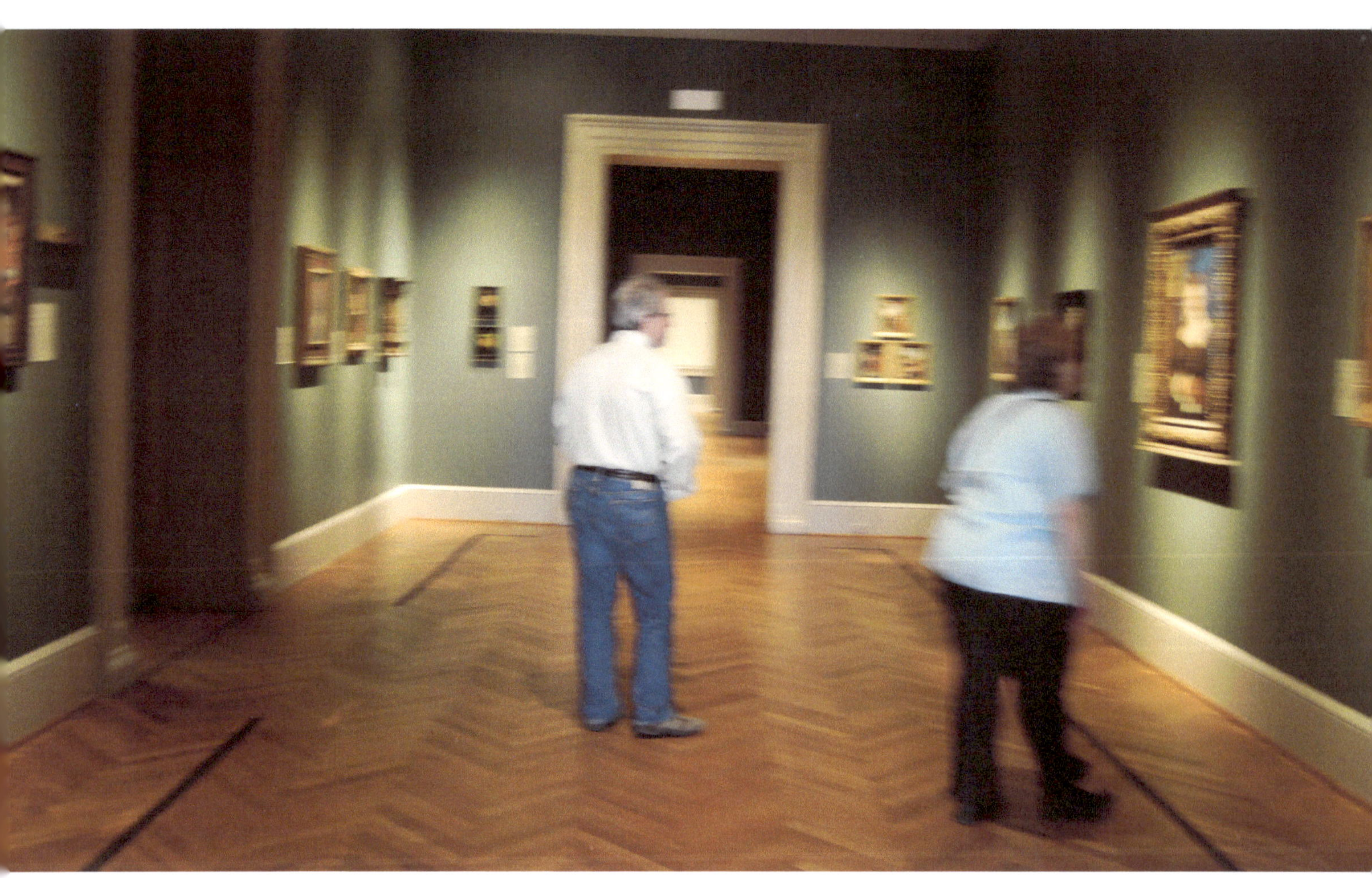

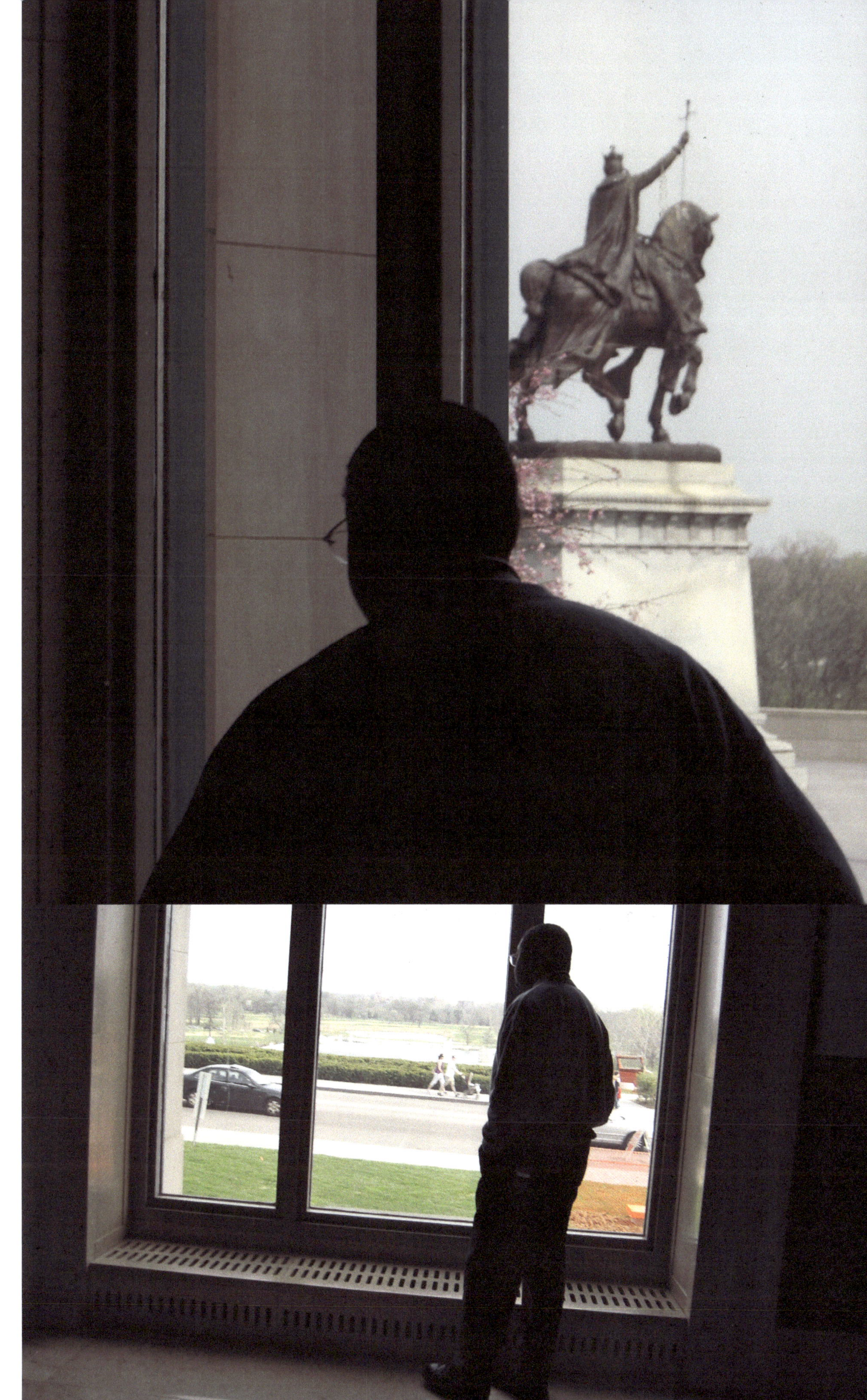

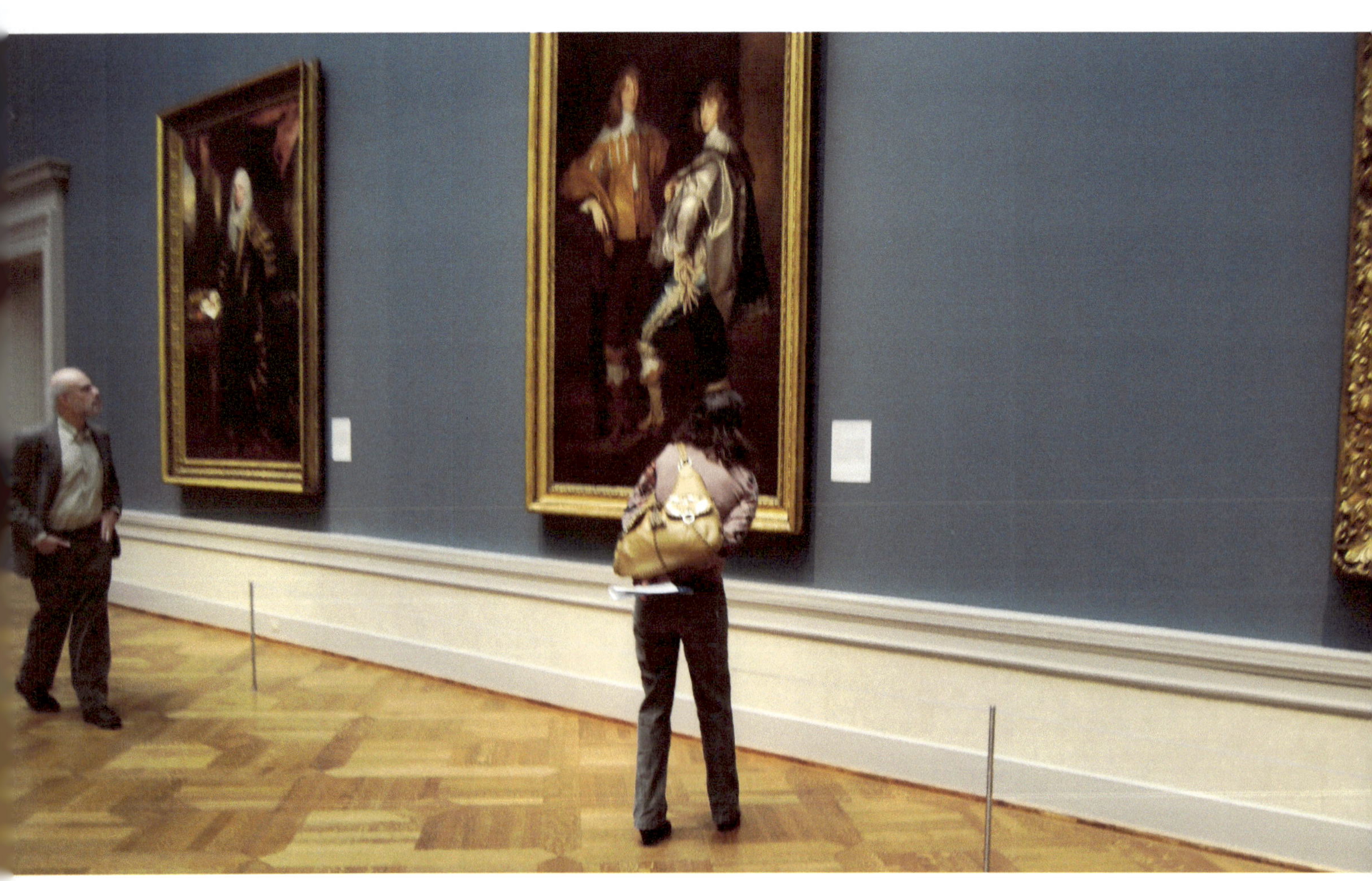

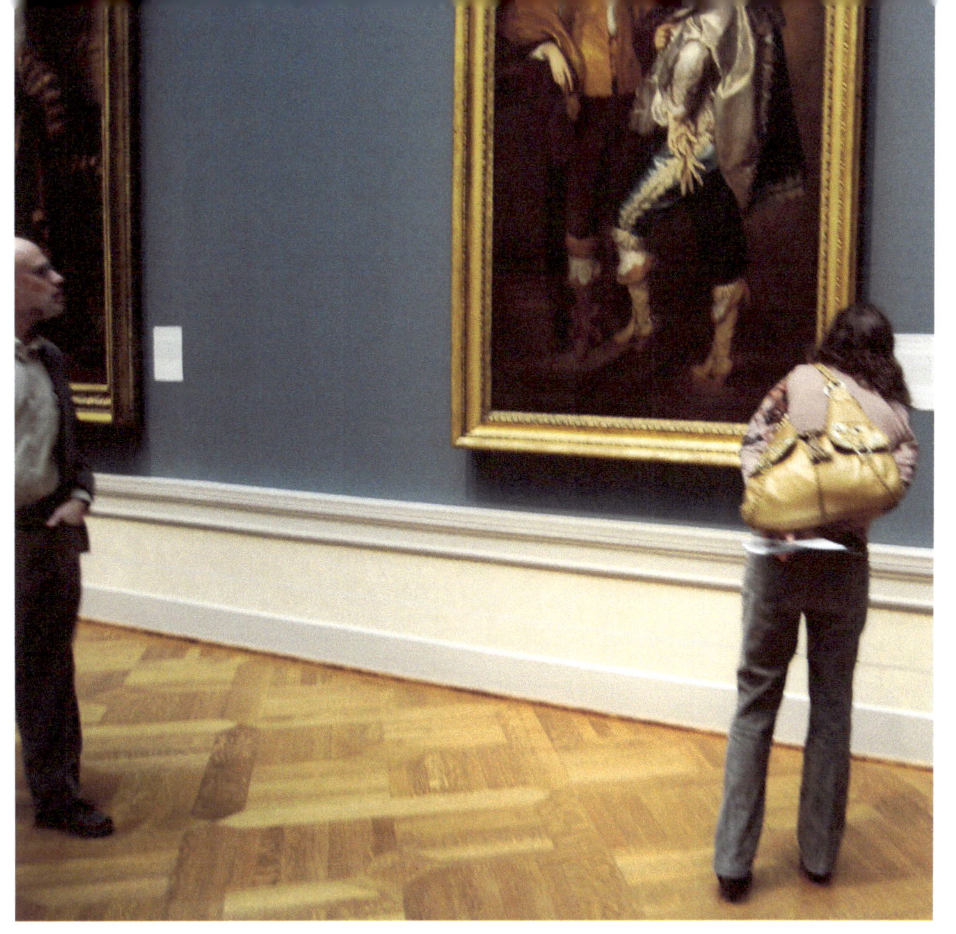

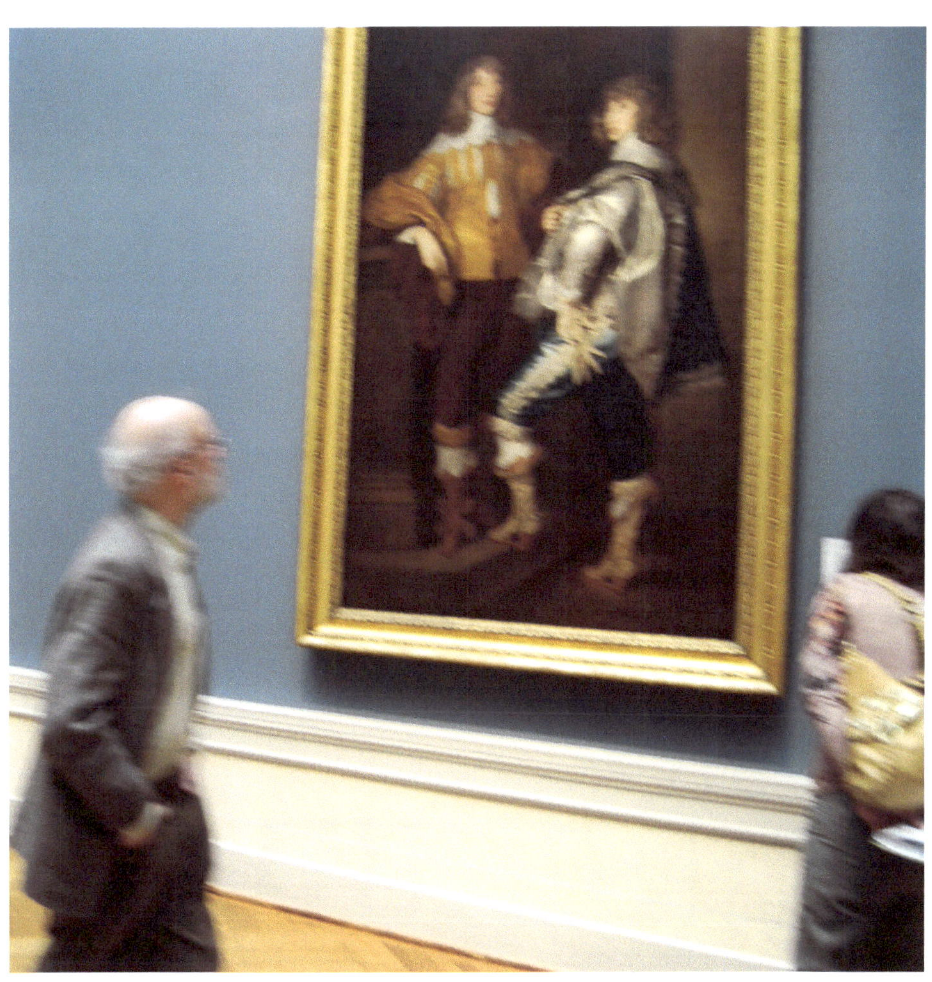

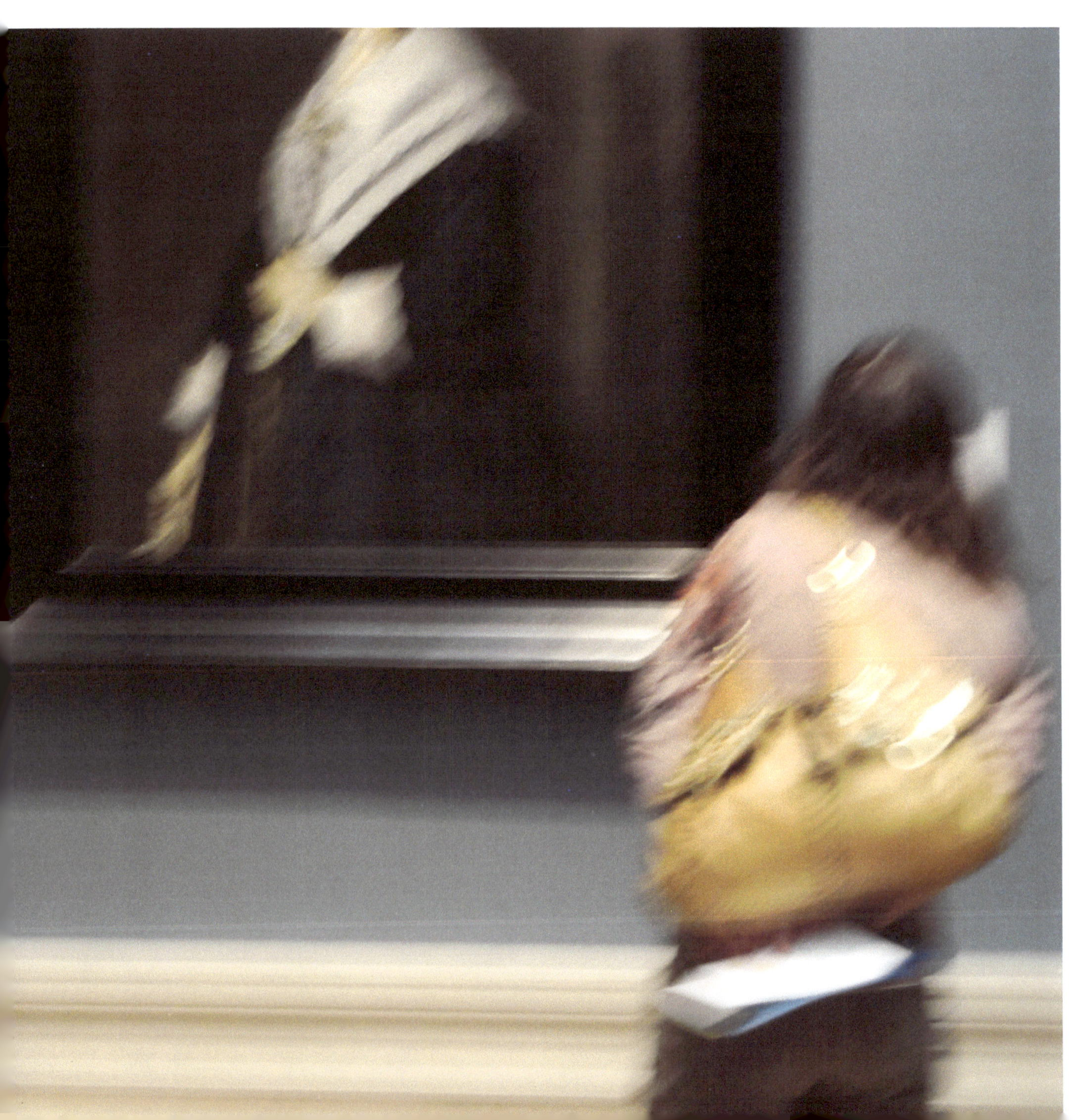

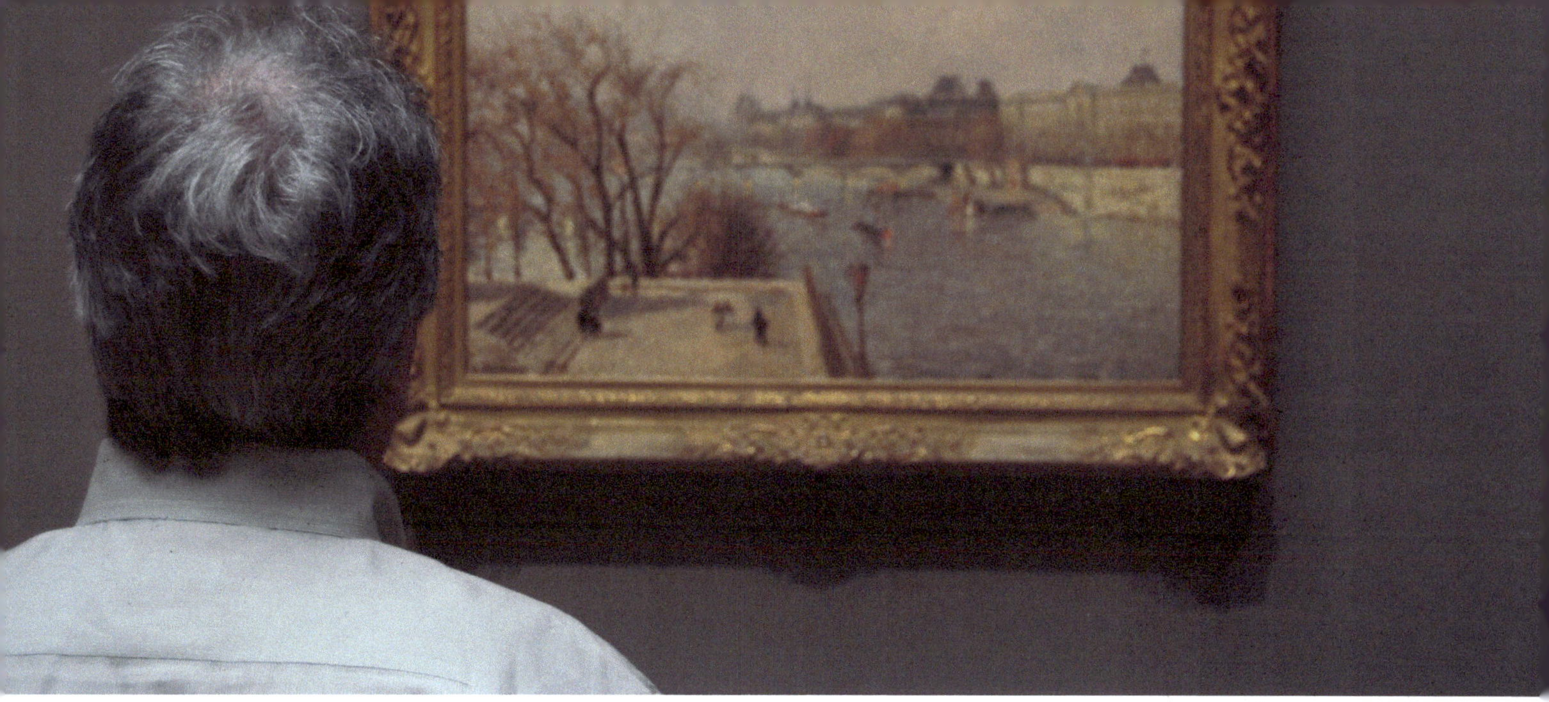

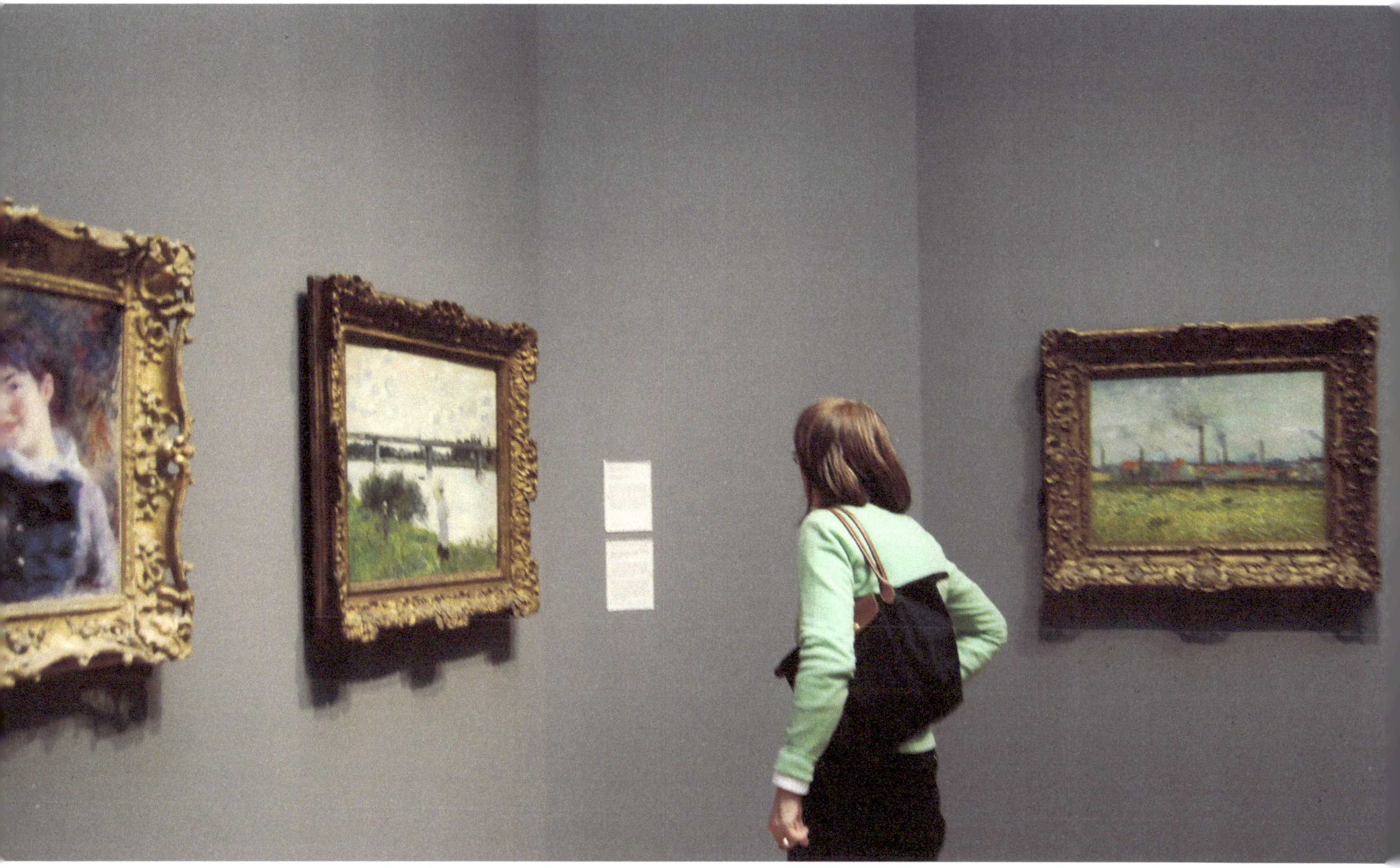

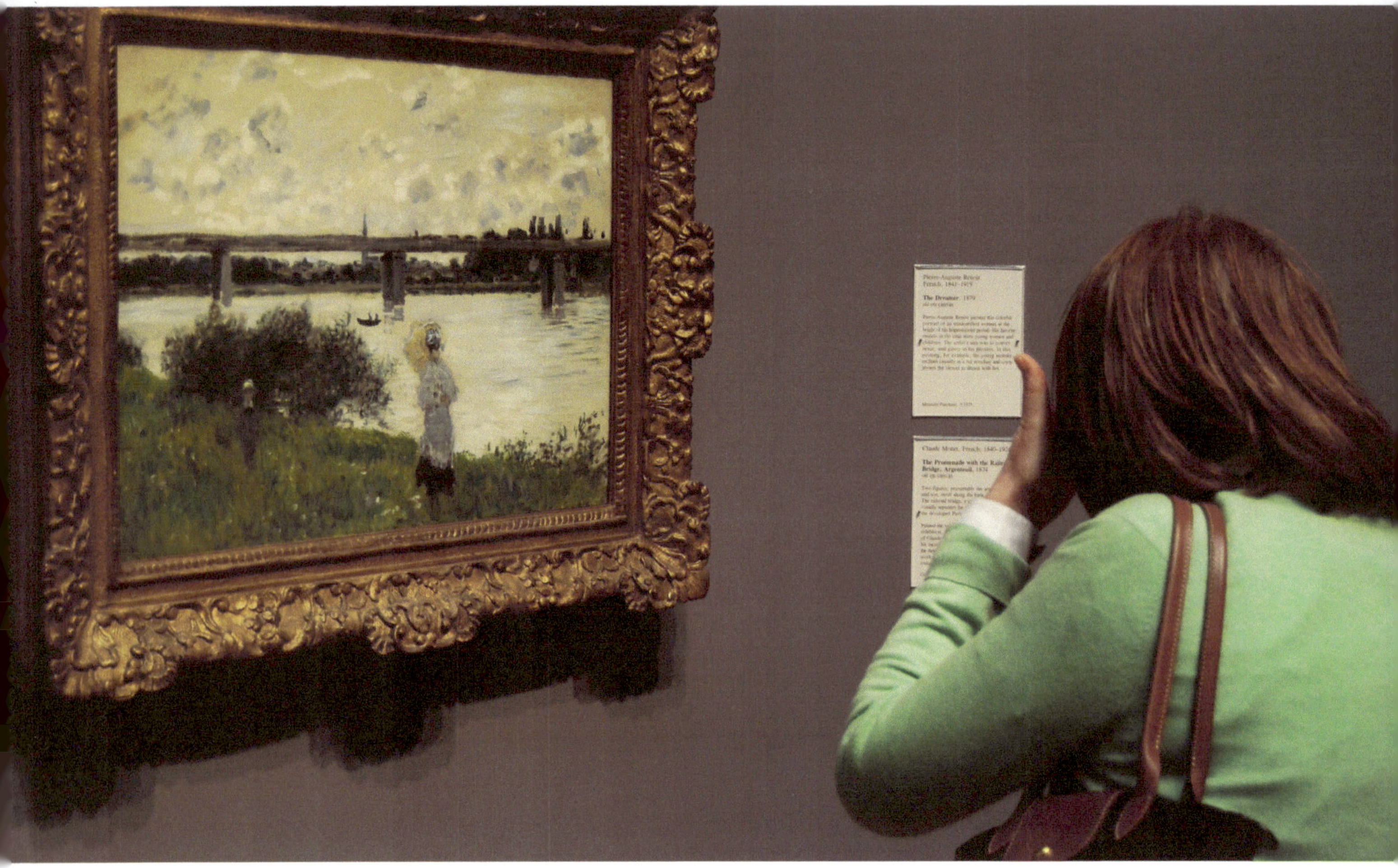

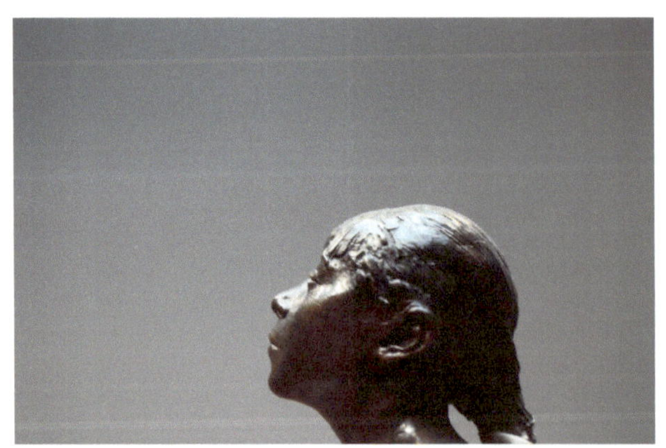

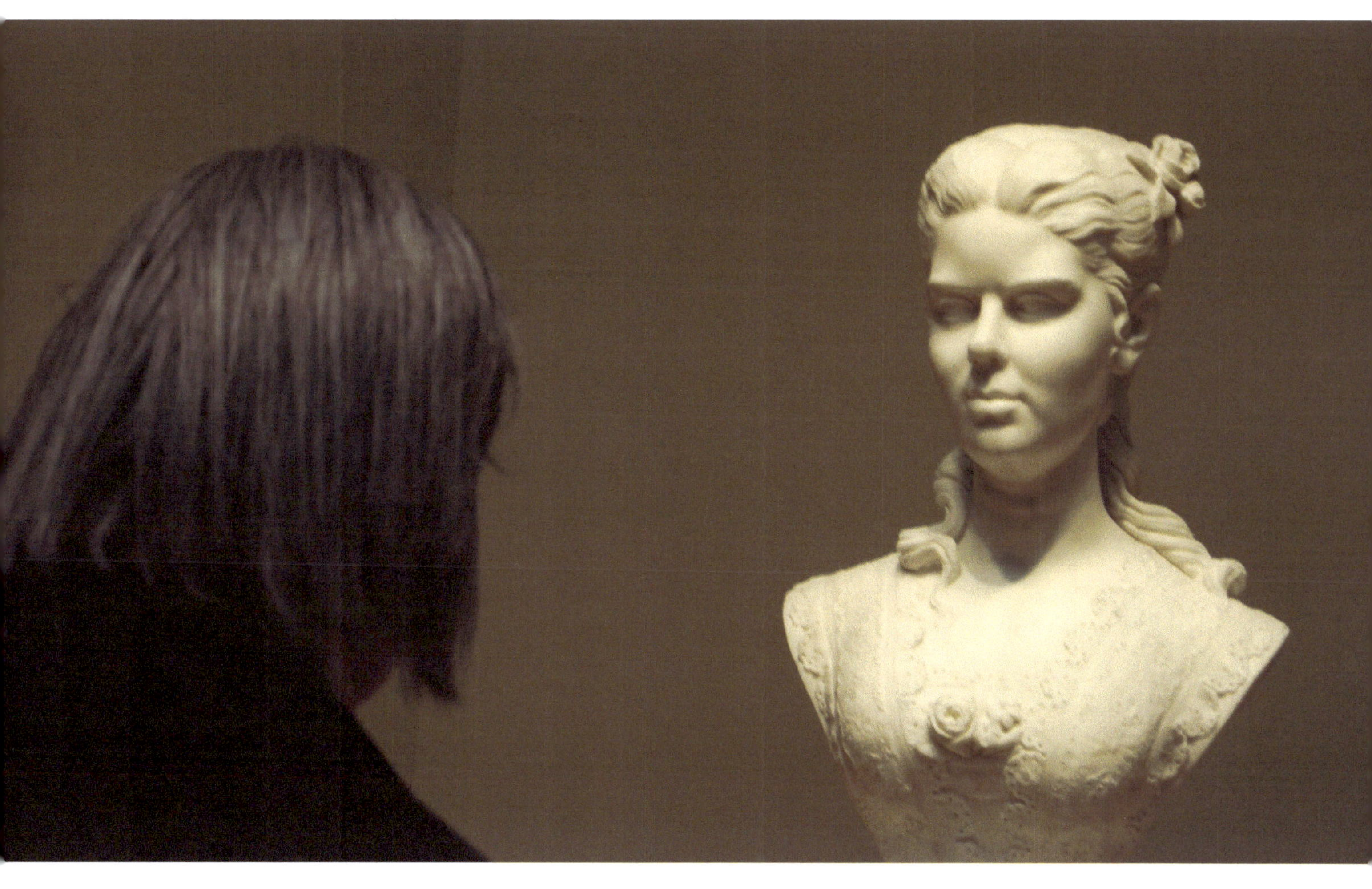

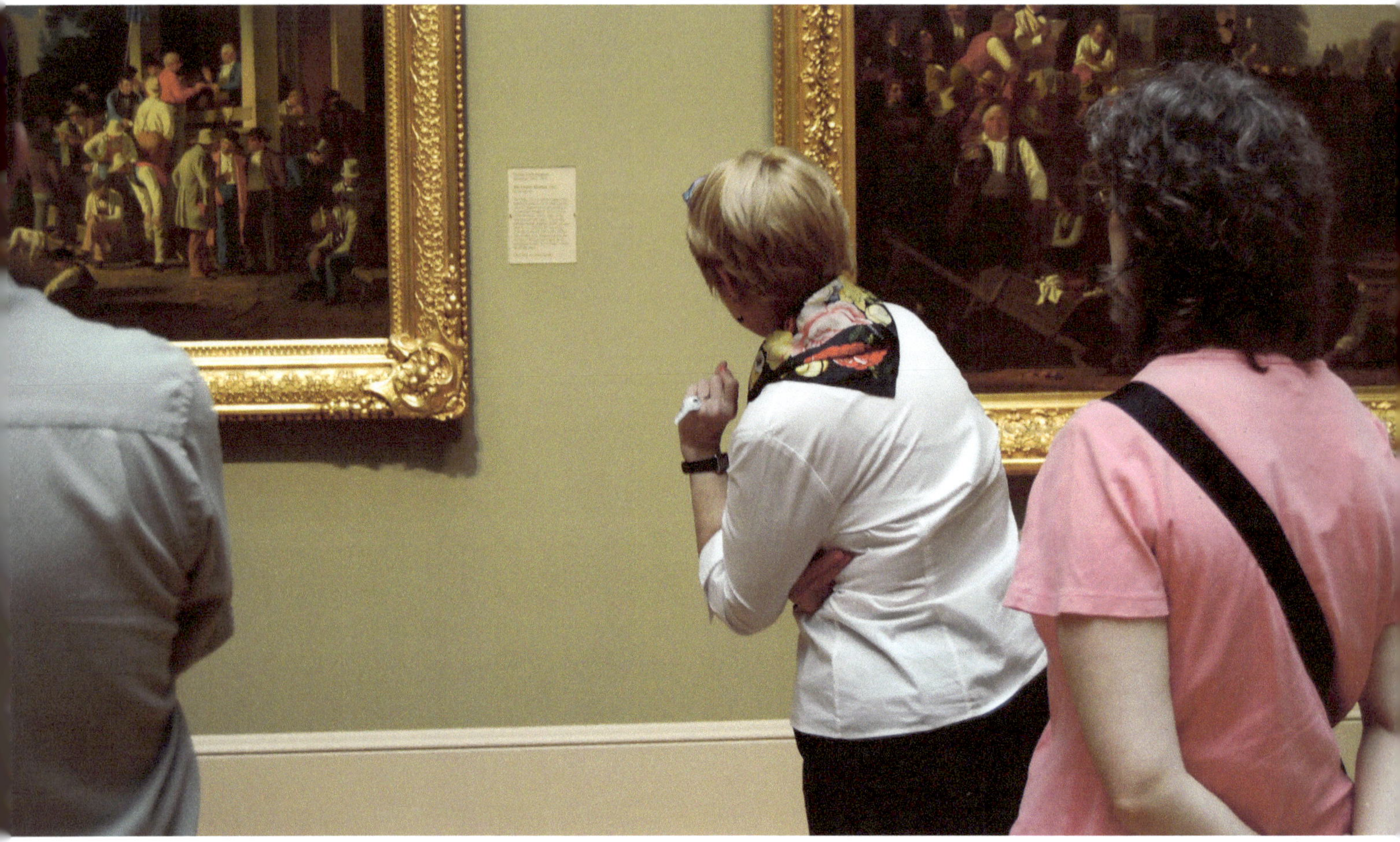

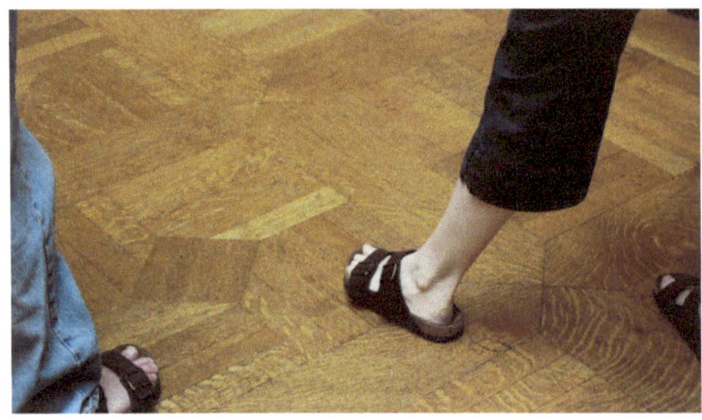

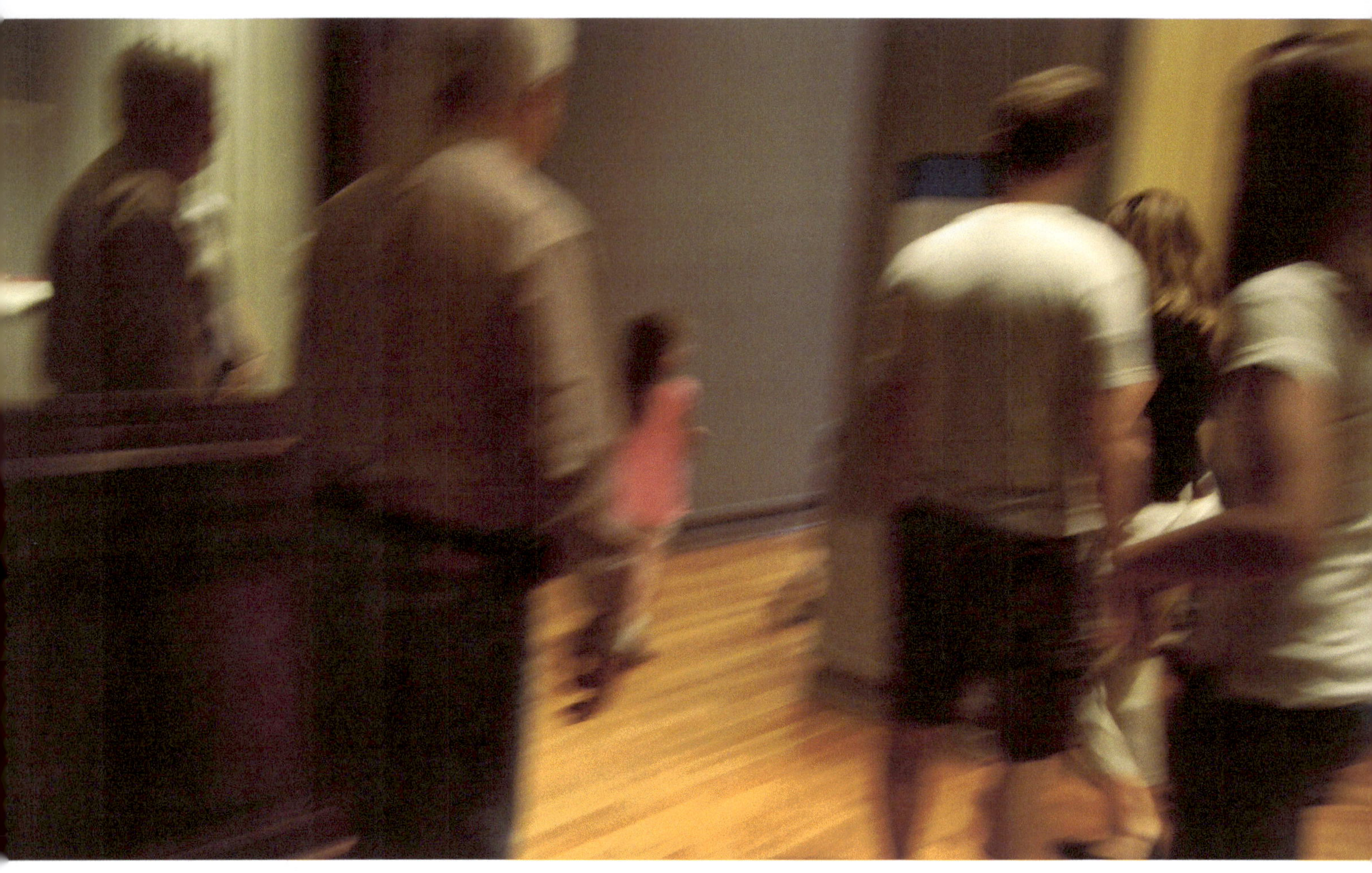

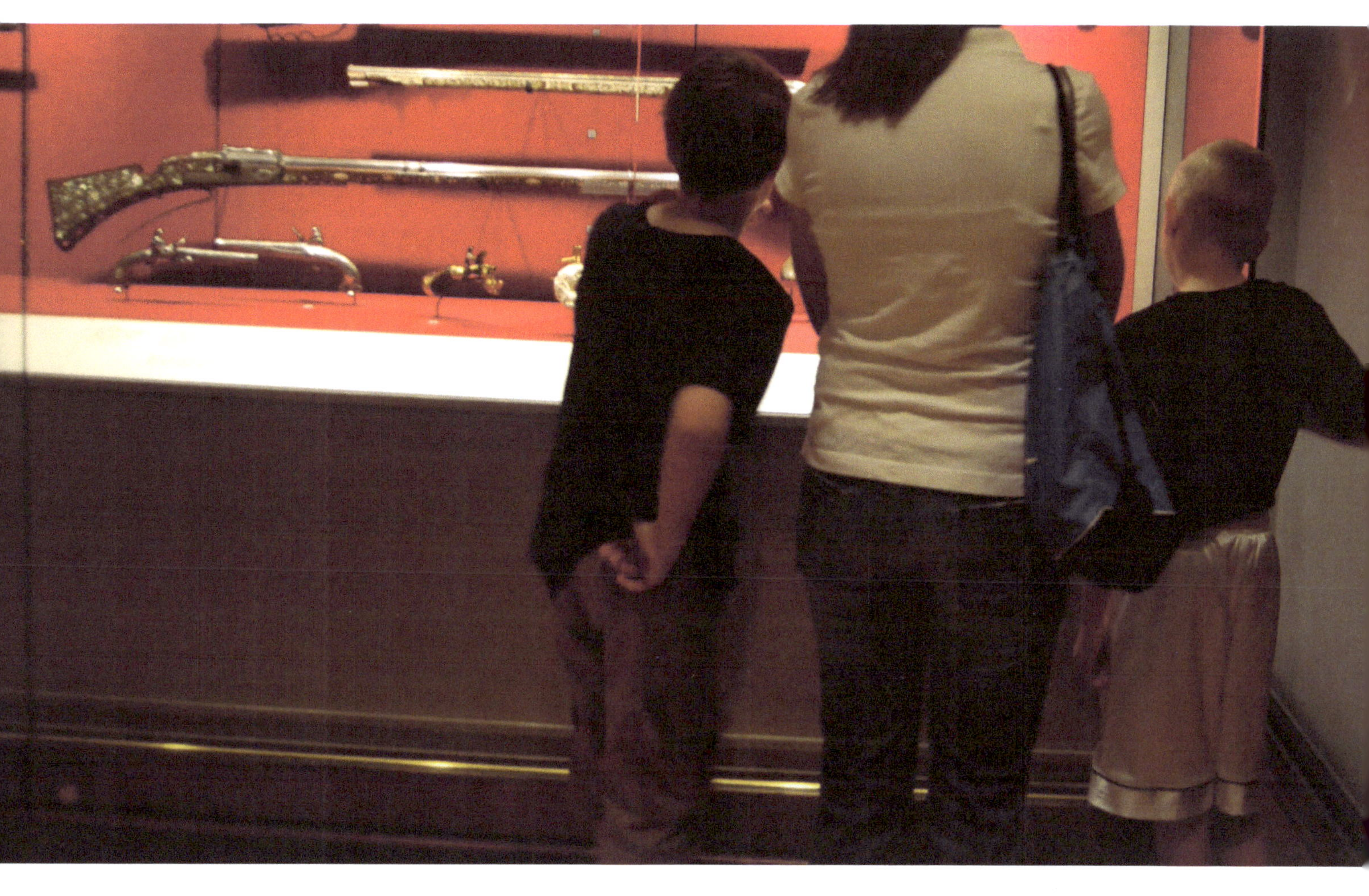

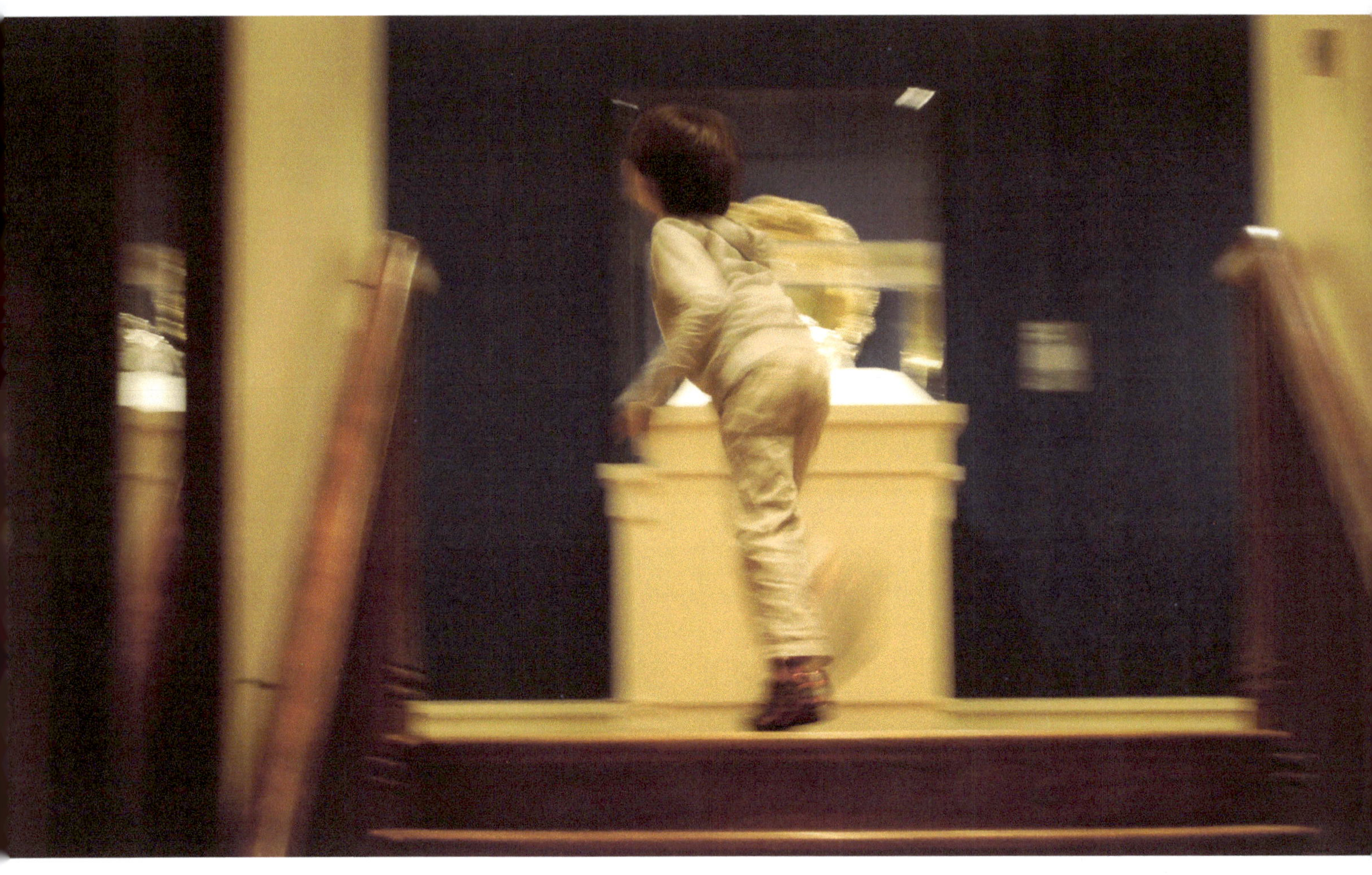

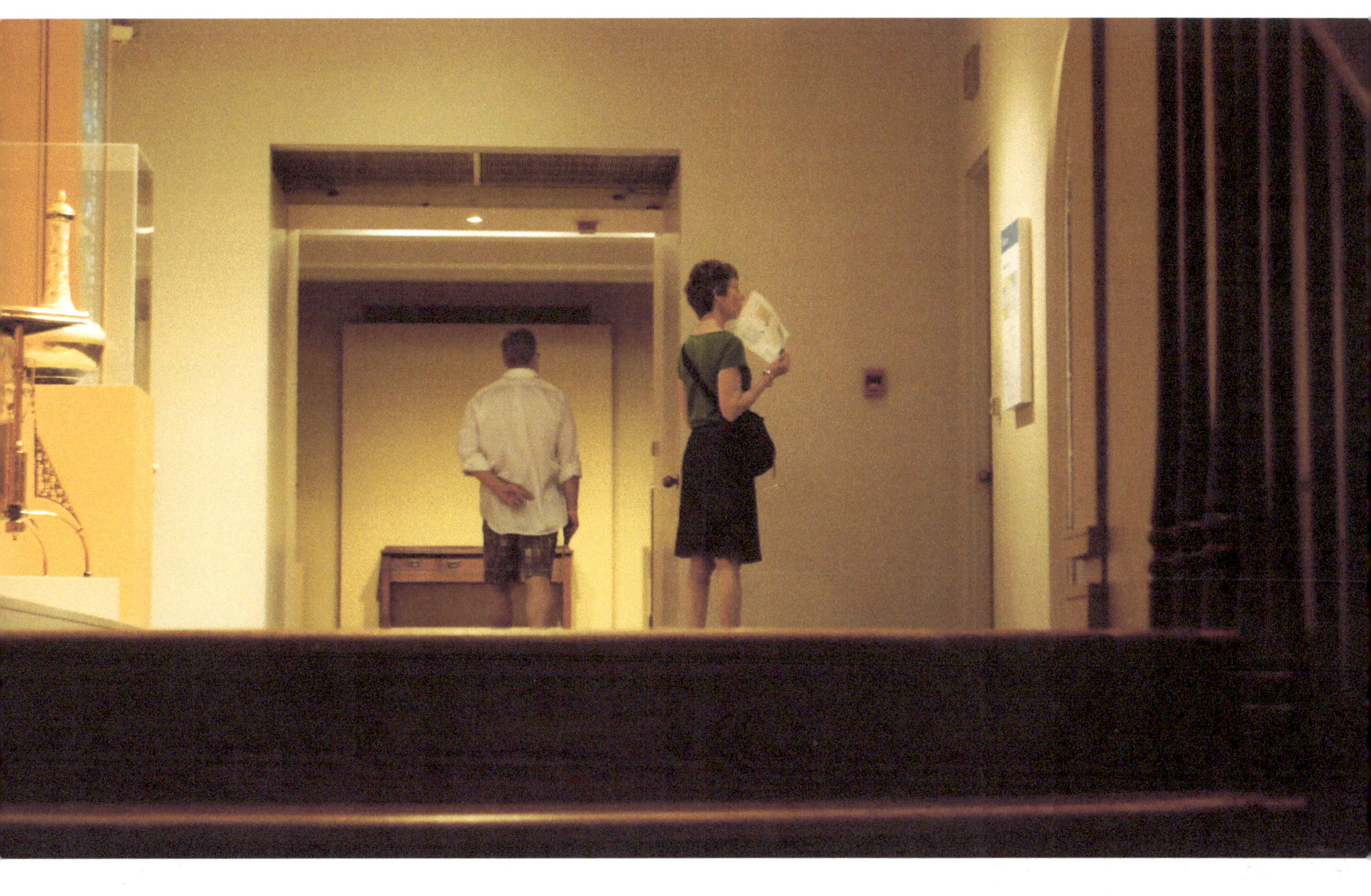

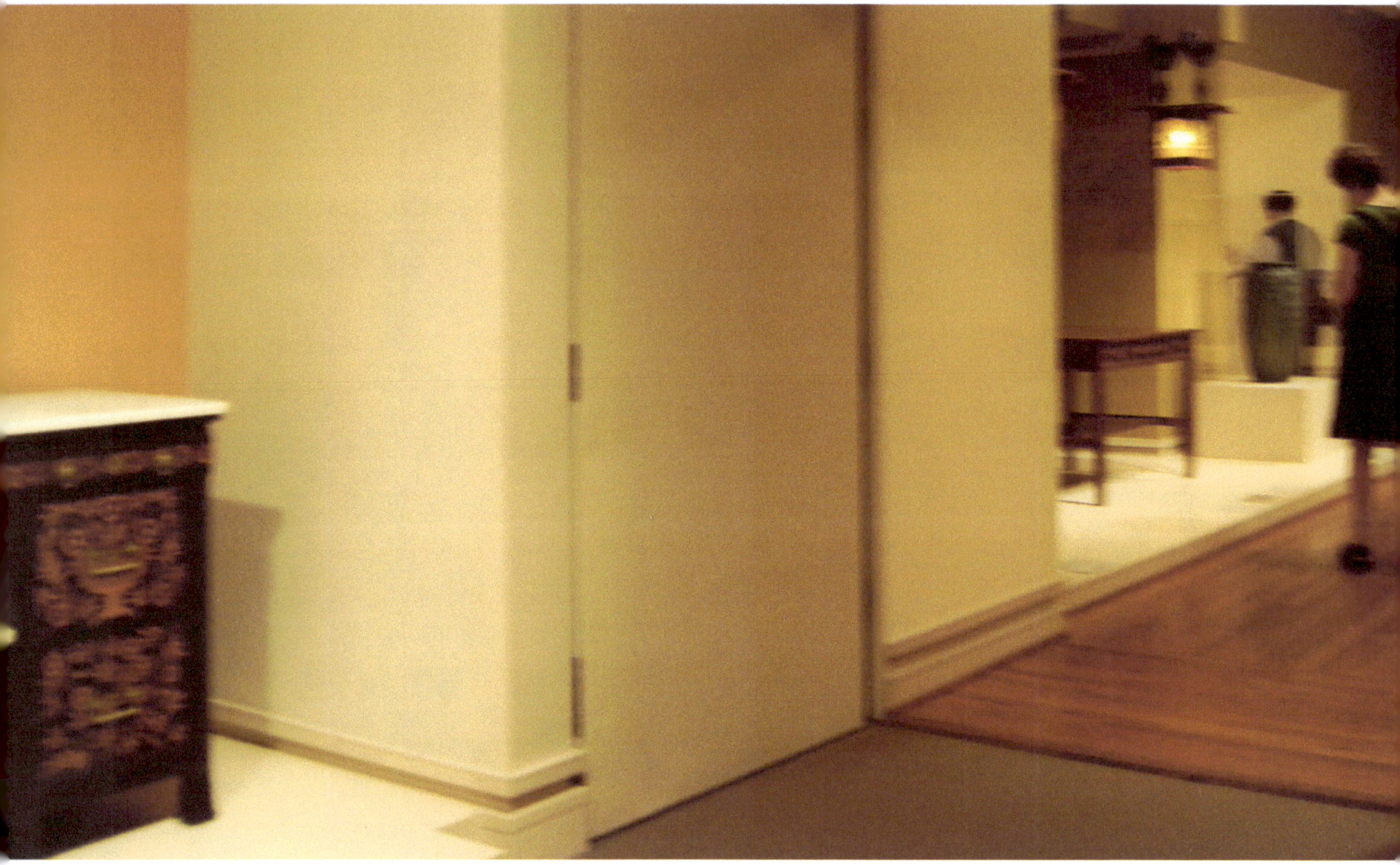

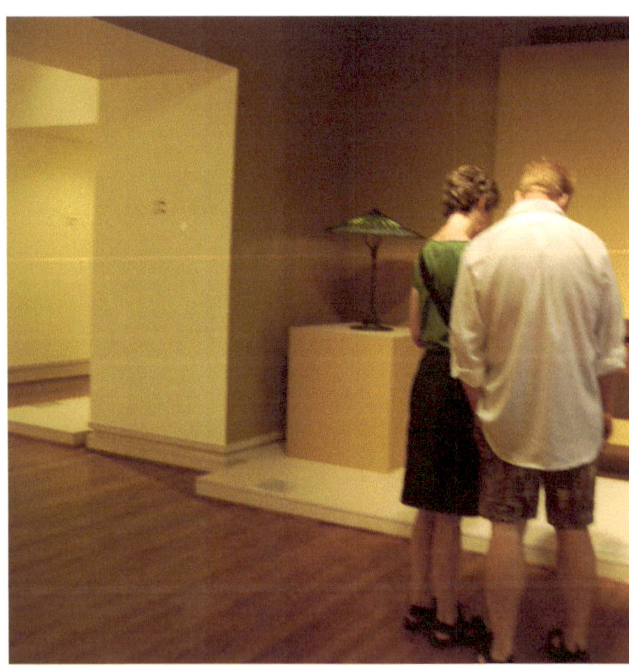

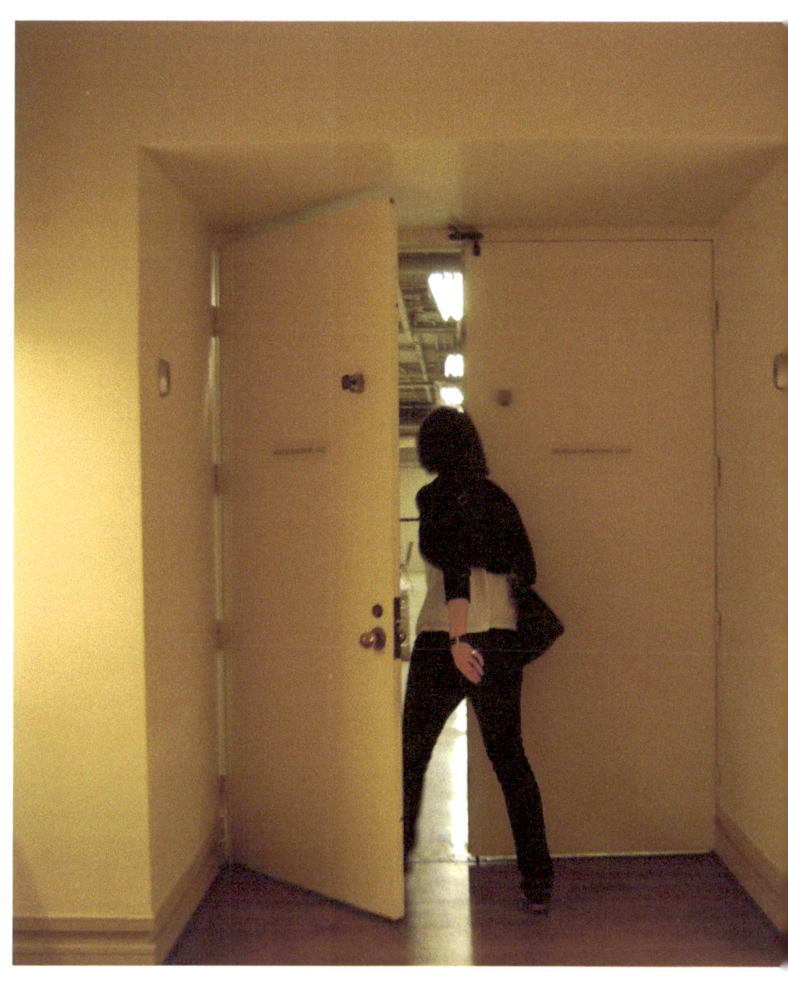

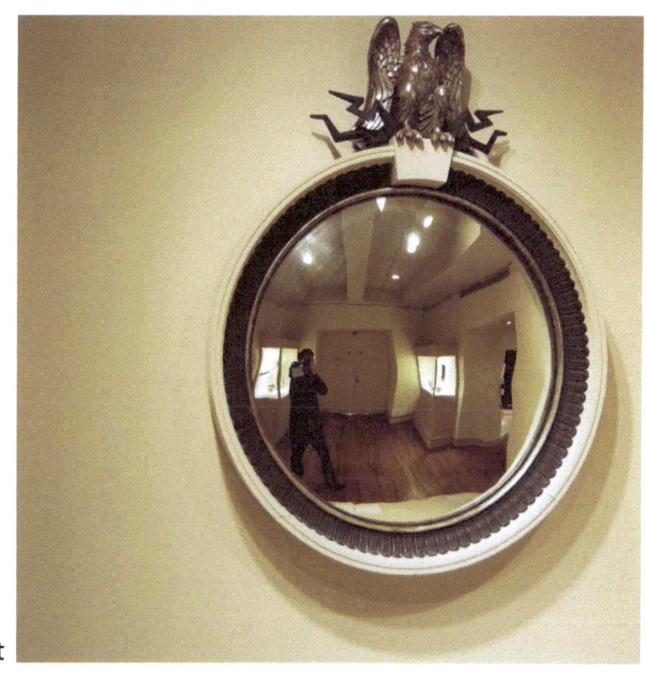

Self portrait

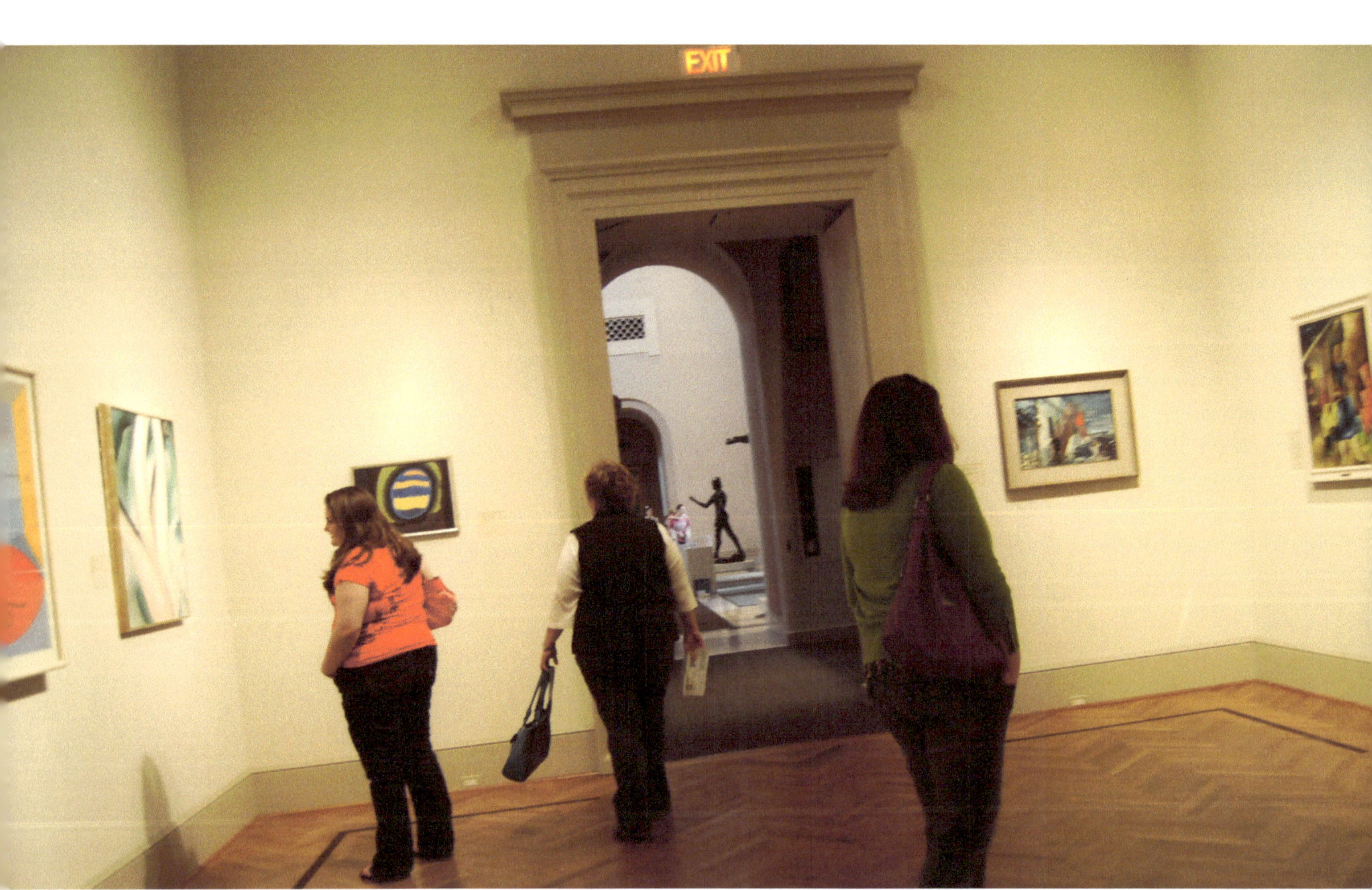
EXIT

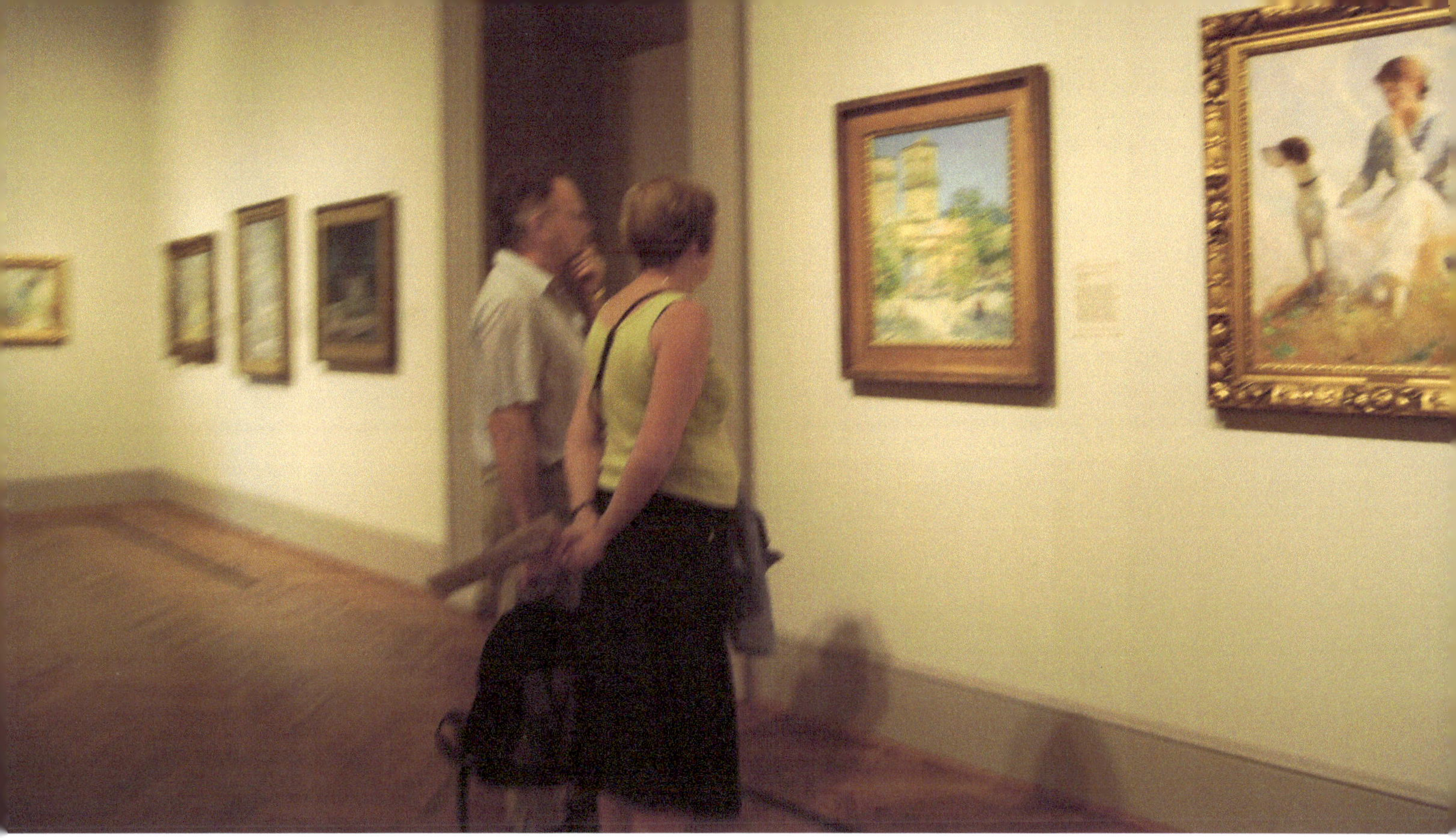

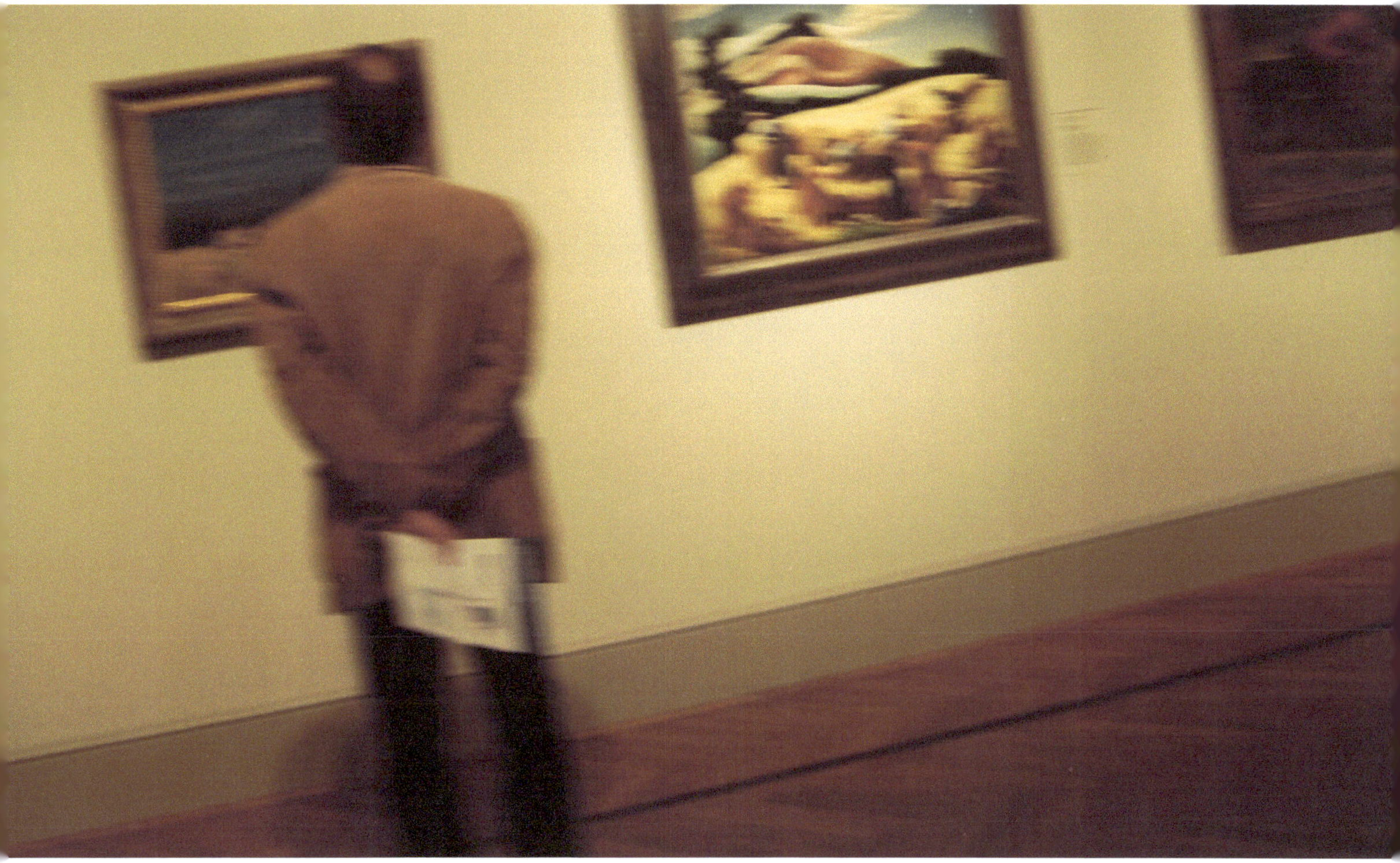

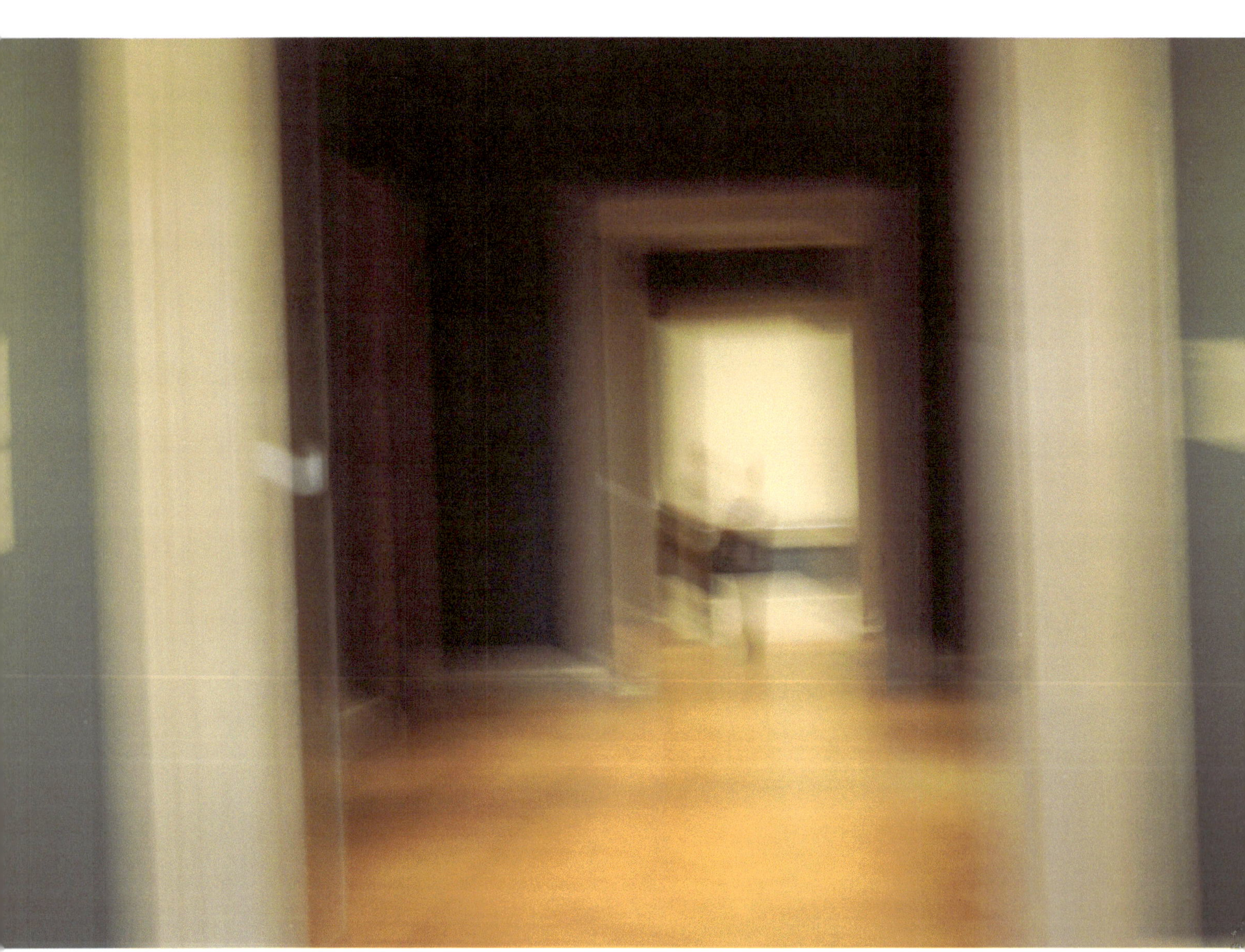

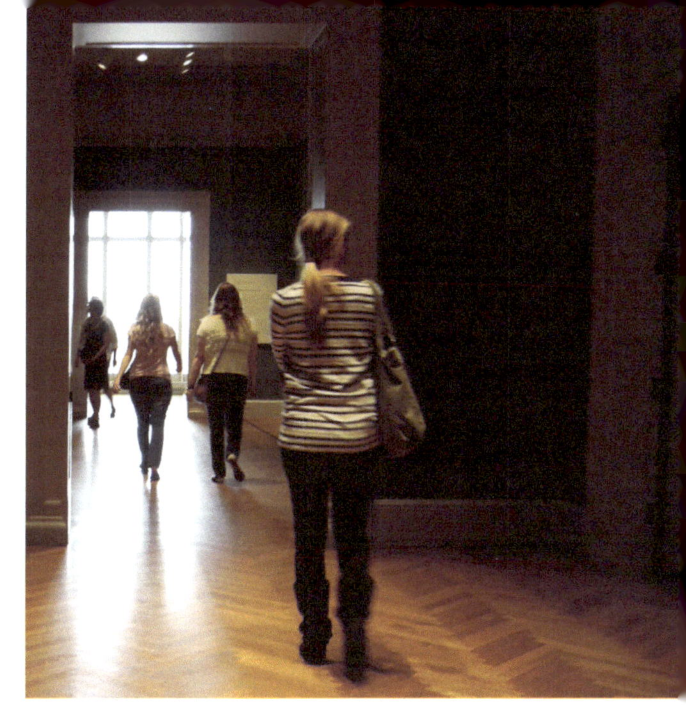

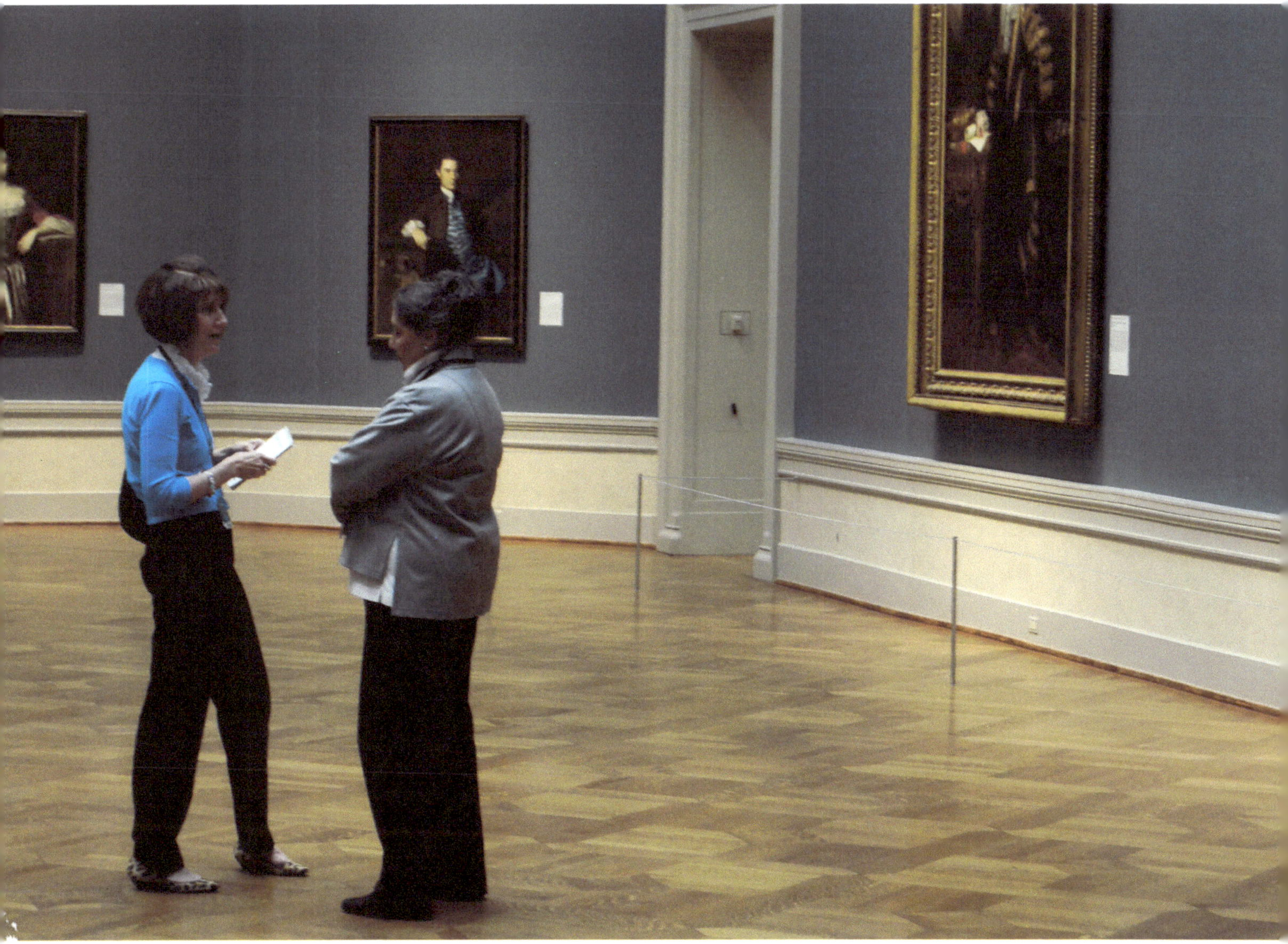

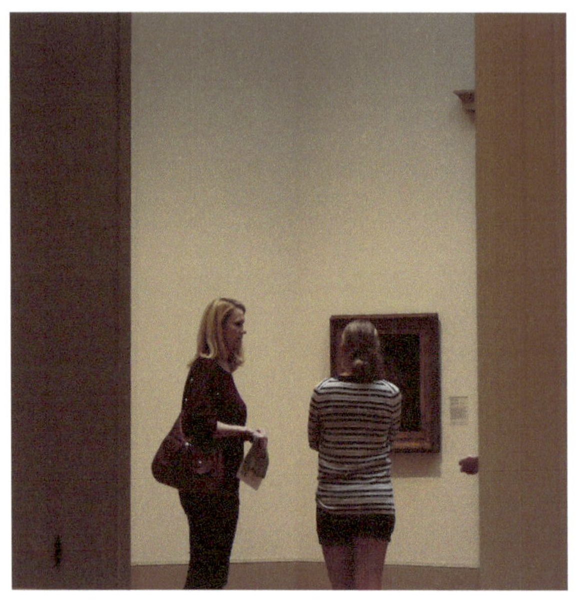

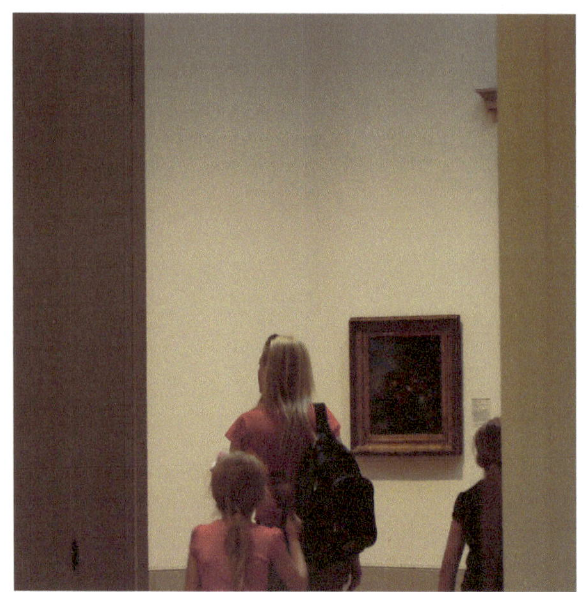

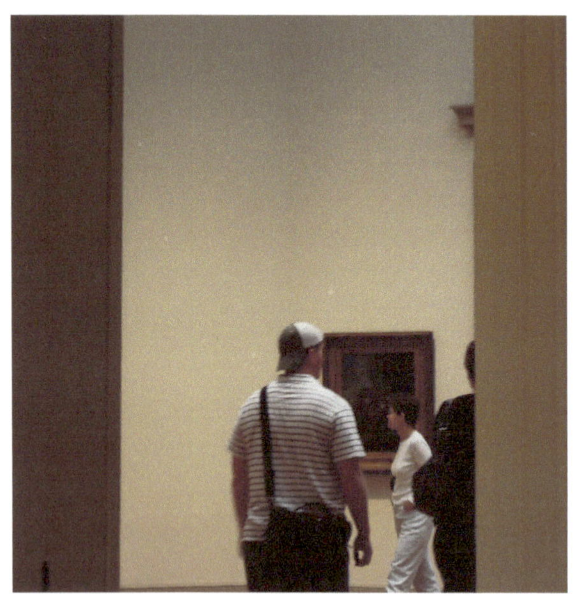

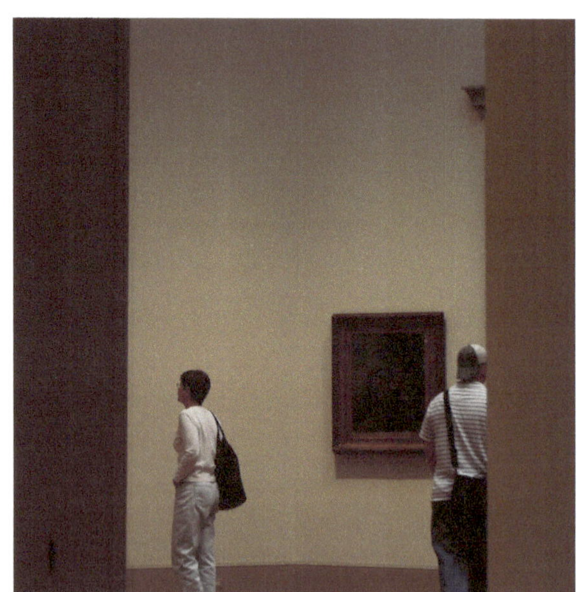

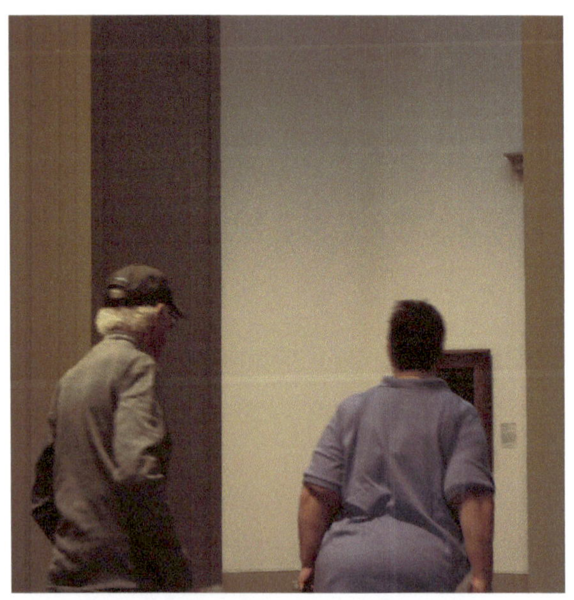

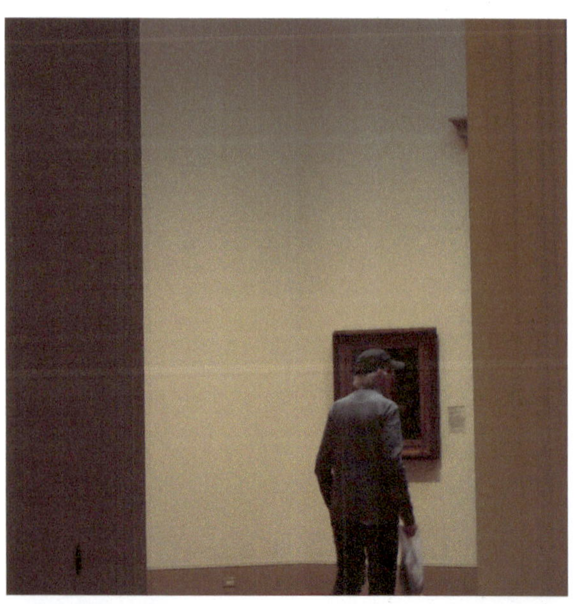

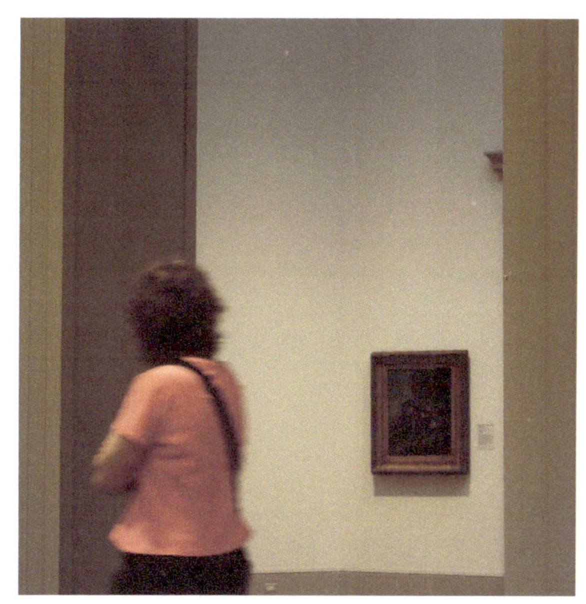

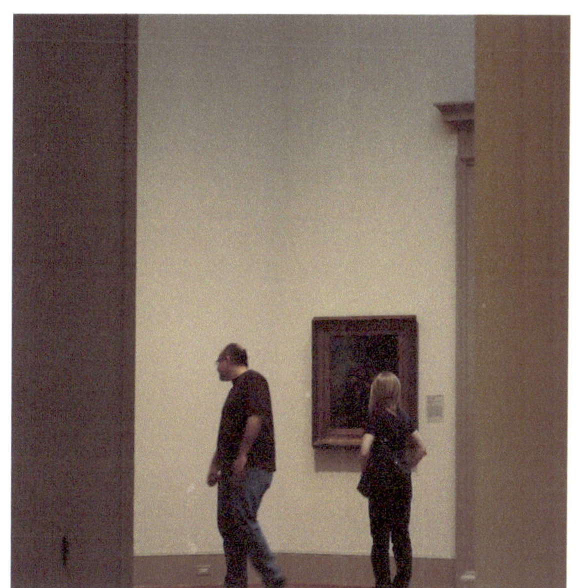

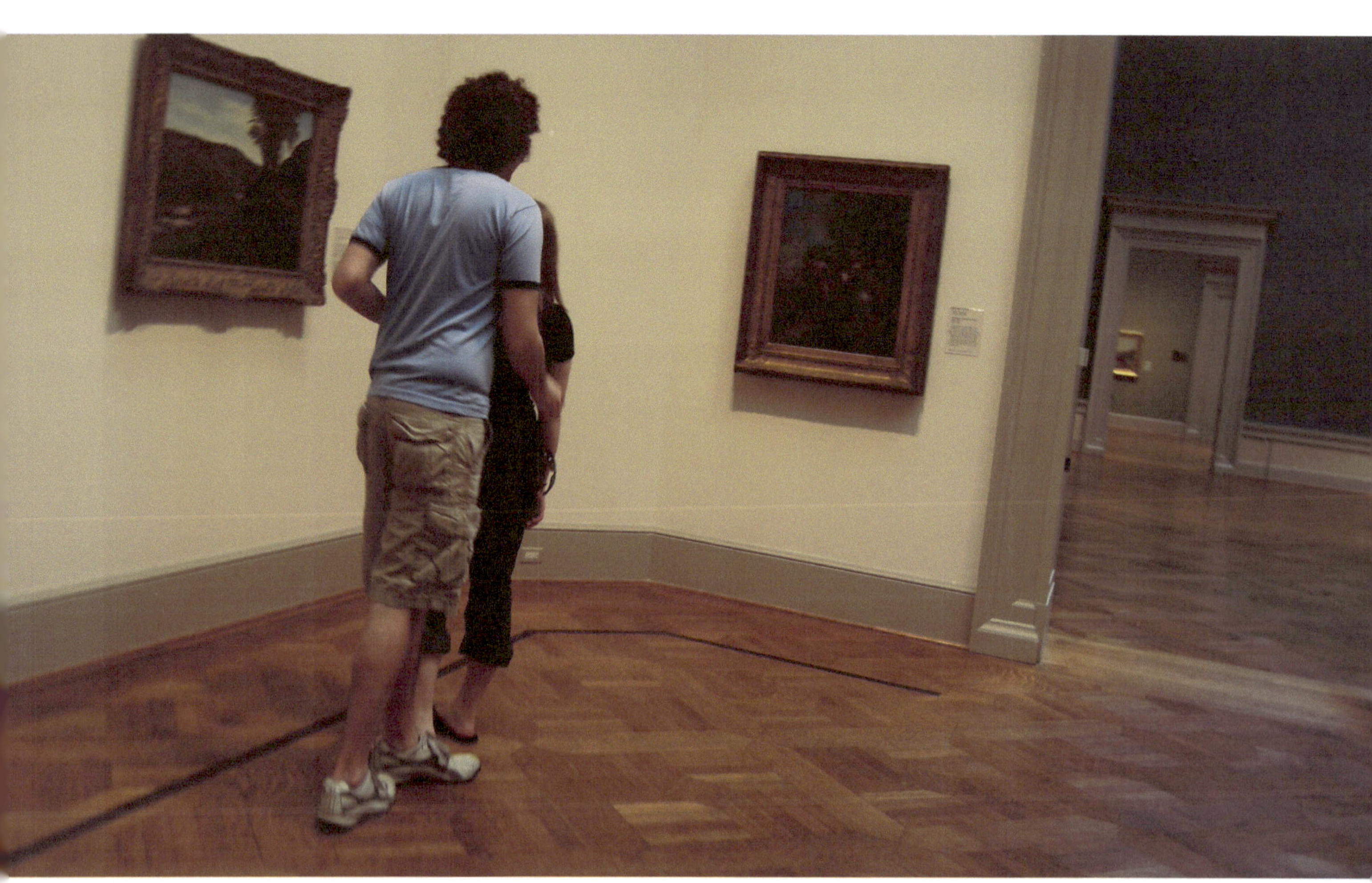

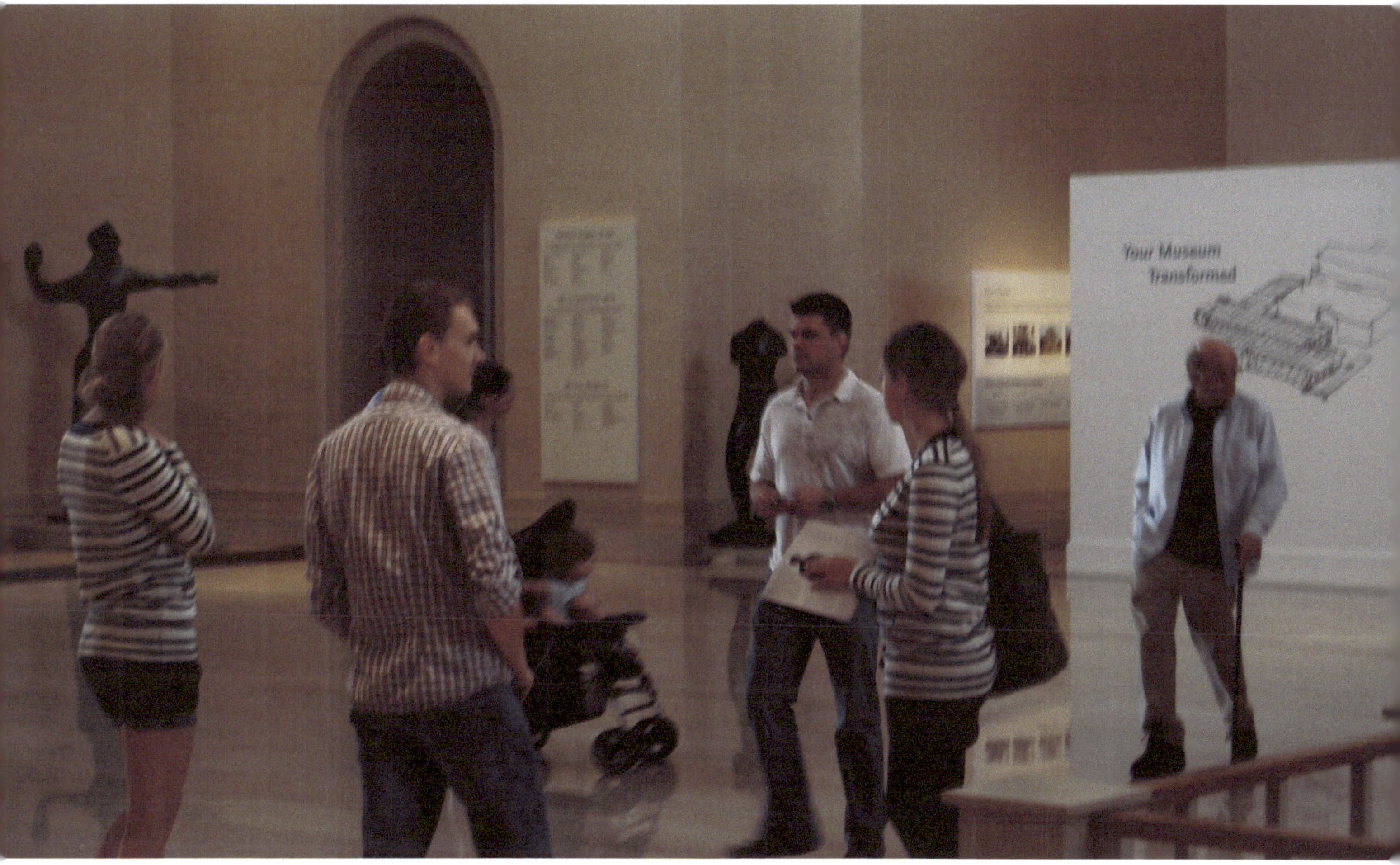

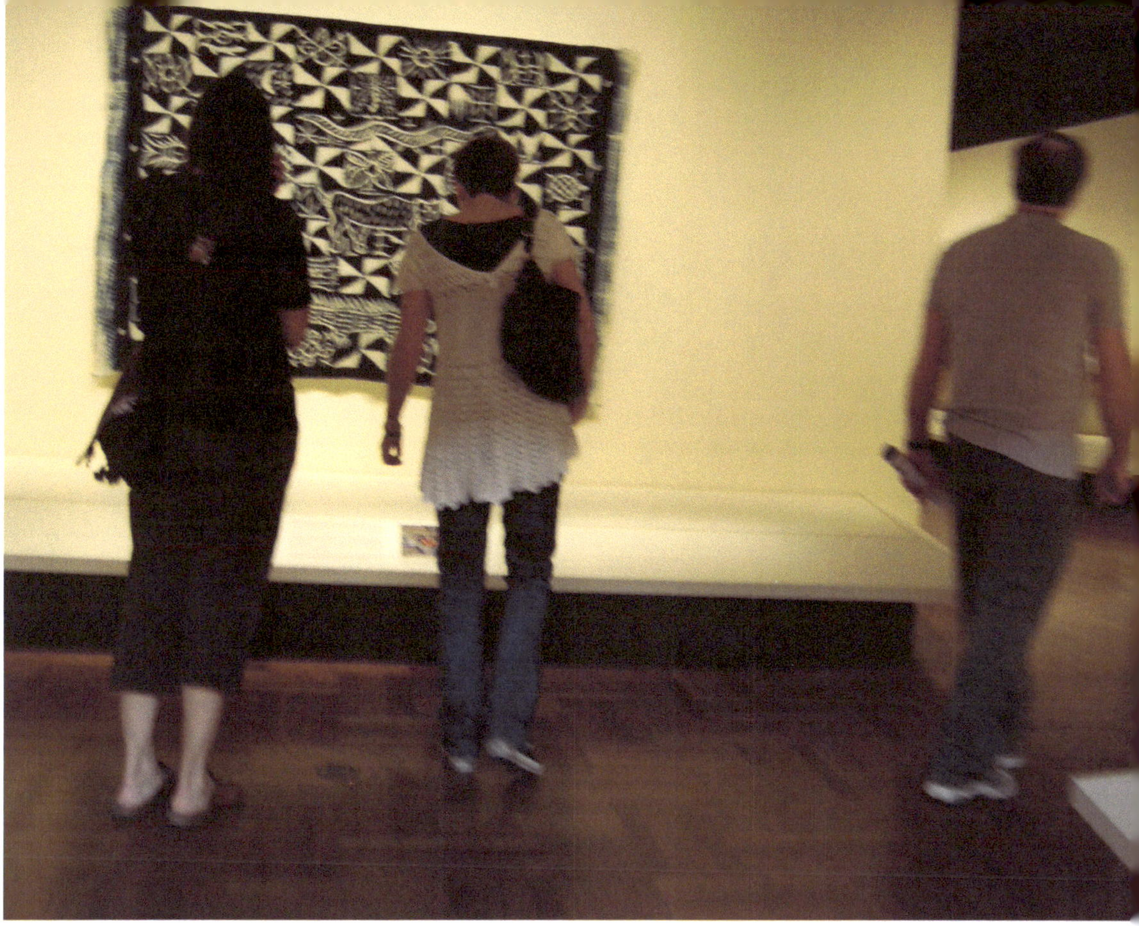

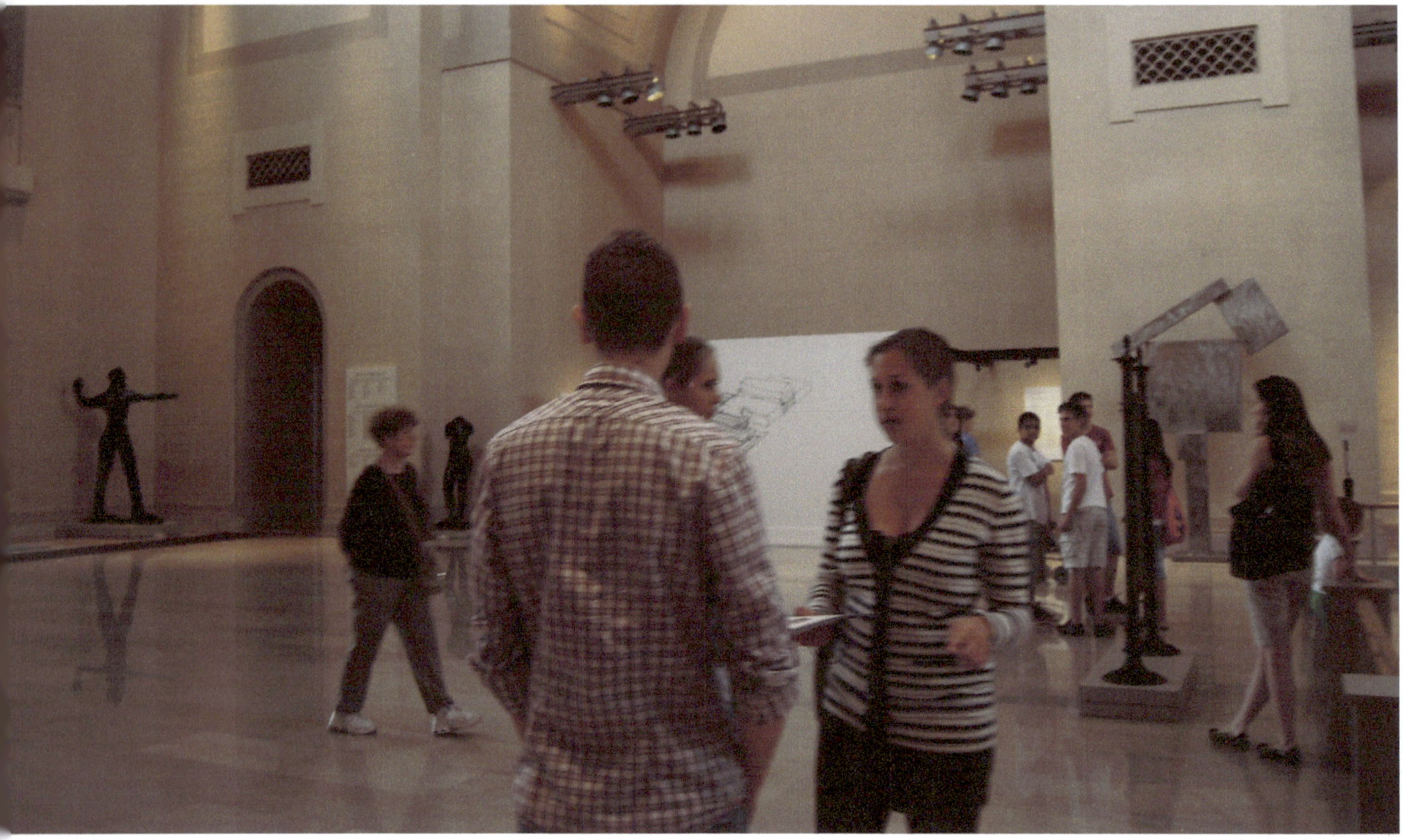

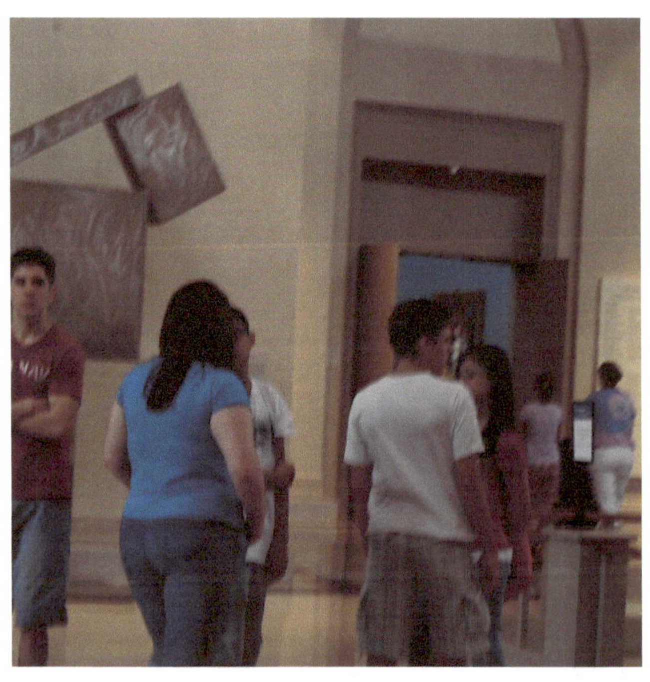

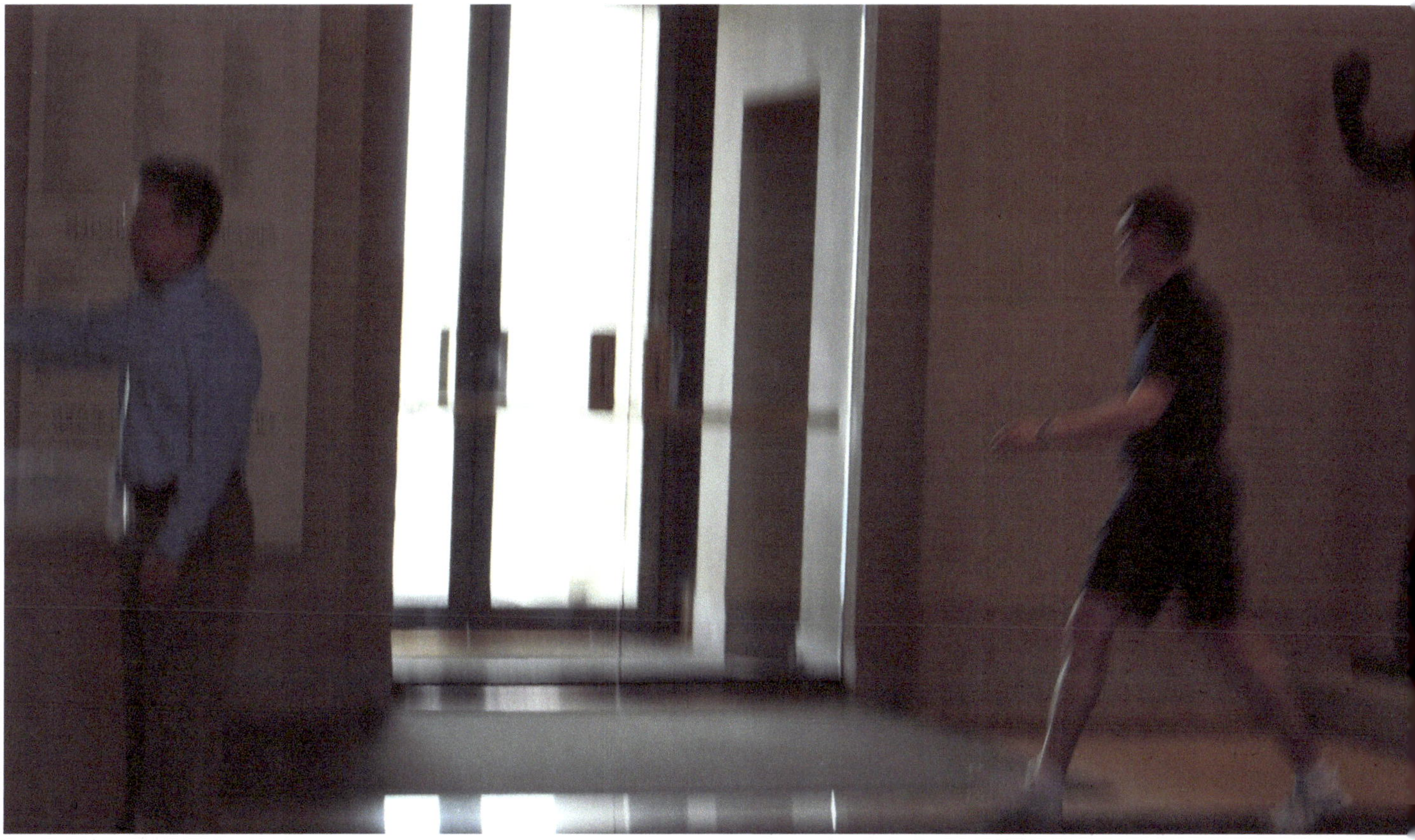

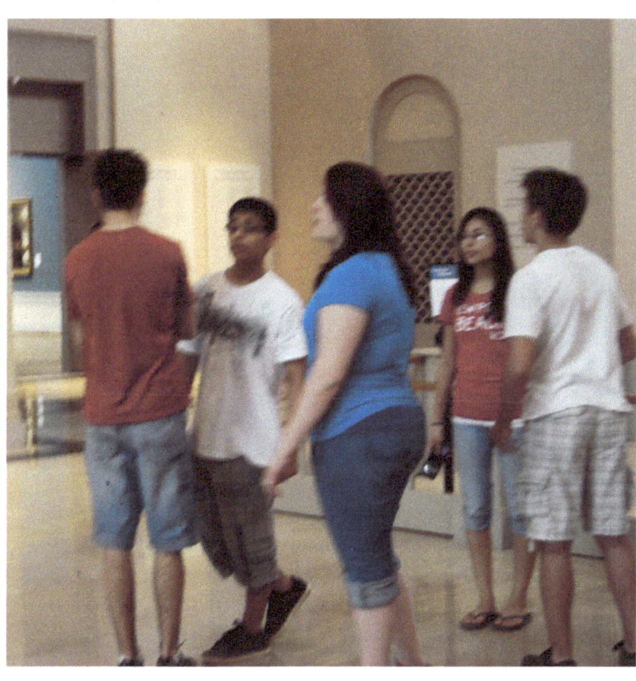

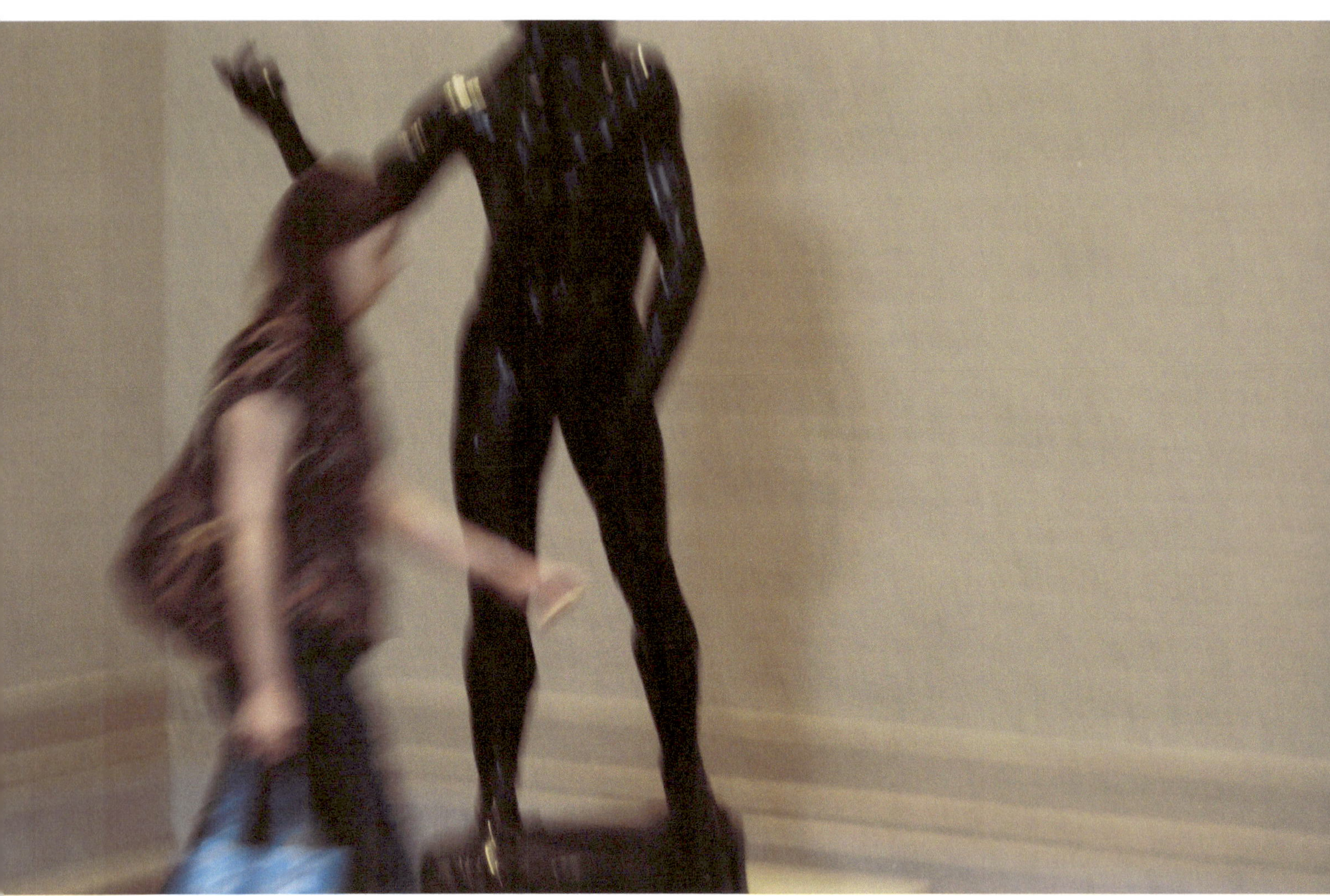

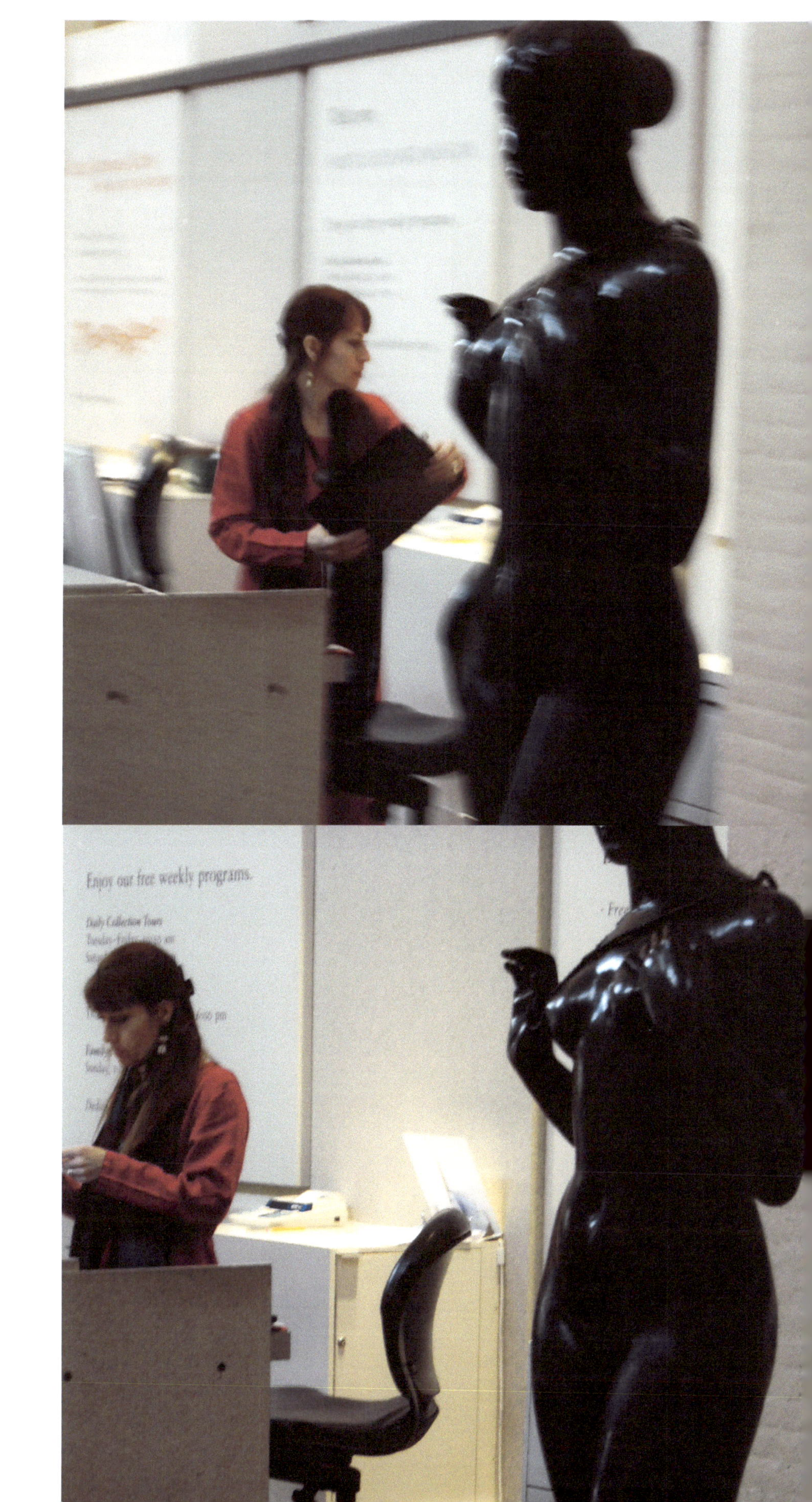
Enjoy our free weekly programs.
Daily Collection Tours

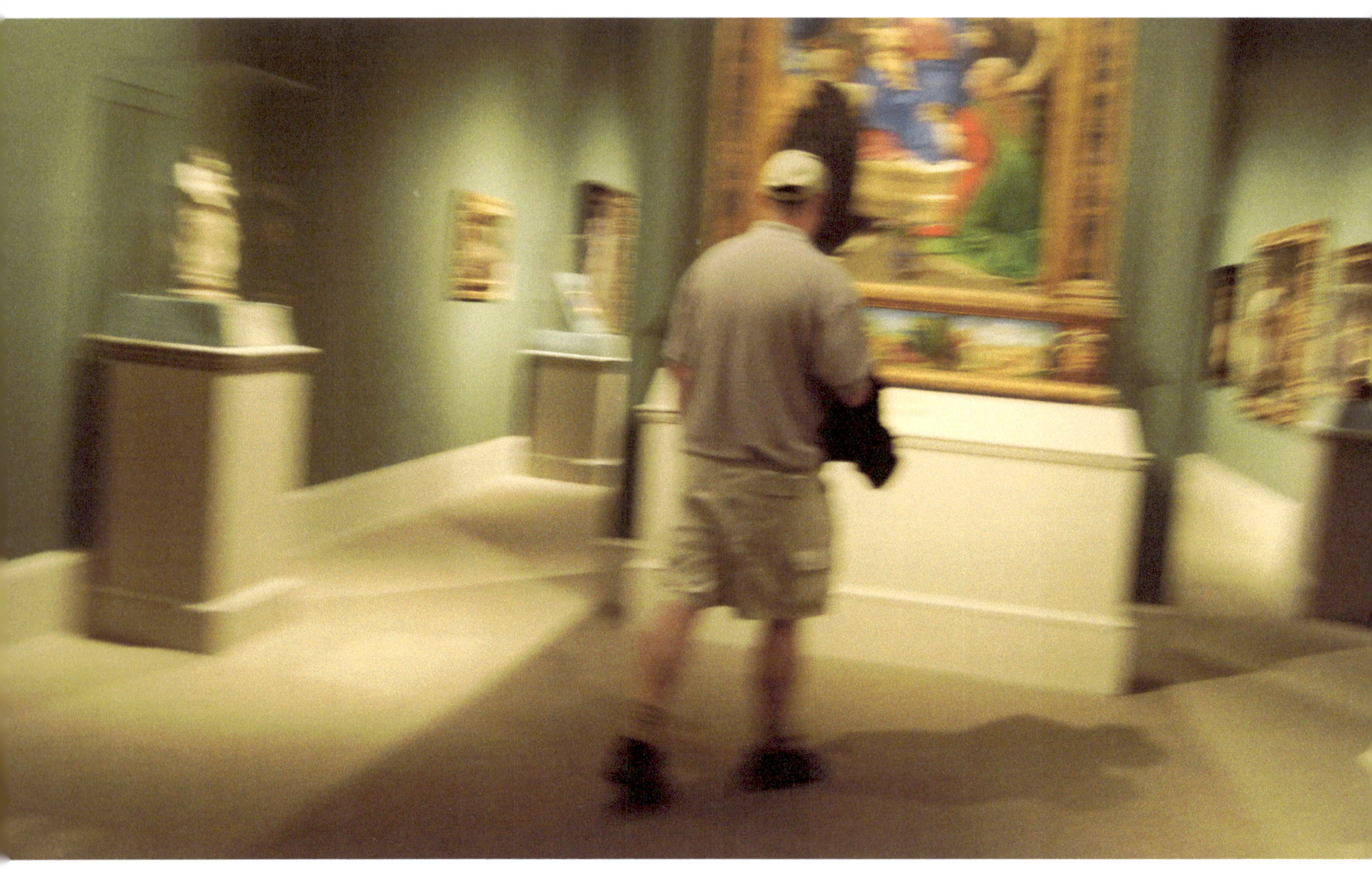

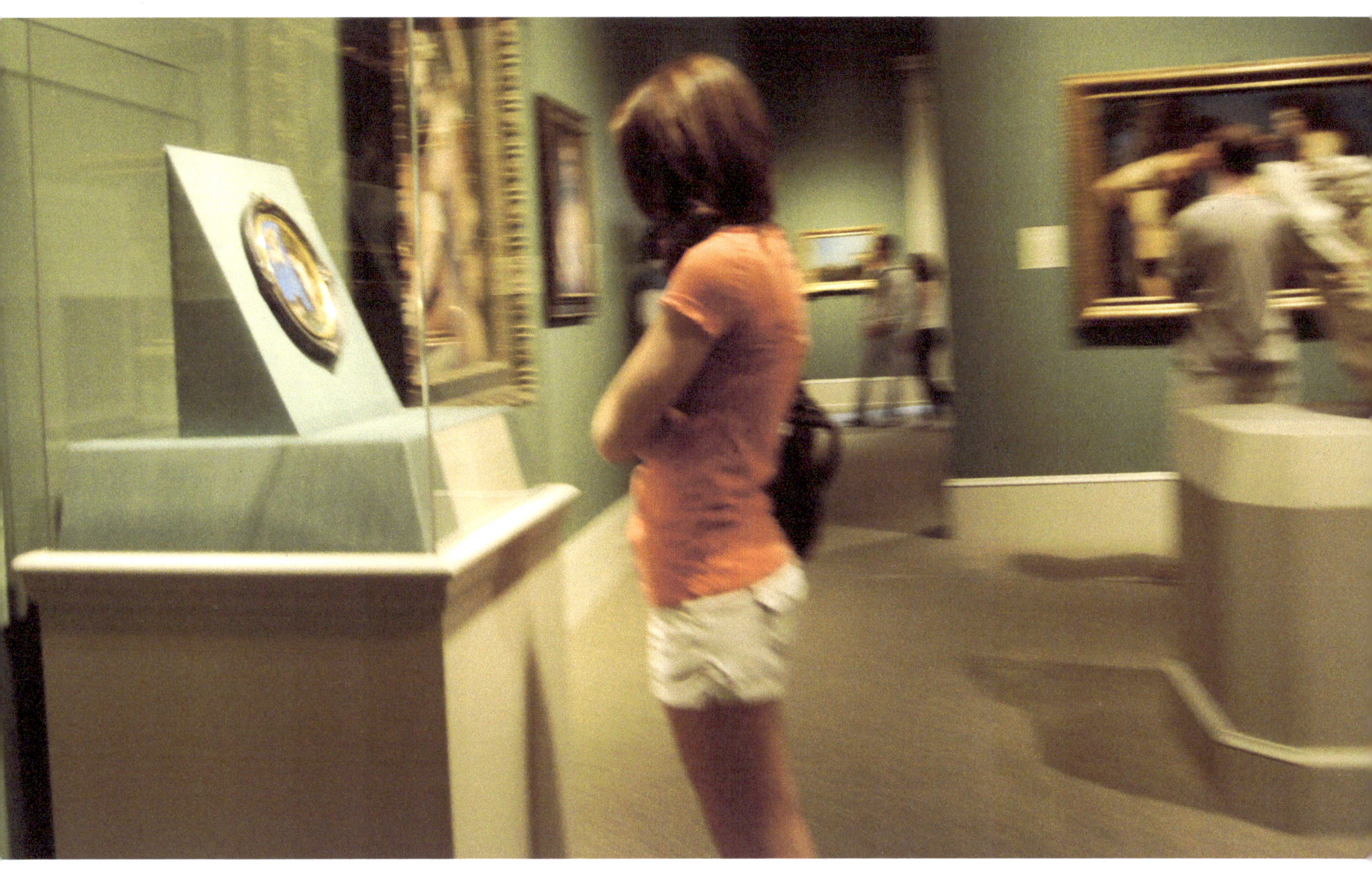

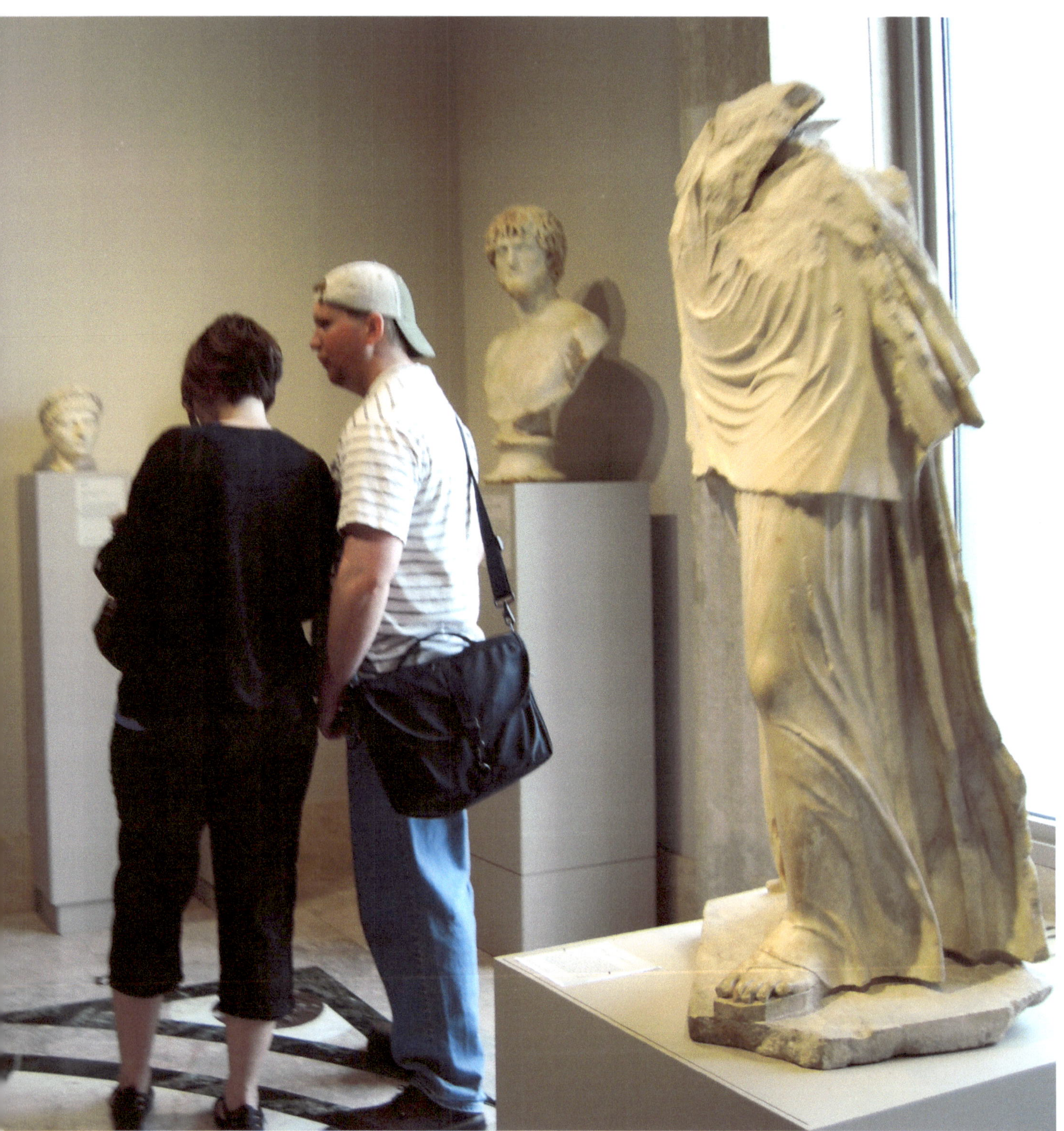

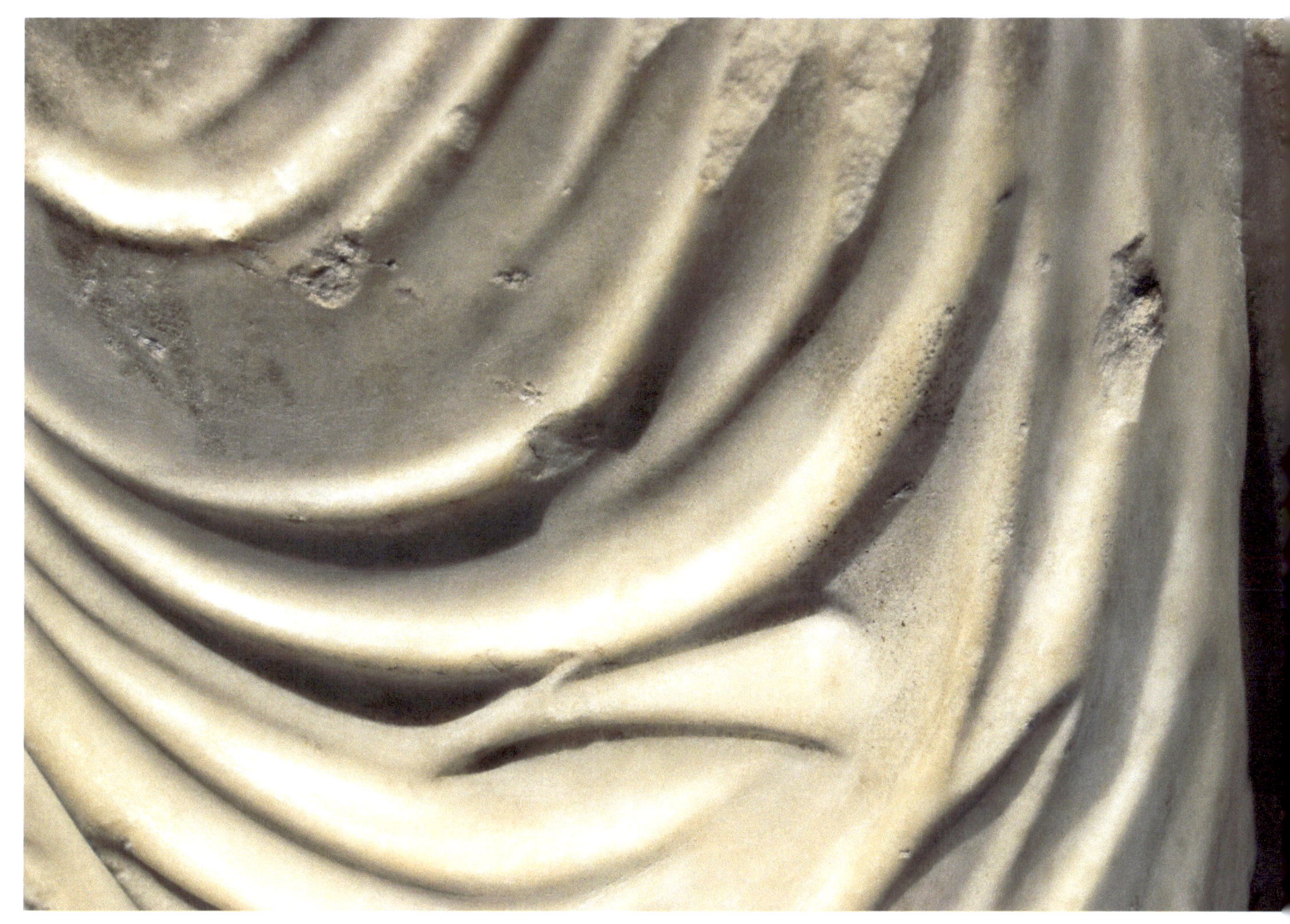

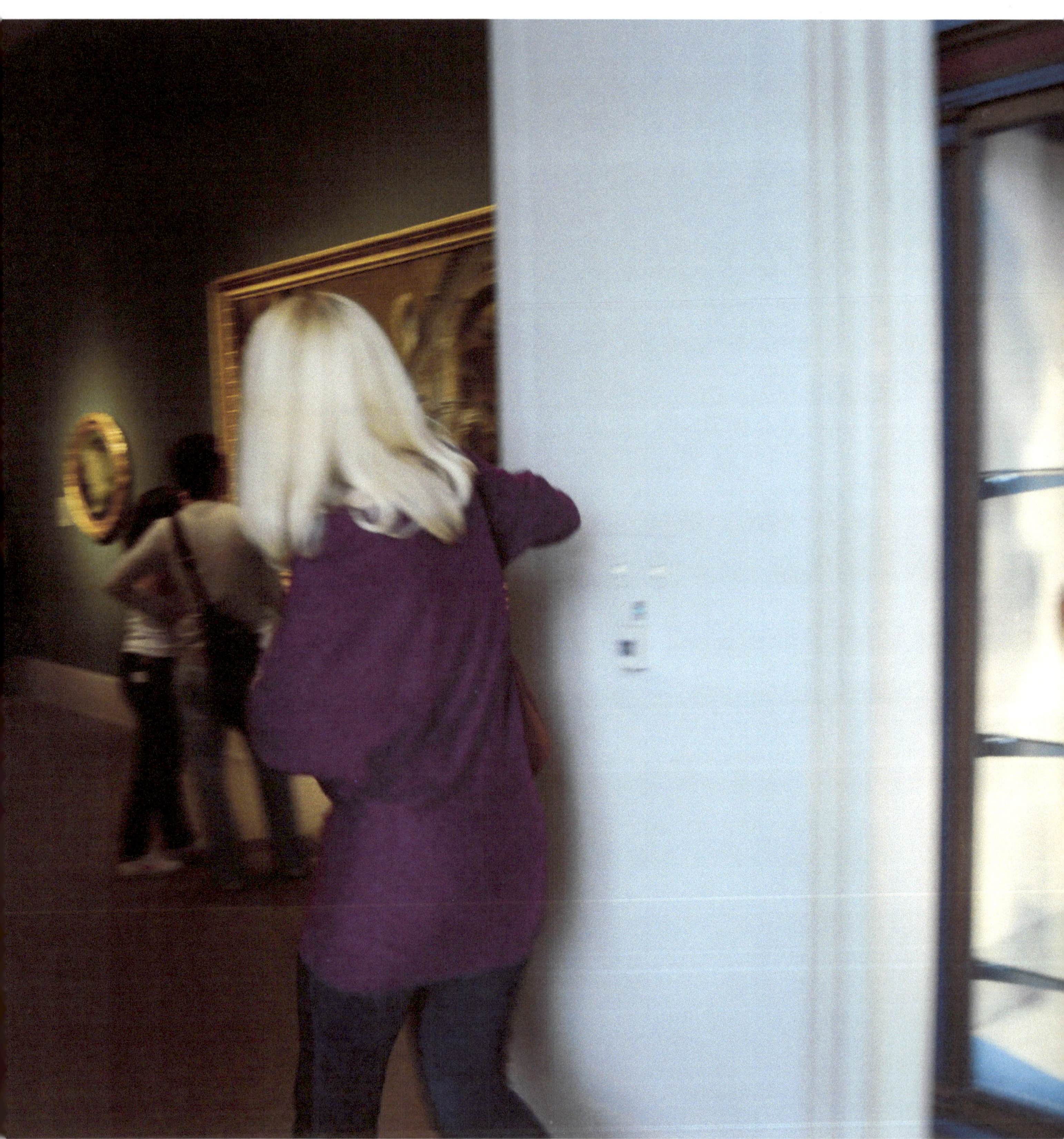

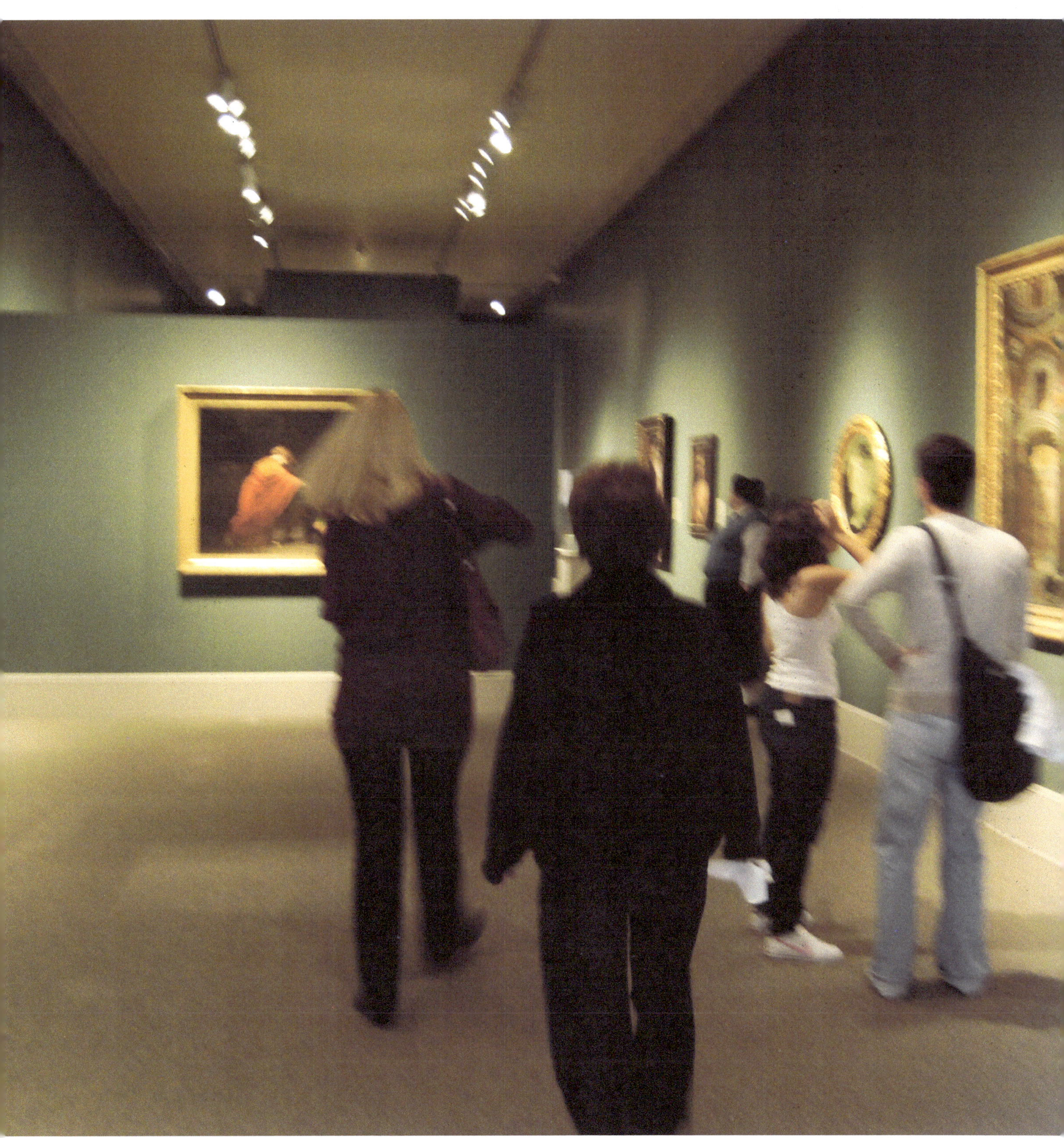

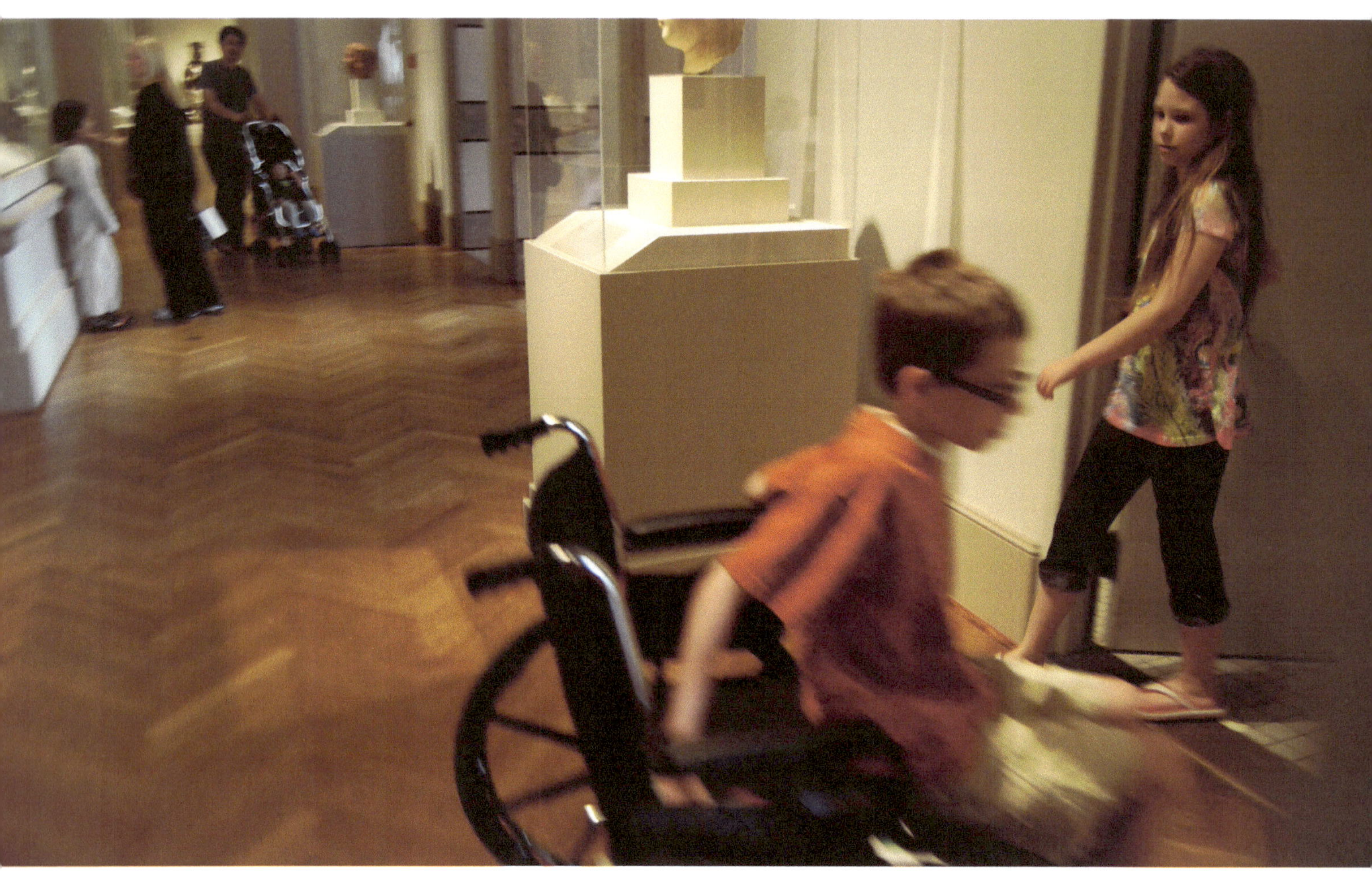

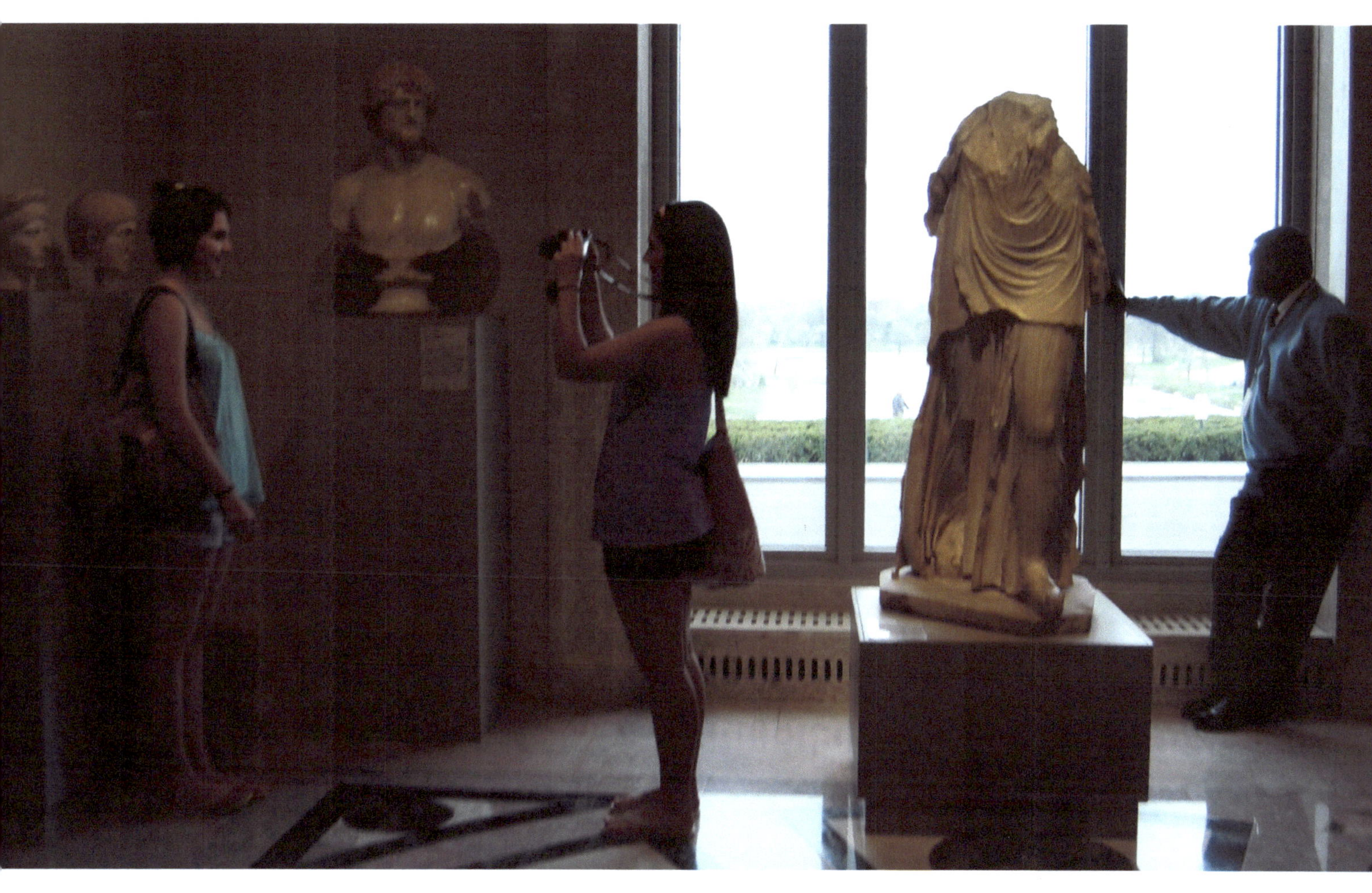

Nelson-Atkins Museum of Art in Kansas City, MO

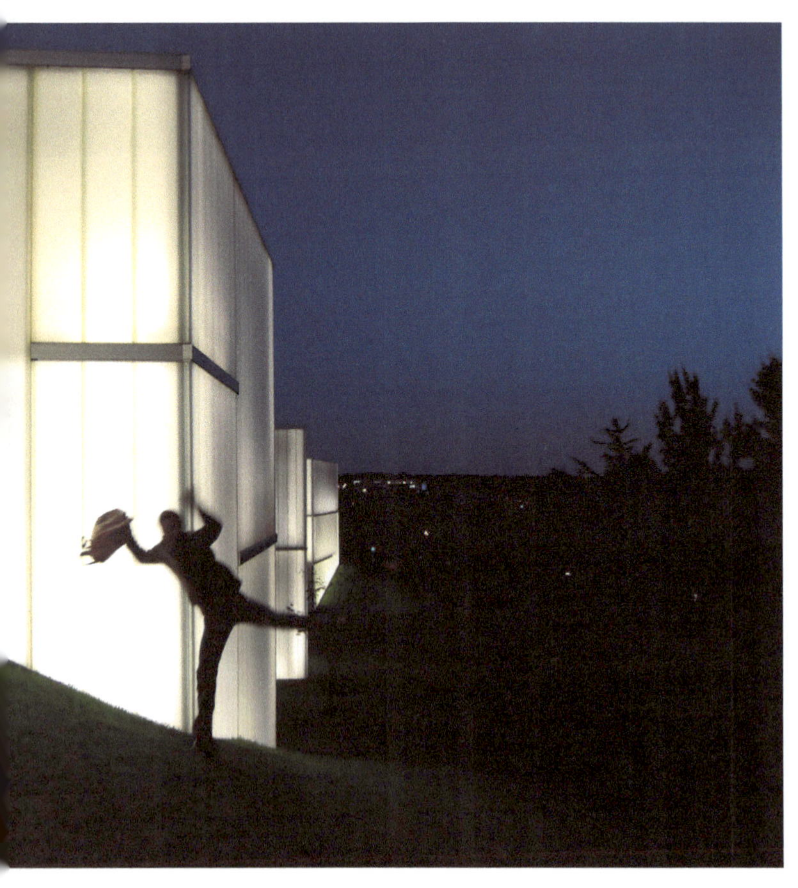

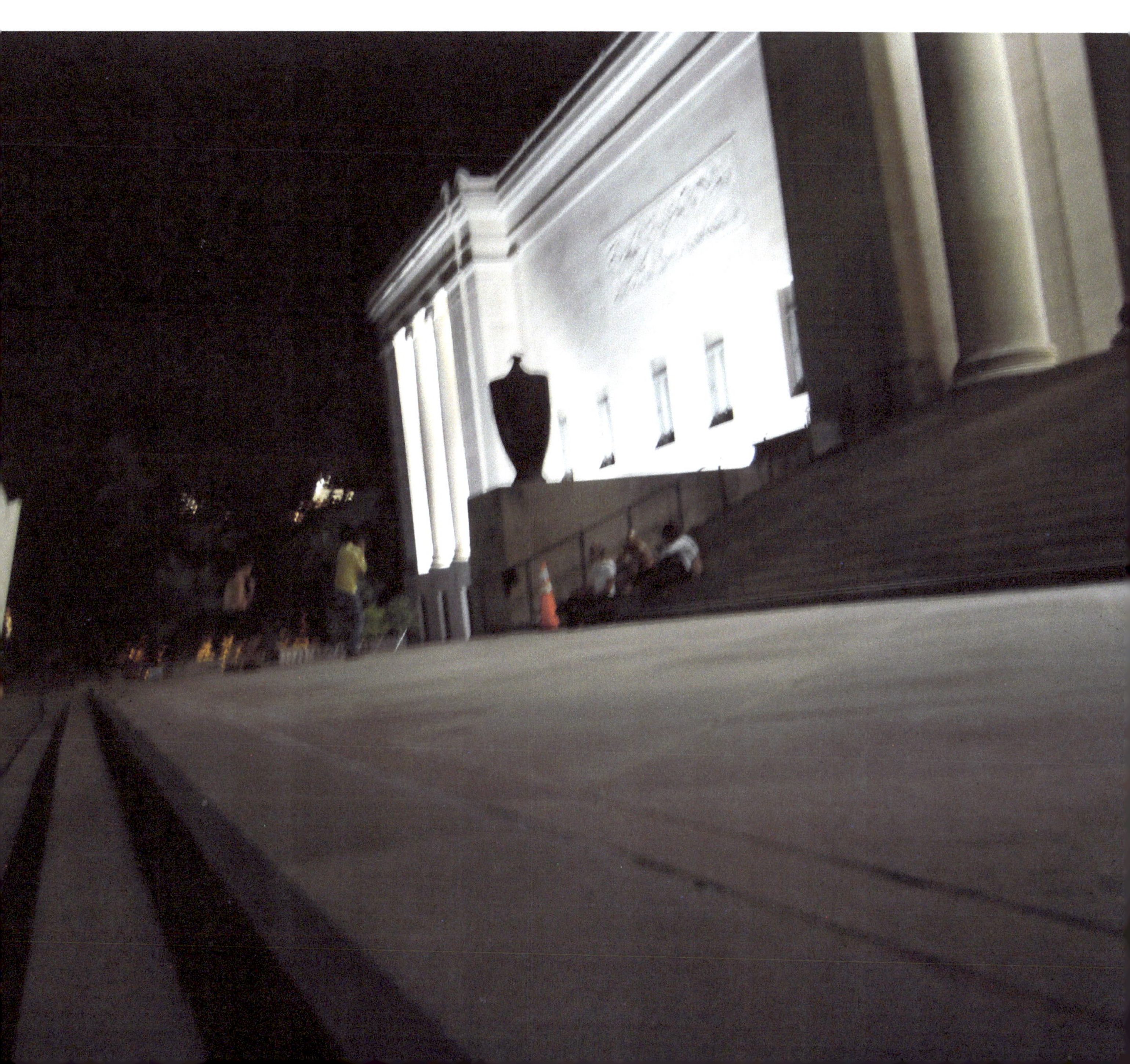

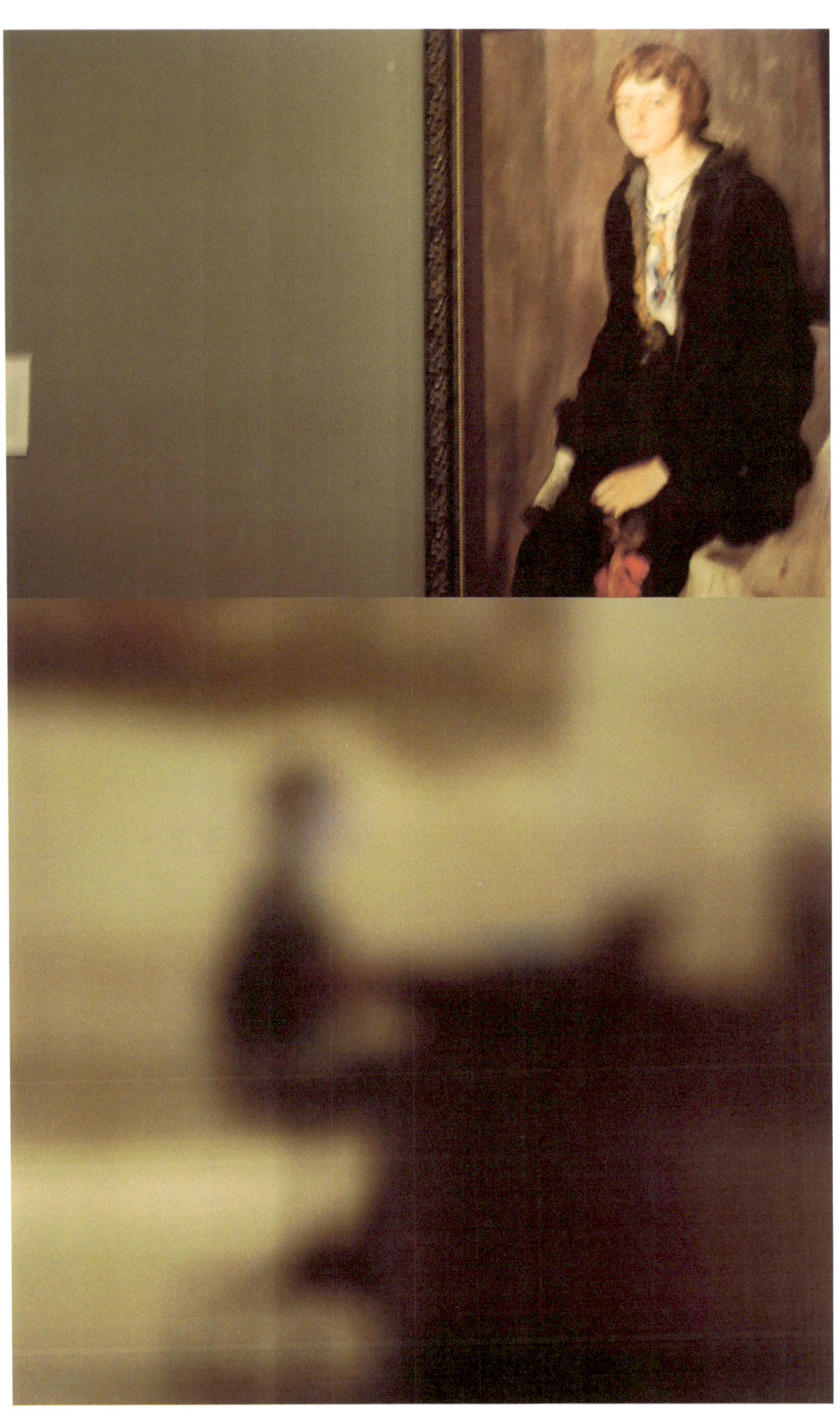

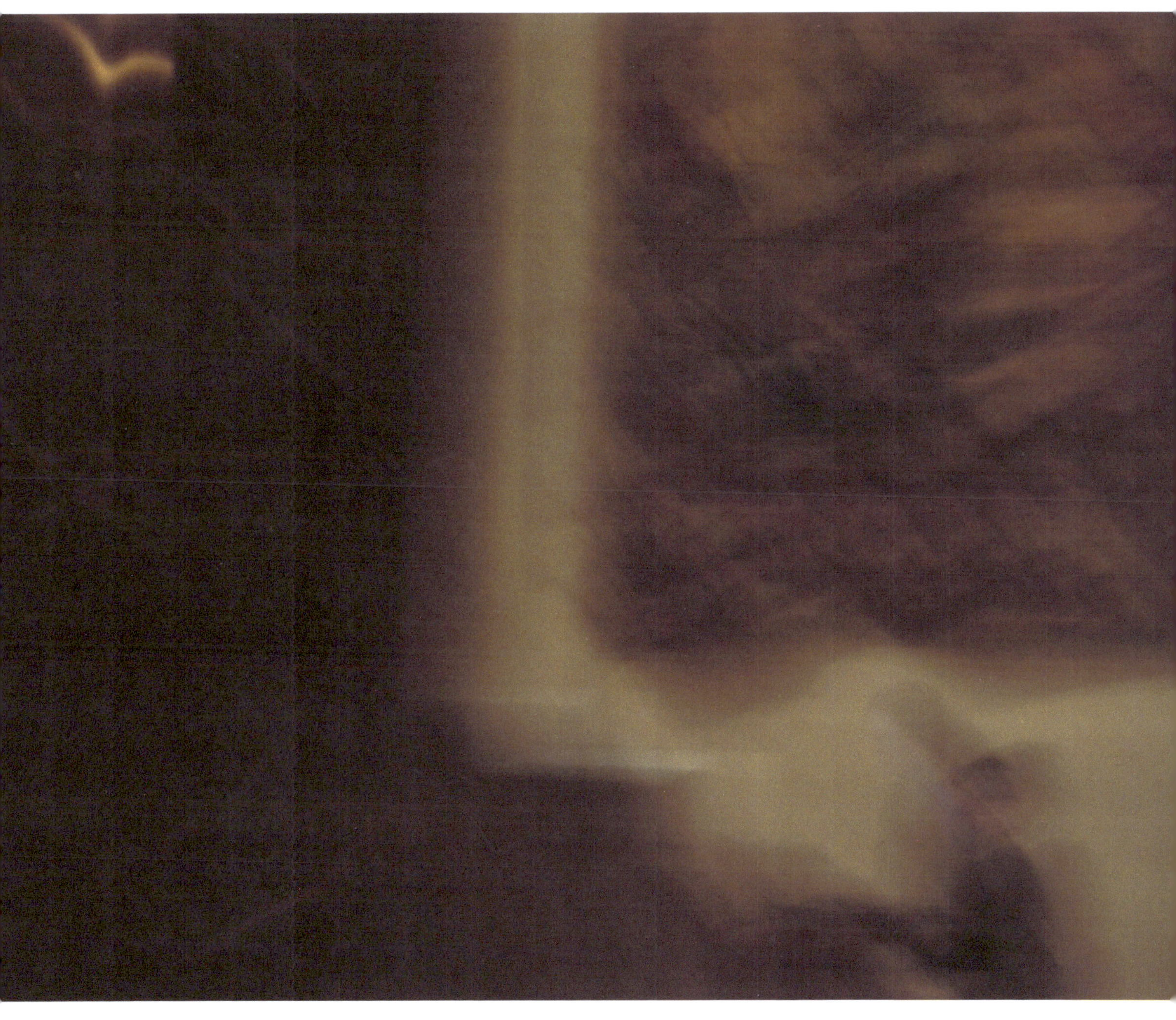

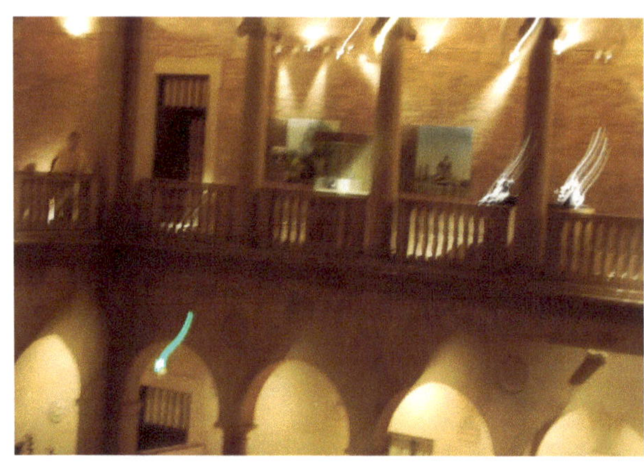

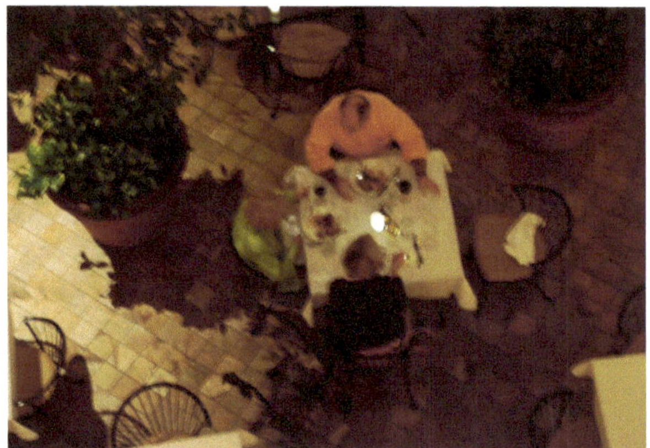

Violinist in Rozelle Court

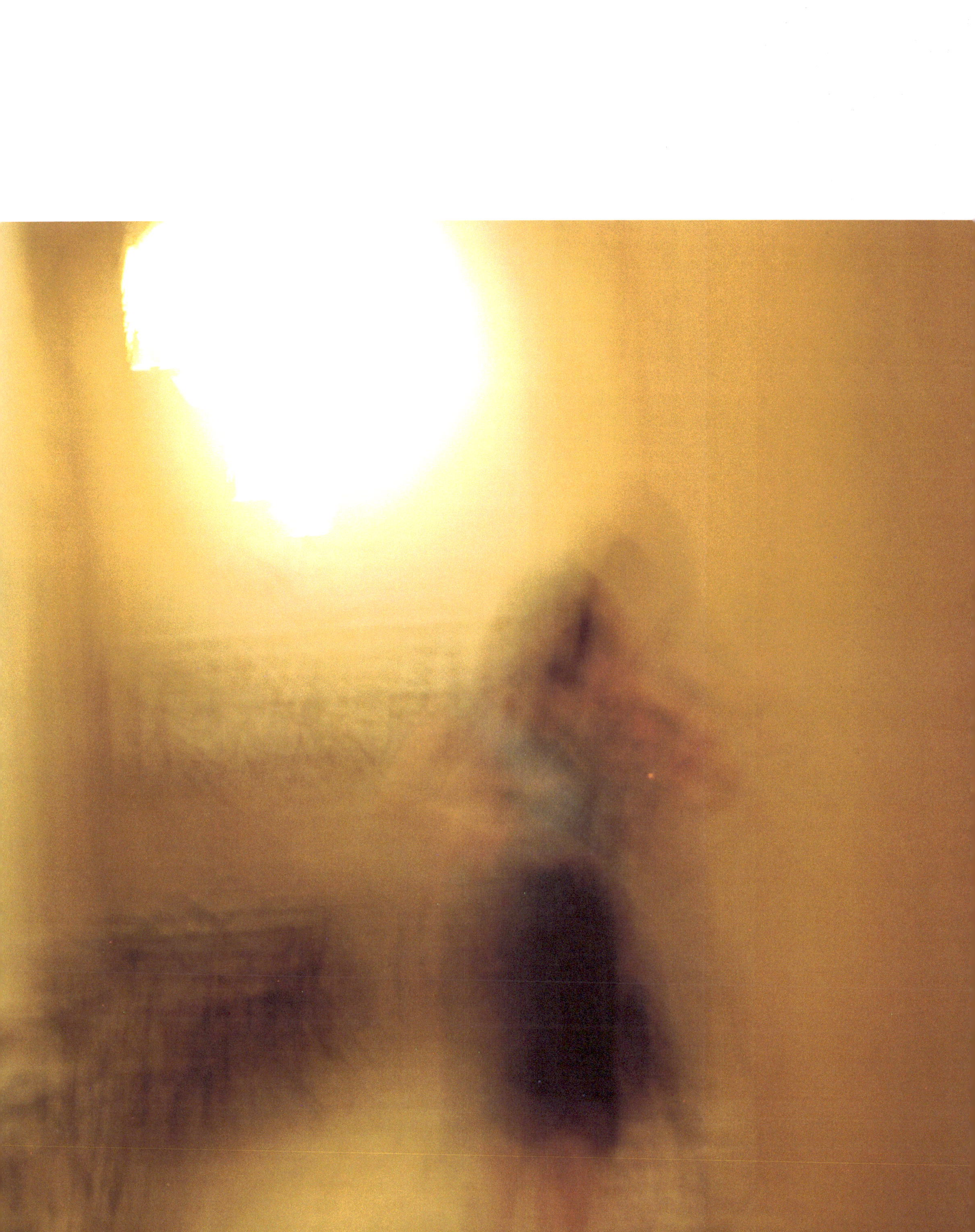

Joseph Wright of Derby (1734-1797)
Sir George Cooke, Bart., ca. 1766-1768 >

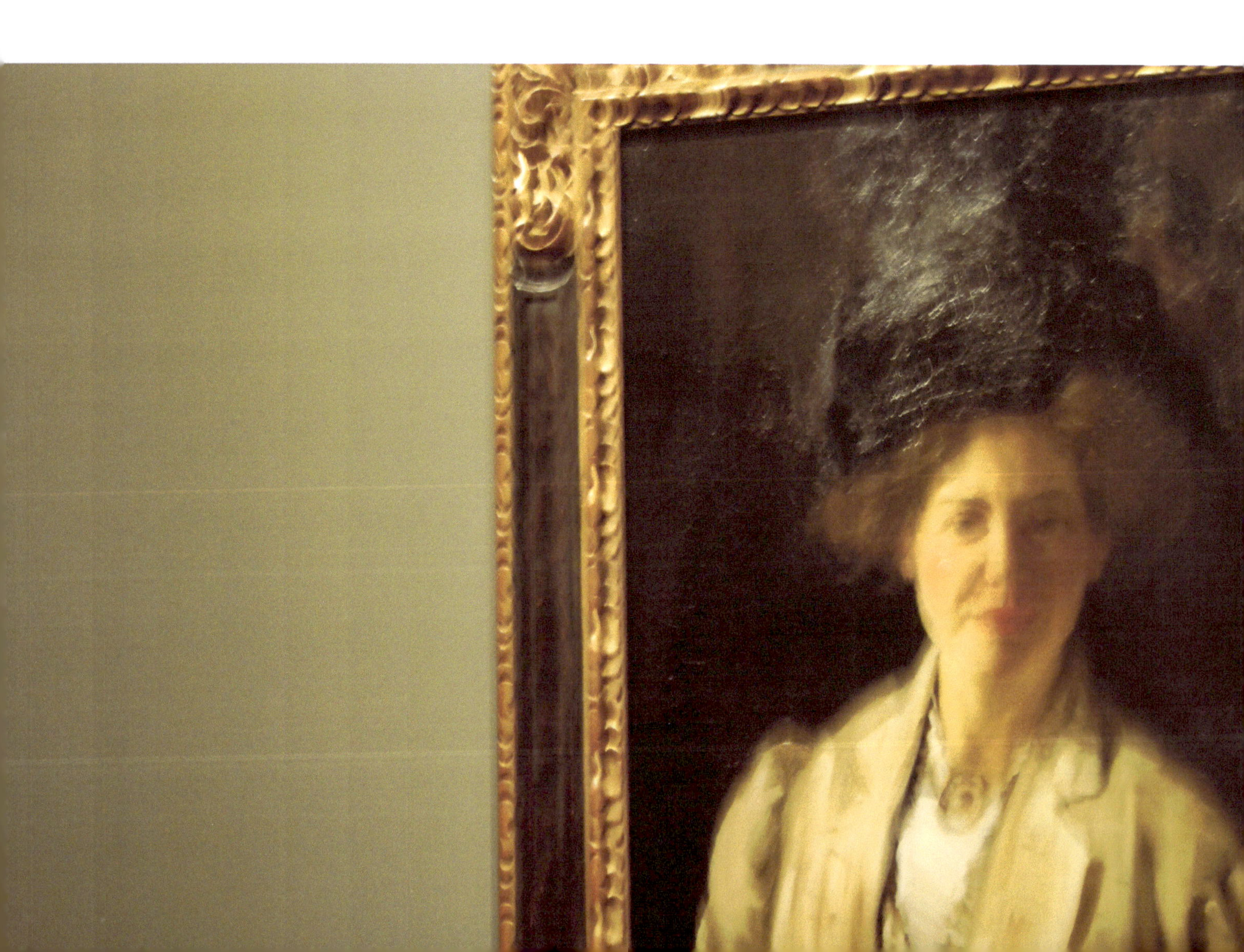

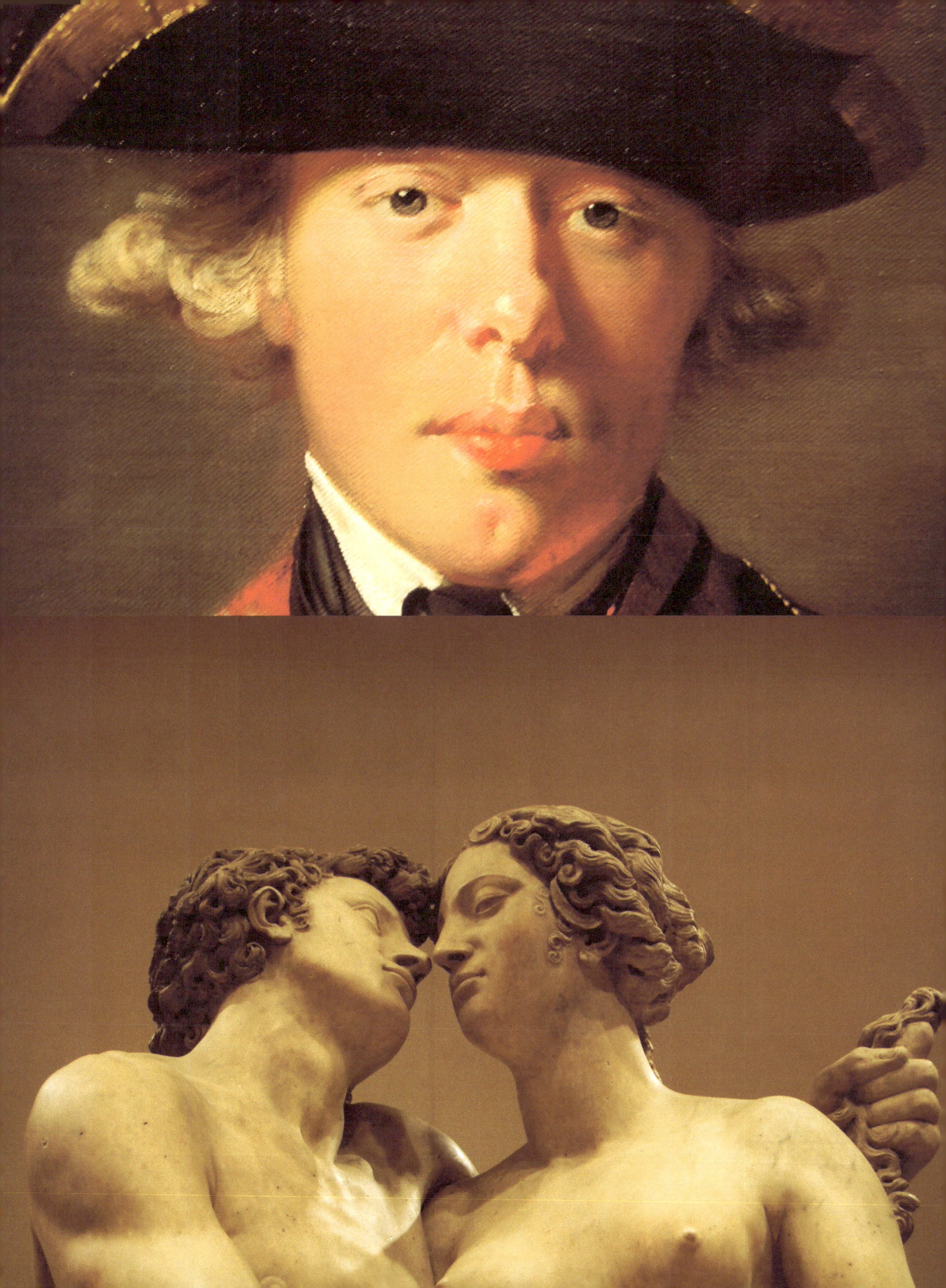

Nelson-Atkins Museum of Art in Kansas City, MO

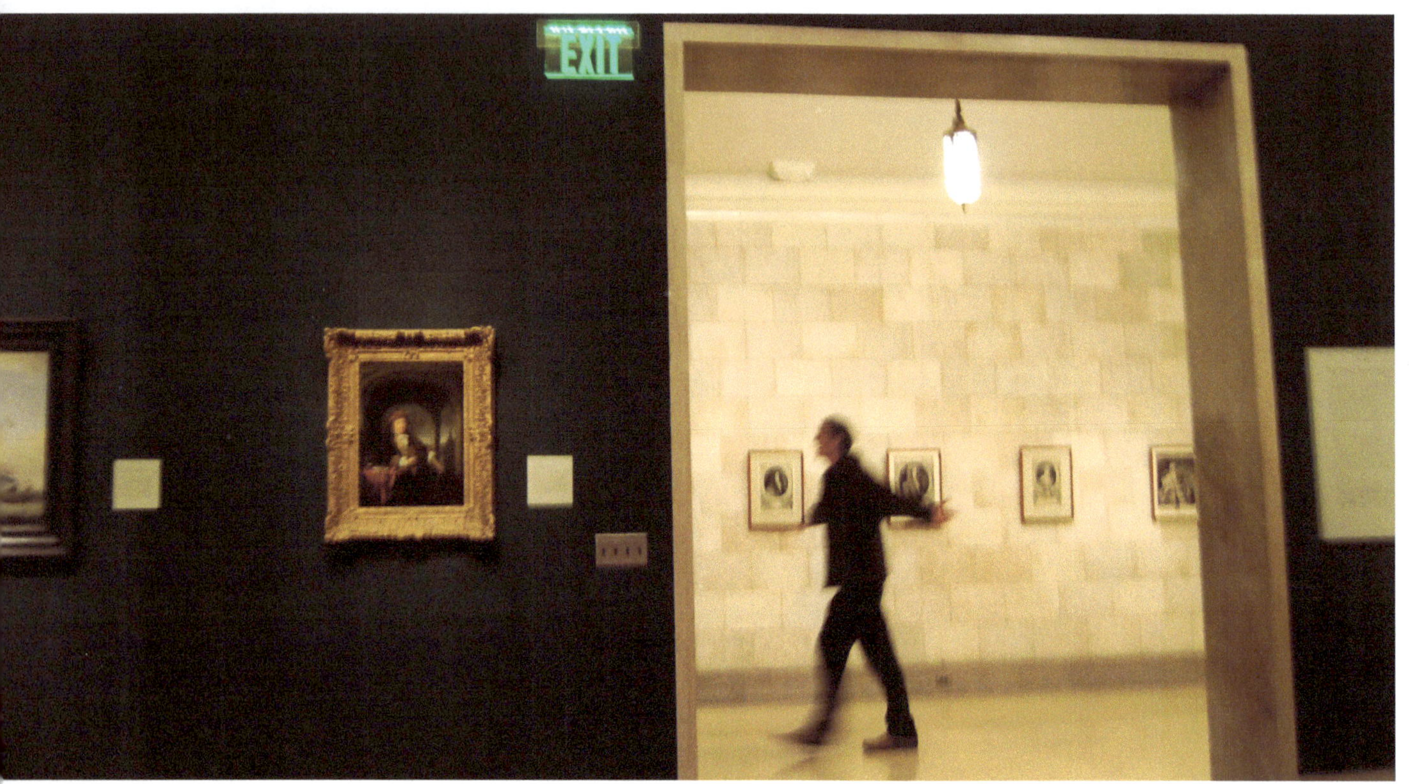

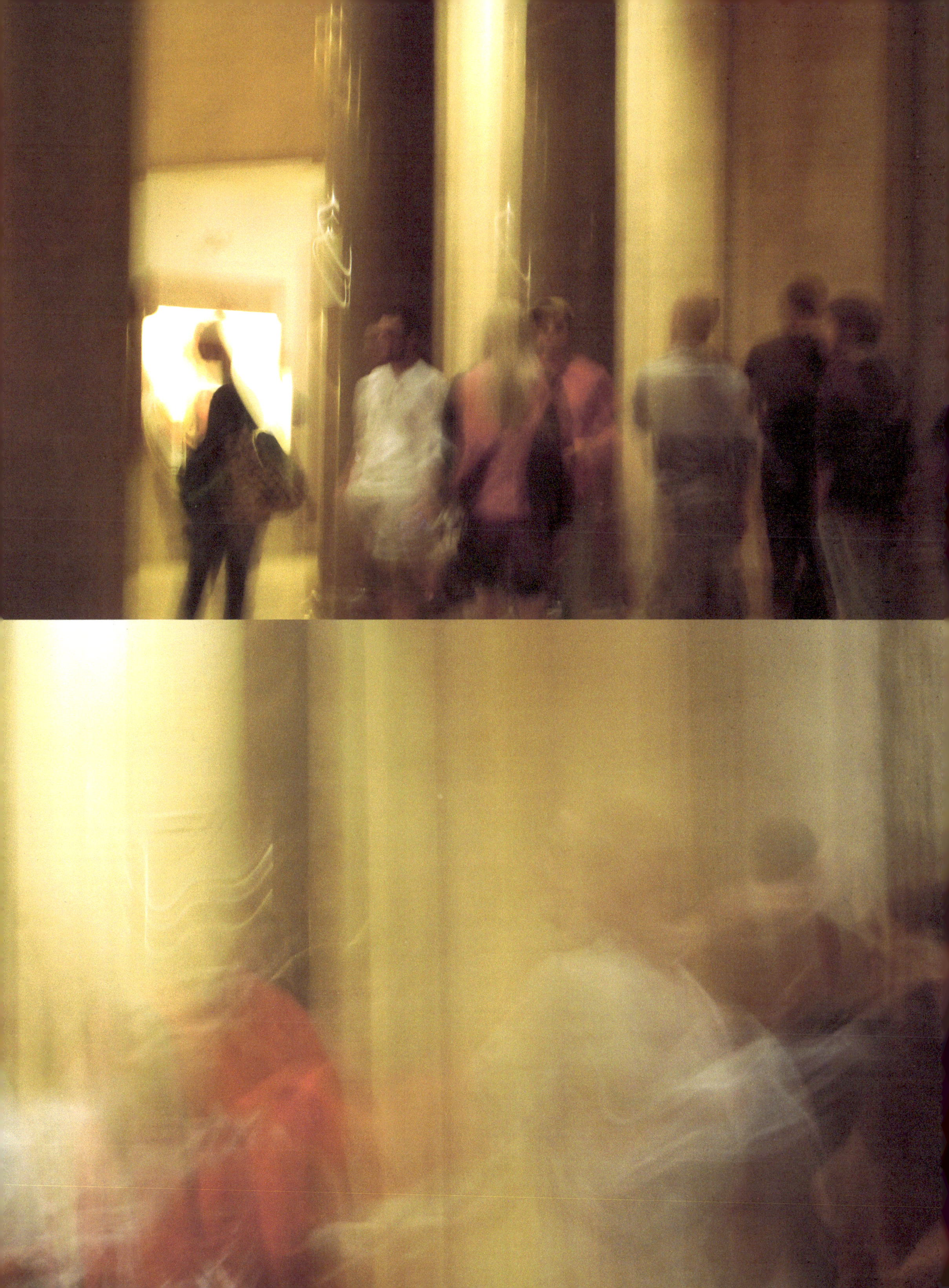

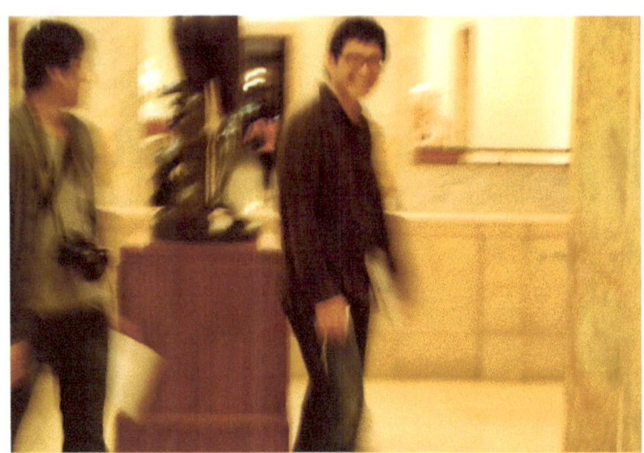

Second-year architecture students from Iowa State University exploring the Nelson-Atkins Museum of Art (pages 184-190)

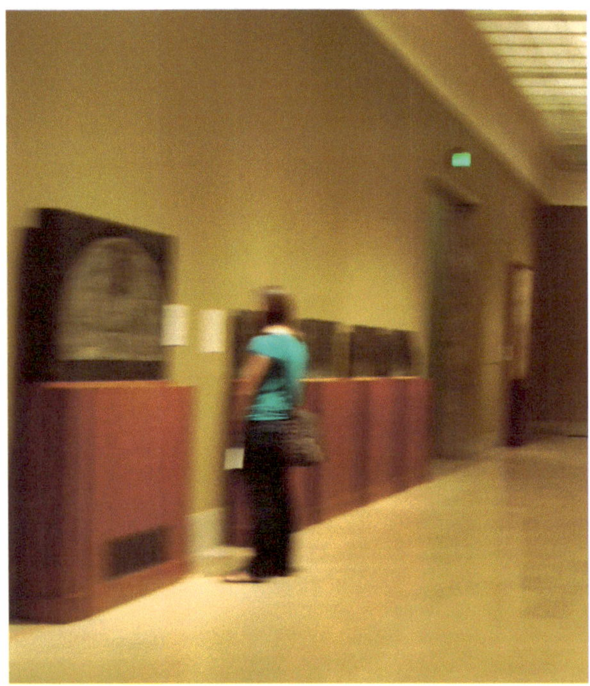

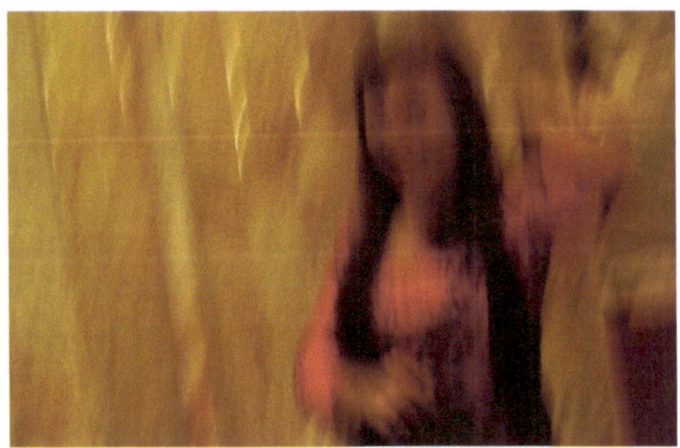

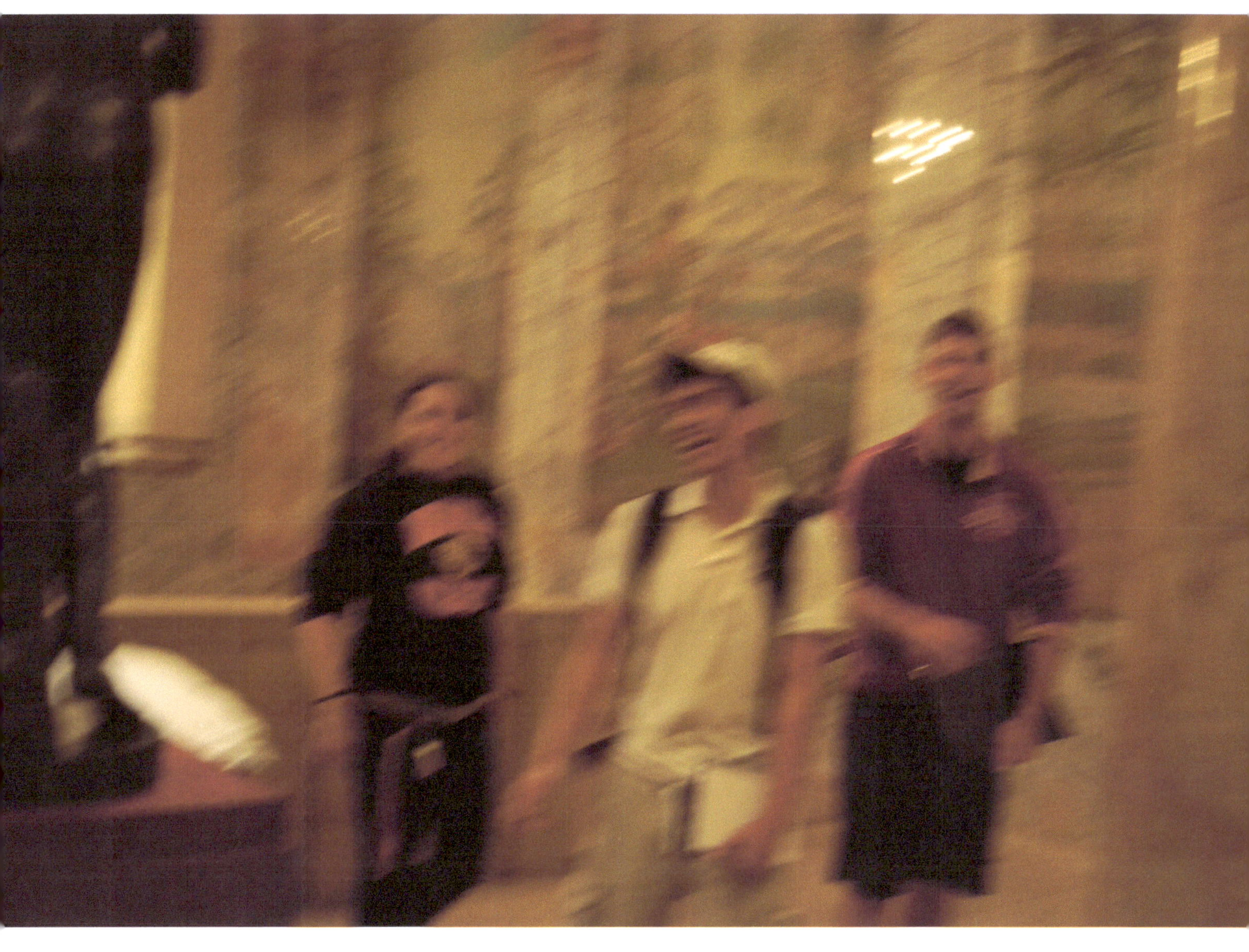

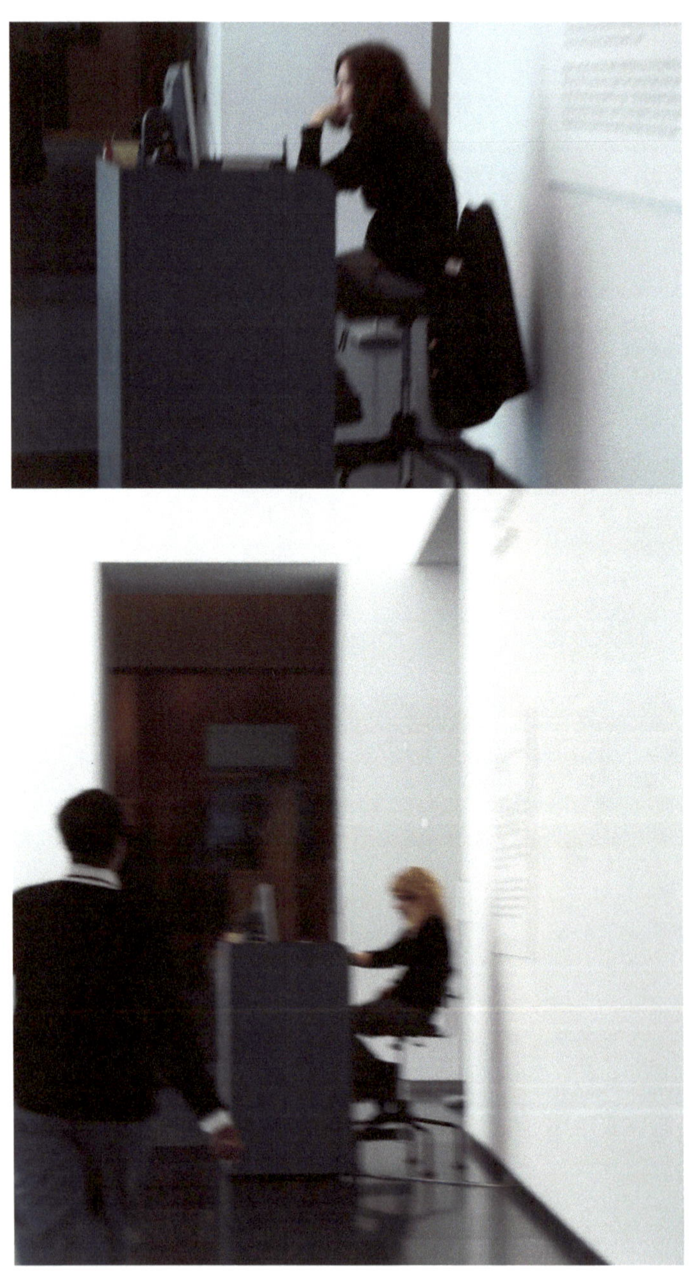

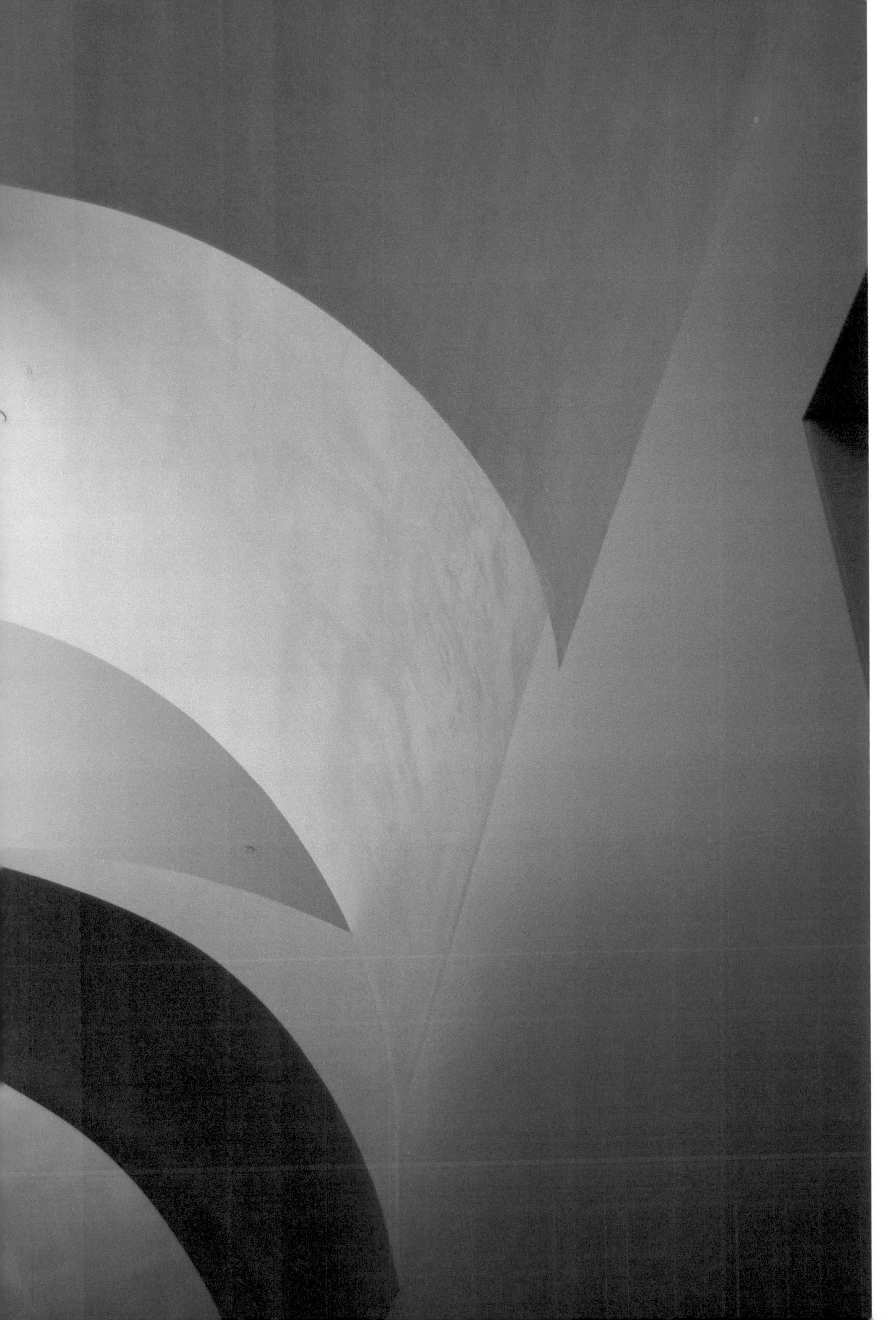

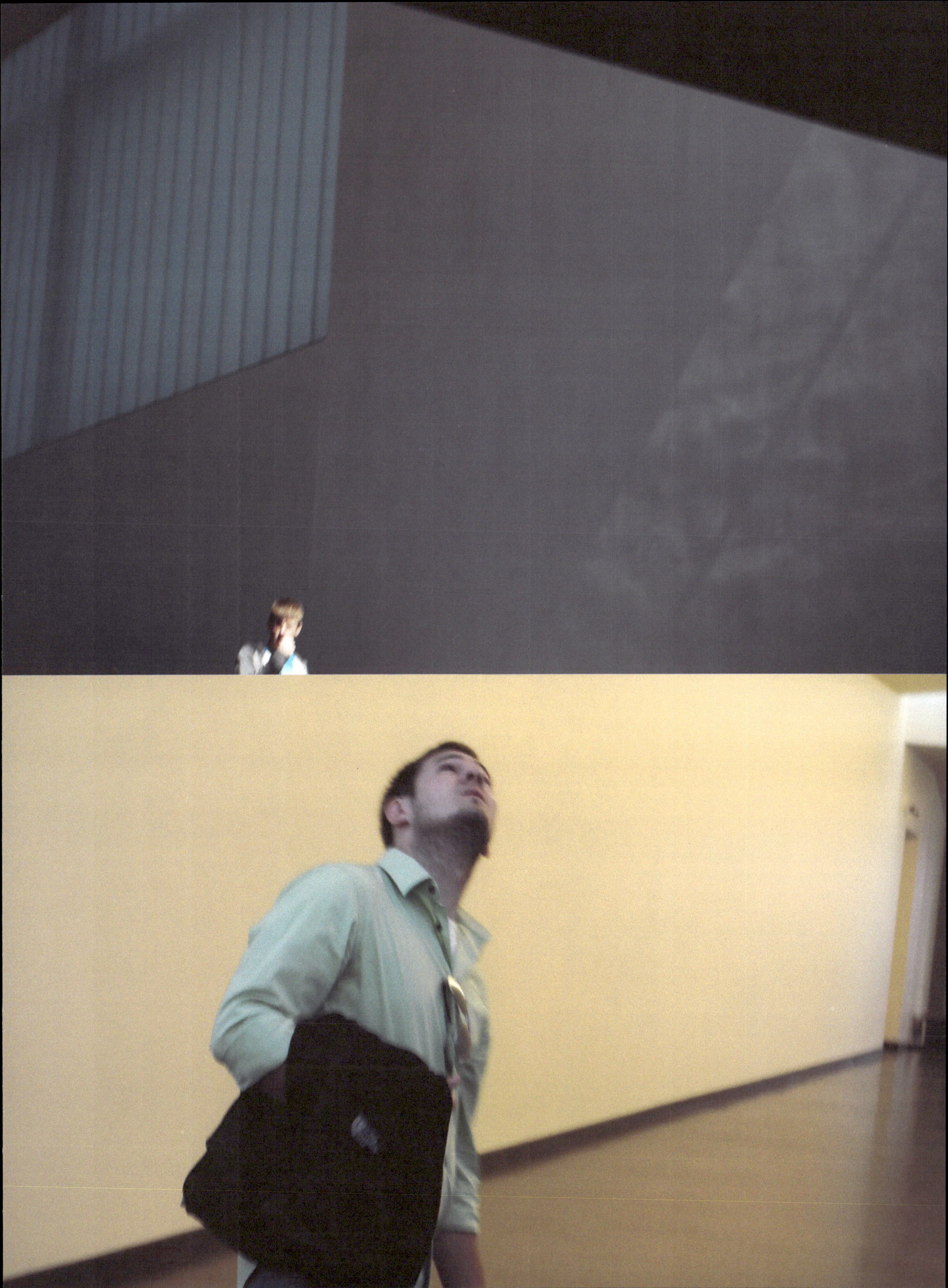

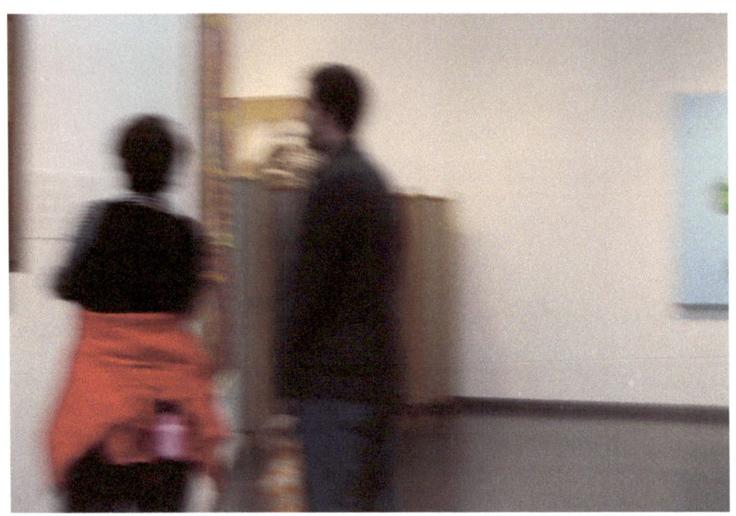

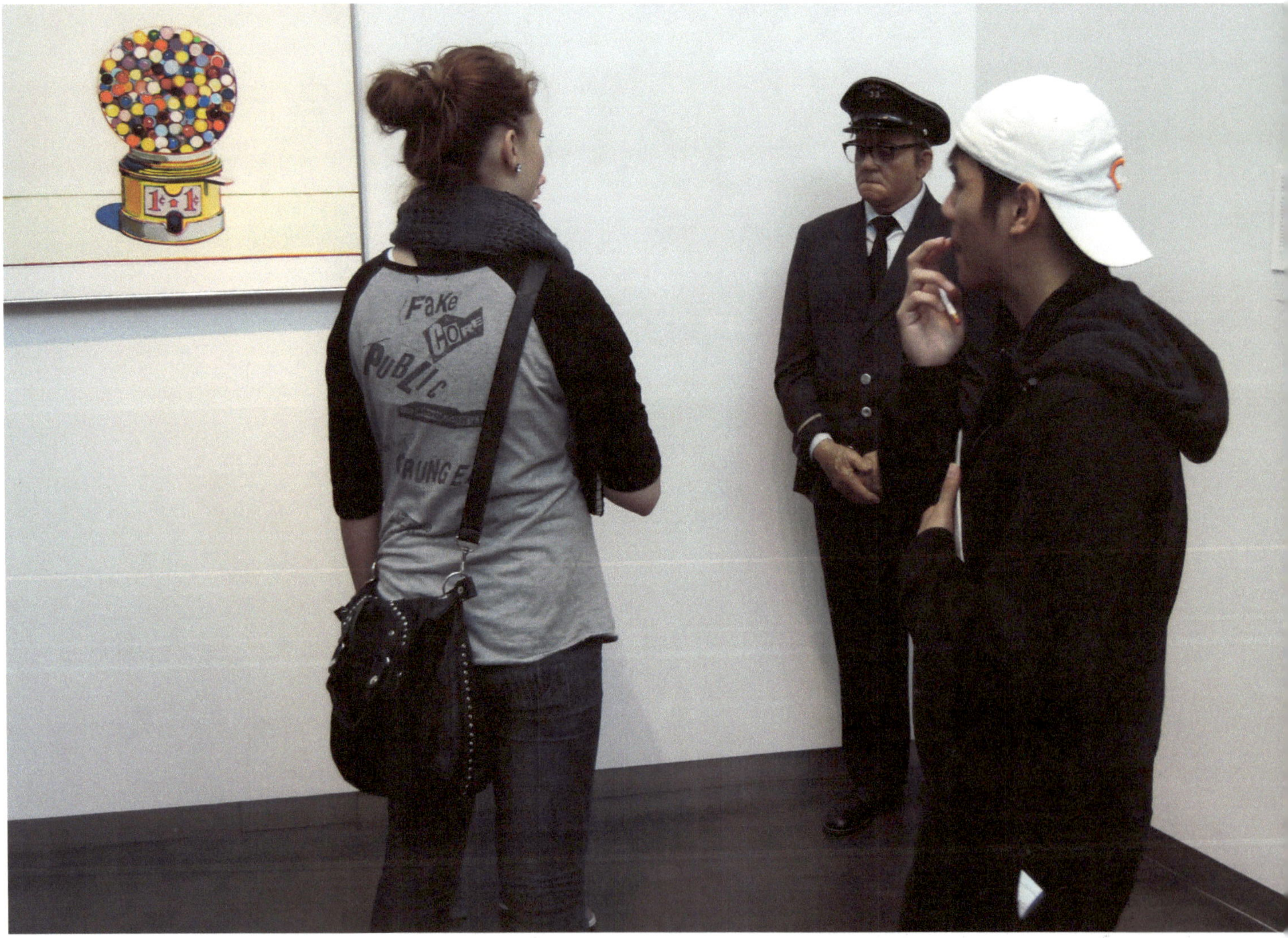

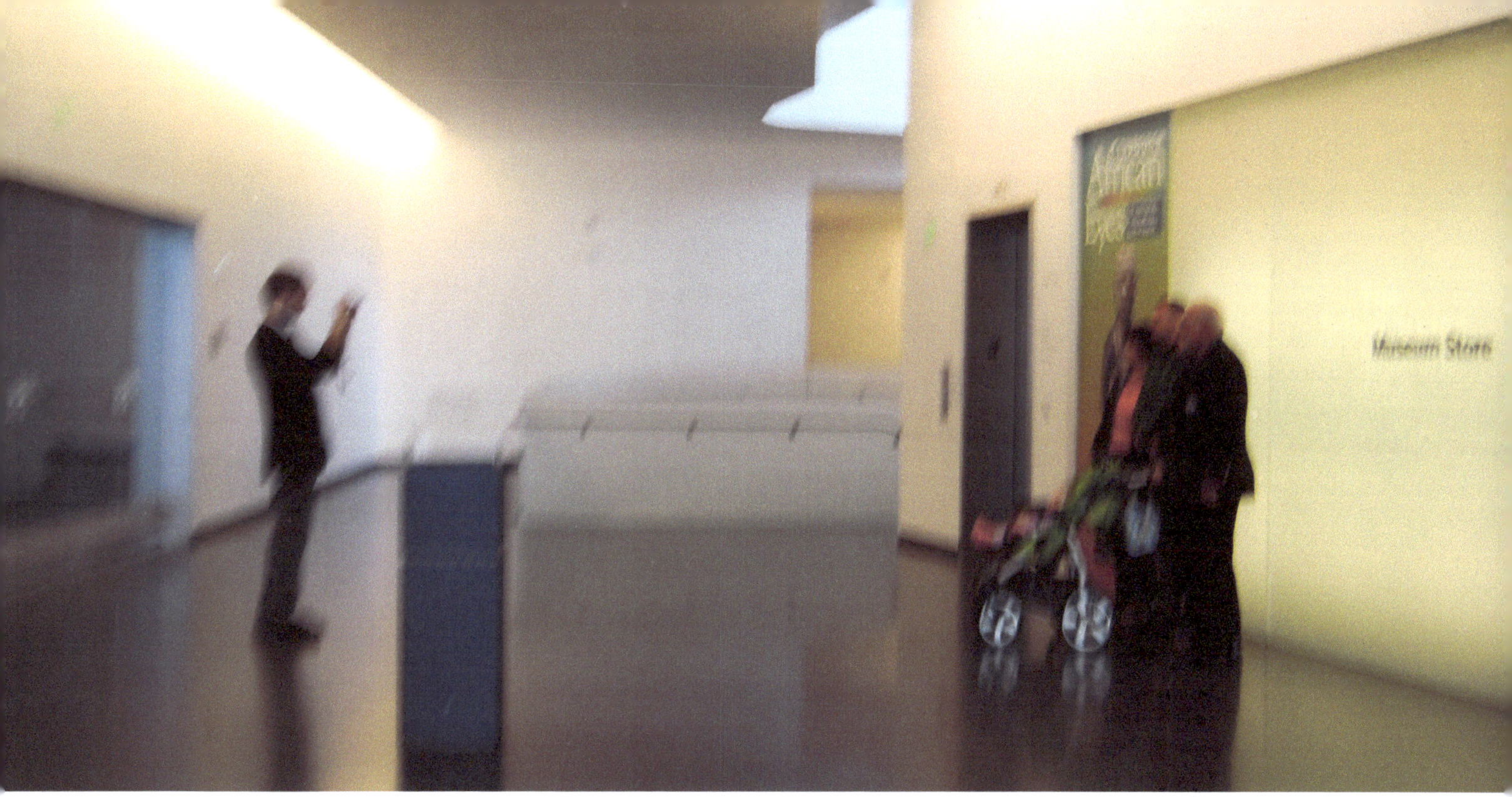

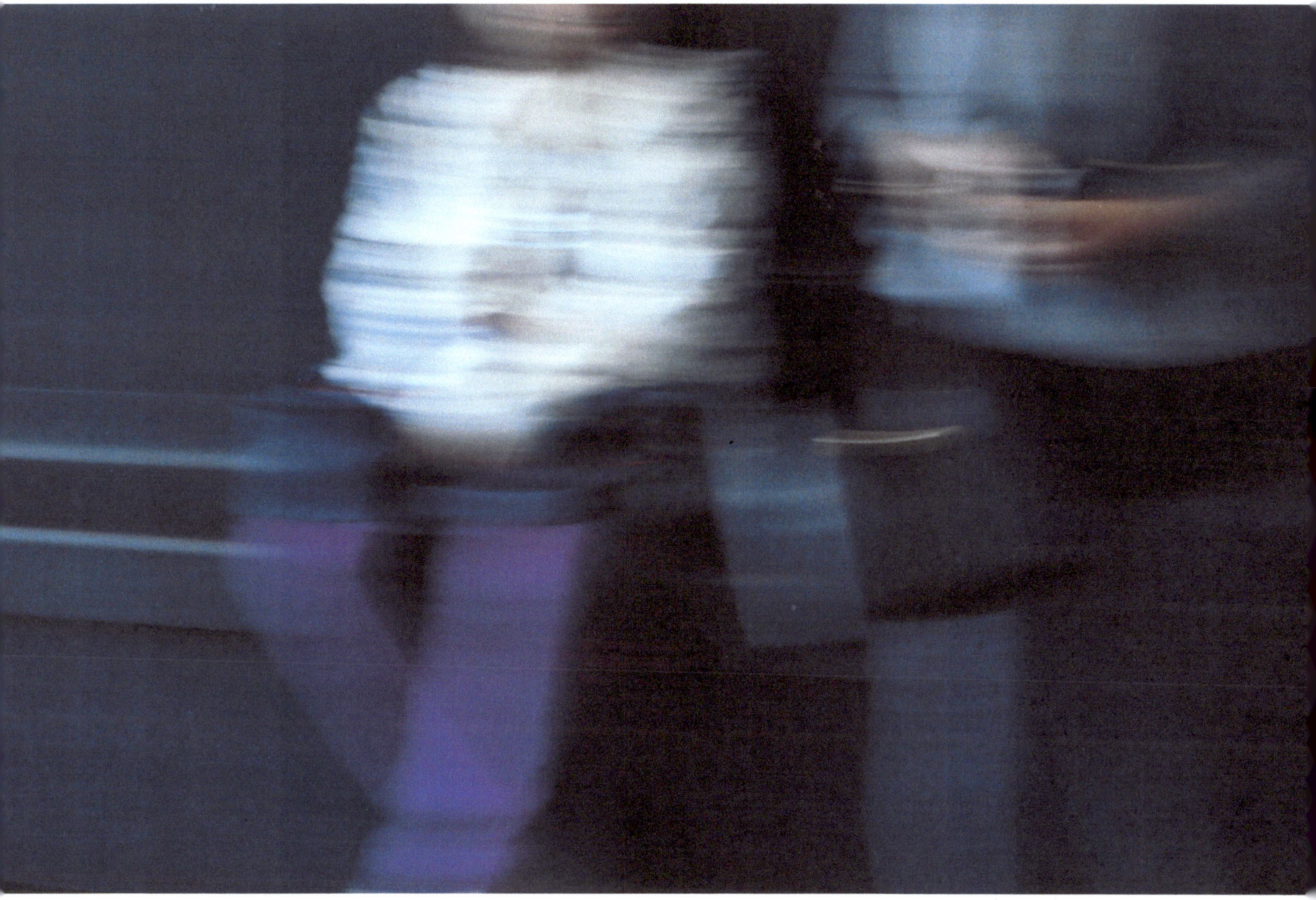

Nelson-Atkins Museum of Art in Kansas City, MO

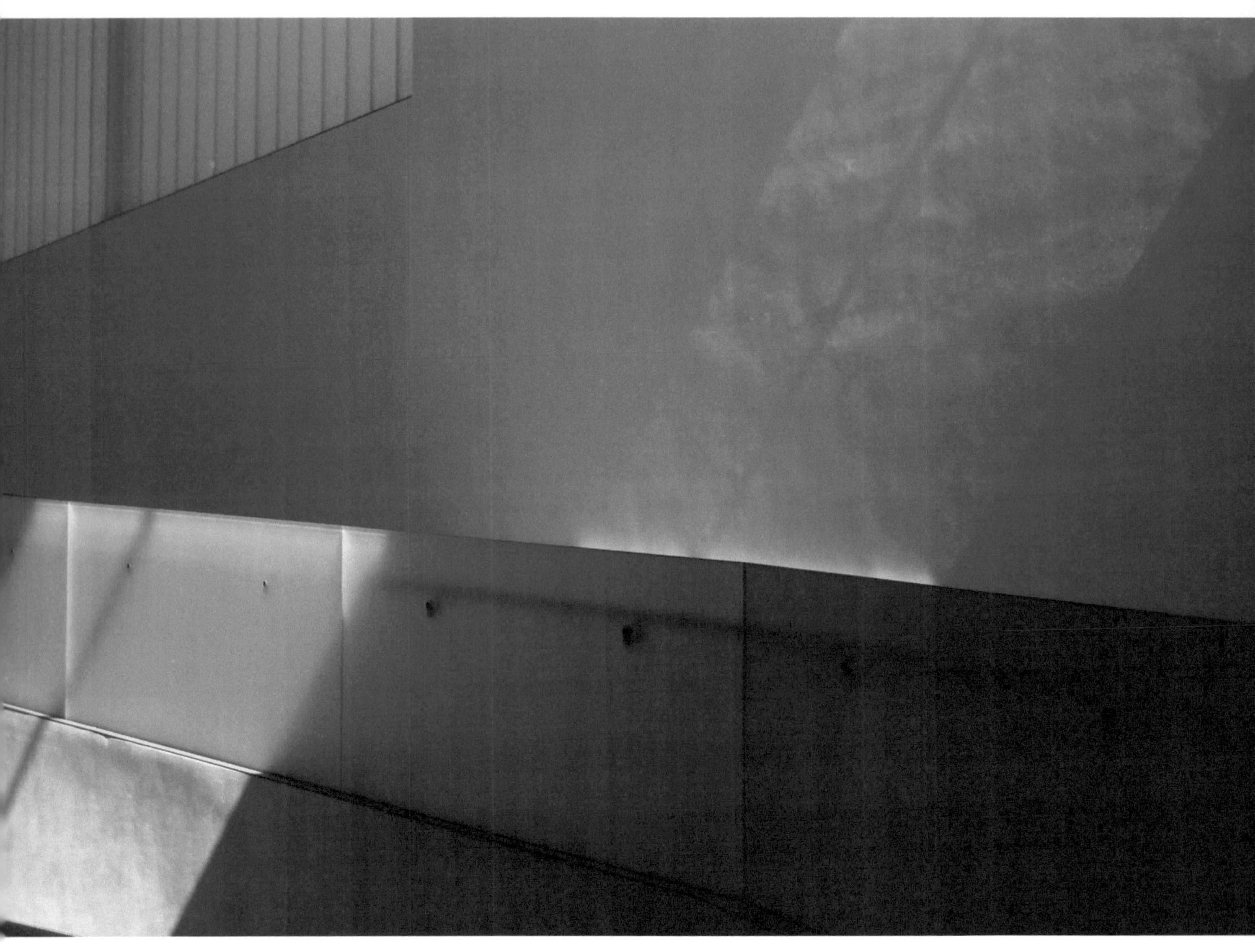

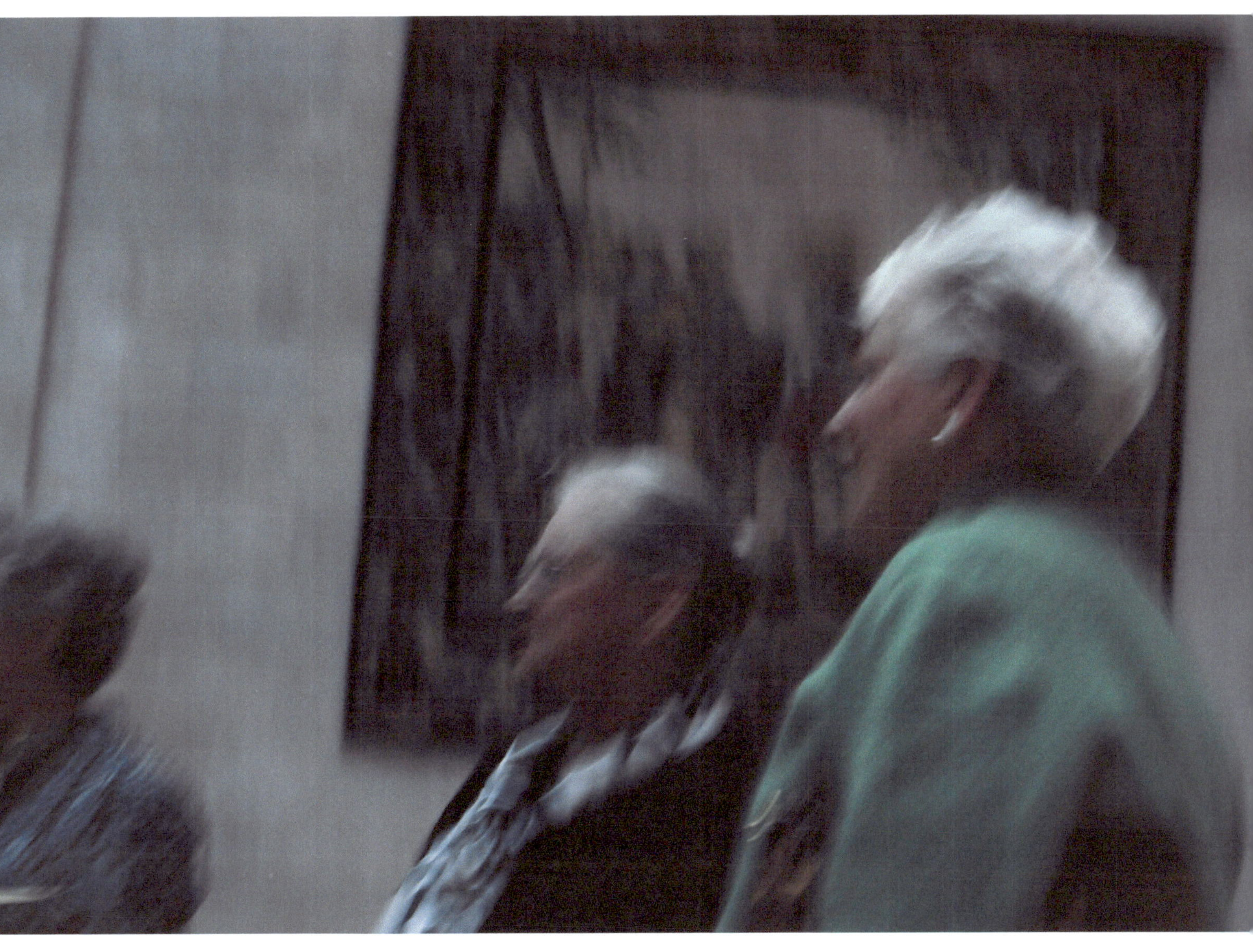

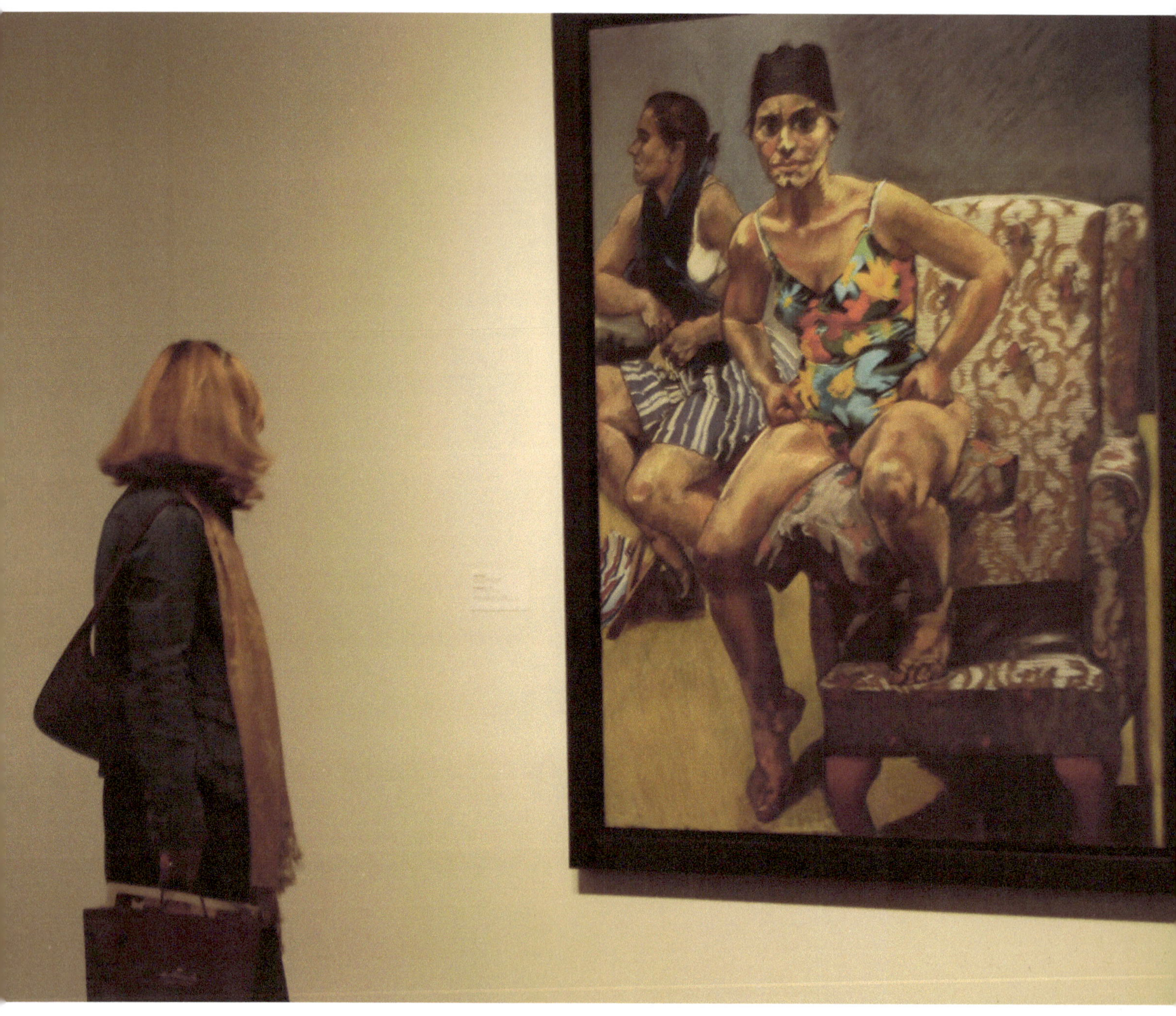

Gao Brothers
The Execution of Christ (detail) >

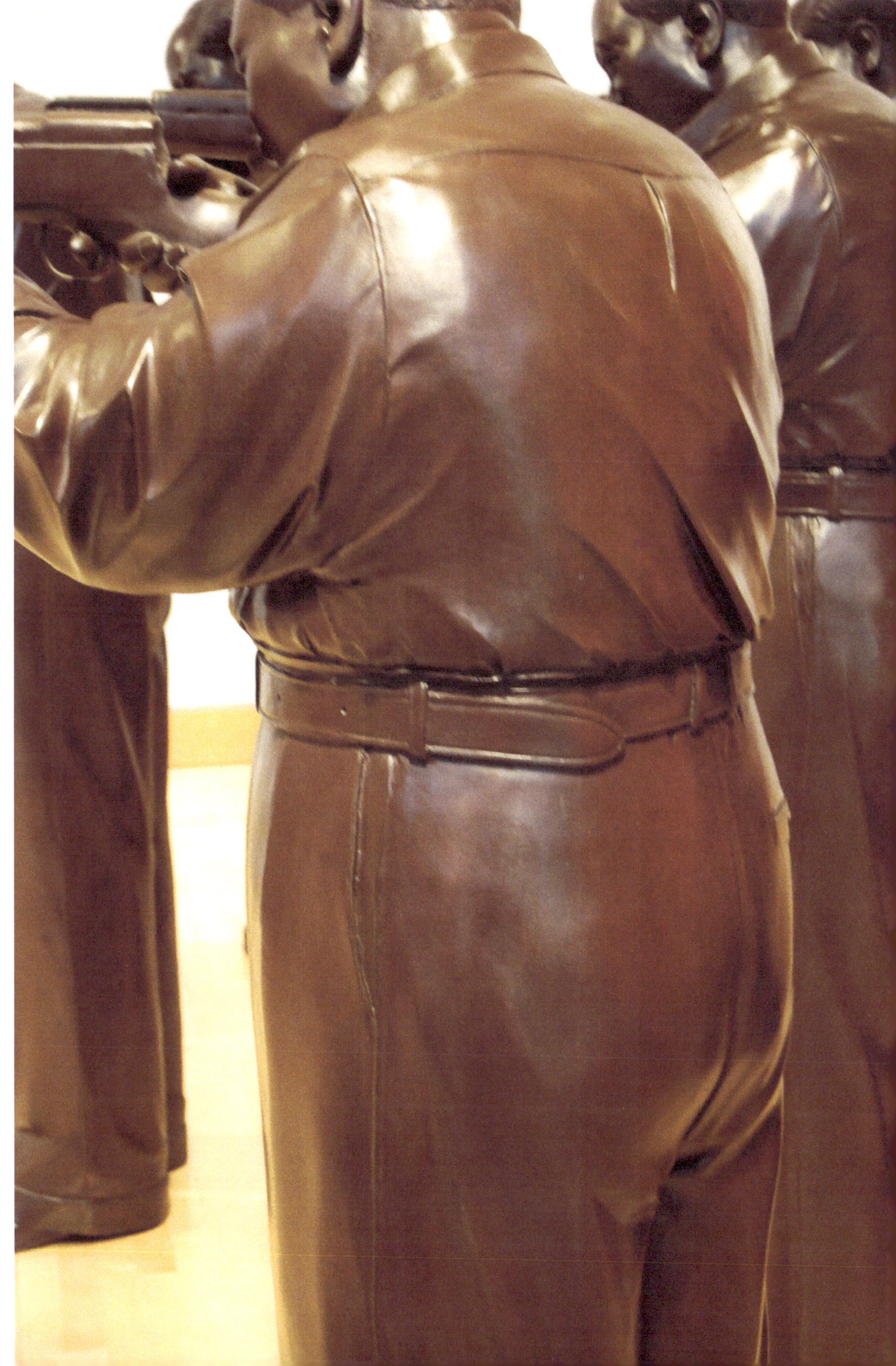

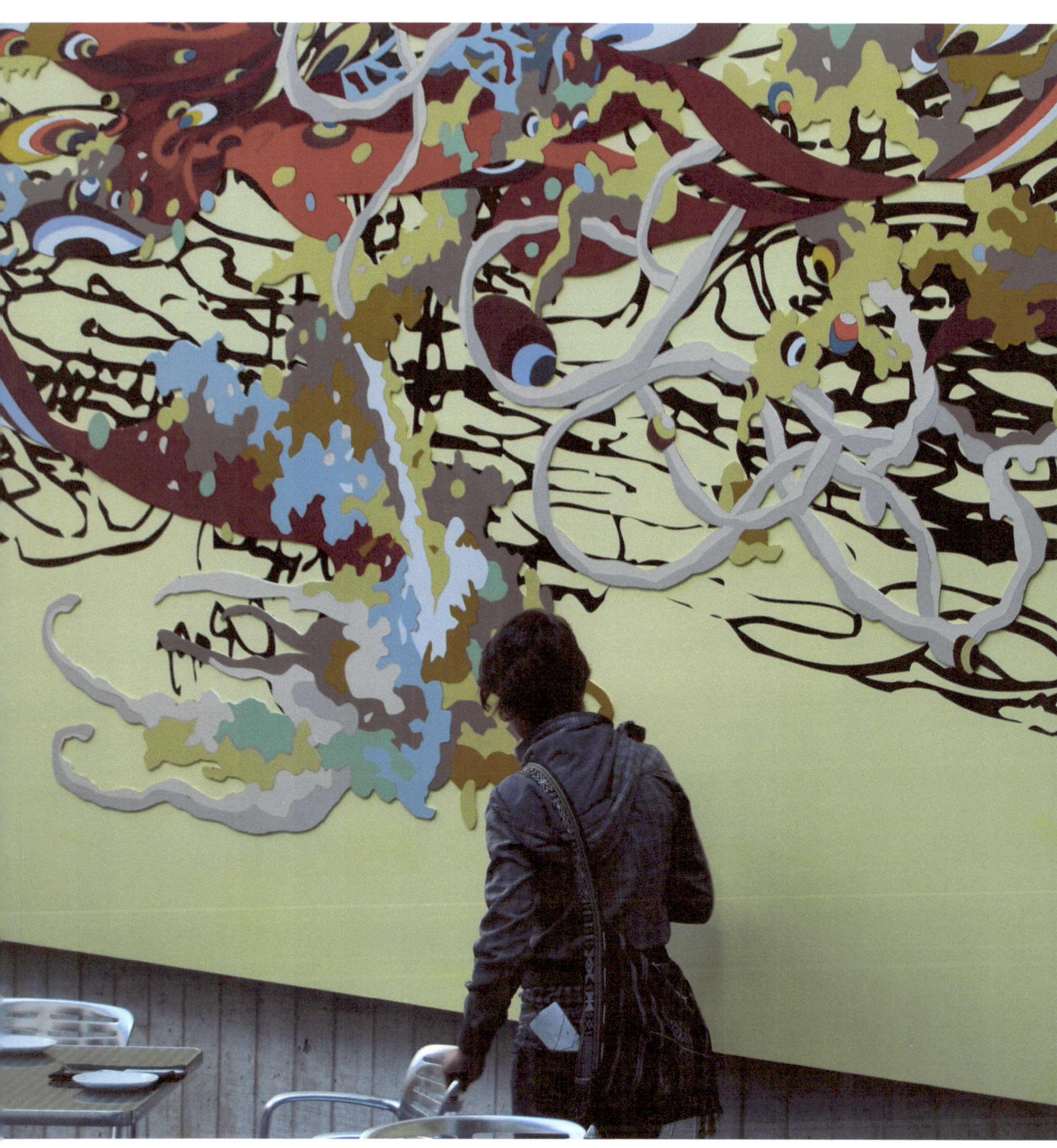

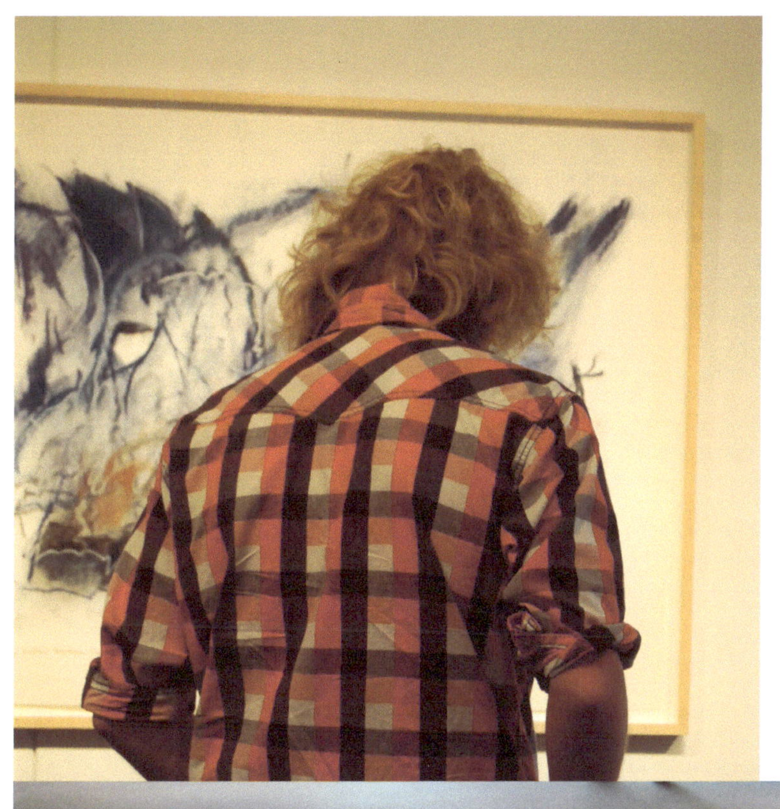

Second-year architecture students and faculty from Iowa State University exploring the Kemper Museum of Contemporary Art (pages 196-199)

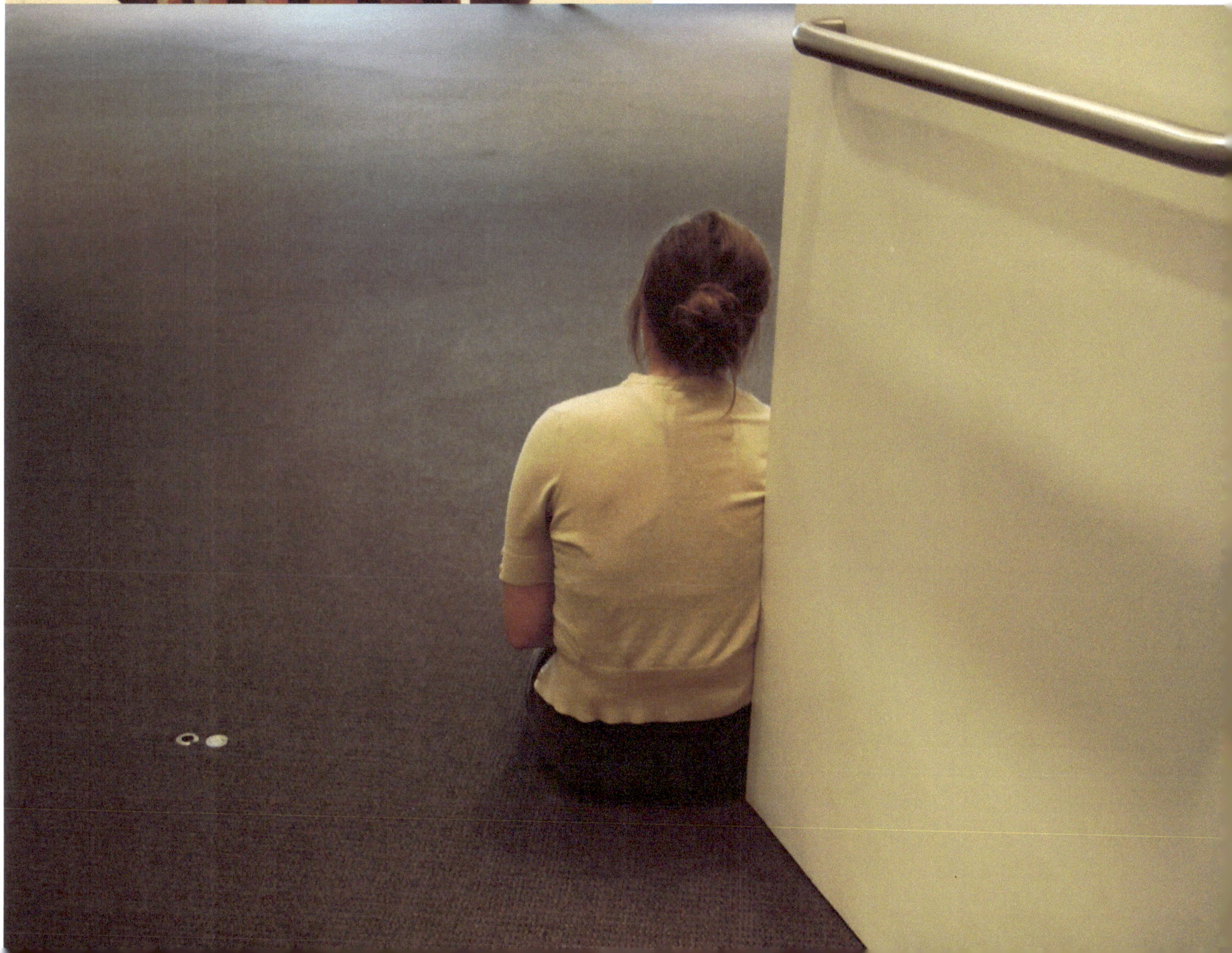

Kemper Museum of Contemporary Art in Kansas City, MO

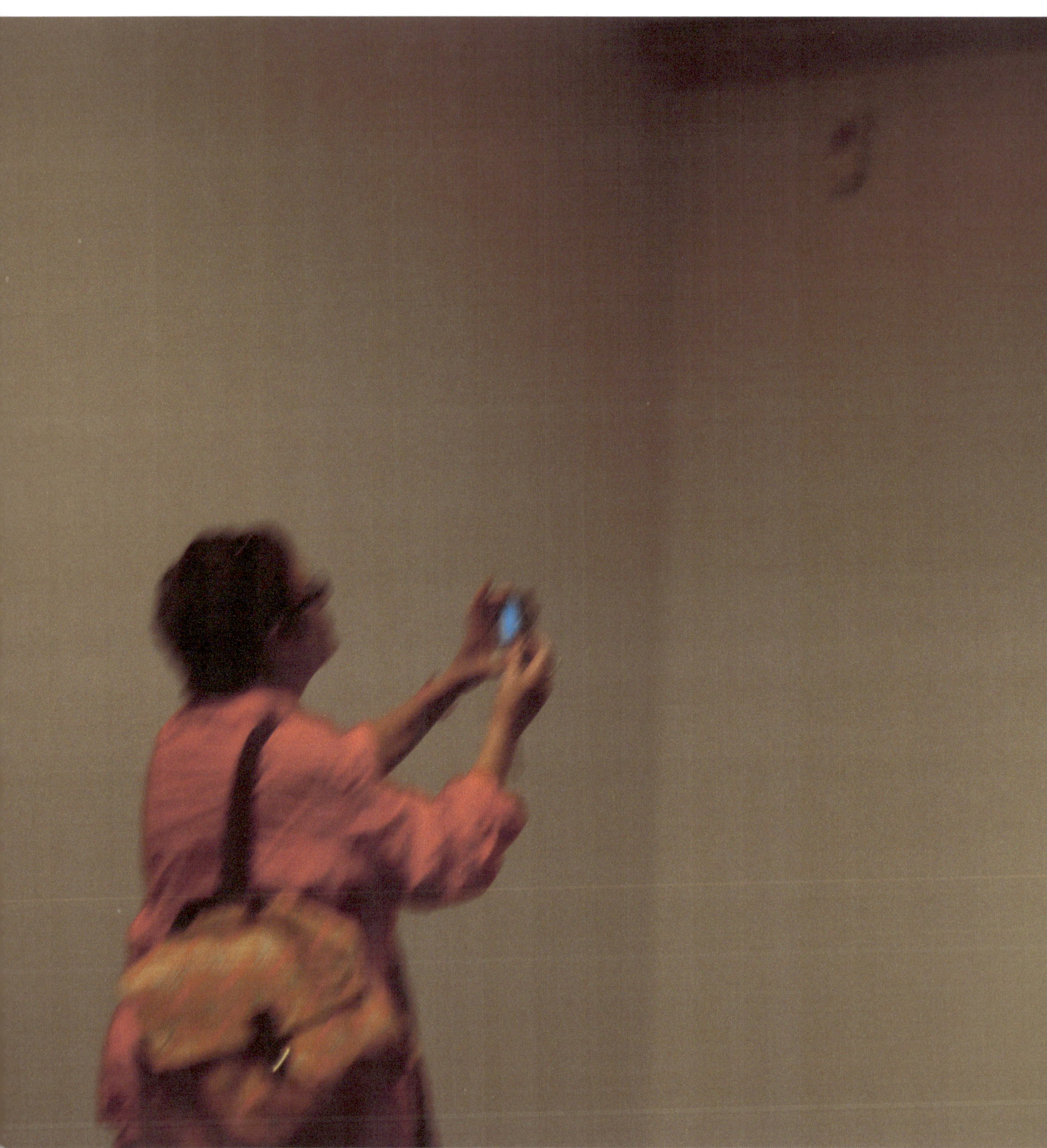

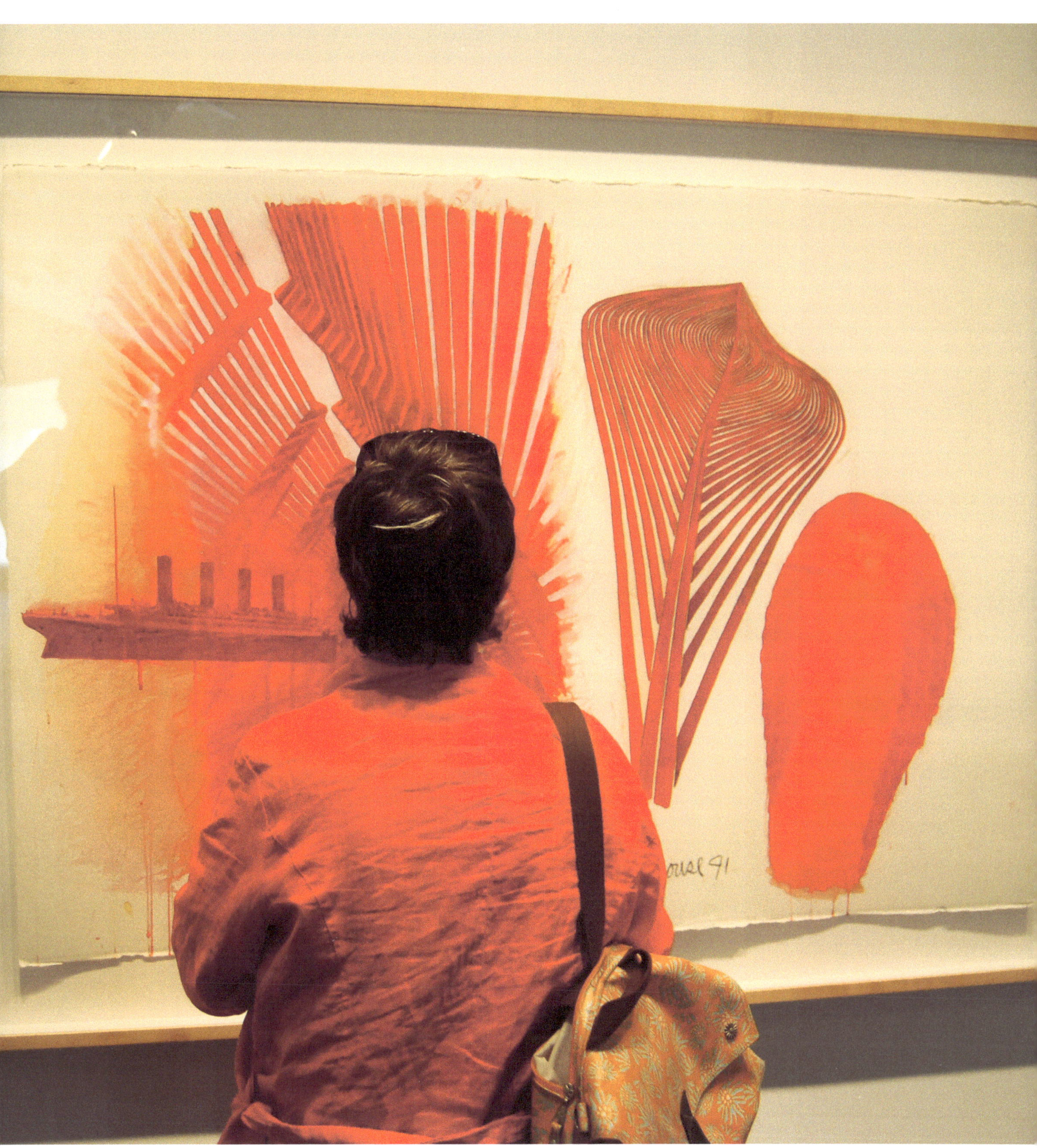

www.ingramcontent.com/pod-product-compliance
Lightning Source LLC
LaVergne TN
LVHW070212110826
845147LV00003B/560

* 9 7 8 1 9 4 1 8 9 2 1 5 2 *